SECOND
EDITION

INTERRACIAL
COMMUNICATION

SECOND
EDITION

INTERRACIAL COMMUNICATION

Theory into Practice

MARK P. **ORBE**
Western Michigan University

TINA M. **HARRIS**
The University of Georgia

SAGE Publications
Los Angeles • London • New Delhi • Singapore

For information:.

Sage Publications, Inc.
2455 Teller Road
Thousand Oaks, California 91320
E-mail: order@sagepub.com

Sage Publications Ltd.
1 Oliver's Yard
55 City Road
London EC1Y 1SP
United Kingdom

Sage Publications India Pvt. Ltd.
B 1/I 1 Mohan Cooperative Industrial Area
Mathura Road, New Delhi 110 044
India

Sage Publications Asia-Pacific Pte. Ltd.
33 Pekin Street #02-01
Far East Square
Singapore 048763

Printed in the United States of America

Library of Congress Cataloging-in-Publication Data

Orbe, Mark P.
Interracial communication: theory into practice/Mark P. Orbe,
Tina M. Harris.—2nd ed.
        p. cm.
Includes bibliographical references and index.
ISBN 978-1-4129-5458-7 (pbk.)
    1. Pluralism (Social sciences)—United States. 2. Intercultural communication—United States.
3. United States—Race relations. 4. United States—Ethnic relations. I. Harris, Tina M. II. Title.

E184.A1O68 2008
305.800973—dc22   2007007889

This book is printed on acid-free paper.

07 08 09 10 11 10 9 8 7 6 5 4 3 2 1

Acquisitions Editor:	Todd R. Armstrong
Editorial Assistant:	Katie Grim
Production Editor:	Catherine M. Chilton
Copy Editor:	Teresa Wilson
Typesetter:	C&M Digitals (P) Ltd.
Proofreader:	Doris Hus
Graphic Designer:	Candice Harman
Marketing Manager:	Amberlyn Erzinger

Contents

Preface

The 1970s witnessed a surge of books on the topic of communication and race: *Transracial Communication* (1973) by Arthur Smith, *Interracial Communication* (1974) by Andrea Rich, and *Crossing Difference . . . Interracial Communication* (1976) by Jon Blubaugh and Dorthy Pennington. We draw our inspiration from these authors who worked to set a valuable foundation for current work in interracial communication. *Interracial Communication: Theory Into Practice* (2nd edition) uses this scholarship, as well as that of countless other scholars and practitioners to provide you with a textbook that focuses on communication and the dynamics of race.

The primary objective of this book is to provide a current, extensive textbook on interracial communication that promotes moving from the theoretical to the practical. We provide a resource to professors teaching an undergraduate course on interracial communication by focusing our efforts on the ways that existing literature can be applied to everyday interactions. For those teaching a related course (i.e., intercultural communication, race relations, communication and racism, etc.), we provide a substantial component dedicated to the interactions of diverse racial/ethnic groups. We also hope that persons outside of academia will find the book a valuable resource for facilitating interracial dialogue in their respective communities. As clearly demonstrated through current and projected demographic trends, the ability to communicate across racial and ethnic groups will be crucial to personal, social, and professional success in the 21st century.

Overview

Interracial Communication: Theory Into Practice emphasizes the valuable contribution that communication theory and research can make to improve the existing state of race relations in the United States. The first section of the book provides a foundation for studying interracial communication. Chapter 1 offers an introduction to the subject area and the book; it also discusses the importance of cultivating a sense of community in the classroom. Chapter 2 presents a history of race, an important beginning to understand current race relations. Chapter 3 focuses on the critical role that language plays in interracial communication. In this chapter we highlight the role that power dynamics play in why and how one gets labeled. Chapter 4 features information on how racial/ethnic identity is developed and maintained and how we perceive ourselves and others. In Chapter 5, we discuss how other elements of culture (such as gender, age, socioeconomic status, and spirituality) can also play an important role during interracial interactions. The final chapter in Part I is Chapter 6. This chapter introduces nine different theories and models that can help you understand interracial communication from a variety of different perspectives. As you will see, each chapter draws heavily from existing scholarship in and outside the field of communication. To complement this information, personal reflections from the authors, case studies, and other opportunities for extended learning are provided in each chapter.

In Part II, the conceptual foundation provided in Part I is used to understand how interracial communication is played out in a number of contexts. In other words, each chapter presents a specific context where the ideas from Part I can be applied. Chapter 7 focuses on the challenges and rewards of friendships that negotiate racial and ethnic differences. Chapter 8 looks specifically at interracial romantic relationships and offers insight to facilitate a productive discussion on this sometimes "touchy" subject. In the next two chapters, we turn to the situational contexts that are somewhat more formal. In Chapter 9, we discuss the interracial communication that occurs in various organizations. Chapter 10 continues this direction by focusing particularly on interracial conflict; it also includes a case study on interracial unity. Chapter 11 provides insight to the important role that the mass media play in terms of perceptions of interracial communication. In addition to Author Reflections, Case Studies, and Opportunities for Extended Learning, each of these chapters also contains TIP (Theory Into Practice) boxes to guide you toward more effective interracial communication. Chapter 12 highlights the primary objective of the book: to make the connection between theory and practice for you explicitly clear and concrete. It also features insight into the importance of facilitating dialogue among diverse racial/ethnic group members.

Changes to the Second Edition

The first edition of our text was written in 1999–2000 and published in 2001. Since that time we have had the opportunity to use the book, for both undergraduate and graduate courses, several times each. Through our own teaching experiences, interactions with students, and conversations with colleagues across the United States, we recognized several different ways in which we could improve the effectiveness of the text. Consequently, we have made several significant changes to our general approach to the second edition; these have been incorporated throughout the text. First, we updated information from the first edition, including statistics, research studies, and contemporary examples. Here, we were able to draw from the most recent U.S. Census statistics and other current sources to capture the changing nature of race in the United States. Second, we have doubled the number of Author Reflections and added multiple Student Reflections—based on what our students have shared the past couple of years—throughout the text. This was done in response to the positive feedback that we received on how the Author Reflections helped to contextualize our interests in studying interracial communication. In the spirit of honoring multiple perspectives, we also included reflections collected from students over the past couple of years. Third, in order to encourage more effective learning, we have indicated key concepts in bold and included them in a glossary at the end of the book. We hope that this resource assists students in becoming familiar with all of the terminology introduced.

In addition to all of these changes, we have also made more specific changes to particular chapters in Part I. While the content in the first chapter largely remains the same, we have added two important sections to Chapter 2, Migration/Immigration Tensions and Post–September 11 Tensions, to our discussions of the significance of race today. Both of these issues have become increasingly salient since the publication of our first edition and are necessary to capture the realities of contemporary issues. In Chapter 3, we have enhanced our discussions of White privilege, especially as it relates to how European Americans remain relatively "race neutral" in terms of labels. We have also added particular sections on Middle Eastern Americans and multiracial Americans in this chapter. Chapter 4 has undergone significant revision. Consistent with Chapter 3, we have enhanced our discussion of Whiteness and White privilege. We have also revised the sections on identity development models and introduced Hecht's communication theory of identity. Given our focus on identity emergence—rather than identity development—this shift in focus is logical. We continue our discussion of societal privilege in Chapter 5 and added significant explanation of how race intersects with other salient aspects of cultural identity. The sixth, and final, chapter in Part I also was significantly revised. In particular we updated each of the theory descriptions based on recent research. We also added another theory, McPhail's complicity theory, a framework that reflects many of the ideas promoted throughout the text.

The chapters in Part II also underwent significant revision. Chapter 7 was revised to include a review of the contact hypothesis, which was used at length to discuss how interracial friendships emerge, evolve, and are maintained, thus warranting the integration of information about friendship selection and an informal discussion of interracial alliances. Chapter 8 introduces the idea of mental models of interracial romantic relationships. Other previous sections were relabeled to reflect the findings and pertinent information discovered from current research. Chapter 9 was restructured to address the issue of illegal immigration and its impact on organizations. The chapter focuses on diversity management in relation to organizational communication. One of the most obvious changes from the first edition can be found in Chapter 10. In our second edition, we replaced the chapter on public speaking and small group communication with a chapter focusing on interracial conflict. This new chapter seemed like an obvious change given its relevance to present-day society and coverage in recent research. In Chapter 11, we added sections on Middle Eastern Americans and European Americans as well as greater discussion of the digital divide. More attention has been directed toward popular culture and television. Finally, Chapter 12 involves enhanced discussions about the practical application of theory to interracial interactions. We added discussion about another barrier that impedes interracial communication, metastereotypes (Sigelman & Tuch, 1997), and commentary on the "racial tirades" involving actors Michael Richards and Mel Gibson as catalysts for personal reflection and social change in racist ideologies.

Note to Our Readers

This book truly represents a labor of love for us. We have attempted to author a book that simultaneously reflects our professional and personal interests in interracial communication. As you read the book, we hope that you come to see our sense of passion for this subject area. Both of us have spent considerable time thinking about race/ethnicity issues and "doing race" during our daily interactions. We also have spent our academic careers engaging in scholarship that promotes greater understanding of the inextricable relationships between race, culture, and communication. Between the two of us, we have taught more than a dozen different interracial communication classes and made presentations to various groups across the United States and beyond. Yet we hesitate when others identify us as "experts" in this area. While our achievements reflect a significant level of competency, there is so much more to learn that such a label seems hardly appropriate. So, as we progress through the 21st century, we invite you to join us in a life journey that promises to be full of challenges *and* rewards.

Authoring a book on a topic such as interracial communication is not an easy task. Trying to reach a consensus among all concerned parties (colleagues, editors, authors, reviewers, students, practitioners) was fruitless. Some agreed on *which* topics should be covered, but disagreements arose in terms of *how* they should be treated and *where* they should appear. As you read through the text, you may find yourself agreeing and/or disagreeing with different approaches that we have taken. In fact, we don't believe that there will be any person who will agree with everything that is included. What we do believe, however, is that the book provides a comprehensive foundation from which dialogue on interracial communication can emerge. In other words, we don't claim to provide "the" answers to effective interracial communication. Instead, we have designed a resource that provides a framework for multiple answers. As the reader, then, you are very much an active participant in this process!

It was our intention to create a book that is "user friendly" to educators who bring a diverse set of experiences to teaching interracial communications. We have completed this task with specific attention to student feedback from past interracial and intercultural communication classes, most of which indicated a greater need for opportunities for extended learning. Students wished to become more actively engaged in the topics of discussion. In light of this recommendation, and others collected from professors, students, and diversity consultants, we have written a book that is both theoretical and practical. Before you begin reading, there are a couple of things that we would like to draw your attention to:

• Existing research and discussions of interracial communication has given a hypervisibility to European American/African American relations (see Frankenberg, 1993). We have attempted to extend our discussion beyond this particular type of interracial interaction to include insights into Latino/as, Asian Americans, and Native Americans (this is especially true for Chapter 10). However, this was not easy because existing research has largely ignored these groups. As scholars broaden their research agendas, we hope that a more balanced coverage of all racial/ethnic groups can be achieved with each edition.

• Different racial/ethnic group members will come to discussions about race and communication with different levels of awareness. They will also come with different levels of power and privilege (see Chapter 3). Regardless of these differences, however, we believe that ALL individuals must be included in discussions on race (see Chapter 1 for guidelines). Throughout the book, we have attempted to strike a tone that is direct and candid, but not "preachy." Our goal is to provide a resource that prepares individuals for a dialogue about race openly and honestly (see Chapter 12). This is not an easy task, but we hope that we were able to negotiate these tensions effectively.

• We have worked hard to address issues that were raised by scholars who reviewed the manuscript in various stages of development. In this regard, we attempted to include some discussion on a large number of topics and focused our attention on those that seemed to be most important. However, like the first edition, we see this second edition of *Interracial Communication: Theory Into Practice* as an ongoing process of discovery. We invite you to contact us with your suggestions, criticisms, and insights.

Mark P. Orbe

mark.orbe@wmich.edu

Tina M. Harris

tmharris@uga.edu

Acknowledgments

Together we have several people to acknowledge for providing crucial support for the completion of the second edition of this text. We are especially indebted to Todd Armstrong, the senior editor for communication titles at Sage Publications. We couldn't be happier publishing our second edition with Sage, and Todd was instrumental in making the process timely, seamless, and relatively painless. In addition to the entire Sage staff, we would like to thank the countless number of reviewers who committed their expertise, time, and experience to provide invaluable feedback to us. For the second edition, they are Sakile K. Camara (California State University, Northridge), Patricia S. E. Darlington (Florida Atlantic University), Eleanor Dombrowski (Cleveland State University), Patricia S. Hill (University of Akron), Frank G. Pérez (University of Texas at El Paso), and Anntarie Lanita Sims (College of New Jersey). At each stage of production, we were able to benefit from their insights. This book is a much stronger one due to the efforts of many scholars and practitioners across the United States.

We would also like to thank these colleagues and reviewers of the first edition: Brenda Allen (University of Colorado–Denver), Harry Amana (University of North Carolina at Chapel Hill), Cecil Blake (University of Pittsburgh), Guo-Ming Chen (University of Rhode Island), Joyce Chen (University of Northern Iowa), Melbourne Cummings (Howard University), Stanley O. Gaines, Jr. (Pomona College), Gail A. Hankins (North Carolina State University), Michael Hecht (Pennsylvania State University), Felecia Jordan-Jackson (Florida State University), Venita Kelley (Spelman College), Robert L. Krizek (Saint Louis University), Marilyn J. Matelski (Boston College), Mark Lawrence McPhail (Southern Methodist University), Betty Morris (Holy Names College), Dorthy Pennington (University of Kansas), Laura Perkins (Southern Illinois University–Edwardsville), Pravin Rodrigues (Ashland University), Jim Schnell (Ohio Dominican College), William J. Starosta (Howard University), Nancy Street

(Bridgewater State College), Angharad Valdivia (University of Illinois at Urbana–Champaign), Jennifer L. Willis-Rivera (University of Wisconsin–River Falls), Julia T. Wood (University of North Carolina at Chapel Hill).

Individually, additional acknowledgments should also be made.

Mark P. Orbe: Writing the second edition of this book was both a professional and a personal journey for me. In revising it, I could not believe how much I have learned about interracial communication since teaching my first course in 2000. In this regard, I am indebted to all my students who made sure that I learned something new each and every semester. As with the first edition, I could not have coproduced such a book without the support, inspiration, and love of lots of folks. In addition to the rewards of working with an anointed coauthor, the never-ending blessings that come from my wife, Natalie, played a pivotal role in this process. While many can see her outer beauty, fewer individuals understand just how beautiful she really is . . . and I'm the luckiest one of them all because I get to experience it up close and personal every day of my life! Although they may not understand it, other friends and family members also helped me with this project. Talking on the phone and chatting online with best friends—Michele, Damon, and Rex—helped me stay grounded and avoid "intellectualizing" things. If nothing else, I'm proud that we've produced a book that "keeps it real." To my past, current, and future students, Dumela!

Tina M. Harris: The process of writing the second edition of this book has been a phenomenal experience for me, a true test of faith! Undoubtedly, this book, the process, and all that they entail are part of a plan much bigger and greater than I. By the grace of God, Mark and I were yoked up to do an awesome work that has been very rewarding and humbling in numerous ways. There are several people who supported and encouraged me throughout this endeavor who deserve special thanks. Mom, I continue to thank God for you. You supported me all the way, having faith that everything would get done, decently and in order. Dad, I wish you were here to share in the work God is doing through your Baby Girl! I can hear you saying, "Chip off the old block!" and that is so true! This book's for you and all that you stood for. I am thankful for my siblings, Greg, Sonya, and Ken. Each of you encouraged me in your own special way, and for that I am grateful. To Venessa and Jennifer (Wood), I praise God for placing each of you by my side as I did the work I was commissioned to do. Your listening ear, feedback, and encouragement mean more to me than you'll ever know. Thanks to all other family members and friends who have supported me on this journey. I love you and thank God for blessing me with such wonderful family. You are a Godsend!

PART I

Foundations for Interracial Communication Theory and Practice

Studying Interracial Communication

In 1902, African American historian W.E.B. Du Bois predicted that the primary issue of the 20th century in the United States would be related to the "problem of the color line" (1982, p. xi). From where we stand today, his words—written more than 100 years ago—appear hauntingly accurate. Without question, race relations in the United States continue to be an important issue. But do you think that W.E.B. Du Bois could have anticipated all of the changes that have occurred in the last century? Take a minute to reflect on some of these events and how they have changed the nature of the United States: Land expansion and population shifts westward. The Great Depression. World wars. The Cold War. Civil rights movements. Race riots. Multiple waves of immigration. Drastic migration patterns. Technological advances. Population explosions. A competitive global economy. This list is hardly conclusive, but it does highlight some of the major events and developments that the United States experienced during the 20th century. Clearly, the world that existed in 1902 when W.E.B. Du Bois wrote his now famous prediction is drastically different. Yet "the problem of the color line" (or, in other words, racial/ethnic divisions) still remains a difficult issue in the United States.

It would be an understatement to say that race continues to be a sensitive issue in the United States (Marable, 2005). Some researchers regard racial coding as the dominant feature of social interaction (A. D. James & Tucker, 2003). Discussions regarding race and ethnicity issues remain difficult, in part, due to significantly different perceptions and realities. Case in point: A national poll conducted by *ABC News* and the *Washington Post* in 2003 found that 54% of European Americans thought that race relations were "good" or "excellent," and 80% felt that African Americans have "an equal chance at jobs." In the same poll, only 44% of African Americans described race relations as good/excellent, and only 39% perceived equal opportunity in employment. Significant gaps between European American and African American perceptions (more than 30 percentage points) were also found in items related to "equal treatment from police," "equal treatment from merchants," "equal chance in housing," and "equal chance at good public schools" (as discussed in Marable, 2005). Such differences in perceptions present a challenge for effective interracial communication.

The basic premise of this book is that the field of communication, as well as other related disciplines, has much to offer us in working through the racial and ethnic differences that hinder effective communication. U.S. Americans from all racial and ethnic groups must learn how to communicate effectively with one another. During the early to mid-1970s, several books emerged that dealt specifically with the subject of interracial communication (Blubaugh & Pennington, 1976; Rich, 1974; A. Smith, 1973). These resources were valuable in setting a foundation for the study of interracial communication (see Chapter 6). Given the significant societal changes and scholarly advances in the communication discipline, however, their usefulness for addressing race relations in the 21st century is somewhat limited. Our intention is to honor these scholars, as well as countless others, by creating an up-to-date interracial communication resource guide that provides theoretical understanding and clear direction for application.

Toward this objective, the book is divided into two parts. Part I focuses on providing a foundation for studying interracial communication and includes chapters on the history of race and racial categories, the importance of language, the development of racial and cultural identities, and various theoretical approaches. In Part II, we use this foundation of information to understand how interracial communication is played out in a number of contexts (friendship and romantic relationships, organizations, conflict, and the mass media). The final chapter in Part II (Chapter 12) makes the connection between theory and practice explicit, especially as it relates to the future of race relations in the United States.

In this opening chapter, we provide a general introduction to the topic of interracial communication. First, we offer a specific definition of interracial communication, followed by a clear rationale of why studying this area is important. Next, we explain the concept of racial locations and encourage you to acknowledge how social positioning affects perceptions of self and others. Finally, we provide some practical insight into how instructors and students can create a positive, productive climate for discussions on issues related to race. Specifically, we advocate for cultivating a sense of community among discussion participants and suggest several possible guidelines toward this objective.

Two important points should be made before you read any further. First, we initially authored this book to be used in interracial and intercultural and communication classes at the undergraduate level. As our vision for the book developed, we realized it could be a valuable resource in any number of courses, including those in sociology, psychology, ethnic studies, and education (both undergraduate and graduate). In addition, we hope *Interracial Communication: Theory Into Practice* will be useful for individuals and groups outside the university setting who are interested in promoting more effective race relations in the United States. Much of our focus in highlighting how communication theory and research is applicable to everyday life interactions occurs within the context of a classroom setting. However, in our minds, *a classroom is any place where continued learning/teaching can occur*. In this regard, the principles shared in this book can apply to community-based groups and formal study circles, as well as long-distance learning and other types of learning that occur through the cyberspace community. In a very real sense, the world is a classroom, and we hope this book is a valuable resource for those committed to using effective communication practices to improve the relationships between and within different racial/ethnic groups.

Second, we acknowledge the power of language, and therefore we have been careful about using specific terms and labels. Chapter 3 focuses on the importance of language in interracial communication and discusses why we use certain racial and ethnic labels over other alternatives. We think it is vital that you can understand why labels are important beyond issues of so-called political correctness. Both scholarly and personal evidence clearly shows that in most cases, one universally accepted label for any specific racial or ethnic group does not exist. So, in these cases, we have chosen labels that are parallel across racial and ethnic groups (e.g., Asian American, African American, European American, Latino/a American, and Native American). In addition, we have decided to use both racial and ethnic markers (instead of focusing on race alone). This decision may initially seem odd, given that this is a book on interracial, not interethnic, communication. But according to most scientific information on race—including how the U.S. government currently defines it—Latino/a Americans (Hispanics) represent an ethnic group with members that cut across different racial groups. Thus, in order to include "interracial" communication that involves Latino/a Americans and other "racial" groups, we consciously use descriptors such as "race/ethnicity" or "race and ethnicity."

Defining Interracial Communication

Early writing on **interracial communication** defined it specifically as communication between Whites and non-Whites (Rich, 1974) or more generally as communication between people of different racial groups within the same nation-state (Blubaugh & Pennington, 1976). Interracial communication was distinguished from other types of communication. **Interpersonal communication** traditionally refers to interactions between two people regardless of similarities or differences in race; the term is often synonymous with **intraracial communication**. **International communication** refers to communication between nations, frequently engaged through representatives of those nations (Rich, 1974). **Intercultural communication** was used specifically to refer to situations in which people of different cultures (nations) communicated. **Interethnic communication**, sometimes used interchangeably with interracial communication, referred to communication between two people from different ethnic groups. Some scholars (e.g., Graves, 2004) use this term to expose the myths of racial categories (see Chapter 2). Others use interethnic communication to illustrate the differences between race and ethnicity and highlight how interethnic communication could also be intraracial communication (e.g., interactions between a Japanese American and Filipino American or between a German American and French American).

Over time, the study of intercultural communication has gained a prominent place within the communication discipline. It also has emerged as an umbrella term to include all aspects of communication that involve cultural differences. Currently, this includes researching interactions affected by age, race/ethnicity, abilities, sex, national origin, and/or religion. Interracial communication, then, is typically seen as one subset of many forms of intercultural communication. We believe this framework has been a mixed blessing for interracial communication study. On one hand, scholars interested in studying how communication is experienced across racial lines are able to draw from a significant body of existing intercultural research and theory. Because of this, we have a "home" in the discipline complete with various frameworks to use in our research. On the other hand, such a positioning appears to have had a marginalizing effect on interracial communication study. Because intercultural theoretical frameworks are designed to apply generally to a variety of contexts, they do little to reveal the unique dynamics of any one type of intercultural communication. In addition, intercultural communication study has become so broad that minimal attention is devoted to any one particular aspect. Teaching a class on intercultural communication is challenging, because most instructors attempt to include materials from various areas of intergroup relations. Thus, issues of race are oftentimes covered in insubstantial ways. One of the major points of this book is that interracial communication is such a complex process—similar to, yet different from, intercultural communication—that existing treatments of it as a form of intercultural communication are not adequate.

For our purposes here, we are operating from the following definition of interracial communication: the transactional process of message exchange between individuals in a situational context where racial difference is perceived as a salient factor by at least one person. This working definition, like those of other communication scholars (e.g., Giles, Mulac, Bradac, & Johnson, 1987), acknowledges that interracial communication can be seen as situated along an interpersonal/intergroup continuum. For instance, can you think of examples of communication that have occurred between two individuals who may be from different racial groups, but whose relationship seems to transcend these differences? If racial differences are not central to the interaction, these individuals' communication may be more interpersonal than interracial. As you will see in Chapter 6, the idea of **transracial communication** (interactions in which members are able to transcend their racial differences) was first generated by Molefi Kete Asante (A. Smith, 1973). However, the more central role that perceived racial differences play within an interaction—from the perspective of at least one participant—the more intergroup the interaction becomes.

❖ **BOX 1.1**

RACISM BREEDS STUPIDITY

The headline in the local newspaper read "Study Finds That Racism Can Breed Stupidity" (Cook, 2003). While three words—"racism," "breed," and "stupidity"—seemed to sensationalize the scientific study that was the basis of the article, the findings were interesting. Researchers at Dartmouth College (Richeson et al., 2003) studied how racial bias, and interaction with African Americans, affected European Americans' ability to perform basic tests. According to the findings of the study, "the more biased people are, the more their brain power is taxed by contact with someone of another race" (Cook, 2003, p. A4). This was because interracial contact caused racially biased European Americans to struggle not to say or do anything offensive. Researchers found that the effect was so strong that even a 5-minute conversation with an African American person left some European Americans unable to perform well on a basic cognitive test. Based on the findings, the researchers concluded that when racially biased European Americans were involved in interracial interactions—even briefly—it taxes the part of their brain in charge of executive control. The result is a temporary inability to perform well on other tasks.

- What do you make of these research findings?
- Do you agree that this happens, and if so, to what effect?

Why Study Interracial Communication?

For the past couple of decades, several basic arguments have emerged to justify attention to cultural diversity when studying various aspects of human communication. Most of these have related more directly to intercultural communication than interracial communication (e.g., Martin & Nakayama, 1997). Although some of these arguments appear equally applicable to interracial communication, others do not seem to fit the unique dynamics of race relations. Therefore, within the context of these general arguments and more specific ones related to the cultural diversity in the United States (e.g., Chism & Border, 1992), we offer four reasons why the study of interracial communication is important.

First, race continues to be one of the most important issues in the United States. From its inception, U.S. culture has reflected its multiracial population (even though political, legal, and social practices have valued certain racial groups over others). Because of the contradiction of the realities of racism and democracy (e.g., equal opportunity), the United States has often downplayed the issue of race and racism. We believe that in order to fulfill the democratic principles on which it is based, the United States must work through the issues related to racial differences. Racial and ethnic diversity is a primary strength of the United States. However, it can also be the country's biggest weakness if we are unwilling to talk honestly and openly. Although calls for advocating a "color-blind society"—one in which racial and ethnic differences are downplayed or ignored—are admirable, they are largely premature for a society that still has unresolved issues with race. Unfortunately, segregation between

European Americans and people of color has reached shockingly high levels. According to Maly (2005), the average European American in the United States lives in a neighborhood that is more than 80% White, while the average African American lives in one that is vastly African American. Asian Americans and Latino/as are less segregated from European Americans; however, they now live in more segregated settings than they did just two decades ago. Such massive racial and ethnic segregation prohibits the type of sustained, meaningful interaction that is crucial to develop interracial communication skills.

❖ **BOX 1.2**

DEFINING IMPORTANT CONCEPTS

Because of your interest in the topic, we assume you are familiar with many of the basic ideas central to understanding the interracial communication processes. But we acknowledge the importance of not assuming that everyone is operating from the same definition for certain terms. Therefore, we have defined some basic concepts related to interracial communication as a way to provide a common foundation. Throughout the text, we have included definitions whenever we introduce concepts that you may not be familiar with (e.g., discussions of privilege in Chapter 4). As you read each description, think about how it compares to your personal definition. It is comparable or drastically different? We recognize that differences may occur, but we want to make sure you understood how we are conceptualizing these terms. These definitions draw from a great body of interdisciplinary work (e.g., Allport, 1958; Hecht, Collier, & Ribeau, 1993; Jones, 1972; Rothenberg, 1992), but not necessarily any one in particular.

Culture: Learned and shared values, beliefs, and behaviors common to a particular group of people. Culture forges a group's identity and assists in its survival. Race is culture, but a person's culture is more than her or his race.

Race: A largely social—yet powerful—construction of human difference that has been used to classify human beings into separate value-based categories. Chapter 2 describes the four groups that make up a dominant racial hierarchy.

Ethnicity: A cultural marker that indicates shared traditions, heritage, and ancestral origins. Ethnicity is defined psychologically and historically. Ethnicity is different from race. For instance, your race may be Asian American, and your ethnic makeup might be Korean.

Ethnocentrism: Belief in the normalcy or rightness of one's culture and consciously or unconsciously evaluating other aspects of other cultures by using your own as a standard. All of us operate from within certain levels of ethnocentrism.

Microculture: Term used to describe groups (in our case racial/ethnic groups) that are culturally different from those of the majority group (macroculture). We generally use this term to refer to African, Asian, Latino/a, and Native American cultures instead of **minorities.**

Racial prejudice: Inaccurate and/or negative beliefs that espouse or support the superiority of one racial group.

Racial discrimination: Acting upon your racial prejudice when communicating with others. All people can have racial prejudice and practice racial discrimination.

Racism: Racial prejudice + societal power = racism. In other words, racism is the systematic subordination of certain racial groups by those groups in power. In the United States, European Americans traditionally have maintained societal power and therefore can practice racism. Because of their relative lack of institutional power, people of color can practice racial discrimination but not racism.

Second, changing shifts in the racial and ethnic composition of the United States will increase the need for effective interracial communication. In mid-October, 2006—as we were working on the second edition of this text—the U.S. population hit a milestone when it increased to over 300 million (Ohlemacher, 2006b). As you can see in Table 1.1, the U.S. population continues to become more and more diverse. Based on current census reports, one out of every three U.S. residents is part of a racial/ethnic group other than European American (Dart, 2006). People of color, then, total 98 million including: 42.7 million Latinos, 39.7 million African Americans, 14.4 million Asian Americans, 5.5 million multiracial Americans (two or more races), 4.5 million Native Americans and native Alaskans, and 990,000 native Hawaiians and other Pacific Islanders.

According to estimates, 60% of the population growth is the result of the number of births outweighing the number of deaths; the remaining 40% is tied to immigration (Ohlemacher, 2006b). By 2050, census estimates project that only half the population will be non-Hispanic White. The Hispanic and Asian populations will both triple, the African American population will almost double, and the European American population will remain consistent (Frey, 2004b). Given current migration within the United States (Frey, 2004b), being an effective interracial communicator will soon be necessary for all U.S. citizens (Halualani, Chitgopekar, Morrison, & Dodge, 2004).

Third, the past, present, and future of all racial and ethnic groups are interconnected. In tangible and not so tangible ways, our successes (and failures) are inextricably linked. To paraphrase an African proverb, "I am because we are, and we are because I am." Long gone is the general belief that the country is a big melting pot

❖ **Table 1.1** U.S. Racial Diversity and Population Milestones

Race	1915 100 million people	1967 200 million people	2006 300 million people
Whites	88.0%	76.6%	56.6%
Blacks	10.7%	13.8%	15.3%
Hispanics	n/a	6.5%	20.5%
Other	0.3%	3.2%	7.6%

where citizens shed their racial, ethnic, and cultural pasts and become (simply) "Americans." Instead, metaphors of a big salad or bowl of gumbo are offered. Within this vision of the United States, cultural groups maintain their racial and ethnic identities and, in doing so, contribute unique aspects of their culture to the larger society. Learning about different racial and ethnic groups is simultaneously exciting, intimidating, interesting, anxiety provoking, and transformative. It can also trigger a healthy self-examination of the values, norms, and practices associated with our own racial/ethnic groups. Remember, without this process we cannot take advantage of all the benefits that come with being a racially diverse society. To paraphrase Rev. Dr. Martin Luther King, Jr., we can either learn to work together collaboratively or perish individually.

Fourth, and finally, productive race relations are only feasible through effective communication practices. Look to past examples of successful interracial collaboration. We would surmise that at the base of each example lie varying aspects of a productive, positive communication process. This book seeks to highlight the central role that effective communication plays in the future of race relations. We recognize that race relations are an important aspect of study for all nations, not simply the United States. Yet we believe that attempting to discuss interracial communication in a larger (international) context would be counterproductive. Although some similarities obviously exist, each country has a relatively unique history in terms of race. We have chosen to focus on the importance of interracial communication within the United States because that is what we know and where we believe we can have the greatest impact. In short, this book represents a scholarly, social, and personal mission to contribute to interracial understanding. We are not simply reporting on abstract ideas related to communication. We are, in essence, talking about our lived experiences and those of our family, friends, colleagues, and neighbors. Communication theory and research has much to offer in terms of the everyday interactions of racially/ethnically diverse people. Our explicit goal is to advocate for using this body of knowledge to improve race relations in the United States. In other words, we want to practice what we preach and give others a resource so they can do the same.

One last comment about the importance of bringing the issue of race to the forefront of human communication: Given the history of race relations in the United States (see Chapter 2), most people appear more willing to discuss "culture" than "race." Simply put, studying intercultural communication is safer than studying interracial communication. And it is this very point that makes centralizing the issue of race so important for all of us. Race cannot be separated from interpersonal or intercultural communication processes. Scholars who study race as part of research in these areas have provided some valuable insights. Nevertheless, we argue that research that does not centralize issues of race cannot get at the unique ways that race affects (to some extent) all communication in the United States. Starting here, and continuing throughout the entire book, we hope to increase your awareness as to the various ways that race influences how individuals communicate.

❖ **BOX 1.3**

AUTHOR REFLECTIONS

One of the important keys to promoting effective interracial communication is the recognition that each of us experiences life from a particular racial location. Because we have asked you to identify your racial location, it is only fair that we also publicly acknowledge our own. This is important because it helps identify us, the authors of this book, as human beings with a particular set of life experiences. Clearly, our racial locations inform our understanding of interracial communication. Therefore, throughout the book, we share our personal experiences through a series of personal reflections. This first reflection serves as an introduction to how I give consciousness to my racial standpoint.

A central component of my racial standpoint revolves around the fact that I don't fit neatly into any one racial category. My grandfather came to the United States from the Philippines in the early 1900s; the Spanish lineage is clear given our family names (Orbe, Ortega). Some of my mother's relatives reportedly came over on the *Mayflower*. Like many European Americans, her lineage is a mixture of many different European cultures (Swiss, French, English). So, my racial standpoint is informed by the fact that I am biracial and multiethnic. However, it is not that simple. Other factors complicate the particular perspective I bring to discussions of interracial communication.

I am a forty-something man who was raised in a diverse low-income housing project (predominantly African American with a significant number of Puerto Ricans) in the Northeast. In this regard, other cultural factors—age, region, socioeconomic status—also inform my racial standpoint. Except what I've seen reproduced through the media, I don't have any specific memory of the civil rights movement. I've always attended predominantly African American churches (initially Baptist, but more recently, nondenominational ones) and have always felt a part of different African American communities. For instance, in college, I pledged a predominantly Black Greek affiliate organization; these brothers remain my closest friends. My wife also comes from a multiracial lineage (African, European, and Native American); however, she identifies most closely with her Blackness. We have three young people who are being raised to embrace strongly all aspects of their racial and ethnic heritage. Over time, they will develop their own unique racial locations.

Through these descriptions it should be apparent that my racial location (like yours) is closely tied to age, gender, spirituality, family, sexual orientation, and region. So, what's your story? How are our racial perspectives similar yet different? As we explained earlier, acknowledging and coming to understand self and other racial locations are important steps toward effective interracial communication.

—MPO

Acknowledging Racial Locations

An important starting point for effective interracial communication is to acknowledge that individuals have similar and different vantage points from which they see the world. These vantage points, or standpoints, are the result of a person's field of experience as defined by social group membership (Collins, 1990). Standpoint theories are based on one simple idea: The world looks different depending on your social standing (B. J. Allen, 1998). Standpoint theories have largely been used by scholars to understand how women and men come to see the world differently (Harding, 1987, 1991; Hartsock, 1983; D. E. Smith, 1987; Wood, 1992). Given the assumption that societal groups with varying access to institutional power bases have different standpoints, standpoint theories appear to offer a productive framework to link existing interracial communication theory and research to everyday life applications. In fact, the value of using standpoint theories as a framework for studying race relations has not gone unnoticed by scholars (Orbe, 1998b; Wood, 2005).

A key idea of standpoint theories is that social locations—including those based on gender, race, class, and so forth—shape people's lives (Wood, 2005). This idea is grounded in the analyses of the master–slave relationship that realized that each occupied a distinct standpoint in terms of their lives (Harding, 1991). Within this text, we focus on the social location primarily defined through racial and ethnic group membership. In simple terms, this concept helps people to understand that a person's racial/ethnic identity influences how that person experiences, perceives, and comes to understand the world around him or her. Everyone has a **racial location**, defined primarily in terms of the racial and ethnic groups to which that person belongs. However, according to standpoint theory, there is an important distinction between occupying a racial location and having a racial standpoint (O'Brien Hallstein, 2000). A racial standpoint is achieved—earned through critical reflections on power relations and through the creation of a political stance that exists in opposition to dominant cultural systems (Wood, 2005, p. 61). Being a person of color does not necessarily mean that you have a racial standpoint. In other words, racial standpoint can, but does not necessarily, develop from being a person of color. Racial standpoints are not achieved individually; they can only be accomplished through working with other people of color (O'Brien Hallstein, 2000). **Racial standpoint**, then, refers to more than social location or experience; it encompasses a critical, oppositional understanding of how one's life is shaped by larger social and political forces. By definition, European Americans cannot achieve a racial standpoint; however, they can develop multiple standpoints shaped by membership in traditionally marginalized groups defined by sex, sexual orientation, and socioeconomic status (Wood, 2005).

Standpoint theory is based on the premise that our perceptions of the world around us are largely influenced by social group membership. In other words, our set of life experiences shape—and are shaped by—our memberships with different cultural groups like those based on sex, race/ethnicity, sexual orientation, and so on. According to standpoint theorists (Collins, 1986; Haraway, 1988; Hartsock, 1983), life is not experienced the same for all members of any given culture. In explicit and implicit ways, our racial locations affect how we communicate as well as how we perceive the communication of others. Acknowledging the locations of different social groups, then, is an important step in effective communication. Part of this involves recognizing that different U.S. racial and ethnic group members perceive the world differently based on their experiences living in a largely segregated society. Simply put, racial and ethnic groups share common worldviews based on shared cultural histories and present-day life conditions. The largest difference in racial standpoints, it is reasoned, is between those racial and ethnic groups that have the most and least societal power (Collins, 1990). In the United States, this means Native Americans, African Americans, and Latino/a Americans have more similar racial locations. European Americans, in comparison, have had greater access to societal power, which has resulted in dominant group status. Based on the arguments of standpoint theorists (Swigonski, 1994), European Americans and U.S. Americans of color have different—even possibly oppositional—understandings of the world. In other words, they see life drastically differently based on the social standing of their racial/ethnic group membership (e.g., the O. J. Simpson trial or the Hurricane Katrina evacuation efforts). Understanding how racial locations create different worldviews, in this regard, assists in beginning the process toward more effective interracial understanding.

In the past, some scholars have criticized standpoint theories because they focused on the common standpoint of a particular social group while minimizing the diversity within that particular group. For instance, traditionally, standpoint theorists have written extensively about the social positioning of women with little attention to how race/ethnicity further complicates group membership (K. Bell, Orbe, Drummond, & Camara, 2000; Collins, 1998). The challenge for us is to use standpoint theories in ways that encourage identifying the commonalities among a particular racial, ethnic group while simultaneously acknowledging internal differences (Wood, 2005). Balancing these two—seeing a person as an individual and seeing him or her as a member of a particular racial/ethnic group—is difficult, but necessary to achieve effective interracial communication. This point is extremely important because it helps us avoid mass generalizations that stereotype all racial and ethnic group members as the same. As such, standpoint theories remind us to see the great diversity within racial and ethnic groups based on individual and other cultural elements like age, education, gender, sexual orientation, and socioeconomic status (Wood, 2005).

According to most standpoint theorists (e.g., Harding, 1991), the marginalized position of U.S. racial/ethnic minorities forces the development of a "double vision" in terms of seeing both sides of interracial communication. Because of this, they can come to understand multiple racial standpoints. How and why do they do this? According to Collins (1986) and others (e.g., Orbe, 1998c), people of color are relative outsiders within the power structures of the United States. In addition to their own racial location, they must develop the ability to see the world from European American locations in order to function in dominant societal structures (e.g., a predominantly White college or university). Learning the ropes from an outsider's position, some argue, creates a better grasp of that racial location than even insiders can obtain (Frankenberg, 1993). Although this has typically been required for the "mainstream" success of people of color, it can also be true for European Americans who are motivated to understand the perceptions of different racial/ethnic groups. However, standpoint theorists remind us that given the existing power and privilege structures, the levels of reciprocal understanding are hardly equal (Wood, 1997b).

Through this brief overview of standpoint theories, you can see why identifying your racial location is an important ingredient for effective interracial communication. Such a move is invaluable because it helps you acknowledge a specific life perspective and recognize its influence on how you perceive the world. In addition, it promotes an understanding that different racial locations potentially generate contrasting perceptions of reality. Nevertheless, remember that standpoint theories also require a conscious effort to pay attention to the various locations within any one particular racial or ethnic group. In other words, this approach to interracial communication hinges on your abilities to understand the possible commonalties of people who share a common racial group while simultaneously recognizing intragroup differences. Focusing on how racial identity is just one aspect of our multicultural selves, Chapter 5 discusses the cultural diversity *within* different racial and ethnic groups.

❖ BOX 1.4

AUTHOR REFLECTIONS

In the first section of this textbook, we discussed the importance of history and multiple identities in understanding interracial/interethnic communication. As my coauthor has indicated in his personal reflection, it is important for you, the reader, to understand our racial/cultural standpoints. Here, I will share with you my journey for self-understanding.

By all appearances, I am African American; however, my family history will tell you otherwise. I am in my thirties and for many years have wondered about the details of my heritage. My father (who passed away in 1996) was in the navy. After I was born in Detroit, Michigan, my family and I lived there for 2½ years until we were stationed in Rota, Spain. For 4½ years, I was immersed in Spanish culture. During the day, both my father and mother worked, and my older brother and sister were in school. Our maid, Milagros (no, we were not rich), kept me during the day, and she taught me how to speak Spanish fluently and all about the rituals of the Spanish people. I felt as if I were a part of the culture.

After living in Spain, we moved from Pensacola, Florida, to Atlanta, Georgia, to be closer to my parents' families. As we moved across the world, it was my age, family status, and interpersonal interactions that shaped who I was. It was not until I was around family and peers with southern dialects, different life experiences, and few interracial/interethnic interactions that I became aware of my racial standpoint. I was accused of "not being Black enough" because I spoke "proper" English. One vivid memory involves being left out of the "best friend game" by my Jewish friend and a Pentecostal European American friend. They both decided that they were each other's friend because they knew each other longer than they knew me. I was the odd person out: Everyone had a best friend except me. I knew immediately that the reason I was not chosen was because of my race/ethnicity.

My quest for learning about my family's history and realization of how we are socialized to view racial/ethnic groups has challenged me to explore the significance of racial/ethnic identity in a society that values a racial hierarchy. Although we do not have a family tree that shows us where we came from, I do find some peace in knowing a few pieces of the puzzle have been completed. I am aware that both of my grandmothers are of Native American and European descent. However, there is a big puzzle piece that does not complete the picture of who my family and I are. For this very reason I am committed to becoming continually aware of the importance of our multiple identities in an increasingly diverse society. I want to have knowledge of my rich ethnic heritage to pass on to my future children.

—TMH

Setting the Stage for Discussions of Race

In many interracial contexts—social, professional, family—the issue of race and racism continues to be a taboo topic. Lack of opportunity and high levels of anxiety and uncertainty decrease the likelihood that honest discussions on racial issues will take place. Ironically, such discussions are typically the primary way that anxiety and uncertainty are reduced. Thus, a vicious cycle is created. People generally do not have sufficient opportunities to discuss issues related to race outside their largely intraracial network. Different racial and ethnic groups live among each other in the same residential districts more than ever, yet, ironically, have limited quality interaction with one another (Halualani et al., 2004). According to this line of research, most interracial contact occurs in two specific locations: on-campus in class and off-campus at work. As you might expect, we believe that the classroom holds the greatest potential for producing high-quality, productive discussions on race.

Unfortunately, in the past, "the issue of race on college campuses has been one of the most profound and controversial topics in higher education" (Muthuswamy, Levine, & Gazel, 2006, p. 105). Because of this, many colleges and universities have enacted strategies to create multicultural campuses; these include proactive initiatives, multicultural programming, and race relations dialogue in and outside of class. Gurin (1999) reports that classroom diversity, combined with opportunities for informal interactions, resulted in positive learning outcomes, such as academic engagement, active thinking, and greater appreciation for differences. Racial and ethnic diversity alone, according to McAllister and Irvine (2000), is not enough—formal and informal opportunities for interaction are necessary. On most campuses, these opportunities must be cultivated by university faculty and staff, given that cultural segregation on campuses is common (Yates, 2000).

Accordingly, we turn next to the importance of classroom climate in promoting effective interracial communication. Race can be an emotional and personal topic for both students and instructors. This is especially true for European American (White) students who "feel that they cannot honestly discuss racially charged issues without fear of the ultimate social shame—being labeled as racist" (A. N. Miller & Harris, 2005, p. 238). A positive, productive classroom climate is, therefore, essential to maximizing discussions related to race, racism, and interracial communication. Consider the reflections of Navita Cummings James, a University of South Florida professor who has extensive teaching experiences in the areas of race, racism, and communication:

> Perhaps the most critical step for me is creating a classroom climate where students can learn from each other, develop their critical thinking skills by agreeing and disagreeing with each other, with assigned readings, and even the professor; where students can live with each other's anger, pain, and other emotions and not personally be threatened by it; where they can "let down" their own defenses and begin to explore and better understand other people's lived experiences . . . and where at least some can move away from the stereotypical "us against them" mentality and begin to see potential allies across the racial divide. (N. C. James, 1997, p. 200)

Based on our own teaching philosophies and past experiences teaching about race and racism in our classes, we agree wholeheartedly with these sentiments (see also

Duncan, 2002). Interracial discussions, in and outside of the classroom, that are attempted without a supportive communicative climate can actually do more harm than good. Thus, we encourage cultivating a sense of community in the interracial communication classroom.

Building Community in the Classroom

Under ordinary circumstances, there is no such thing as "instant community" (Peck, 1992). We tend to use the label **community** to describe any number of settings (e.g., neighborhoods, colleges, churches). In most instances, these characterizations involve a false use of the word (Orbe & Knox, 1994). A single working definition of community is difficult to pinpoint (Gudykunst & Kim, 1992). Nevertheless, Peck's (1987) writings on what he calls "true community" appear to offer the most productive approach, especially in terms of the interracial communication classroom. He restricts the use of community to a "group of individuals who have learned how to communicate honestly with each other" (Peck, 1987, p. 50). Those who are part of a true community have relationships that go deeper than typical interactions that only involve "masks of composure." They also involve a significant level of commitment to "rejoice together" and "to delight in each other, make others' conditions our own" (Peck, 1987, p. 50).

Building a sense of community in any classroom is ideal. It appears essential for courses that involve topics related to issues of culture, race, and oppression (Orbe, 1995). Sometimes it can seem like an impossible task, especially given the time and commitment it takes. Because race continues to be a volatile issue in the United States, studying interracial communication typically involves some tension. The most productive instances of interracial communication, at least initially, work to sustain rather than resolve this tension (Wood, 1993). This involves probing the awkwardness that sometimes comes with learning new perspectives, especially those that appear to conflict with a person's existing views. It also includes dealing with a range of emotions— anger, fear, pride, guilt, joy, shame—associated with understanding your own racial location. Negotiating the tensions that accompany such strong emotions can encourage classroom participants (including both instructors and students) to recognize racial/ethnic differences while also seeing the commonalities among different cultural groups. Julia T. Wood (1993) explains how her philosophy supports this approach:

> Realizing that humans are both alike and different—simultaneously diverse and common—allows us to honor and learn from the complexity of human life. . . . I hope to create a productive discomfort that provokes more holistic, inclusive, and ultimately accurate understandings of human communication and human nature. (p. 378)

Cultivating a sense of community in the classroom is facilitated by the instructor, but is the responsibility of each member of the class (Orbe, 1995). A major aspect of building classroom community involves establishing relationships. According to Palmer (1993), "real learning does not happen until students are brought into relationship with the teacher, with each other, and with the subject" (p. 5). So, how do we go about cultivating a sense of community in interracial communication classes? Peck

(1987, 1992) identifies six characteristics of "true community": inclusiveness, commitment, consensus, contemplation, vulnerability, and graceful fighting. As you will see, each of these elements of community contributes to maximizing the potential for interracial communication interactions.

Inclusiveness refers to a general acceptance and appreciation of differences, not as necessarily positive or negative but just as different (Crawley, 1995). First and foremost, "community is and must be inclusive" (Peck, 1992, p. 436). Maintaining ingroup/ outgroup status within the interracial communication classroom is counterproductive to cultivating a sense of community (Gudykunst & Kim, 1992). Community members must establish and maintain a sense of inclusiveness.

Commitment involves a strong willingness to coexist and work through any barriers that hinder community development (Peck, 1992). Part of your commitment to community is a faithfulness to work through both the positive and negative experiences associated with the tensions of racial interactions. In other words, being committed to community involves "hang[ing] in there when the going gets rough" (Peck, 1987, p. 62). Typically, it is exactly this sense of commitment that allows people to absorb any differences in racialized standpoints as a healthy means of community development and preservation (Peck, 1987).

Consensus is another important aspect of community. Interracial communities, in the true sense of the word, work through differences in opinions and seek a general agreement or accord among their members. Racial and ethnic differences are not "ignored, denied, hidden, or changed; instead they are celebrated as gifts" (Peck, 1987, p. 62). In every situation, developing a consensus requires acknowledging and processing cultural differences. In the interracial communication classroom, reaching a consensus does not imply forced adherence to majority beliefs. Instead, it involves collaborative efforts to obtain a win–win situation or possibly "agreeing to disagree."

Contemplation is crucial to this process. Individuals are consciously aware of their particular racial location as well as their collective standing as a community. This awareness involves an increased realization of self, others, and how these two interact with the larger external surroundings. Becoming more aware of your multicultural selves is an important component of this process, and Chapters 4 and 5 are designed to facilitate greater self-discovery in this area. Note that the "spirit of community" is not something forever obtained; instead, it is repeatedly lost (Peck, 1992, p. 439). Constant reflection of the process toward community is necessary.

For community to develop, individuals must also be willing to discard their "masks of composure" (Gudykunst & Kim, 1992, p. 262) and expose their inner selves to others (Peck, 1987). In other words, a certain degree of **vulnerability** must be assumed. For interracial communication instructors, this means creating a relatively safe place where students are accepted for who they are (Orbe & Knox, 1994). It also involves assuming the risks associated with sharing personal stories related to culture, race/ethnicity, and social oppressions. Vulnerability is contagious (Peck, 1992). Students are more willing to take risks and make themselves vulnerable when they perceive the instructor as personally engaged in the process of building community.

The final characteristic of community, according to Peck (1987, 1992) is **graceful fighting**. As described earlier, tension in the interracial communication classroom is to be expected. Conflict is a natural process inherent to any intergroup setting and should not be avoided, minimized, or disregarded (Hocker & Wilmont, 1995). The notion that "if we can resolve our conflicts then someday we will be able to live together in community" (Peck, 1987, p. 72) is an illusion. A community is built *through* the negotiation (not avoidance) of conflict. But how do we participate in graceful fighting? The next section explores this important question.

❖ **BOX 1.5**

THE PROBLEM WITH STEREOTYPES

According to the literature (e.g., Leonard & Locke, 1993; H. Waters, 1992) as well as our personal experiences, stereotyping is a major barrier to effective communication. **Stereotypes** are generally defined as overgeneralizations of group characteristics or behaviors that are applied universally to individuals of those groups (e.g., Allport, 1958). Despite the negative impact that racial stereotypes have on interracial communication (Leonard & Locke, 1993), research suggests that greater exposure to racial group members has positive effects in dispelling stereotypes (Sigelman & Welch, 1993). This line of logic matches what our personal experiences tell us.

It is fairly easy to stereotype racial and ethnic members who belong to groups to which you have little exposure. The greater the number of Mexican Americans you know, for instance, the more difficult it will be for you to accept mass generalizations about this diverse group. However, here is the catch. The way to move beyond stereotyping is to increase authentic communication between racial groups; however, the existence of stereotypes is a significant barrier to authentic communication. Stereotyping others based on race/ethnicity discourages the recognition of the great diversity *within* racial and ethnic groups. Therefore, one key element for effective interracial communication is clear. We must come to terms with the overt and covert stereotypes we have of other racial and ethnic groups and then continue to seek out opportunities to increase our exposure to different facets of other cultures. It appears that the most effective guideline is to create a balance where people are seen simultaneously both as individuals and as members of larger cultural groups.

Ground Rules for Classroom Discussions

We do not particularly like the term graceful fighting to describe the type of communication that we want to promote during interracial interactions. The word *fighting* has such a negative connotation because it triggers images of nasty disagreements, physical confrontations, or screaming matches. Nevertheless, we do believe that our ideas of a positive, productive interracial communication classroom climate are consistent with Peck's writings on graceful fighting. In short, we see it as referring to an expectation that agreements and disagreements are to be articulated, negotiated, and possibly resolved, productively. One point needs to be raised before outlining the process of creating ground rules for discussion: some general differences in how different racial/ethnic groups engage in conflict.

A number of general ground rules exist that commonly are adopted to guide effective group discussions. Chances are, based on your experiences with working with different types of groups, you could generate an elaborate list of conversational guidelines. Be open minded. Be an active listener. Use "I" statements when articulating thoughts, emotions, and ideas. Act responsibly and explain why certain things people say are offensive to you. Assume that people are inherently good and always do the best they can with what information they have. Over the years, we have come across a number of lists of ground rules, many of which overlap significantly. In terms of discussion specifically involving issues of race and racism, we offer selected ground rules offered by N. C. James (1997, pp. 197–198). As you read each of the following items, think about how it contributes to a productive communication climate. We hope you will see the importance of each ground rule in overcoming some of the potential barriers associated with interracial communication.

1. Remember that reasonable people can and do disagree.

2. Each person deserves respect and deserves to be heard.

3. Tolerance and patience are required of all.

4. Respect the courage of some who share things we may find highly objectionable. We may learn the most from their comments.

5. Understand the rules for civil discourse may need to be negotiated on individual, group, and class levels (e.g., gender-linked and race-linked styles of communication may need to be considered explicitly).

6. Acknowledge that all racial/ethnic groups have accomplishments their members can be proud of and misdeeds they should not be proud of (i.e., no racial/ethnic group walks in absolute historical perfection or wickedness).

7. Each person should understand the privileges that he or she has in the United States based on skin color (e.g., Whites and lighter skinned people of color) and other social assets such as social class, gender, level of education, and so on.

8. "Equality" between and among discussants should be the relational norm.

Do you agree with each of these ground rules? Why or why not? Consistent with the characteristics of cultivating a sense of community, it is important to recognize that a consensus of all participants must be gained in terms of classroom discussion ground rules. If just one person does not agree with a ground rule, it should not be adopted. Of course, some members may provide convincing arguments that persuade others to adopt certain guidelines. This, however, should not translate into peer pressure or intimidation. Again, after some extended discussion on each ground rule, a consensus needs to be reached or the ground rule is not adopted by the classroom community. Because the dynamics of each community are different, ground rules are likely to be different from group to group. We must also take into consideration the specific situational context (dyadic, small group, open discussion) and communication channel used by the group. For instance, think about the interracial communication occurring on the Internet. Individuals sitting at computer terminals all over the world are interacting via chat rooms and other means without ever seeing the other people and hearing their voices. Given this type of cyberspace interaction, do you think the ground rules for discussions would be the same? Or would they be different because of the absence of face-to-face interaction? One of the Opportunities for Extended Learning at the end of this chapter allows you to explore this idea further.

Another factor that should be recognized when creating ground rules for class discussions is the readiness levels of the participants of the group (including the instructor). In this regard, it is important not to simply adopt the various ground rules that we have generated here. Each community must create a set of communication norms that meet the expectations and competencies for their particular members. In some instances, different groups will be willing and able to incorporate additional guidelines that reflect their deeper understanding of race, racism, and race relations in the United States. For instance, some interracial communication classes may decide to adopt one or more of the following guidelines:

1. Communicate with the assumption that racism, and other forms of oppression, exist in the United States.

2. Agree not to blame ourselves or others for misinformation that we have learned in the past; instead, assume a responsibility for not repeating it once we have learned otherwise.

3. Avoid making sweeping generalizations of individuals based solely on their racial/ethnic group membership (e.g., I can't understand why Asian Americans always. . .).

4. Acknowledge the powerful role of the media on the socialization of each community member.

5. Resist placing the extra burden of "racial spokesperson" or "expert" on anyone.

6. Respect, patience, and an appreciation of diverse perspectives is required (Note: Can you see how this guideline is at a different level than number 3 in the more basic list?).

Each of these six examples represents another guideline that your classroom community may want to adopt as they engage in meaningful interracial communication. What other ground rules, relatively unique to your situation, might you also adopt? Once a consensus has been reached on a workable set of guidelines, post them in the class so members have access to them. Over the course of the life of the community, review, reemphasize, challenge, and/or revise your ground rules. As the relational immediacy of the students and instructors increases, so might the need for additional guidelines for classroom discussions. Other rules may no longer seem relevant. The key is to create and maintain a set of communication ground rules that serve to guide your discussions on race and racism.

Conclusion

Chapter 1 was designed to introduce you to the study of interracial communication in the United States and outline the importance of cultivating a sense of community to maximize the potential for productive dialogue on topics related to race. Interwoven throughout this chapter are several important assumptions that are central to effective interracial understanding. We summarize them here to facilitate your navigation of future chapters.

The first assumption deals with the history of race. Although race is largely a socially constructed concept, it must be studied because it is such an important external cue in communication interactions. Race matters in the United States. Ethnic differences may be a more credible marker (scientifically), but people see and react to race differences. Second, relying on racial and ethnic stereotypes when communicating with individual group members is counterproductive. Seeing others as individuals, while maintaining an awareness of general cultural norms, promotes effective interracial communication. The third assumption has to do with honest self-reflection in terms of the social positioning that your particular racial/ethnic group occupies. Acknowledging, and coming to understand, self and other racial locations is crucial to effective interracial communication. Fourth, research and theory within the field of communication has significant contributions to make in terms of advocating for productive communication within and across different racial and ethnic groups. And while we do not assume that communication is a cure-all, it does appear to be the primary means to advance race relations in the United States.

OPPORTUNITIES FOR EXTENDED LEARNING ❖

1. Some communication scholars do not necessarily agree with our definition of interracial communication. For instance, Marsha Houston (2002) contends that the history of race (and racism) is integral to U.S. history. As such, she states that race is always a salient issue—either explicitly or implicitly—when people from different racial and ethnic groups interact. Break into small groups and discuss the issue raised by Dr. Houston; what are your thoughts about the saliency of race in everyday interactions?

2. Some suggest that the key to effective race relations in the 21st century is to become color-blind. Break into intraracial and interracial groups and discuss that feasibility and effectiveness of this guideline. As a whole, does the group believe that transracial communication is possible? Or is race such a prominent feature of identity that it always serves as a central marker during human communication?

3. In an attempt to understand your particular racial location, create a list of statements in response to the question, What does it mean to be _____ [insert racial/ethnic group] in the United States? Once you have compiled your list, share it with others within and outside your racial/ethnic group. What similarities and differences exist? Learning about others' racial locations is an excellent way to generate an increased level of understanding of your own racial location.

4. Find out more about the racial and ethnic composition of your local community by visiting American FactFinder at http://factfinder.census.gov. At this Web site sponsored by the U.S. Census Bureau, you can get current demographic information about particular communities (by zip code or city) and states, as well as the entire United States

5. As indicated within the chapter, guidelines for classroom discussions should reflect the specific dynamics of a particular group. Think about what guidelines might be necessary for computer chat rooms or classes conducted via the Internet. How might these be similar to, yet different from, more traditional classrooms?

6. One strategy for facilitating discussions relate to race, racism, and communication is to generate a list of propositions and see if the class can reach a consensus in terms of their agreement or disagreement (N. C. James, 1997). First, break the class into groups. Then give each group one of the following statements (or create your own), and instruct them to reach a consensus if at all possible.

    a. In the contemporary United States, people of color cannot be racist.

    b. Racism can be unconscious and unintentional.

    c. Many European American men in the United States are currently the victims of reverse discrimination.

    d. All European Americans, because of the privilege in the United States, are inherently racist.

    e. Asian Americans can be racist against other people of color, like African and Latino/a Americans.

2

The History
of Race

The presence of race in the United States is like the presence of the air we breathe—something always around us that we use constantly, sometimes without much thought. Have you ever thought about the racial categories that you and others are placed in? Chances are some of you have and others have not. This chapter is designed to give you a brief historical overview of the concept of race. Tracing the history of the evolution of race and racial classifications is important in identifying the various ways that current designations affect our everyday communication.

The concept of race is a highly complex one, reflected in the great body of literature that deals with issues associated with race. In fact, some might suggest the issue of race is central to nearly every aspect of the national agenda of the United States. Thus, we acknowledge that this text is simply an introduction to the various perspectives on race. We have included a number of references that will give you a more in-depth treatment of the issues discussed here. Our hope is that you will take the initiative to do further reading (see Opportunities for Extended Learning at the end of each chapter for some direction).

As evidenced throughout this book, the United States is a country where, in the words of Cornell West (1993), *race matters*. Attempts to promote a deeper understanding of the complexities inherent in interracial communication must begin with an exploration of the idea of race and racial designations.

History of Racial Classification

The concept of race as we know it did not exist in the ancient world (Snowden, 1970). Over the years, many scholars have examined the emergence of the idea of race and attempted to document the developmental history of racial classifications. Some suggest (e.g., Gosset, 1963) that a French physician, Francois Bernier, was the first to write about the idea of race in 1684. Bernier created a racial categorization scheme that separated groups of people based on two elements: skin color and facial features. The result was the formulation of four racial groups: Europeans, Africans, Orientals, and Lapps (people from northern Scandinavia). Other scholars (e.g., West, 1982) point to the work of Arthur de Gobineau (1816–1882), whose work divided the human race into three types (White, Black, and Yellow), with the White race described as the most superior of the three. But the most influential of all racial classifications, especially as they relate to the ideas of race in contemporary times, was established by Johann Friedrich Blumenbach in the late 1700s. When tracing the history of race, nearly all scholars point to Blumenbach's typology, first created in 1775 and then revised in 1795, as a central force in the creation of racial divisions (Lasker & Tyzzer, 1982; Montagu, 1964, 1997; Spickard, 1992). Because his ideas served as a foundation for much of the subsequent work on race, our coverage of the history of race begins with a focus on his work.

Blumenbach (1752–1840) was a German anatomist and naturalist who had studied under Carolus Linnaeus. In 1758, Linnaeus constructed a system of classification of all living things (Bahk & Jandt, 2004). According to the Linnaean system, all human beings are members of a certain kingdom (Animalia), phylum (Chordata), class (Mammalia), order (Primates), family (*Hominidae*), genus (*Homo*), and species (*sapiens*) (Spickard, 1992). Each level of this pyramid-like typology contains a number of specific subdivisions of the level above. Blumenbach's (1865/1973) work was based on the premise, supplied by Linnaeus, that all human beings belonged to a species known as *Homo sapiens*. His work focused on extending this system down one more level to human *races*, primarily based on geography and observed physical differences. His identification of five distinct races, as well as other fundamental work on race, appeared in the third edition of his book *De Generis Humani Varietate Nativa* (On the Natural Variety of Mankind; Blumenbach, 1865/1969).

It is important to note that Blumenbach's original text (made available in 1775) recorded only four races based primarily on the "perceived superior beauty" of people from the region of the Caucasus Mountains. Interestingly, these four groups were defined primarily by geography and not presented in the rank order favored by most Europeans (Gould, 1994). Instead the Americanus, describing the native populations of the New World, were listed first. Second were the Europaeus (**Caucasians**), who included the light-skinned people of Europe and adjacent parts of Asia and Africa. The Asiaticus, or Mongolian variety, were listed third. This grouping included most of the other inhabitants of Asia not covered in the Europaeus category. Finally listed were the Afer (Ethiopian) group, who represented the dark-skinned people of Africa. This initial taxonomy, like the earlier work of Linnaeus, did not imply any inherent form of social hierarchy. Blumenbach is cited as the founder of racial classification, because unlike his predecessors he purportedly advanced the earlier work by rearranging races along a hierarchical order with Caucasians occupying the most superior position.

In the most simple terms, Blumenbach's 1795 work incorporated an additional ordering mechanism into his classification of race. This one addition would set in motion a series of developments that led to our current state of racial relations. In essence, "he radically changed the geometry of human order from a geographically based model without explicit ranking to a hierarchy of worth . . . [based on] a Caucasian ideal" (Gould, 1994, p. 69). He accomplished this by recognizing one particular group as closest to the created ideal and then characterizing the remaining groups as progressive derivations from this standard. In order to create a symmetrical pyramid, Blumenbach added the Malay classification in 1795. This grouping included the Polynesians and Melanesians of the Pacific, as well as the aborigines of Australia. In his own words, Blumenbach (1865/1973) describes the process of creating a social hierarchy:

> I have allotted the first place to the Caucasian . . . which makes me esteem it the primeval one. This diverges in both directions into two, most remote and very different from each other; on the one side, namely into the Ethiopian, and on the other the Mongolian. The remaining two occupy the intermediate positions between the primeval one and these two extreme varieties; that is the American between the Caucasian and Mongolian; the Malay between the same Caucasian and Ethiopian. (p. 131)

The result was an implied racist ranking of Europeans first, Africans and Asians last, and Malays and Americans between them (see Figure 2.1). Over the years the implied worth of human races—as indicated by the conventional hierarchy created by Blumenbach—has permeated the various attempts at racial classification. Most systems of classification divide humankind up into at least four groups based primarily on skin color and physical features: Red, Yellow, Black, and White (Native Americans, Asians, Africans, and Europeans, respectively). Whether or not brown-skinned peoples are considered a separate race depends on who is doing the categorizing (Lasker & Tyzzer, 1982; Spickard, 1992). Subsequent sections in this chapter explore the biological and social nature of racial classifications, as well as how these perspectives inform our current perceptions of race and interracial communication. However, before doing so, we need to explore the ways that earlier racial classifications were used in terms of world, national, and local events.

Economic and Political Expansion and Race

The history of race is intertwined with one of the major themes of the past five centuries of world history: economic and political expansion of European countries (Lasker & Tyzzer, 1982; Tolbert, 1989). As a way to justify their domination of Native populations of land they deemed desirable, Europeans developed and maintained ideologies and belief systems that supported their policies. (At this juncture, it is not productive to label these endeavors as intentionally oppressive or not. The bottom line is that such systems were created and maintained.) In addition, existing racial classifications, and the inherent cultural values associated within a hierarchy of race, served to fuel certain behaviors. Promoting a greater understanding of how race has been used by some as a means of economic and political expansion is an important aspect of the history of race. According to Tolbert (1989), three specific ideologies warrant attention: (1) the idea of a "chosen people," (2) racism, and (3) colonialism.

A Chosen People

The first ideology that helps us understand the role of race in international affairs is a version of the Judeo-Christian concept of a **chosen people**. This idea appears both in the Hebrew Scriptures and the New Testament. Within this interpretation

Figure 2.1   Blumenbach's Geometry of Human Order (1795)

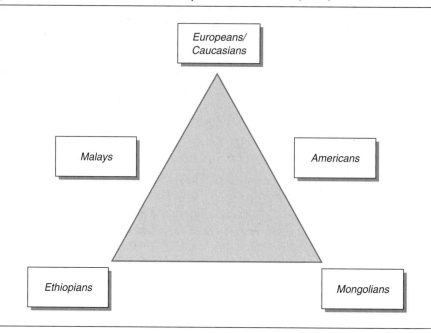

(C. E. Jackson & Tolbert, 1989), Europeans were the race chosen by God. It was their responsibility, therefore, to reclaim the world in his name. One movement related to this idea become known as Manifest Destiny.

Throughout the history of European expansion into the "new world," the idea that their efforts were consistent with spiritual teachings was prevalent. Yet the term **Manifest Destiny** began to appear in print regularly within the United States around the mid-1800s. At that time it referred to the idea that the United States had the right—granted by God—to spread across the entire North American continent (S. Brewer, 2006). The religious sentiment of U.S. Americans at this time in history was extremely high; in fact, many believed that the land across North America was sacred land that had been given to them by God.

It was in the name of Manifest Destiny that Europeans proceeded with their expansion in North America. Although initially embracing Europeans as potential traders, Native peoples faced grave adjustments in the face of a relentless encroachment by these strangers. The principles inherent in a Manifest Destiny clearly clashed with the nearly universal Native American belief that the land was a living entity the Creator had entrusted to them for preservation and protection (C. E. Jackson & Tolbert, 1989). Years of wars, disease, and negotiations, including the 1830s national "removal policy," which called for the resettlement to Oklahoma of all Native Americans living east of the Mississippi, had a devastating impact on America's Native populations. By 1850, for instance, the estimated 12 million Native people in North America at the time of Columbus's arrival had been reduced to 250,000 (Tolbert, 1989). By 1914, the 138 million acres that Native peoples "oversaw" had been reduced to 56 million acres.

> ## ❖ BOX 2.1
>
> ### STUDENT REFLECTIONS
>
> Although I am 100% German, I carry very little of the German culture in my blood. After all, my family moved to America when I was only 3 years old, and I have assimilated to the culture and its values quite well since then. However, I always felt a sense of shame and embarrassment whenever grade school kids found out that I was German. Maybe it is because the only time the teacher discussed anything German was when World War I and World War II came up on the lesson plan. My mother also felt a little embarrassed at times when in public, because whenever my siblings or I misbehaved, she would speak in German to us. . . . While I was taught to respect all people, no matter what color their skin, I was never taught of the injustices happening in the world around me. Sure, I went to high school and learned all about the civil rights movement and slavery, but I was never enlightened to how bad things still were in today's world. As much as I hate to say this, I feel that my high school has left me behind when it comes to social issues and the injustices surrounding them.

Native Americans were not the only people who were engulfed by the Europeans' expansion of the Americas (S. Brewer, 2006). The U.S. annexation of Texas from Mexico, the U.S. war with Mexico, and the subsequent acquisition of the New Mexico and California territories all were completed under a general charge of Manifest Destiny (Parrillo, 1996). Although Mexicanos were guaranteed, as new U.S. citizens, the protection of basic rights, discrimination and racism were commonplace. During prosperous times, with an urgent need for workers in agriculture, railways, and industry, Mexicans were welcomed by employers. In times of scarcity, however, they have been dismissed as "disposable field hands"—oftentimes without hearings or confirmation of their U.S. citizenship (West, 1982). Much of the land in the southern and western regions of the United States was gained through efforts related to Manifest Destiny. According to S. Brewer (2006), additional expansions—in Puerto Rico, the Philippine Islands, Alaska, and Hawaii—also can be included. However, at this point in history, "some had dropped the phrase Manifest Destiny and replaced it with a shorter one: Imperialism" (p. 42).

Racism

According to Hodge (1989), racism is "the belief in, and practice of, the domination of one social group, identified as a 'race,' over another social group, identified as of another 'race'" (p. 28). To justify their economic and political expansion in the New World, European Americans relied on the perpetuation of racist thinking. Because Europeans believed that races were genetically different, most did not see the exploitation of Native people, Africans, and others as any different from the use of farm animals (Graves, 2004). Manifest Destiny, in this regard, had a significant impact on how people, and by extension institutions, regarded Native Americans, Africans, and others living in the Americas. Three important components of early racist thinking are especially relevant to understand the foundational years of the United States.

First, Europeans maintained that humankind consists of well-defined races. This basic belief was evident in the ways that diverse ethnic and cultural groups, like those included in the larger groupings known as Native Americans and African Americans, were regarded as similar when contrasted to European American norms. This ignored that in many instances great diversity existed within the various ethnic groups contained in one racial category; in fact, the diversity within groups was larger than between groups (Bahk & Jandt, 2004).

Second was a belief that some races are inherently superior to others. In order to support the idea of a chosen people—one that is superior over other groups—they attempted to prove the inferiority of other racial groups by ignoring the achieved levels of learning, wealth, community, and established spirituality of Native American and African civilizations. The history of European–Native relations, for example, was situated within a superiority–inferiority dynamic (Corbett, 2003). Labels for indigenous people reflected negative stereotypes (e.g., Savages, Barbarians, Wild-men) and rationalized the enactment of policies designed to transform them into "proper citizens" (Stromberg, 2006).

❖ BOX 2.2

STUDENT REFLECTIONS

For the past few years, some of my relatives have been tracing our generational roots. Not to our surprise, we have traced our ancestry back to the McFadden Plantation of Sumter, South Carolina. It was not surprising because as an African American, I figured that my ancestors were slaves. It just amazed me to get a true and visible example of where my ancestors lived and experienced such harsh treatment. Bitterness did not overwhelm me, but I was negatively affected in the beginning. I felt a little angry about how many people's ancestors were robbed of their pride, dignity, tradition, and most importantly their sense of family and togetherness—things that seem to plague our community today.

Third, the belief that the superior race should rule over inferior races was viewed as good for both European Americans (who were fulfilling their responsibilities as the so-called chosen people) and other racial groups (who would benefit from the European influences). For example, European Americans believed that Africans had a natural defect that made it nearly impossible for them to function as free women and men. Using this reasoning, slavery was deemed productive in partially civilizing these "savages" and introducing them to a faith by which they could achieve salvation (Tolbert, 1989).

Colonialism

Colonialism is a formal system of domination that removes the power of self-determination from one group and gives it to another. Given the examples provided in earlier sections, it should be relatively clear how colonialism was central to European economic and political expansion. Comments from Paul R. Spickard (1992), an expert on issues of race and ethnicity, offer a nice point of summary for how this works:

> From the point of view of the dominant group, racial distinctions are a necessary tool of dominance. They serve to separate the subordinate people as Other. Putting simple, neat racial labels on dominated peoples—and creating negative myths about the moral qualities of those people—makes it easier for the dominators to ignore individual humanity of their victims. (p. 19)

Spickard goes on to explain how categorizing various African peoples all in one racial group, "and associating that group with evil, sin, laziness, bestiality, sexuality, and irresponsibility," (p. 19) made it easier for European slave owners to rationalize treating them in inhumane ways.

As you can see within our descriptions, the ideals of a "chosen people," Manifest Destiny, racism, and colonialism are closely woven together. Understanding the history of race is important, because as you will see throughout this text, contemporary issues are oftentimes rooted within a long-standing history of racist thinking. With this foundation in place, the remainder of this chapter discusses race as a biological and/or social construct, and the role of racial classifications in the contemporary Americas.

The Biological Foundations of Race

By definition, a race is a "subdivision of a species; it consists of a population that has a different combination of gene frequencies from other populations of the species" (Lasker & Tyzzer, 1982, p. 458). In the 19th century, the popularity of Darwinian theory served as a catalyst for scientists who were attempting to prove the existence of racial differences. Throughout history, the so-called commonsense view of race was based on the idea that at one time a handful of supposedly pure races existed. These subgroups had physical features, blood, gene pools, and character qualities that diverged entirely from one another (Zuberi, 2000). Over the years, some racial group members mixed with others outside their racial group, which resulted in some overlapping in racial characteristics. Clear distinctions remain in the identifying markers of each group, however. For instance, popular thought is that most observers can still distinguish a Caucasian type by his or her light skin, blue eyes, fine sandy or light brown hair, high-bridged nose, and thin lips. In contrast, a Negroid type is identified by dark brown skin, brown or black eyes, tightly coiled dark hair, broad flat nose, and thick lips (Diamond, 1994). Similar prototypical classifications could be generated for the Mongoloid and other races.

Over time, the increased number of interracial unions has contributed to a blurring of the distinct boundaries between "pure" races. However, additional problems arise within this commonsense approach when we look at specific examples within each racial category. For instance, Europeans who reside near the Mediterranean have dark, curly hair. The Khoisan peoples of southern Africa have facial features that closely resemble the people in northern Europe (Diamond, 1994). The !Kung San (Bushmen) have epicanthic eye folds, similar to Japanese and Chinese people (Begley, 1995).

Various scientists have engaged in countless studies searching for proof for the biological differences that exist in different racial groups. Some researchers, for example, conducted extensive analyses of geographical differences, only to come away with inconclusive findings. Once blood was ruled out as a possible distinguishing trait, some researchers began to study genetic composition (Bahk & Jandt, 2004). Others measured body parts—brains, calf muscles, jaws, lips, and noses—in attempts to link the more "inferior" races with apes (Valentine, 1995). In 1965, researchers studied gene clusters and proposed the formulation of hundreds, even thousands, of racial groups (Wright, 1994). Alternative bases for designating racial groups (e.g., by resistance to disease or fingerprints) have also generated a wide variety of equally trivial divisions (Diamond, 1994). Regardless of what was being measured and how, scientists were not able to come up with consistent evidence or proof of biological differences between racial groups (Begley, 1995).

In fact, extensive research indicates that pure races never existed (Lasker & Tyzzer, 1982; Montagu, 1997; Spickard, 1992), and all humankind belongs to the same species, *Homo sapiens.* National, religious, geographic, linguistic, and cultural groups do not necessarily coincide with racial groups. The cultural traits of such groups have no demonstrated genetic connection with racial traits. Because of this, the genetic variability within populations is greater than the variability between them (Bahk & Jandt, 2004). In other words, the biggest differences are *within* racial groups, not *between* them. This is not to say that physical features have no connection to geographical and genetic factors (the two primary factors in Blumenbach's work). But it is now understood that the few physical characteristics used to define races account for only a very tiny fraction of a person's total physical being (Graves, 2004). The differences that are apparent in different racial groups—but not exclusive to any one racial group—are better understood by considering environmental influences and migrations, as well as genetic factors.

Ashley Montagu (1964, 1997) was one of the first, and clearly the most successful, researcher to make use of scientifically established facts in debunking what he referred to as "man's most dangerous myth." His work has revealed how existing "racial mythologies" have supported countless attempts of "superior races" to prevail over more "inferior" ones. For example, think about the basic premises for slavery, Manifest Destiny, and cheap labor, discussed earlier. In the 20th century, Adolf Hitler and others who believed in the notion of White supremacy have accounted for millions of deaths. A review of current events or even a quick search on the Internet indicates that such beliefs still exist across the United States. All of these ideologies have one characteristic in common: They reflect attempts to foster the advancement of a superior race. In fact, the power of **eugenics** (the idea that intergroup breeding is a desirable mechanism to ensure the existence of superior races) has been used to explain the brilliance of African Americans such as Booker T. Washington, Frederick Douglass, and George Washington Carver. Each man's highly regarded accomplishments, it has been argued, were achieved through the genes inherited from the "white bloodlines" of a European American parent (Spickard, 1992).

As much as existing research has revealed the illogical notion of racial classifications as a means of self- and other identity, most people in the United States continue to use race as a way to distinguish human qualities, potential, and behaviors. Despite a lack of scientific evidence, race continues to be a largely accepted means of categorization. This is true for many people—not just those with racist ideas—who wrongly believe that racial differences are real (Graves, 2004). Now that we have debunked the myth of racial difference, we explain race as a sociopolitical construct. One point of caution first: Accepting that racial differences are not real does not make the effects of racism any less damaging. This point should make itself evident throughout future chapters.

The Sociopolitical Construction of Race

In the most basic sense, race cannot be considered a scientific construct if its categories are constantly being changed depending on laws, history, emotions, and politics (Nakashima, 1992). Instead, race is best understood as a product of social, political, and economic dynamics (rather than as a phenomenon based on biology). Through identifying and discussing the various ways that different social, political, national, and regional groups define racial classifications, exactly how political these decisions are becomes readily apparent.

The Fluid Nature of Racial Categories

Roughly speaking, race has become a way to describe human variation created by the interplay of geography, migration, and inheritance (Lasker & Tyzzer, 1982). However, the ways in which we have categorized people by race has changed over time (Bahk & Jandt, 2004). For example, in the late 19th and early 20th centuries, some newly arrived European Americans, including Italians and the Irish, were defined as distinct racial groups (National Research Council, 2004). Over time, these groups have been accepted, along with other Europeans as "White." In short, the fluid nature of racial categories over time speaks volumes about its existence as a social-historical construction (A. D. James & Tucker, 2003). As seen in Table 2.1, the U.S. Census Bureau has used a wide variety of racial categories to classify its citizens. In addition, different definitions historically have been used to designate who should belong to which group. For instance, some individuals who share a common national origin, such as Mexicans and Filipinos, have been counted as racial groups. Such persons represent cultural groups whose descendants originate from two or more of the traditionally accepted races (Fernandez, 1992). Over the years, changes have ranged from ones largely expected to others that appear illogical. For instance, did you realize the following?

- From 1920 to 1940 some Asian Indians were counted as members of a "Hindu" race.
- In the 1960 U.S. census, Latin Americans were counted as White.
- The U.S. census has stopped asking about race in their count of the residents of Puerto Rico because of the contrasting definitions of racial designations.
- Prior to 1977, Asian Indians were considered White but are now designated as Asian/Pacific Islanders.
- Current categories consider persons with origins traced to North Africa and the Middle East to be White.
- Latino/Hispanic people (from Mexican, Puerto Rican, Cuban, Central or South American, or other Spanish culture or origins) can be of any race.

In addition, racial categories vary in different social networks. Historically, they have been defined with regard to geographical, cultural, economic, and political factors. In many cases, social distinctions based on race develop when two or more groups of people come together in a situation of economic, political, or status competition (Spickard, 1992). Through a competition for perceived limited resources, a sense of us-versus-them is created and maintained. Depending on the introduction of additional players into the competition, these distinctions may change. People indigenous to the New World, for instance, did not experience themselves as Native Americans prior to the arrival of Europeans. Instead, they were Pequot, Osage, Mohegan, Sioux, or Oneida, for example.

❖ **BOX 2.3**

AUTHOR REFLECTIONS

For most of us, challenging existing ideologies about race is not easy. Such a process involves letting go of some basic ideas that have been commonly accepted as fact by the larger society. I vividly remember the first time that someone confronted me with the idea that there was only one human race and what we have come to recognize as different racial groups were not, in fact, different races at all. It occurred in the early 1990s during a graduate seminar that I participated in as part of my doctoral program in interpersonal/intercultural communication. I remember publicly nodding in agreement to my fellow classmate's comments, but privately thinking that she was playing around with the semantics of the word *race*, or trying to intellectualize our conversation by using abstract academic jargon that had no relevance to everyday living.

But, somehow, that brief encounter planted a seed that would be nurtured as I continued to explore the complex dynamics of culture, race, and communication. In various places, I found other scholars and practitioners who embraced the idea of one human race. "Race, an idea whose time has passed," was a phrase I saw on T-shirts, bumper stickers, and posters. Upon greater exploration of this issue, I found more and more evidence that indicated the concept of race was a social construction, with little or no biological foundation. Trying to communicate this idea to others was not easy, nor always well received. During discussions with family, friends, and colleagues, I got a chance to see a wide variety of reactions, including those that mirrored my own initial response.

Not to be deterred from embracing this newly founded idea, I consciously avoided using the term *race* and instead used *ethnicity*. I subsequently found out that this substitution was first suggested in 1950 (Montagu, 1972)—was I behind the times! Nevertheless, I began to use *interethnic* to describe the communication between African Americans and European Americans, *biethnic* to describe my cultural identity, and *multiethnic* to describe my family. Recently, I have shifted back to using racial terminology, especially in my teaching and research (or adopting a combination of the two: *race/ethnicity*). Race is a powerful concept in the United States, and whether a scientific or social phenomenon, it is one that must be acknowledged when exploring the relationships between culture and communication. Not to use the term would be ineffective and unrepresentative in describing the type of research that I do.

What has your personal journey been like, in terms of understanding your own and others' racial/ethnic identity? What role has this book played in the process?

—MPO

This underlying principle is also evident in how various counties and states officially define and designate their population in terms of race. Given the world's attention on its historic fight against apartheid, South Africa has probably one of the best known systems of racial classification. Four racial groups are commonly designated there: Whites, Coloureds, Asians, and Blacks. Within this system, two groups—the racially mixed Coloureds and the Asians—act as buffers between the historically dominant Whites and native Blacks (F. J. Davis, 1991). Although this type of racial classification may seem remote to most people living in the United States, several examples closer to home also illustrate the inconsistencies of racial designations. The following examples from North, Central, and South America may seem strange, alien, or confusing. Such reactions are natural, especially for those of you who have always accepted the rigid racial designations (Black/White) of the United States.

- In the United States any degree of African ancestry has historically made a person Black. Such is not the case in Latin America or the Caribbean. In some societies, any degree of non-African ancestry means that a person is not Black (Winn, 1995).
- The same person defined as Black in the United States may be considered Coloured in Jamaica or Martinique and White in the Dominican Republic (Hoetink, 1967).
- In Brazil, a survey of Blacks generated 40 different words to describe their race/color (C. Page, 1994). The possibilities between Black and White are many: *preto, cabra, escuro, mulato escuro, mulato claro, pardo, sarara, moreno*, and *branco de terra* (Degler, 1971). Some "Blacks" in Brazil change their designations as they move to different social classes.
- Three-fifths of Puerto Ricans who come to the mainland and are identified as Black were defined differently in their homeland. Most were considered *blanco* (white), *mulato* (mulatto), *trigueño* (wheat colored, olive skinned), or any of a number of color designations other than Black (F. J. Davis, 1991).
- To a West Indian, Black is a literal description: You are Black if your skin is black. If you are lighter—like the coloring of Gen. Colin Powell—you would describe yourself as "middle-class brown" or "a light chocolate." (Gladwell, 1996)

These examples clearly illustrate the ambiguous ways that race has been defined in various American societies. How race is designated in each culture is best understood within its national, political, and economic history (for a comprehensive treatment, see F. J. Davis, 1991).

Race Designations in the United States

Another means of critically examining the sociopolitical construction of race in the United States is to trace the ways that different racial group members, including multiracial persons, have been designated. The first census, supervised by Thomas Jefferson in 1790, had three categories: "free Whites," "slaves," and "Other free persons." This last category included free Blacks and "taxable Indians," referring to those Native Americans living in, or in close proximity to, European settlements (Wright, 1994). For most of the 19th century, distinctions were made between gradations of enslaved Blacks, including **mulattos** (one-half Black), **quadroons** (one-quarter Black), and **octoroons** (one-eighth Black) (F. J. Davis, 1991). After 1920, such distinctions were eliminated with the estimation that nearly three-quarters of all Blacks in the United

❖ **Table 2.1** U.S. Census Racial Categories, 1790–2000

Year	U.S. Census Racial Categories
1790	Free Whites, Other Free Persons, Slaves
1800–1810	Free Whites, Other Free Persons except Indians not taxed, and Slaves
1820	Free Whites, Slaves, Free Colored Persons, Other Persons Except Indians not taxed
1830–1840	Free White Persons, Slaves, Free Colored Persons
1850	White, Black, Mulatto
1860	White, Black, Mulatto, Indian
1870–1880	White, Black, Mulatto, Chinese, Indian
1890	White, Black, Mulatto, Quadroon, Octoroon, Chinese, Japanese, Indian
1900	White, Black, Chinese, Japanese, Indian
1910	White, Black, Mulatto, Chinese, Japanese, Indian, Other (plus write-in)
1920	White, Black, Mulatto, Indian, Chinese, Japanese, Filipino, Hindu, Korean, Other Races (plus write-in)
1930	White, Negro, Mexican, Indian, Chinese, Japanese, Filipino, Hindu, Korean, Other Races (spell out in full)
1940	White, Negro, Indian, Chinese, Japanese, Filipino, Hindu, Korean, Other Races (spell out in full)
1950	White, Negro, Indian, Japanese, Chinese, Filipino, Other Races (spell out)
1960	White, Negro, American Indian, Japanese, Chinese, Filipino, Hawaiian, Part Hawaiian, Aleut, Eskimo
1970	White, Negro or Black, Indian (American), Japanese, Chinese, Filipino, Hawaiian, Korean, Other (print race)
1980	White, Negro, Japanese, Chinese, Filipino, Korean, Vietnamese, Indian (American), Asian Indian, Hawaiian, Guamanian, Samoan, Eskimo, Aleut, Other (specify)
1990	White, Black, Indian (American), Eskimo, Aleut, Chinese, Filipino, Hawaiian, Korean, Vietnamese, Japanese, Asian Indian, Samoan, Guamanian, Other Asian Pacific Islander, Other Race
2000	White, Black or African American, American Indian or Alaska Native (specify tribe), Asian Indian, Chinese, Filipino, Other Asian (print race), Japanese, Korean, Vietnamese, Hawaiian, Guamanian or Chamorro, Samoan, Other Pacific Islander (print race), Some Other Race (individuals who consider themselves multiracial can choose two or more races)

NOTE: From *Measuring Racial Discrimination* (p. 31), by National Research Council, 2004, Washington, DC: National Academies Press.

States were racially mixed and that "pure" Blacks would soon disappear. This assumption, coupled with the socially accepted principles of hypodescent and the "one-drop rule," resulted in more exclusively rigid categories of White and Black persons.

Unlike many other countries, the United States has historically embraced a **one-drop rule**, whereby a single drop of Black blood makes a person Black (Rockquemore & Laszloffy, 2005). This idea was grounded in the ideal of a pure "White race," one that would be forever tainted by even the most minuscule addition of Black blood. The rules of **hypodescent** were based on a similar assumption. According to Root (1996), this principle occurs in a "social system that maintains the fiction of monoracial identification of individuals by assigning a racially mixed person to the racial group in their heritage that has the least social status" (p. x). Both of these commonly accepted practices led to the continued social separation between Black and White worlds, despite the blurring of these distinctions (F. J. Davis, 1991; Root, 1992). For instance, some scholars (C. E. Jackson & Tolbert, 1989; Spickard, 1992) believe that attempts to cling to these sociopolitical distinctions, in addition to clear economic reasons, led many White slave owners to regard some of their children (born to female slaves) as slaves. Recent DNA evidence suggests this was the case with the children of President Thomas Jefferson and Sally Hemmings (who was one of Jefferson's slaves). Ironically, it was Thomas Jefferson who wrote extensively on how the government should categorize mixed-race persons (see Box 2.4).

❖ BOX 2.4

EARLY WRITINGS ON MIXED RACE PEOPLE

Racial designations have always been salient in the United States. As the founding fathers began to write key documents, complex definitions for what constitutes racially mixed people were created. The formulas provided below were written by Thomas Jefferson.

Let the first crossing be of "a," pure Negro, with "A," pure white. The unit of blood of the issue being composed of the half of that of each parent, will be $a/2 + A/2$. Call it, for abbreviation, h (half blood)

Let the second crossing be of h and B, the blood of the issue will be $b/2 + B/2$, or substituting for $h/2$ its equivalent, it will be $a/4 + A/4 + B2$ call it q (quateroon) being ¼ Negro blood.

Let the third crossing be of q and C, their offspring will be $q/2 + C/2 = a/8 + A/8 + B/4 + C/2$, call this e (eighth), who having less than ¼ of a, or of pure Negro blood, to wit ? only, is no longer a mulatto, so that a third cross clears the blood. ("What Constitutes a Mulatto?" 1995)

Given the idea that racial designations are socially constructed, it is important to understand that different states had varying legal specifications as to the degree of Black ancestry that qualified residents as "officially Black" (see Spickard, 1989). Many states, especially those in the Northeast, did not have such legal definitions. Others were quite specific in their statutes. For instance, a person with one "Negro or Mulatto" great-great-grandparent was defined as "Negro" in North Carolina or Louisiana. However, this same person could be "White" in several states where racial lineage was only traced to great-grandparents (e.g., Indiana, Tennessee, Maryland, and Florida) or grandparents (e.g., Oregon). All of these state laws, to varying degrees, attempted to legalize the one-drop rule. Many of us would like to believe that such statutes are relics of an embarrassing past. However, many of these state laws remained on the books— if not in practice—until the late 20th century. Consider the following case: In 1986, the U.S. Supreme Court refused to review a ruling from a lower court in Louisiana. In this case, a woman, whose great-great-great-great-grandmother was a Black slave, sued over the right to change her race legally from Black to White (Wright, 1994). Although she could trace her lineage to the point where she could conclude that no more than 3/32 of her genetic heritage was Black, the state court's decision that she was legally Black in Louisiana was upheld.

In the absence of such supposedly clear definitions for other racial groups, the process of racial designation was even more inconsistent. Even with these state laws regarding African Americans, most designations historically were completed by what was commonly known as the **eyeball test** ("No Place for Mankind," 1989). This non-scientific, random measure involved various untrained laypersons (e.g., census takers, hospital staff, educational administrators) making decisions about others' racial makeup based on their own perceptions of race-based physical characteristics (see Orbe, 1999). Without question, such common practices resulted in numerous classifications that are largely ambiguous, illogical, and inconsistent.

This point is best illustrated through the example of three brothers who lived in Dulac, Louisiana, in 1969. Part of the Houma nation, the brothers shared the same father and mother. Each man was given a racial designation by the hospital staff that had assisted with his birth. The oldest brother was born with the help of a midwife at home. Because the state of Louisiana did not recognize the Houma as an official Native American nation prior to 1950, he was classified as a Negro. Born in a local hospital after 1950, the second brother was designated as an Indian. The third brother was assigned to the White category. Born in a New Orleans hospital 80 miles away, his designation was primarily based on the French family name (Stanton, 1971). Do such designations make sense to you? Or do they seem absurd? Much has changed in the past 50 years; however, many U.S. Americans still operate from such dated ideologies (see, for example, Orbe, 1999).

As we saw earlier, an analysis of the ways that individual states treated racial classification provides some insight into the unscientific nature of these designations. The examples described thus far have focused on the experiences of African American, Native American, and biracial people. But note that certain states needed ways to name and define groups of people who were relatively unique to their geographical location, for example, the Creole of Louisiana and the Mestizo of Texas and New Mexico. The state of Hawaii, added to U.S. territories at the end of the 19th century, also provides an interesting insight into the social construction of race (Tolbert, 1989). Unlike the remainder of the United States, which traditionally embraced the one-drop rule with little question, Hawaii has a long tradition of treating race designations more fluidly and inclusively because of the multiracial background of its native population.

The original Hawaiian settlers can be traced back some 1,500 years. The first inhabitants came initially from the Marquesas Islands and then from Tahiti (Howard, 1980). Hawaii's earliest residents were Polynesians, whose racial/ethnic composition represented a blend of Southeast Asia, Indonesia, and possibly the Middle East (F. J. Davis, 1991). After the arrival of several Spanish ships in the late 18th century, the Hawaiian Islands have been the adopted home for a number of other racial groups, including those from China, Japan, the Philippines, Puerto Rico, and Portugal (Day, 1960). Unlike other parts of the United States, Hawaii has a history of greater acceptance of ethnic and racial intermarriages, which has resulted in an affirmed melting pot of cultures. Steeped in a strong tradition opposing rigid racial categories, residents have long used a variety of ways to describe themselves, including the creation of multiple ethnic and racial configurations. Despite this localized sociopolitical system, official racial designations changed when Hawaii became the 50th state in 1959. At that time, the U.S. Census Bureau imposed its monoracial categories on a population that up until then had had little use for such categories (Lind, 1980). The strong tradition of affirming multiracial heritages continues in Hawaii despite the attempts of the government agencies. This was demonstrated in the 1980 census when close to 70% of Hawaiian residents, not satisfied with the unrepresentative sampling of separate race categories, defined themselves as "Other" (F. J. Davis, 1991).

The Significance of Race Today

Once students come to understand the myth of racial difference, some ask about the relevancy of using race as a concept. More specifically, they ask: Why can't we all be of one human race? Why do we still need to pay attention to race? Doesn't that simply reinforce racial and ethnic differences? While the ideals of living in a color-blind society are definitely attractive, we cannot achieve this goal until issues of race, ethnicity, and racism are identified, understood, and eliminated. This will take a significant amount of work—by individuals, groups, organizations, and society as a whole. In other words, we cannot become color-blind until we raise a sufficient level of color-consciousness. As Bahk and Jandt (2004) state, we need to pay attention to racial and ethnic categories "until practices of racial injustice are completely obviated in every sector of our society" (p. 66).

In 1950, the United Nations Educational, Scientific, and Cultural Organization (UNESCO) spoke about the constantly changing ideas related to classifications of race: "These divisions," they concluded, "were not the same in the past as they are at present, and there is every reason to believe that they will change in the future" (Montagu, 1972, p. 72). Historically, the maintenance of racial categories has been similar to a game of musical chairs: Each round always seems to be a little different from the first, and someone inevitably is left out! Concurrently, traditional racial categories have experienced problems with the millions of U.S. citizens who identify their heritage as multiracial (Root, 1996). As we move to a "minority–majority country" (Halualani et al., 2004), the inherent problems of attempting to classify a multiracial, multiethnic population along rigid racial categories continues.

Race continues to be a significant sociopolitical marker in the United States because, in most people's minds, race is a fundamental way to understand human diversity. Regardless of its unscientific and illogical foundation, thinking along long-established racial categories dominates national discussions. And although racial categories have served as a means of discrimination throughout U.S. history, they have also facilitated a sense of identity and common experiences for many racial groups (Spickard, 1992). In the face of historical uses of racial classification systems, many African Americans, for instance, have embraced their Blackness as a source of pride, unity, sense of belonging, and strength. In this regard, race and ethnicity function as a double-edged sword. Before concluding this chapter, we highlight two issues in the contemporary United States—immigration and post-September 11 tensions—that illustrate this point.

Immigration and Migration Tensions

In many ways, the United States is a country of immigrants. In fact, U.S. history has been shaped by four distinct waves of immigration (Pedraza, 2006). The first wave—covering the 18th to the middle of the 19th century—saw a large influx of immigrants from Northern and Western Europe. These were in addition to the forced migration of persons from Africa, as well as Native Americans. The second wave of immigrants came from Eastern and Southern Europe at the end of the 19th and beginning of the 20th century. Between 1924 and 1965, the period described as the third wave witnessed an internal migration involving African Americans, Native Americans, Mexicans, and Puerto Ricans relocating from the south to the north. The final wave of immigration, covering the past 40 years, has witnessed a large influx of immigrants from Asia and South and Central America (Pedraza, 2006).

Contemporary immigration patterns are significantly different from those of the past. For example, in 1960 the top five countries represented in the foreign born population in the United States were from (in order from largest to smallest) Italy, Germany, Canada, the United Kingdom, and Poland. In 2000, the top five countries of origin were Mexico, China, the Philippines, India, and Cuba. This reflects a dramatic shift in terms of nationality, with the largest number of immigrants coming from Central America and Asia (Huntington, 2005). As such, Latinos, with a U.S. population that reached 41.3 million in 2005, are now the largest and fastest growing minority group in the United States (Acosta-Belen & Santiago, 2006). Puerto Ricans make up over 9% of this number—and double that if you count those living on the island of Puerto Rico. Currently, they are the second largest Latino group, after Mexican Americans.

The number of foreign-born individuals residing in the United States amounts to 33.5 million people, which represents almost 12% of the country's population (Larsen, 2004). This does not include the 11 to 12 million undocumented immigrants (Ohlemacher, 2006a). While nearly 90% of all immigrants living in the United States until the middle of the 20th century were of European or Canadian descent, more than half of today's immigrants come from the Asian and Latin American countries (Suarez-Orozco, 2000). In fact, in the year 2003, 53% of immigrants were born in Latin

America, 25% in Asia, and only 14% in Europe (Larsen, 2004). While early waves of immigrants experienced a process of natural, continuous, and irreversible assimilation, such is not the case for those persons who are more recent immigrants (Suarez-Orozco, 2000). Many immigrants continue to function, in varying degrees, in both "new" and "old" cultures (Mahalingam, 2006).

Scholars have critically examined immigration over time and concluded that resistance to immigration is grounded in the politics of race (Merrill, 2006). Interestingly, the U.S.–Canadian border is over two times the size of the U.S.–Mexican border; yet in 1995, 330 Border Patrol agents were assigned to the northern border and 4,300 assigned to the southern border (Demo, 2005). Growing anti-immigration sentiment has been understood by some as covertly reflective of racial and ethnic tension (Domke, McCoy, & Torres, 2003). Interestingly, research reports that the percentage of adults with an unfavorable impression of immigrants from Mexico has tripled in the last decade, with no similar negative trend for immigrants from other countries. This statistical pattern is situated within a larger belief that Hispanic immigrants "mostly take low-paying jobs Americans don't want" (quoted in Domke, McCoy, & Torres, 2003, p. 137). Not surprisingly, the popular stereotype of the contemporary immigrant is one of "a poor and unkempt young Mexican male worker" (Demo, 2005, p. 292). In this regard, immigrants from certain geographical regions—mostly those in Africa and Central and South America—are perceived in more negative terms than those who are from Europe or Asia.

Post–September 11 Tensions

Middle Easterners have lived in the United States since the mid-1800s; most of the earliest immigrants were Chaldeans—Roman Catholics from present-day Iraq (Reimers, 2005). In the following years, other groups immigrated to the United States in substantial numbers from the late 1800s to the early to mid-1900s, including those from Armenia, Lebanon, and Syria (Reimers, 2005). In 2000, the 2.5 million immigrants from the Middle East constituted about 1% of the U.S. population and approximately 5% of the foreign born. While these people continued to come from countries such as Armenia, Lebanon, and Syria, they also represented significant numbers from Turkey, Iraq, Iran, Israel, Palestine, and North Africa (Egyptians are usually perceived as Middle Eastern despite being a part of Africa) (Reimers, 2005).

Prior to September 11, 2001, the label *Arab* was used to emphasize the commonality of all individuals of Arab descent regardless of national origin. However, after the terrorist attacks, the use of national labels such as Palestinian, Egyptian, or Lebanese were more frequently used (Witteborn, 2004). This was done to highlight the important distinctions in terms of religion, nationality, and ethnic origins—an important consideration given the general ignorance about this diverse group. Consider the comments of author Douglas Brinkley, during a National Public Radio interview, when he was talking about Dearborn, Michigan—a city that has the largest Arab community in the United States: "You see Lebanese restaurants and Iraqi bakeries all over. It's like you have a big Muslim world right there" (as quoted in Witteborn, 2004, p. 84). According to Witteborn (2004), the misconception lies in equating Arabs with Muslims when only 23% of

Arabs living in the United States are Muslims. Like Brinkley, most U.S. Americans could not make similar distinctions.

Immediately following 9/11, Middle Easterners—and/or individuals perceived to be Arab Muslims—experienced a backlash of discrimination, harassment, and violence. In fact, according to an FBI report, anti-Islamic religion incidents increased by more than 1600% between the years 2000 and 2001 (Swahn et al., 2003). The same report documented that a significant number of targets of this backlash were not Arab Muslims; instead, they included Sikhs, Arab Christians, South Asians, and Moroccans. Merskin (2004) reports that in several different speeches by President Bush, his rhetoric built on stereotypical words and images of Arabs. Consistent with existing media and popular culture images, he portrayed Arabs as evil, bloodthirsty, animalistic terrorists. Such representations negate the diversity and multiplicity of diverse groups of people united by a cultural identification (Witteborn, 2004).

Not surprisingly, immediately following September 11, the decrease in support for immigration was documented by national polls. For instance, one poll conducted in October 2001 found that 58% of adults in the United States wanted immigration reduced—a sharp increase from 41% just four months earlier ("Keep America's Gates Open," 2001). As described, earlier perceptions are skewed for non-European immigrants.

Conclusion

One central task of the study of interracial communication is to describe what we mean when we discuss race and racial categories. This chapter was designed to give you a historical perspective on these concepts. Specifically, we provided insight into the complex ways that designations based on race and ethnicity have been tied to social, political, and economic events. In addition, we focused on how the progression of race categories is tied to interracial communication in the 21st century.

Distinctions attributed to racial differences were initially used by Europeans in the 18th century to justify political and economic expansion. This continued well into the 20th century as the political and economic systems in the New World continued to take shape. Despite a lack of scientific evidence, race continues to be a largely accepted means of categorization in the United States. Various attempts to prove the existence of racial differences have only resulted in revealing the myth of "pure" races. In fact, it is commonly accepted that the greatest variability of human differences occurs within traditional racial categories, not between them. The most compelling evidence indicates that race is a sociopolitical construction, one that is actively maintained by our communication in various contexts, including interpersonal, small group, organizational, and mass media (to be highlighted in Part II). The reality remains, however, that most people continue to utilize this framework as a marker to distinguish human qualities, potential, and behaviors.

This foundation is important in setting the stage for our understanding of the complexities inherent in interracial communication. First, it allows us to debunk the myths of superior and inferior racial groups. Second, it helps us affirm the existence of some differences when comparing different racial/ethnic groups while at the same time recognizing the similarities of all people belonging to one human race.

OPPORTUNITIES FOR EXTENDED LEARNING ❖

1. Request a copy (if you do not already have one) of a form that your college or university currently uses to collect racial/ethnic information. What directions or guidelines are provided for this section? What categories are included? How are they defined? Inquire about whether these forms strictly follow federal guidelines or incorporate changes specific to state legislation. If you can, compare different forms from past years. How have questions pertaining to race and ethnic designations changed?

2. Can you think of real-life or hypothetical examples of racist acts? Independently generate a list of three different examples of racism. Then break into groups and share examples. Take special note of those examples that you would not consider racist and explain why. See if the group can ultimately come to a consensus as to what is, and what is not, racist behavior. It may be helpful, for instance, to differentiate behaviors that reflect prejudice, discrimination, and racism (see definitions in Chapter 1).

3. While on the *Oprah Winfrey Show* in the spring of 1997, champion golfer Tiger Woods explained that as a youngster he coined the term *Cablinasian* to capture the essence of his multiracial heritage (Caucasian, Black, American Indian, and Asian ancestry). His comment seemed to raise the consciousness level of the nation in terms of embracing the idea of a multiracial identity. Use an Internet search engine to get different sources discussing issues related to multiracial Americans. (Using the keyword *Cablinasian* will only result in one or two hits. Instead, use the keywords *biracial Americans* or *multiracial Americans.*). What impacts might a new multiracial identity have on our society? How do traditional civil rights groups feel about such a move?

4. Are you familiar with the fairly recent work of Leonard Jeffries? Jeffries, a professor of Black studies at the City University of New York, made the argument that the key determinant of personality is the skin pigment melanin (Adler, 1991). Using this guide, he divided humanity into "Ice People" (the greedy warlike inhabitants of the North) and "Sun People" (the generous, communal natives of the South). What is your reaction to his basic ideas? How are they similar, (yet different), from the basic ideas of such groups as the Ku Klux Klan and the Aryan Nation?

5. Use the Internet to locate different Web sites that support and oppose stiffer immigration laws. Based on what you find, what are the major arguments that inform both sides of this important societal issue? Summarize and create a classroom debate where groups can argue their support or rejection of the following: The United States, as a nation of immigrants, should remain committed to immigration rights.

6. Take the role of the director of the Office of Management and Budget, the federal agency given the task of determining how racial and ethnic groups will be defined. (If you are working in a small group, assume you are a member of the OMB committee given the same task.) Given your increased knowledge of the history of race, how would you construct categories (if at all) for the 2010 U.S. Census? Spend some time discussing the rationale for your resolution, because this decision has direct consequences for the country. In addition, be sure to identify what values, if any, are to be served by your suggestions for designating race. Share your ideas with your professor and classmates.

B

The Power of Language, Labels, and Naming

While reading Chapters 1 and 2, how conscious were you of the terms used to describe different racial/ethnic groups? Did some labels offend you? Confuse you? Enlighten you? One of the challenges in writing a book on interracial communication involves the various decisions that must be made in terms of language, labels, and naming. Such decisions are difficult because racial/ethnic groups are not static entities (A. Rodriguez, 2002). Instead, the ways in which ingroup (as well as outgroup) members identify and label themselves change and evolve over time (Larkey, Hecht, & Martin, 1993). Throughout the book, we have attempted to determine and utilize those terms and labels that are most currently used by the particular racial/ethnic group we are discussing.

We have also maintained a high level of consciousness in our labeling and naming choices. As you will undoubtedly come to realize, if you have not done so already, language is a powerful element in communication processes. Unlike the popular old adage, we do believe "sticks and stones may break your bones *and* that names can and will hurt you." Historically, the process by which racial/ethnic groups—as well as those cultural elements central to their locations—were labeled has in fact had a tremendous effect on self- and other perceptions. For example, did you notice in Chapters 1 and 2 we avoided using the terms *America* or *American* to describe the land or people of the United States? Instead we used phrases like North, Central, and/or South America or American to help specify the particular people/land to which we were referring. The term Americas is used to alert you that we are describing more than simply the United States. Is all this simply splitting hairs, lingering examples of the destructive legacy of political correctness? As you will see in this chapter, our response to this question is, "No, not necessarily." Using the term America to describe the United States—or using American to describe U.S. citizens—is egocentric and reduces the visibility, attention, and importance given to other diverse countries in the Americas (Canada, Mexico, Argentina, Brazil, etc.). In a historical sense, it is also important to recognize that "America" was the home to civilizations of people years prior to the arrival of Europeans. What became known as the New World to European settlers was, in the experiences of the indigenous people of the land, not "new" at all. Many knew it as Turtle Island (M. C. Gonzalez, 2002).

Our objective here is not to provide a laundry list of "politically correct" language for you to use when interacting with individuals who are racially/ethnically different. Given the complexity of interracial communication processes, such a list would be limited, ungeneralizable, and possibly counterproductive. Instead, we want you to recognize the inherent power of language choices in determining levels of communication effectiveness. Specifically, this chapter discusses the importance of language in interracial communication, and how societal power is directly related to issues of labeling and naming specific cultural groups. Before offering some general guidelines, we discuss the centrality of other communication elements, such as nonverbal cues and situational context, in making language choices. Our treatment of the power of language, labels, and naming begins with exposing some of the myths surrounding the phenomenon that has become known as political correctness.

The furor over **political correctness** (PC) has died down some in recent years. However, it is still common to hear references to the concept as it has become associated with a specific set of ideologies and, in turn, a collection of socially accepted terms. For instance, students commonly begin their comments in class by stating, "I know this isn't PC, but . . . " Other students use certain terms, and following the nonverbal reactions of others, immediately add, "Oops, I guess that's not the politically correct term nowadays. Sorry, but you know what I meant!" During the early 1990s, discussions of political correctness took place mainly on college and university campuses (Ethridge, 1991; J. Taylor, 1991). However, the issue of "being PC" soon spread to other aspects of society, such as corporate organizations, which were also experiencing an increased number of traditionally underrepresented group members entering their ranks (Aamidor, 1994).

So, exactly what is politically correct language? In its most basic form, it refers to the elimination of speech that oftentimes works to exclude, oppress, demean, or harass certain groups (Remar, 1991). However, being PC developed into a media phenomenon that clearly expanded beyond its original intentions. In the early 1990s, media attention to what was described as the "political correctness movement" on college and university campuses made it into a national issue. As described in the major national outlets, political correctness was "an umbrella term that describes what is deemed acceptable by an eclectic group of radical feminists, homosexuals, Marxists, and 'multiculturalists'" (J. Taylor, 1991, p. 100). While the term is not used as frequently in recent years, the tensions behind the debates of political correctness can still be seen in more contemporary issues such as efforts to eliminate affirmative action programs.

❖ **BOX 3.1**

AUTHOR REFLECTIONS

One of the most difficult aspects of coauthoring a book on interracial communication involves the careful ways in which many topics must be handled. Our goal is to provide sufficient knowledge, theories, and experiential application that promote a greater understanding of the complexities of culture, race/ethnicity, and communication. When it comes to verbal and non-verbal cues, much of the existing literature focuses on highlighting the various differences that were found in cross-group comparative studies. Based on these findings, a significant amount of literature offers generalizations on how African/Asian/Latino/a/Native Americans communicate both verbally and nonverbally. In almost all cases, European Americans are used as the point of comparison. Although this type of information may be helpful in the creation of a general body of knowledge, it offers little practical value for everyday interactions. In fact, I believe the result of such studies has contributed to a well-documented characterization of a "stereo-typical African American" (see Orbe & Everett, 2006). Such generalizations, communicated in "black-and-white" terms (pun intended!), do not encourage persons to recognize the great diversity *within* particular ethnic groups based on other salient issues such as gender, class, or age. Instead, the focus is on generalized differences *between* racial/ethnic groups.

In light of this unproductive trend, this chapter avoids giving significant attention to such research. Instead, we focus on the central role that social power plays in the usage and effects of language choices. Through the discussion presented, we hope you will achieve an increased awareness. In terms of generalized differences across ethnic groups, we believe the ultimate means for determining their value is through actual interracial communication!

—(MPO)

At this point, we want to be explicit about why we are including a chapter on language. Embracing one or the other interpretations of what it means to be PC is not important. Regardless of your particular perceptions of political correctness, we hope you will recognize the importance of language choices (terms, labels, names) on communication effectiveness in general, and interracial communication effectiveness specifically. Teaching others how to be politically correct is not our objective. Instead, we hope to increase your awareness and sensitivity to the power of language when communicating with others. In addition, we will help you understand why certain racial/ethnic groups prefer some terms over others. Through the insights shared throughout the remainder of the chapter, you will be able to make informed decisions about what language choices you incorporate into your everyday interactions. One important aspect of the idea of making an informed choice includes an awareness of the history of racial/ethnic terms and insight into how others might interpret contemporary use of specific labels.

The Power of Language

Language is central to human communication processes. Although certainly it is incorrect to equate language with communication itself, the important role of language in communicative effectiveness cannot be denied. For most individuals, however, their native language is a ubiquitous entity, one that is constantly in use but seldom critiqued or questioned consciously. Their language—their words, gestures, phrases, and styles—is natural and effortless when used with others who share a common speech community (see Chapter 6). In this regard, language is an abundant public resource that many utilize with little attention to its powerful nature. In terms of interracial communication, the power of language can be seen in the ways it has been used to label, and subsequently define, some *groups* of people while leaving others—the dominant or "standard" group—unlabeled. Prior to our discussion of the power of labels and naming, some background information is needed. Specifically, we want you to see the important role that language plays in human communication processes. This is best achieved describing language as (1) a tool, (2) a prism, and (3) a display.

Language as a Tool

In its most basic form, language is a tool that humans have utilized, sometimes effectively, sometimes not so effectively, to communicate their ideas, thoughts, and feelings to others. Language systems include semantic, syntactic, pragmatic, and phonetic patterns and are accessed through either written or spoken channels. Language is the means by which our internal cognitions (beliefs, values, attitudes, emotions, etc.) can be shared with others. As described earlier, this process is central to human communication as seen in the word's origin. Communication comes from the Latin **communicare**, which means "to make common." Without any common experiences, human communication would be impossible. The ability to share even our most basic internal cognitions with others as a means to establish and locate common experience is central to the human experience. Without these common experiences to draw from (some use the term **homophily** to describe the common experiences you share with others), communication would be impossible.

❖ **BOX 3.2**

AUTHOR REFLECTIONS

As we have discussed in this chapter, language is a prism or tool we use on a daily basis to communicate, and depending on a number of variables and factors, that language can be very powerful in shaping our identities and affecting how racially different people interact with and perceive each other. We must be sensitive to the fact or reality that, as racialized individuals, we will indeed have different interpretations of our shared experiences. We also need to be aware of how our language can manifest that power and cause even greater division between the races.

One example of this is the phrase "jungle fever," which entered popular culture vernacular as a result of Spike Lee's film of the same name. Stevie Wonder even wrote the theme song. The movie was incredibly popular and played a very critical role in articulating for its audience, and society at large, the historical framing of Black/White love. According to Paulin (1997), the title

> reiterates dominant representations of interracial relationships . . . [as evidenced by] the underlying discourse of contamination implied by the clichéd title. . . . Thus, *Jungle Fever* effectively reinscribes the notion that interracial love is the result of irrational, racialized, heated passion. . . . The film serves to reproduce the notion that interracial desire is transgressive and that it contaminates pure blood lines. (p. 168)

As you can see, the phrase has an incredibly negative connotation, and when the movie was released, very few people took the time to deconstruct its meaning and power.

Use of the phrase "jungle fever" permeated everyday conversation, and the lyrics seem to speak to the pressures interracial romantic relationships oftentimes face. It is lost on the listener that the very title of the song invokes thoughts and visions of savagery bestowed upon the African American person in the relationship, whose very presence seems to "infect" the European American partner with a disease that will ultimately kill him or her. Fifteen years have passed since the movie was released, and the term remains a part of Black culture. I have personally chosen *not* to use the term as a reference to interracial romantic relationships. It gives too much power to a phrase that subconsciously demonizes relationships between the races. Let's all be proactive in being careful about the words we use and the power we give insensitive and offensive language—one word at a time.

—TMH

The analogy used here can be productive in understanding how a language system is similar to a tool box. Language systems are comprised of a set of tools used to communicate in different settings. No limitations are put on the number of tools that a person is capable of acquiring, nor is any one person restricted from learning how to use any one set of tools. In fact, we would guess that many U.S. Americans find themselves using different language systems (tool boxes) for achieving different objectives in various communities of which they are a member. For instance, a student may draw from one set of tools when interacting with family members and another when discussing his or her chemistry test with a professor. In order to communicate effectively, the same or different tools might be necessary when in the company of friends, professional colleagues, or those with a common interest or hobby. In essence, a well-stocked tool box (language system) is essential to getting the job done (communicating effectively). Trying to complete a job without the proper tools is possible, but increasingly more complex and time consuming. And even when all of the right tools are available, most jobs are more difficult than they initially appear to be, in part because of the imperfection of the tools. It also can be the result of a person's lack of ability to use the tools properly. In similar ways, these tool issues impact language and interracial communication effectiveness.

One aspect of language that sometimes hinders effective interracial communication is the **arbitrary nature of words.** As is commonly discussed, words do not have any inherent meaning. Instead, they are abstractions of the things they represent and, subsequently, are always incomplete representations. In other words, a person uses a word or phrase in an attempt to capture the essence of an idea or thing. Assuming a phrase exists that comes close to representing one's ideas, the key for effective communication lies with the other person's ability to decode the phrase in a manner consistent to that in which it was encoded. Meaning is created not by the words themselves, but how the words are interpreted by *both parties.* Some responsibility for specific language, therefore, must be assumed by both the senders and the receivers. The ability to communicate effectively with others depends on our language capabilities as well as the commonality of experiences (homophily), which lends to the increased likelihood of shared meaning. Generally speaking, the wider and more divergent the language communities in which we normally reside, the more difficult mutual understanding becomes.

Language as a Prism

Language is more than simply a passive, neutral tool that we use to communicate our internal cognitions to others (Hymes, 1974). In addition to serving as an "instrument for voicing ideas," it also provides a guide for an individual's mental activity (Hoijer, 1994, p. 194). In other words, language serves a central role in providing linguistic, semantic, and verbal categories that have a direct relationship to how we come to understand abstract ideas. Within this perspective, language can be regarded as a prism in the way it helps shape the ways in which we perceive reality. One of the central ideas associated with this interpretation of language is the Sapir-Whorf hypothesis (sometimes referred to as simply the Whorfian hypothesis).

The **Sapir-Whorf hypothesis,** a major proponent of linguistic relativity, suggests that language structure is necessary in order to produce thought (Fong, 2000). Within this perspective, language is a guide to social reality. Although it helps articulate our experiences, it also plays a central role in defining them. In its most extreme form, this approach to language suggests that the particular elements of a language system predispose us to think in particular ways and not in others. Edward Sapir explained that "human beings do not live in the objective world alone, nor alone in the world of social activity as ordinarily understood, but are very much at the mercy of the particular language which has become the medium for their society" (Sapir quoted in Mandelbaum, 1949, p. 162).

You may need a set of examples to help you understand this abstract concept. A significant amount of research has been completed on color terms and perceptions (e.g., Kay & Kempton, 1984) and provides support for the Sapir-Whorf hypothesis. An easy experiment serves as a great illustration of how a person's language capabilities in terms of color act as a prism for his or her reality. Select a piece of clothing that is a really unusual color. Ask several of your friends, both women and men, to identify its color. Inevitably a variety of different terms will be generated to describe one item. For instance, you may hear the same item called blue, green, bluish green, teal, turquoise, seafoam green, or malachite. Depending on the particular person's set of life experiences (e.g., working as a salesperson for J. Crew clothing), perceptions of the item probably differed greatly. According to the Sapir-Whorf hypothesis, varying perceptions of reality are due to the differences in language abilities (color terms) of specific people. In other words, the ways in which a person thinks about a particular thought, object, or emotion is confined by the terms to which she or he has access. If one of your friends does not have the term *seafoam green* in her repertoire of color terms, she will not be able see something as seafoam green (even if others do). In this regard, her reality is shaped by her language structures.

Along this same line of inquiry, other research (e.g., Fong, 2004) has revealed how varying elements (semantics or syntax, for example) of different language systems (English, Spanish, Japanese, etc.) impact the specific worldviews of those who were raised using a particular language. But the Sapir-Whorf hypothesis also has its critics. Other scholars (e.g., Carroll, 1992) have found it difficult to test the strength of the relationship between structure of language and perceptions of reality. Given the varying reports about the relationship between language structure and thought processes, a precise understanding of the exact impact of language structure on thought processes is inconclusive. However, what is not in question is that our language capabilities do have *some* tangible effect on how we come to understand reality.

Language as a Display

As you can see, the importance of language in the communication process can be seen through the many roles it plays. In addition to its use as a tool and a prism, language also serves as a display for our internal thoughts. Humans utilize their language capabilities to communicate their thoughts. In this regard, language is a tool. However, the language choices we make as a means to communicate certain ideas do more than simply articulate those ideas. Although oftentimes unintentional, they provide additional information—beyond the presentation of our ideas—about internal cognitions regarding a particular subject. It has often been said that language is an index to, or reflection of, our internal thought patterns (Hymes, 1974). Consider the following example to help you understand how individuals' language choices sometimes communicate more about them than they always recognize.

In the English language, several words (synonyms) can be used to communicate any one idea. The unconscious or conscious choice of words can provide a great deal of insight in terms of how one feels about the idea—in some cases, even more than is directly communicated. Olsen (2006) describes the power of language in his article critiquing the treatment of Japanese Americans during World War II. In particular, he criticizes the ways in which the government, media, and historians used words and phrases that downplayed the harsh reality of actual treatment. As such, he urges educators to use appropriate terms to teach students about how Japanese American citizens (and not "non-aliens") were forcibly removed (as opposed to "evacuated") to concentration camps (more accurate than past reports that described the sites as relocation centers or internment camps). These shifts in language are important to avoid neutralizing the racist activities of the U.S. government, which also included violating the Japanese citizens' First Amendment rights by outlawing reading and writing in Japanese, worshipping in Japanese, and other cultural and recreational activities (Mizuno, 2003). Do you see any parallels between this example and the language that was used to describe those who lost their homes during Hurricane Katrina (e.g., "refugees" versus "evacuees")?

The phrase **semantics of prejudice** can be used to describe how language choices can unintentionally reveal information about individuals' internal thoughts (regardless of other unconscious attempts to shield them in public). For those persons who have spent considerable amounts of time involved in varying forms of interracial communication (like the authors of this book), language choices often serve as a way to understand the perspectives of others (see, for example, Houston, 2004). When you hear a new acquaintance refer to a third party as "Oriental" (as opposed to Asian, Korean, or Laotian), do you draw any conclusions about how she regards people of Asian descent? How about if a person commented on the "savage-like behaviors of some Blacks" or how he thought that "biracial women are exotic"? Would these language choices impact your perceptions of this person's views on race, ethnicity, and interracial communication? It is safe to say that for those experienced in interracial communication—including both authors of this text—such a display of language choices would certainly send up red flags!

This is not to say that the use of certain phrases is a direct reflection of certain thoughts, beliefs, and/or values. Nor is it accurate to conclude that everyone who uses a specific term has similar internal cognitions regarding any one particular topic. Remember, however, what the Sapir-Whorf hypothesis suggests: Our language structures predispose us to think in certain ways. For those persons interested in becoming effective communicators within racially and ethnically diverse settings, a clear consciousness of language choices must be maintained.

❖ **BOX 3.3**

ADVOCATING FOR ONE UNIVERSAL LANGUAGE, ESPERANTO

Article 2 of the Universal Declaration of Human Rights clearly states that all persons are entitled to basic human rights without distinction to race, sex, religion, and language (among others). Consequently, scholars across the world are advocating for the adoption of one universal language that can be used throughout the world (Chong-Yeong, 2002). **Esperanto** is the most widely spoken constructed international language; created in 1887, it is used in world travel, correspondence, cultural exchange, conventions, literature, language instruction, television, and radio broadcasting ("Esperanto: The International Language That Works!" 2006). According to Sikosek (2003), Esperanto speakers are more numerous in East Asia and Europe (compared to the Americas, Africa, and Oceania) and are particularly prevalent in northeastern European countries, in China, Korea, Japan, and Iran, as well as in Brazil, Argentina, and Mexico.

Esperanto is not designed to replace anyone's native language; instead, it is designed to serve as a common second language ("Esperanto: The international language that works!" 2006). According to Chong-Yeong (2002), it is currently used by millions of people across 120 countries in the world. Esperanto is an effective common auxiliary language because it: (1) does not belong to any one particular cultural group, (2) is easy to learn, and (3) has sufficient linguistic complexity to reflect diverse human experiences.

- Have you heard of Esperanto?
- What are some of the advantages and disadvantages of adopting it as a common universal language?
- If your university offered it as an option for a foreign language requirement, would you take it? Why, or why not?

The Power of Labels

Part of human nature is to use labels to refer to other people and ourselves. Systems of classifications are a natural means by which we make sense out of a complex world. But we must critically examine the genesis and development of labels for particular categories. Labels communicate on many levels of meaning. They also implicitly work to establish, maintain, or challenge specific kinds of relationships between individuals and/or groups of individuals. Labels, as a form of language, can be used strategically to communicate closeness or distance among individuals depending on the intentions and effects of the speech act. In the context of our discussion revolving around the power of language, it is important to recognize that the labels designated for specific racial/ethnic groups in the United States reflect this reality.

As illustrated in Chapter 2, the contextualization of language is itself very much a political act. Asante (1998b) explains that whenever categories and labels are created in an effort to make certain concepts functional, certain choices are made from many different possibilities. Typically the categories ultimately chosen can create mechanisms that benefit some groups to the disadvantage of others. Some suggest that persons with political, social, and economic power occupy positions that allow them to label less powerful groups of people. In many instances this is completed in ways that maintain or increase the power bases of those already in the most powerful societal positions.

White Privilege

Over the course of U.S. history, European American men have held most of the social, economic, and political power. From this position of privilege, they have consistently created and used labels to define other ethnic groups in ways that have benefited their own existence. Chapter 2 described how Africans, Asians, Latinos, and those indigenous to North America never defined themselves as such until coming in contact with Europeans. Prior to European influences, the labels that were used reflected the diversity of particular groups of people based on ethnicity and culture. Think about how one label based on race (e.g., Oriental or Asian) has come to represent a multitude of diverse ethnic and cultural groups (e.g., Chinese, Filipino, Hmong, and Indonesians). Each label created a category that served the purpose of defining these groups from a European perspective.

This critical line of thinking provides a vivid illustration of Asante's argument that the choice of certain labels (over others) is situated in a political context, one in which dominant power bases are maintained or increased. Why didn't Europeans recognize and account for the diversity within different racial groups? Some scholars, focusing on the ideas of linguistic relativity (i.e., Fong, 2004), would point to the effect of their relative ignorance in terms of these differences. It is apparent that European perspectives were informed by the language that was created and maintained in terms of pure, distinct races. Can you understand how their language systems included racial terms that had a direct influence on the ways individuals come to understand others who are different? Other scholars (e.g., Frankenberg, 1993), taking a more critical perspective, might conclude that Europeans' positions of privilege worked to render this labeling process "natural" and "logical" while *unintentionally* reaping the benefits of such a language system.

The idea of **societal privilege** is an important concept in terms of the ways that certain groups have the power to label others while remaining unlabeled. Based on the work of Peggy McIntosh (McIntosh, 1995a, 1995b), a greater understanding of how societal privilege operates within specific contexts has been advanced in terms of its effect on perceptions of "reality." McIntosh initially wrote on male privilege; however, her recognition of White privilege (McIntosh, 2002) is especially relevant to discussions on interracial communication. Societal privilege, in this vein, refers to a general favored state, one that has been earned or conferred by birth or luck. Unlike that which is earned, power from unearned privilege can look like strength, but what it typically represents is an *unearned entitlement*. According to McIntosh, part of White privilege is seeing racism in terms of individual acts and not as largely invisible systems that confer dominance on European Americans (McIntosh, 1992). In terms of the power of labeling, a position of privilege is a position that remains largely unnamed and racially "neutral" (A. C. Rowe & Malhotra, 2006). White privilege can be seen in the ways that most people of European descent think of themselves as Americans with no race (A. N. Miller & Harris, 2005).

The remainder of this section presents an overview of the labels that have been used to describe the major racial/ethnic groups in the United States. Recognize that such groups are not merely static entities. As you will see, racial/ethnic groups—as we have come to understand them—are products of a lengthy process of labeling and identification. Our primary objective in including this material is to create awareness of how labels have evolved over time. Through exposure to this information, you will obtain some additional insight into our rationale for the language choices in this book. Ultimately, these insights will contribute to your increased awareness and understanding of the complexity of labels and help each of you make informed choices about the language you use.

African Americans

Research on the evolution of labels to describe persons of African descent is well documented (R. A. Davis, 1997; Holloway, 1990; Larkey, Hecht, & Martin, 1993). Variations have included African, Colored, Negro, **Black**, Afro-American, and African American.

According to Holloway (1990), the different labels reflect changes in how persons of African descent negotiated their identity in the United States. This ranges from strong African identification, nationalism, integration, and attempts at assimilation to a renewed sense of cultural identification. Larkey et al. (1993) see recent shifts of African American self-identification as connected to issues of self-determination, strength, progress, and control. One major issue in labeling, for all racial/ethnic groups generally and people of African descent specifically, is the general preference for labels that have been generated from within the community (as opposed to those imposed by others). For many African Americans, language preferences reflect a personal and/ or cultural choice.

Given the variety of choices, which term—Black or African American—is correct? Because of the diversity of thought within this heterogeneous group, one term is not necessarily more correct than the other. Much has to do with the specific personal choices of the individual. The most recent research found that people of African descent were equally divided in the preference for the label "Black" or "African American." Interestingly, this was consistent across gender and level of education. However, those individuals who were younger, attended integrated schools, and were from larger non-Southern cities were more likely to prefer "African American" rather than "Black" (Sigelman, Tuch, & Martin, 2005).

❖ BOX 3.4

LINGUISTIC PROFILING

When communicating on the phone with someone whom you do not know, it is natural to make judgments about that person's race, gender, age, and other demographic elements (Groscurth, 2003). Recent research has indicated that this is especially true in terms of race; according to Rickford and Rickford (2000), an average U.S. American can correctly identify the race of speakers 80–90% of the time. While the process of making judgments is natural, it is illegal when individuals discriminate against others based on those judgments. In fact, this discriminatory act has been given a name, linguistic profiling.

Linguistic profiling occurs when individuals listen to a person's voice on the phone, make conclusions about a person's race/ethnicity, and then discriminate against the person based on assumed race/ethnicity (Baugh, 2000b). Recently, several African Americans across the United States have sued apartment managers who, they claim, correctly assumed their race by their vocal patterns and then violated fair housing practices. Oftentimes these plaintiffs were not identified because of their use of Ebonics—something that for some signals ignorance (Baugh, 2000a) and triggers negative reactions (Groscurth, 2003). Instead, they used "standard" English but in ways in which their intonations and vocalics reflected the African American culture.

- Do you think that linguistic profiling is prevalent?
- In what contexts?
- Do you think that there is such a thing as "sounding Black" or "sounding White?"
- How does society perceive individuals whose language use does not "match" their racial and ethnic identity?
- Is this becoming more, or less, common?

R. A. Davis (1997) argues that African Diasporans anywhere in the world need to be designated with great clarity. He believes that an all-inclusive term like **African American** is not appropriate given the increasing diversity of people of African descent living in the United States. According to Reimers (2005), more Black immigrants have entered the United States than during the slave era. Recently, the largest numbers have come from the Caribbean (most notably the Dominican Republic, Cuba, Jamaica, and Haiti) and secondly from Africa (most notably Nigeria, Ethiopia, Morocco, Ghana, and Kenya) (M. Waters, 1999). Because of this we need terms that embrace the diversity for Black Americans while also recognizing the differences in terms of culture, language, and national origin (El Nasser, 2003). In the end, Davis argues that people of African descent born in the United States should be labeled as Black Americans; those born in Africa and gaining U.S. citizenship are best described as African Americans.

Asian Americans

Most scholars trace the first wave of Asian immigrants in the United States back to Chinese laborers who arrived in California between 1850 and 1882 (Min, 2006). However, the first recorded Asians arrived in the United States prior to the signing of the Declaration of Independence; this small group of "Manila men" arrived in New Orleans in the 1760s (Gudykunst, 2001). We make this point to draw attention to the fact that particular immigration patterns of different Asian American groups is varied and covers 250 years (Chan, 2003) and three different eras (Min, 2006).

In recent years, the label Asian has replaced the use of other terms, including "Mongolian," "Asiatic," and "Oriental." Still, Asian American is imprecise since it includes a number of different cultural groups under one umbrella term: Chinese Americans, Filipino Americans, Japanese Americans, Korean Americans, Vietnamese Americans, Asian Indian Americans, Cambodian Americans, Laotian Americans, Hmong Americans, and Thai Americans (Gudykunst, 2001). Because of the great diversity represented within this commonly used label, it is often helpful to use more specific identifiers when possible. This practice recognizes and distinguishes Asian Americans from Asian nationals, and it also helps differentiate among different Asian nationalities. Such distinctions are important given the wide variety of cultures and experiences of those commonly referred to as a single entity. For instance, recognizing a person as a Korean American, rather than more generally as an Asian American, allows greater insight into that individual's cultural heritage (Sing, 1989).

While Asian American is a convenient label, J. Lee and Zhou (2004) report that few U.S. Americans of Asian descent actually identify themselves as such. Instead, they identify with their particular countries of origin. Still, many U.S. Americans treat Asian Americans as a panethnic group—seeing all Asian Americans as similar and with little, or no, recognition of differences within particular ethnic groups (Gudykunst, 2001). Cultural differences, like those related to age, generation status (J. Lee & Zhou, 2004), and spirituality (Min, 2006), are given little consideration to how they affect identity and communication. A key factor in how Asian Americans communicate has to do with the experiences within the United States—for instance, are they immigrants, first generation, or born in the United States? These important issues impact things like language ability, cultural values, and cultural identification (Gudykunst, 2001).

❖ **BOX 3.5**

STUDENT REFLECTIONS

I cannot count how many times I have been told I talk or act White or have been called an "Oreo" (Black on the outside, White in the inside). I had no Black people around me besides my family since I moved to the suburbs. I did a 180 when I moved from the city to the burbs. I found myself trying to act "less Black" because I was young and I wanted friends even though there wasn't another Black girl in my entire elementary school. In second grade, all of the girls in my class told me they wouldn't play with me because I was Black, and I was called a nigger more in elementary school than in the rest of my life. Since then I embrace my race and love me for me. I know I speak properly, and unfortunately the way I speak is being mistaken for talking White; however, I see it as representing Black people in the most positive way I know how. I know many people who dumb themselves down because they think that excelling in school or speaking correctly is a White thing, and that is a disgrace. We, as Black people, should be ashamed of ourselves when we equate success to acting White. We need to lift our fellow Black people up and be proud of our educated brothers and sisters.

European Americans

As we discussed earlier, European Americans have historically remained unnamed because of their positions of privilege in the United States. In fact, this privileged social positioning results in little conscious awareness of their racial/ethnic identity for most persons of European descent (Frankenberg, 1993). Unlike other racial/ethnic groups, the identity of this dominant group is not seen as central to everyday life interactions. Hence, when faced with the question of self-identification (e.g., "What are you?" or "What race do you consider yourself?"), a common response from many European Americans is simply to label themselves as "Americans." Although this label can be seen as focusing on their current standing in the United States, it indicates how their self-identity is void of any consciousness of their particular racial/ethnic identity.

It is important to recognize that labels for European Americans, like the other labels discussed in this section, have evolved over time. For instance, many groups that were not initially considered White (e.g., Catholic Irish immigrants or persons from eastern Europe) over time have "achieved" status as White/European American (Roedieger, 1994). Researchers (Martin, Krizek, Nakayama, & Bradford, 1996) have done some significant work in the area of exploring how people of European descent describe themselves. Specifically, they examined which terms (Anglo, Caucasian, Euro-American, European Americans, WASP, White, or White American) were most commonly used in self-identification. Based on extensive research conducted throughout the United States, they found that when forced to use a racial/ethnic marker, people of European descent most often chose "White," followed by "Caucasian." Labels that were least reported were "WASP" (White Anglo-Saxon Protestant) and "Anglo." More recent research supported these findings (Bahk & Jandt, 2004). Are you surprised by these results? For European American readers, do they coincide with the labels you use?

As noted by Martin et al. (1996), the labels most commonly used by persons of European descent reflect terms that are significantly vague and general (as compared to those that are most historically and geographically based). You have probably noticed that we have opted primarily to use **European American** in attaching a label to this group. This is done in attempts to use parallel terms that are geographically based, as reflected in the headings of this section. Although this rationale is strong, it—along with other language choices in terms of interracial communication—is not invoked without some concerns. For instance, some scholars, such as Frankenberg (1993), warn that using parallel terms "falsely equalizes communities, who are, in terms of current reality, unequally positioned in the racial order" (p. 231).

Latino/a Americans

As we illustrated and discussed earlier, naming is not a neutral act. In many cases, we have seen how racial/ethnic labels have been used to downplay microlevel differences in order to maximize the distance between certain groups and European Americans. Such is the case for the term **Hispanic**, a label first sanctioned for official and generalized use in the United States in 1968 (Melville, 1988). *Hispanic American* is a term that has come to represent persons with a similar use of the Spanish language and other aspects of a Spanish culture, regardless of the distinct differences of the many groups that it includes. For instance, the label refers to those U.S. citizens from Mexico, Cuba, Spain, Chile, the Dominican Republic, and many other countries (Pino, 1980; Spielberg, 1980). In this regard, both of the designations—Hispanic and Latino/a—group people of Spanish-speaking descent into a single category and thereby erase any designations based on national origin.

Research by Rinderle (2006) illustrates the complexity of names over time. Specifically, she traces the names for people of Mexican descent back to times before Spanish explorers arrived in the Americas. At this time, between 9 and 25 million people were living in what is now Mexico: Mayas in the south, Tarascos in the west, and Mixtecos and Mexicas/Aztecas in central Mexico were most prominent. With the arrival of Columbus, a new term was invented: *Indio* (Indian). Over time, additional terms—some derived from within, and some outside of, the group—have been used. Mexican was introduced following the independence movement in 1810, Mestizo became prominent in the early 1900s, and Mexican American was popular following World War II. Since that time, other terms have emerged to described this large cultural group: Hispanic (created by U.S. government officials), **Chicano** (which emerged from the Chicano movement), and Latino/a (an inclusive term that people choose for themselves) (Melville, 1988).

Currently, Hispanic and Latino/a are umbrella terms, especially in California and New York, used to describe various groups. Hispanic, according to sociologist Edward Murguia, is more acceptable for those people seeking to become a part of U.S. culture; in contrast, Latino/a is typically used by those concerned with preserving language and culture ("Names for Minorities," 2003). According to a survey conducted in 2002 by the Pew Hispanic Center, 53% of respondents found either term acceptable, while 34%

favored "Hispanic" and 13% preferred "Latino/a" (Fears, 2003). When individuals use these terms to describe themselves, different meanings can be attached to the very same label (F. P. Delgado, 1998b). Some Latino/a Americans use La Raza to signify political unity among diverse cultural groups (F. P. Delgado, 1998b). For many, La Raza encourages different Latino/a communities to recognize the power of "one race," something advocated by the Chicano movement.

With the variations of terms to describe this fastest growing segment within the United States, Tanno (2004) reminds us of the "worth of multiple names." She argues that in our personal lives we simultaneously embrace various labels like student, child, friend, employee, and sibling. Such can also be the case with racial and ethnic labels:

> In my case, I resort to being Spanish and all that implies whenever I return to my birthplace, in much the same way that we often resort to being children again in the presence of our parents. But I am also Mexican American when I balance the two important cultures that define me; Latina, when I wish to emphasize cultural and historical connectedness with others; and Chicana, whenever opportunities arise to promote political empowerment and assert cultural pride. (p. 40)

Middle Eastern Americans

The Middle East is a term used to define a cultural area; as such it does not have precise borders. By extension, **Middle Eastern Americans** is a label that encompasses people from a particular region in the world who are descended from multiple cultural groups. As used today, the label Middle Easterner includes individuals from—or persons who can trace their ancestry to—many different countries such as Armenia, Lebanon, Syria, Turkey, Iraq, Iran, Israel, Palestine, and North Africa (Egyptians are usually perceived as Middle Eastern despite being a part of Africa) (Reimers, 2005). Similar to other racial and ethnic labels described in this chapter, this is a term that describes a group that shares one aspect of culture. However, to maximize your communication effectiveness when interacting with Middle Eastern Americans, it is crucial to recognize the diversity within this large diverse group.

For instance, did you realize that Middle Eastern people represent a variety of different religious, linguistic, and cultural groups? Many U.S. Americans automatically, but incorrectly, assume that all Middle Eastern Americans are Arabs—whom they believe are Muslim (Swahn et al., 2003). In particular, the terrorist attacks of the U.S. on September 11, 2001, seemed to prompt this perception because the terrorists were identified as fundamentalist Muslims, or "Islamists." While Arab people are overwhelmingly Muslim, many are not. In fact it has only been in the last two decades that Muslims have come to represent a majority of Arab immigrants to the United States. Many Middle Easterners who came to the United States were Jewish (both Israel and Arab nations), Christian (including large numbers of Lebanese Christians and Egyptian Copts), and members of the Baha'i faith from Iran (Reimers, 2005). According to Witteborn (2004), only 23% of Arabs currently living in the United States are Muslims.

❖ **BOX 3.6**

THINKING CRITICALLY ABOUT THE MODEL MINORITY MYTH

- Asian Americans have the highest percentage of any racial group with a bachelor's degree or higher (49.4%).
- Asian Americans are only 5% of the total U.S. population, yet make up 15% of all U.S. physicians and surgeons.
- Nearly 10% of all engineers in the United States are Asian American.
- Fifteen percent of all computer and mathematical occupations in the United States are held by Asian Americans.
- The median household income for Asian Americans was $57,518—the highest among all racial groups.

While these statistics provide evidence for the Model Minority label, a closer examination reveals inaccuracies with this racial stereotype. For instance, it is important to recognize that Asian Americans are a diverse group of people whose ancestors came from many different cultures (W. Kim, 2006). When analyses consider different Asian ethnic groups separately, the Model Minority stereotype becomes faulty. For instance, while Asian American groups from some particular countries (e.g., China, India, Japan, and Korea) have benefited from high educational achievements, others (e.g., those from Southeast Asia) were refugees from predominantly agricultural countries where education was less emphasized. As such, some Asian Americans—like the Hmong, Vietnamese, Cambodians, and Laotians—have high percentages of people with educational levels far below the national average and larger numbers living in poverty (W. Kim, 2006). While the Model Minority stereotype continues to dominate public thinking, it is most descriptive of members of some Asian American groups, but definitely not all. A more critical approach to understanding this phenomenon would be to recognize that other factors like national origin, age, and socioeconomic status impact educational and professional success.

In addition to religious diversity, Middle Eastern Americans also vary in terms of language (not all come from Arab-speaking nations), socioeconomic status, and professional status. For instance, although Middle Eastern Americans as a group have a higher proportion of college degrees in general, unskilled workers and farmers—like those from Yemen—are also part of this large, diverse group (Reimers, 2005). Despite this diversity, most U.S. Americans have great difficulty differentiating between the various cultural groups from the Middle East. In fact, some scholars have described Middle Eastern Americans as an invisible racial/ethnic group in the United States (Salaita, 2006). However, the events of September 11 drastically changed that social position (Salaita, 2006). Since September 11, 2001, national polls of Arabs and Muslims have revealed increased prejudice, discrimination, and attacks on all Middle Easterners in the United States. While most of these have targeted Muslim Arabs, they have also involved Christian Arabs and Asians, Egyptian Copts, and members of the Sikh faith. In addition, U.S. government officials have targeted Arab Americans and Muslims with campaigns for detainment, incarceration, and deportation. Much of the racial discrimination and racism that this group has faced has developed out of long-standing stereotypes of "evil" Arab Americans (Semmerling, 2006) as "savages and barbarians" (Salaita, 2006, p. 30).

Multiracial Americans

Multiracial Americans, a diverse group of individuals whose parents are from different racial and ethnic groups, have always existed within the United States. While some individuals whose parents come from different racial groups continue to identify in terms of one group, an increasing number of persons are advocating for labels that affirm all aspects of their racial and ethnic heritage. The most significant push toward this goal, including a national march on Washington (Orbe, 1999), was seen immediately prior to the 2000 U.S. Census. Responding to the pressure of this growing population, the government responded by making the 2000 U.S. Census the first in which people could describe themselves as being of two or more races. The result, according to A. D. James and Tucker (2003), was more than 6.8 million U.S. residents describing themselves as multiracial. This accounts for approximately 2.5% of the total population, the majority of which are young children. Based on this, and other data (e.g., growth in multiracial birth rates, interracial marriage), experts agree that multiracial Americans represent a group that will continue to experience tremendous growth.

Contemporary conceptualizations of race have been challenged by the growing number of multiracial Americans, resulting in reconfigurations of historical racial divisions (A. D. James & Tucker, 2003). Unlike in the past, increasing numbers of multiracial Americans refuse to be "boxed in" one racial category; instead, they affirm multiple sources of their racial identities (Root, 2001). This includes individuals whose identities reflect two different races (e.g., Eurasians—a person with one Asian and one European parent), as well as those whose lineage encompasses complex racial and ethnic combinations (e.g., Tiger Woods' identification as Cablinasian, a term he created to refer to his Caucasian, Black, American Indian, and Asian ancestry). Without question, when it comes to multiracial identities, it can be a messy process. This is especially true when these individuals identify differently in different social contexts (D. R. Harris & Sim, 2001) and refuse to respond to attempts by others that they practice "racial allegiance" to one group over the other. According to A. D. James and Tucker (2003), the identity of multiracial Americans is dynamic and experiences changes over time, place, and context.

Many factors are important to consider when understanding how multiracial Americans define themselves. History, and continued social adherence to the one-drop rule, is certainly one. However, scholars point to other factors, such as levels of family identification, physical appearance, friends, relations with extended family members, and composition of neighborhood, as especially important (Rockquemore & Brunsma, 2002). Logically, those families emphasizing multiracial and multiethnic diversity are much more likely to raise children with multicultural identities appreciative of their diverse heritage (Rockquemore & Brunsma, 2002). But as Orbe (1999) points out, depending on the particular circumstances of the individual, it is equally "logical" for families to adopt other descriptors, including the refusal to be labeled as anything other than a member of the "human race."

Native Americans

The story of how the indigenous people of what is now regarded as North America were labeled as "Indians" is common knowledge. Prior to the arrival of European explorers/ settlers, diverse nations of native people—Oneida, Sage, Pequot, Mohegans, Blackfeet, Sioux, Cherokee, Potawatomi, and so on—lived off the land. Early writings of European settlers utilized various labels to describe groups indigenous to what was named "America." Most of these terms—Abergeny men, Wild-men, Pagans, Salvages, Barbarians, Heathens—reflected the European sense of superiority and their condescending views (Stromberg, 2006). In the end, it was Christopher Columbus, thinking he had reached India via a quicker route, who incorrectly labeled these Native persons as Indians.

Like other racial and ethnic groups, there is a lack of agreement among Native Americans on one preferred term (Shaver, 1998). While "Indian" has been reported as the most commonly used by indigenous people (Pratt, 1998), others strongly advocate for "First Nation people" (Heilbron & Guttman, 2000). Other terms used across North America include **American Indian**, Native People, and Indigenous People. Language choices among indigenous people also lead to significant questions in terms of "What is a Native American?" Must one be raised in traditional native culture or speak a native language or be on a tribal roll to identify as a First Nations person (Stromberg, 2006)?

Currently, there are over 545 federally recognized tribes of Native Americans and Alaska Natives in the United States; this includes the two largest tribes, Cherokee and Navajo, and others (Apache, Chippewa, Iroquois, Pueblo, and Sious) (Ogunwole, 2006). Individual Native American communities each have their own rich and complex traditions developed for various ceremonial and decision-making processes (Stromberg, 2006). Approximately 2 million indigenous people can be found across each and every state (Crawford, 2000). Less than half of the native population (34%) continues to live on reservations or other American Indian areas (Ogunwole, 2006); however, because their spiritual beliefs are closely tied to being caretakers of the land, many still refer to their reservation as "home" and continue to return from time to time.

In the past, federal agencies included Alaskan Natives in the same category as American Indians; in some instances, Native Hawaiians and Samoans are also included. Although these groups are lumped together for statistical purposes, they can also be quite culturally diverse (as can particular nations). When describing Alaskan Natives, for example, little attention is given to the diversity of people comprising this group. Not all are Eskimos, an offensive term applied by non-Natives that literally means "raw meat eaters." Indigenous people of Alaska, as well as their descendants from northern Canada, eastern Siberia, and Greenland, prefer Inuk (plural form, Inuit) over Eskimo. Like many of the other racial/ethnic groups discussed in this section, preferences for labeling Native Americans call for naming their specific nation whenever possible.

Nonverbal Communication

In his book *The Silent Language*, Edward T. Hall (1959) first discussed the great importance of recognizing verbal and nonverbal behaviors in intercultural communication contexts. We can easily talk about verbal and nonverbal language in similar terms, although some key differences exist (e.g., the punctuation of verbal exchanges as compared to the continuity of nonverbal cues). However, can you see how our earlier metaphors (language as a tool, prism, and display) also apply to nonverbal language systems? Given the focus of this chapter, some specific attention to the crucial role that nonverbal cues play alongside specific forms of language is warranted. In fact, according to some scholars (e.g., Mehrabian, 1982), the actual meaning of the message carried through the verbal portion of the message is quite low—only 7%. Others (Birdwhistell, 1970) suggest that the majority of the meaning comes through vocal qualities (38%) and facial expressions (55%). The exact science behind attempting to identify precise formulas by which meaning is created are, at best, inconclusive. However, the point of these studies is clear: The role that nonverbal cues play in interracial communication processes is crucial.

In the simplest of terms, nonverbal and verbal communication can be differentiated from each other based on one element: the presence or absence of messages coded through words. Nonverbal research has included studies based on proxemics (space), kinesics (body gestures), haptics (touch), vocalics/paralanguage, and chronemics (time). E. T. Hall's (1959) initial work has stimulated a large body of cross-cultural communication research that examines the nonverbal differences within different cultures, including differences among various racial/ethnic groups. For instance, research has reported the following:

- Puerto Ricans use touch communication much more frequently than North Americans and the British (Knapp, 1973).
- African American speech has more vocal range, inflection, and tonal quality than European American speech (Garner, 1994).
- Native Americans' use of silence is much different than that of European Americans in that it can reflect respect, active listening, or possibly a response to ambiguity (D. O. Braithwaite, 1990; Carbaugh, 2002).
- U.S. Americans are much more likely to use public displays of affection than their Japanese counterparts (Nakane, 1984).

The generalizable conclusions of these few studies are offered here as representative of the hundreds of studies that have explored the nonverbal differences among diverse cultures.

Our objective here is explicitly not to summarize existing studies in interracial nonverbal communication. We align ourselves with Collins (1990), who encourages a critical thinking approach to social scientific research whose "aim is to create scientific descriptions of reality by producing objective generalizations" (p. 205). Because of the great diversity within each group, such "objective, statistically significant" generalizations typically provide little direction in actual face-to-face interactions with persons who are racially/ethnically different (Orbe & Everett, 2006). In most circumstances, generalizations focus on racial/ethnic differences with little attention to other cultural variables such as sex, socioeconomic status, or age. These elements, in fact, may play a more salient role in one's communication in some situational contexts. For instance, research reports that sex differences within and between groups are often lost in cross-cultural comparisons (e.g., Waldron & Di Mare's 1998 work on the impact of sex differences on Japanese–U.S. American communication differences). Sex and/or gender differences, then, are erased within a focus on race/ethnicity. What is ultimately concluded in these studies applies to the "typical" racial/ethnic group member, an entity that is largely a creation of social science (Orbe & Everett, 2006). For instance, do you think you could find a Japanese American who displays all of the verbal and nonverbal qualities generalized to her cultural group? In his early work, Edward T. Hall (1966) made the problematic nature of generalizations apparent when he stated, "It should be emphasized that these generalizations are not representative of human behavior in general—or even of American behavior in general—but only of the group included in the sample" (p. 116).

Problems of generalization notwithstanding, the information generated on patterns of nonverbal behaviors among different racial/ethnic groups can provide an important backdrop to effective interracial communication. Such insight can increase awareness of the possible perceptions of specific behaviors (see Table 3.1). Next we briefly discuss several nonverbal elements that should be acknowledged when choosing appropriate/effective language.

The Context of Language Choices

Oftentimes, people with little experience in intergroup relations desire a quick and easy foolproof list of the "dos and don'ts" for communicating with others who are racially or ethnically different. We have made a conscious attempt to avoid such a simplistic treatment of the complex issues related to interracial communication. We are often approached by colleagues and students who are seeking insight into an interracial communication problem. Typically, they offer a brief summary of a problematic interracial case scenario and then ask the supposedly simple question, "What should I do?" We have found that, in almost all cases, there is never a simple answer to these types of inquiries. Most of the time, the best response we can come up with is, "It depends. . . ." Past experiences reveal that the most productive way to help someone deal with interracial conflict is to provide some applied research guidelines. Then we can help others gain a more complete understanding of what they perceive as a relatively simple problem.

One of the most important considerations in choosing appropriate/effective language centers around the specific relationship between the parties involved, as well as the particular situational context. Where did the interaction take place? Who was present during the interaction? How well do you know the individuals? What past experiences do you share with one another? What do you (they) know about their (your) lived experiences? Within what relationship is the interaction enacted (classmates, coworkers, friends, acquaintances, strangers)? One basic axiom states that communication has both a content and relationship dimension. Within our discussion here, this axiom can be used to understand that certain verbal cues (content) will have varying meanings and effects depending on the status (relationship) of the parties involved. Effective interracial communicators must come to understand the appropriate nonverbal language for the particular interaction *as negotiated by all parties involved.* In this regard, the same relationship can be perceived quite differently from each

❖ **Table 3.1** Guide to Perceptions of Interracial Verbal and Nonverbal Behaviors

The information included in this table highlights some specific examples of how verbal and non-verbal cues can generate various meanings depending on ingroup and outgroup perceptions. They are offered here not as generalizations applicable to all ethnic group members in any one group, but as information to assist you in recognizing potential sources of miscommunication.

Specific behavior	Possible ingroup perception	Possible outgroup perception
Avoidance of direct eye contact by Latino/as	Used to communicate attentiveness or respect	A sign of inattentiveness; direct eye is preferred
An African American who aggressively challenges a point to which she or he disagrees	Acceptable means of dialogue; not regarded as verbal abuse or a precursor to violence.	Arguments are viewed as inappropriate and a sign of potential immediate violence.
Asian American use of finger gestures to beckon others	Appropriate if used by adults for children, but highly offensive if used to call adults.	Appropriate gesture to use with both children and adults.
Interruptions used by African Americans	Tolerated in individual/group discussions; attention is given to most assertive voice.	Perceived as rude or aggressive; clear rules for turn taking must be maintained.
Silence used by Native Americans	A sign of respect, thoughtfulness, and/or uncertainty/ambiguity.	Silence indicates boredom, disagreement, or a refusal to participate/respond.
The use of touch by Latino/as	Perceived as normal and appropriate for interpersonal interactions.	Deemed as appropriate for some intimate or friendly interactions; otherwise perceived as a violation of personal space.
Public displays of intense emotions by African Americans	Personal expressiveness is valued and regarded as appropriate in most settings	Violates U.S. societal expectations for self-controlled public behaviors; inappropriate for most public settings.
Asian Americans touching or holding hands of same-sex friends	Seen as acceptable behavior that signifies closeness of platonic relationships.	Perceived as inappropriate, especially for male friends
Latino/as use of lengthy greetings or the exchange of pleasantries prior to business meetings	Regarded as an important element of establishing rapport with colleagues.	Seen as a waste of time; getting to the business at hand is valued.

person's perspective. For instance, research has indicated that African American women often take offense when European American women assume a position of familiarity with their language cues (i.e., "Hey, girl, how are you?") in their interactions, which they perceive as premature (Orbe, Drummond, & Camara, 2002).

❖ **BOX 3.7**

STUDENT REFLECTIONS

I come from a family that is half Middle Eastern and half Irish. There seem to be very few people who have this mix; in fact, I have yet to meet any. My mother is the Irish person, and of course, my father is Middle Eastern, Chaldean to be exact. In short, Chaldeans are Catholic Iraqis, and many left Iraq in search of a more culturally accepting environment being that they were often mistreated for practicing Christianity rather than Muslim traditions. My mother and father were engaged, but my father's family didn't want to accept my mother because she was a "White girl"—they wanted him to marry a Chaldean woman. My parents ended up getting married in Las Vegas, alone, because no one would come to their wedding.

This line of reasoning is also useful in offering insight into the importance of recognizing cultural ownership of certain verbal cues. Because of shared cultural experiences and an acknowledged relationship status, two members of a particular racial/ethnic group may use language that is appropriate between them but highly inappropriate when others (ingroup and especially outgroup) use it. One example is when Filipino American men use "Pinoy" (pee-noy) to describe one another, but regard the term as derogatory when used by non-Filipinos (Sing, 1989). The use of "niggah" among African Americans (not to be confused with outgroup uses of "nigger") also helps illustrate the idea of cultural ownership. Some argue that, among African Americans, the term reflects the positivity and unity of ingroup relations:

> I have heard the word "niggah" (note the spelling, dig the sound) all of my life. Many of my elders and friends use it with phenomenal eloquence. They say it to express amusement, incredulity, disgust, or affection. These people are very much being themselves—proudly, intensely, sometimes loudly. (J. C. Brown, 1993, p. 138)

Other African Americans argue that any form of the word, given its negative history, should not be used. Regardless of where individuals fall within the debate of ingroup use, clearly it represents a word extremely offensive when used by non–African Americans.

The Context of Nonverbal Cues

Growing up, it was not uncommon for children to be reminded by their parents that, "It's not *what* you said, but *how* you said it." This childhood lesson is a valuable one in terms of the importance of verbal and nonverbal cues in the context of interracial communication. Language choices, and subsequently the meaning they generate among interaction participants, cannot be understood outside of their context. This crucial idea is oftentimes ignored by communicators who focus on the specific language used, with little recognition of the importance of the context. The following real-life example illustrates this point:

> Recently, an African American woman filed charges of racial/sexual harassment against a European American male supervisor. Her major complaint was that he consistently referred to her as a "little African princess." When confronted about his specific language, he could not understand how this phrase could be offensive to someone who identified with her cultural roots as strongly as the accuser.

What is your initial reaction to this case scenario? Were the man's continued remarks the basis for a racial/sexual harassment suit or was the woman being overly sensitive? (This specific example might serve as an excellent resource to explore perceptual differences based on a number of cultural elements, including race/ethnicity, sex, and age.) Gut reactions aside, it is extremely difficult to evaluate this case without the contextualizing power of nonverbal cues. Given the focus of our discussion, a number of questions should have arisen. For instance, think of the value of potential insight gained from the following questions: What vocal qualities were used by the man? Was his tone condescending, sarcastic, or complimentary? What specific context did the phrase occur in? One-on-one interaction? In front of a large group? In a business meeting? Or at the annual holiday party that celebrates Christmas, Hanukkah, and Kwanzaa? What type of eye contact (if any) was maintained during these interactions? Was the man standing over the woman, walking past her, or in her face? As you can undoubtedly see, obtaining answers to these questions helps develop a fuller understanding of meaning associated with specific language choices.

Remember the important point that, despite particular language choices, scholars believe a majority of the meaning of a message is communicated nonverbally. This crucial element of interracial communication does not cancel the importance of making good language choices. However, it does assist us in recognizing the key role that nonverbal cues play within the negotiation of meaning between racially/ethnically diverse persons. An increased consciousness of the meanings that others attach to your nonverbal behaviors—especially given that nonverbal cues are used more unconsciously than verbal ones—is crucial to effective interracial communication.

The most effective communicators, particularly those who are committed to maintaining and strengthening intergroup relations, acknowledge **intentionality** as a key issue in their response to certain language they regard as inappropriate or offensive. The most effective responses for the same language clue may be drastically different for those individuals who are identified as "unconscious incompetents" (naive offenders) as opposed to those whose language choices are more consciously offensive (Howell, 1982). For instance, would your response to a child's use of the word *Chink* to describe a person of Chinese descent be the same if one of your professors used it? This is not to say that intentionality is necessarily more important than the effects that certain language choices have on interactions. However, it does take the motive (or lack thereof) behind using certain terms into consideration. As we discussed earlier, language can be regarded as a tool, prism, and display of internal cognitions. Persons who come to understand how the language, consciously and/or unconsciously, serves multiple roles are at the best vantage point to manage an effective communication interaction.

Conclusion

After reading this chapter, you should have an increased consciousness of the importance of verbal and nonverbal messages within the context of interracial communication. Language is a powerful resource that serves multiple functions in our everyday lives. Throughout this chapter, as well as in the remainder of the text, we have made a conscious attempt to avoid what might result in a definitive laundry list regarding interracial language use. Instead, our discussion resolves around the understanding of the crucial role that language systems play in our everyday lives.

Several general guidelines, however, may help summarize the central points of this chapter. Although these bits of advice offer quick points of reference for everyday interactions, they are best understood within the context of the information provided within this chapter. To summarize, effective interracial communicators do the following:

- Recognize the role that power plays within language, labels, and issues of naming (including ingroup cultural ownership of certain terms and phrases).
- Make informed choices about the verbal/nonverbal cues they use in particular situational contexts *and* assume responsibility for their effects.
- Develop a deep understanding of the similarities and differences of verbal and nonverbal language systems within and between different groups.
- Seek out additional information when needed! If an appropriate relationship has been established, this may mean asking specific people of color their perceptions of particular verbal cues. It may also include using other means, such as books, videos, and/or other educational resources.

OPPORTUNITIES FOR EXTENDED LEARNING ❖

1. In order to gain a more personal understanding of the associative power of labels and names, take the Implicit Association Test developed by Yale University. You can find it at http://www.yale.edu/implicit/. Follow the instructions to the "Black–White IAT." After taking the test (it will take approximately 5 minutes), discuss your impressions of the test with your friends, family, and classmates.

2. Sometimes recognizing one's own position of privilege is difficult. Try to create a list of specific "privileges" that European Americans have in the United States. These are benefits that, because of their dominant group status, European Americans take for granted (e.g., "flesh-colored" bandages matching their skin color). If you need some prompting, check out the work of Peggy McIntosh (1995b). In order to understand how all persons have some positions of relative

privilege, it may be helpful to generate different lists of privilege based on gender, abilities, sexual orientation, or socioeconomic status.

3. Take some time to visit www.esperanto-usa.org. This Web site is a comprehensive resource for those persons interested in learning more about the most widely used international auxiliary language. You might be surprised to see how easy the alphabet, phonology, grammar, vocabulary, and writing systems are. You can also learn useful phrases that may come in handy someday!

4. Generate a list of responses to the following sentence: "I find it offensive when I hear (*name of specific group*) using terms and phrases like (*name specific language*), because . . ." Then share your responses with others. Is there a general agreement among people racially both like, and not like, you? Why or why not?

5. Based on what you have learned from this chapter, create a list of language guidelines to be used in classroom discussion. First, think about certain rules individually. Second, discuss your list with others in groups. Finally, see if all of the groups can come together with a consensus of general (or possibly specific) guidelines. You might also want to reflect back to the guidelines for discussions that were created as you attempted to build community (see Chapter 1). Remember, the value of this exercise is more in the process than the actual results of these discussions!

4

Racial and Ethnic Identity Negotiation

S ome have described the United States as having a general preoccupation with identity issues (Field & Travisano, 1984). According to other scholars, cultural identities are bound to get more, rather than less, complex in the 21st century (Tanno & Gonzalez, 1998). A good place to begin any discussion on racial/ethnic/cultural identity (the topic of both Chapters 4 and 5) is with some honest, straightforward self-assessment. Before reading any further, take a few minutes to reflect on how you would describe your cultural identity. (Box 4.1 can be used specifically for this purpose.) What aspects of "who you are" quickly come to mind? How do these characteristics and/or roles reflect how you have come to define "culture"? Is your response to this line of inquiry relatively easy, extremely difficult, or somewhere between the two? Have there been particular events in your life that have triggered a search for a deeper under-standing of your cultural identity? How comfortable do you feel identifying one spe-cific aspect of your cultural identity as most central to who you are?

This chapter will provide you with some detailed descriptions of theoretical frameworks that explain how racial/ethnic identities, as well as perceptions of racially/ ethnically diverse others, are negotiated over time (Hecht, Jackson, & Ribeau, 2003). Although the information will not directly answer any of the questions just listed for any particular person, it will help you understand your own particular cultural stand-point more easily. The first portion of this chapter presents general information con-cerning identity formation. The remainder of the chapter details the stages that specific racial/ethnic group members experience as they form their particular race/ethnic iden-tities. We conclude by explaining the communication theory of identity.

Approaches to Studying Identity

The concept of identity is universal. Nevertheless, the way in which personal/cultural identities are played out in different cultures varies (Geertz, 1976). Research on how individuals come to understand who they are has generated a significant amount of information regarding what has been established as a complex, intricate, lifelong process (Moss & Faux, 2006). Much of the work in the area of identity development has focused on how young children and adolescents engage in the process of formulating personal/cultural identities.

❖ BOX 4.1

WHO AM I?

A common exercise used to help people self-assess their identity is known as the "Who Am I?" exercise (e.g., Kuhn & McPartland, 1954). Before reading any further, take a few minutes to reflect on how you define yourself. Take a piece of paper and jot down "I am" 20 times down the left side of the paper. Then take a few minutes and complete each statement. Do this with the assumption that no one but you will see the list. The key is not to take a lot of time on this exercise. Just write down what pops into your mind in the order it occurs to you. Do not continue reading until you have completed this exercise.

Take a minute to read through your list and reflect on the descriptors that you provided to the question, "Who am I?" Pay attention to the types of responses you used to complete the sentence.

- How many of your items represent specific roles that you play in life (e.g., student, friend, mother/father, daughter/son)?
- Do others refer to aspects of cultural groups to which you belong (e.g., women, Asian American, Generation X, gay/lesbian/bisexual) and/or personal characteristics (e.g., handsome, intelligent, caring, aggressive)?
- Scholars suggest that the ordering of statements may also be significant in identifying a hierarchy of the most important aspects of your personal/cultural identity (Kuhn & McPartland, 1954). For instance, are the responses at the top of your list the most central to who you are?
- How might your list have changed given a different time, location, and set of consequences?
- If prompted, could you articulate why you listed the particular characteristics in the order they appear?

Most notable in the existing literature is the work and influence of Erik Erikson (1963, 1968). According to Erikson (1963), the major task of adolescence is establishing an independent identity. Central to his ideas about identity formation is the recognition that individuals move through a series of interrelated stages in their psychosocial development. Each stage, according to Erikson (1968), involves a particular aspect of identity crisis. Individuals are able to move to another stage by resolving issues related to current stages. Social science theorists, representing a number of fields, including psychology, sociology, and communication, have applied the funda-mental works of Erikson to a number of contexts.

Consistent with the dominant worldview of the United States and most other Western cultures, much of this work has tended to view identity as an individual entity (Carbaugh, 1987; Geertz, 1976). Within this perspective, self is regarded as a unique, separated whole. This underlying cultural assumption is clear in most of Erikson's (1963) work. He stresses that the formation of a personal identity coincides with estab-lishing autonomy and independence. More recent perspectives have recognized that this work is based on the individualistic notions of Western cultures. In doing so, they have worked to embrace a more collectivistic approach to studying identity, one in which the self is defined in relation to others (Shotter & Gergen, 1989).

For the purposes of this chapter, we identify ourselves as scholars who see the important role that both the individual and the relational serve in identity negotiation. Like Rosenthal (1987), we believe a person's cultural identity develops through inter-action with others—and that identity is continuously negotiated, not developed toward a particular goal. As such, identity negotiation is a function of the individual and his or her relations to a particular cultural reference group and that group's place in larger society. Therefore, we suggest viewing identity as both an individual entity (representative of traditional psychological perspectives) *and* as a relational one (rep-resentative of social communication theory). In other words, we argue that identity development simultaneously involves personal and individual characteristics (e.g., personality characteristics) and cultural identities associated with particular roles, reference groups, and cultural categories.

The Co-Creation of Identity

One of the most influential works in identity development scholarship is *Mind, Self, and Society* (Mead, 1934). In this book, George Herbert Mead described the con-cept of self in terms of its direct relationship to various segments of social life. His work marks a shift from a focus on the self to one on the communication (symbolic interaction) between self and others. Although some communication scholars have identified problems associated with Mead's work (e.g., Tanno & Gonzalez, 1998), his attention to the important relationship between self-identity and social life highlights the central role that communication plays in identity formulation. In this regard, Mead's contributions inform the current perspectives of cultural identity develop-ment, especially those that appear in the literature associated with the field of com-munication. For instance, his approach to identity development is well represented in Goffman's (1967) proposition that identities are both negotiated and enacted through communication and relationships. Mead's work is also fundamental to the current work in symbolic interactionism, both the Chicago and Iowa schools (Meltzer & Petras, 1970). The framework provided in this section draws from these schools of thought, in addition to more current scholarship on racial/ethnic identity develop-ment (e.g., Hecht et al., 2003) that sees identity formation as a co-created entity.

Simply put, cultural identities are co-created and re-created in everyday interac-tions (Yep, 2002). This general idea is grounded in Mead's work and subsequently strengthened by the advances of his students. For instance, Blumer (1969) has championed the idea that the sense of self emerges from a process of definition/redefinition that occurs through social interaction. In other words, identity is negotiated—formed, maintained, and modified—through our interactions with others. Identity also simultaneously influences these very interactions through our expectations and perceptions of others' behaviors (Hecht et al., 1993). In essence, a person's sense of self can be seen as an integral part of that person's social behavior (and vice versa). Part of a person's social behavior includes finding appropriate names and labels (remember the discussion on the importance of language in Chapter 3) that locate the self in socially recognizable categories (Burke & Reitzes, 1981). Most often, we gain our self-identities through a process of contrasting ingroup and outgroup characteristics (J. C. Turner, 1987). In other words, we come to understand who we are as we compare and contrast ourselves with others. Helms (1994) suggests, for instance, that most European Americans largely define their "Whiteness" in terms of the opposite or lack of "Blackness" (see, for example, Morrison, 1991).

Think about how others—especially those that play an important role in your life—interact with you. What messages do they send you about their perceptions of you through both their verbal and nonverbal cues (both directly and indirectly)? Do you accept, reject, or ignore their perceptions of you? Symbolic interactionists would suggest that the images others communicate to you are a central aspect of identity formation. Another central element is your reaction to their communication. Gradually, some of these meanings generated through this interaction are generalized over time and become established as core elements of your identity (Hecht et al., 2003).

Focus on Racial/Ethnic Identity

So far, we have summarized some existing research on identity and identity formation to help you understand how persons come to define themselves culturally. Toward this objective, we have combined research on personal identity and cultural identity issues. This section continues to use these cultural identity perspectives, but we focus our attention more narrowly on racial/ethnic identity development. Specifically, we discuss three fundamental contributors to the co-creation of racial/ethnic identity (family and friends, dominant societal institutions/organizations, and media) to illustrate the process by which perceptions of racialized self and others are formed. One of the premises of this text is that race and ethnicity represent social categories that develop during early socialization and maintain a central place in self, culture, and communication processes (Gordon, 1978). In the next few sections, we discuss how individual racial/ethnic identity is co-created through interactions with family and friends, societal organizations, and the mass media.

Family and Friends

One of the central aspects of Mead's (1934) framework is the idea of a **generalized other**, a concept he uses to refer to the collective body from which the individual sees the self. In other words, it is an individual's perception of the general way that others see him or her. Throughout your life, you have learned these perceptions from years of socialization and interaction with others. Each person has a number of **significant others** who have been particularly influential in her or his identity development. Hecht et al. (2003) refer to these individuals as orientational others. For most individuals, orientational others are family members (not restricted only to blood relations).

How do family and friends help co-create our racial/ethnic identity? The answer to this question is complicated. Racial/ethnic identity is developed in a number of ways, including direct communication about race/ethnic issues, role modeling, and general socialization (see, for example, Harwood, Soliz, & Lin, 2006). An extremely powerful component of the co-creation of race/ethnic identity is reflected in the labels that family and friends use. C. Taylor (1992) notes that "people do not acquire the languages needed for self-definition on their own. Rather, we are introduced to them through interaction with others who matter to us" (p. 32). Think back—as far as your memory allows—to the terms and labels that friends and family members have used to describe you as well as themselves. How does your self-identity reflect some level of conscious or unconscious acceptance of these labels? Can you think of instances when you felt uncomfortable with the racial/ethnic labels used by or about family and friends? Such experiences reflect one aspect of the powerful role that family and friends play in the co-creation of identity (Dodd & Baldwin, 1998). This is supported by Rockquemore and Brunsma (2002), who, in their work on multiracial families, acknowledge the importance of nuclear and extended family in creating healthy identities.

As described by a number of communication scholars (e.g., Gangotena, 1997; N. C. James, 2004; McKay, 2000; Stone, 1996), one of the primary ways that racial/ethnic identity is created for people is through family stories. Most often, but not always, family stories are passed down orally from generation to generation and represent some truth or life lesson. In terms of those particular family stories that focus on race/ethnicity, many provide pertinent information used to develop perceptions of the racial/ethnic identities of self and others. Navita Cummings James (2004) describes how significant stories from her youth (e.g., stories of lynching, murder, slavery) represented a specific set of beliefs and stereotypes about European Americans and African Americans, including the following:

- Black people are "just as good" as White people—and in some ways (e.g., morally) better.
- Black people have to be twice as good as Whites to be considered half as good.
- White people probably have some kind of inferiority complex which drives them to continually "put down" Blacks and anyone else who is not White.
- White men are usually arrogant. White women are usually lazy.
- There are some good White people, but they are the exceptions. (p. 64)

These perceptions were gained through the communication of both European and African American sides of James's family. In addition, she is quick to point out that these childhood beliefs and stereotypes did not immediately become part of her self-identity. Instead, her work on family stories, culture, and identity suggests that family stories represent one source of cultural information used in the co-creation of racial/ethnic identity. This information exists within larger contexts like your local neighborhood (Rockquemore & Brunsma, 2002).

❖ **BOX 4.2**

Author Reflections

While I was lecturing at another university recently, an African American woman described me as a "cultural enigma." Her comment was part of a question she was asking about the presentation that I had just given about my research. Although I probably shouldn't be, I am surprised at the level of intensity that often accompanies people's need to know my racial/ethnic/cultural identity. Within the context of this woman's comments, she seemed to accept the difficulty that occurs when people try to classify my cultural identities in terms of "either/or" categories (see MPO's personal reflection in Chapter 1). However, this is not typically the case. More often than not, people exhibit an intense need to know "what I am." In the past few years, I've experienced acquaintances and colleagues who do the following:

- Use direct questions ("What *are* you?" "Are you Black?" "What's your cultural background?—You have *something* in you, but I can't figure it out!")
- Touch the back of my head in an attempt to measure how "nappy/kinky" my hair is (I had just met this African American woman at a conference; this was her way of trying to figure out my racial background)
- Tell me that "everyone is dying to figure out what you are" and that "some people don't feel comfortable interacting with you until they know"
- Assume they know my race/ethnicity and then try to argue with others (including some of my good friends) when they are corrected!

Part of me wants to respond to these types of inquiries by saying, "What difference does it make?" But of course I realize that race and ethnicity do make a difference in the United States (as well as other countries).

Writing this book has increased my consciousness of how these experiences work in the co-creation of my racial/ethnic identity, especially in terms of how others see me. It's interesting because more often than not people of color typically recognize that I've got "something in me" whereas many European Americans are quicker to designate me as a "White male." When I correct them (which is often, but not always), reactions include shock, apologies, embarrassment, and aggression. "You can say what you want, but I see you as a White man and that's how I'm going to interact with you!" responded one person. Although each of these interactions is both symbolic and significant to me, I imagine that most of these individuals are relatively unaware of the power of their verbal and nonverbal cues. Part of their uncertainty and anxiety is probably fueled by a recognition that their self-identities are tied to how they identify me. As James Baldwin (1990) put it, "If I'm not who you say I am, then you're not who you think you are." So how do these interactions affect my racial/ethnic identity? I'm not exactly sure, but I do recognize that they definitely do have some impact—if they didn't, why would I remember them so vividly?

—MPO

Dominant Societal Institutions/Organizations

As we saw in the descriptions in the previous section, our family and friends typically (but certainly not always) serve an important role in providing information concerning our racial/ethnic identity (Dodd & Baldwin, 1998). For many parents with children of color, cultivating a positive racial/ethnic self-identity in their children is seen as important (Orbe, 1999), especially for those who believe children from racial/ethnic microcultures who lack a strong, positive identity are prone to fail in dominant societal institutions/organizations. What do we mean by "dominant societal institutions/organizations"? This is a phrase that best represents various predominantly European American organizations that reflect the dominant cultural values of the United States (e.g., hospitals, schools, government agencies, police, etc.). Oftentimes the messages that individuals receive from the institutions concerning their racial/ethnic identity either explicitly or implicitly contradict those from friends and family. In other words, certain institutions serve as the "recognition, nonrecognition, or misrecognition" of racial/ethnic identities (C. Taylor, 1992, p. 32). Think about how certain persons in authority—teachers, police officers, doctors, social workers—have interacted with you over the course of your life. How has their communication, both verbally and nonverbally, contained messages concerning their own as well your racial/ethnic identity? Consciously or unconsciously you have dealt with these messages as part of an ongoing process of identity development.

The lived experiences of biracial and multiracial persons in the United States offer a vivid example of how the co-creation of racial/ethnic identity involves ingroup and outgroup perceptions (Harwood, Soliz, & Lin, 2006). Autoethnographical research indicates that multiracial families talk about race and ethnicity issues among themselves differently depending on a variety of interrelated factors. These include the influence/presence of parents, racial/ethnic makeup of neighborhoods, and personal philosophies of race/racism (Rockquemore & Brunsma, 2002). A growing number of parents are raising their children to resist pressure to choose one racial/ethnic identity. Instead, they embrace a multiracial identity that allows them to express all aspects of who they are (Wardle, 1987). Problems occur when orientational others (e.g., a teacher or a social worker) fail to recognize this identity and continue to see them in traditional racial categories that follow a one-drop rule. What happens, then, when a child must deal with conflicting messages in terms of her or his racial/ethnic identity? Take the case of a young girl whose racial lineage consists of African, European, Asian, and Native descent (in that approximate order) whose experiences were described by Orbe (1999). At birth, her parents believed the hospital records should indicate her "race/ethnicity" as multiracial and list all of her racial heritage (as was done with their first child). The assisting records nurse, based on her perceptions of the baby's mother, listed her race/ethnicity as "Black." The family's pediatrician, despite knowing the multiracial family for over a year, recorded "White" in the appropriate box on another hospital form. Her designation was based on the girl's physical features (blond hair, blue eyes, and peach complexion). Despite some initial conflicting perceptions, the little girl has been raised to see herself as multiracial. Nevertheless, distinct differences in how outgroup members describe and perceive her continue to contradict this racial/ethnic identity.

This brief case study helps us understand the complex ways that interactions with authority figures must be negotiated within the context of family and friends' communication about racial/ethnic identities. Only time will tell how her co-created self-identity will ultimately be formed in the context of interactions with family, friends, and members of the larger macroculture. We would suggest that all people experience some conflicting messages about their identities (although at various levels of intensity). This process is aptly described by Hegde (1998) as **identity emergence**. It refers to the multiple, sometimes contradicting, interactions that characterize the experiences of human life. One societal institution that plays a significant role in this process of identity emergence is the mass media. Because of the growing interest in the power of mass-mediated images, we separate it from other dominant societal organizations/institutions.

❖ **BOX 4.3**

THE NEW TREND ON RACIAL AMBIGUITY

Over time, the media have always paid close attention to racial appearance in terms of who was included on screen and in print. Recent articles (e.g., La Feria, 2004) in the mainstream media have commented on a growing trend in the entertainment industry—the promotion of individuals who are racially ambiguous. They argue that actors, models, and other entertainers—Vin Diesel, The Rock, Jessica Alba—whose heritage is difficult to discern are highly marketable. Part of their popularity with younger audiences seems to relate to the lack of certainty about their racial and ethnic composition.

- Think about your favorite movies, television shows, and magazines. Do they feature racially ambiguous persons?
- What were your initial perceptions of these individuals?
- How are they portrayed in the media?
- Have you paid more attention thinking about their racial/ethnic heritage after taking this class?

Mass Media

Considerable research exists on the impact of mass media representations on an individual's perceptions of race, ethnicity, and culture, both in terms of self and others (e.g., R. L. Jackson, 2006). In light of this research, Chapter 11 discusses how mass-mediated communication comes to represent—and ultimately affect—interracial communication in a variety of contexts. Several theoretical frameworks have been created to assess the impacts of the mass media on perceptions of self and others. These include, but are not limited to, cultivation theory, agenda setting theory, critical theory, uses and gratification approach to media, social learning theory, and the theory of a spiral of silence. Each of these theoretical frameworks suggests different levels of mass media influence. However, one consistent idea is common across this diverse set of media theories: Mass media representations do have some impact on societal perceptions of self, culture, and society. According to D. Kellner (1995), media culture "provides the materials not of which many people construct their sense of class, of ethnicity and race, of nationality, of sexuality, or us and them. Media culture helps shape the prevalent view of the world and deepest values. . . . Media culture provides the materials to create identities" (p. 1).

Much of the research on mass media representations and effects has focused on television images and their impact on viewers who watch large amounts of television programming (Stroman, 1991). However, of equal or possibly greater importance are the mass-mediated representations found in mainstream books, films, magazines, newspapers, and music—all of which seem to reinforce those racial/ethnic images found on television. For children of color, these forms of mass media serve as a relentless source of dominant cultural values, beliefs, and attitudes (R. L. Miller & Rotheram-Borus, 1994). Mainstream mass media forms have been largely criticized for simply perpetuating negative racial/ethnic stereotypes (T. M. Harris & Hill, 1998). According to bell hooks, exposure to negative images is unavoidable for African Americans, given the pervasive nature of the mass media. "Opening a magazine or book, turning on the television set, watching a film, or looking at photographs in public spaces, we are most likely to see images of black people that reinforce and reinscribe white supremacy" (hooks, 1992, p. 1).

Clearly, the messages contained in the mass media serve as another source of information concerning racial and ethnic groups that all persons, regardless of cultural background, must deal with. Halualani (1998) describes this process as a "struggle of culture"—the clash between cultural identities produced for us and by us (p. 265). In terms of Mead's (1934) focus on symbolic interactionism, we can see how mass-mediated images might contribute to how an individual understands her or his own "generalized other."

Thus far, we have focused primarily on the co-creation of racial/ethnic self-identity. However, during this time, we also gain perceptions of others who are racially/ethnically different. When opportunities for substantial interracial interaction are limited because of personal, social, or physical distance, mass media representations have a greater impact on outgroup perceptions. The following excerpt illustrates the power of mass-mediated forms of communication. As you will see, this is in terms of not only how an individual perceives himself or herself, but also how others come to perceive and interact with those who are racially/ethnically different from themselves.

> A white woman acquaintance at my university pulled me aside and in a serious voice announced that she understood what I had been talking about all of these months about my ethnicity and race. "I saw the movie THE JOY LUCK CLUB with my husband over the weekend. I feel so close to you now, like I understand you so much better! Chinese women are so lucky to have relationships with their mothers with such deep emotions!" I felt confused and speechless and didn't know where to begin. In addition to the fact that I am not Chinese American, I wondered what in the world this woman and her husband have fantasized about my life and family relations based on this Hollywood movie. (K. Wong, 2002, p. 98)

Our discussion of the co-creation of cultural identities has provided a framework to gain insight into a highly complex process. Individuals come to understand racialized perceptions of self and others through many different mechanisms. This information provides an important backdrop for the next section on cultural identity development models. As you read the descriptions of the various stages in each model, think about the crucial role that these and other information sources play in this dynamic, ongoing process.

Cultural Identity Development Models

According to Phinney (1993), the formation of cultural identity generally involves three phases: (1) unexamined cultural identity, (2) cultural identity search, and (3) cultural identity achievement. Following a description of each of these identity formation components, we turn to the specific ways that scholars have described how macrocultural and microcultural group members (including those persons identifying as biracial) form their racial identities. As you will see, all of the existing racial identity development models (e.g., J. A. Banks, 1976; Hardiman, 1994; Helms, 1994; B. W. Jackson & Hardiman, 1983; Ponterotto & Pedersen, 1993) reflect Phinney's (1993) three general phases.

During the first stage of cultural identity formation, we function in society with an *unexamined cultural identity*. We take our cultural values, norms, beliefs, customs, and other characteristics for granted. Our culture is experienced as "natural" and generates little interest. Microcultural group members tend to become aware of racial differences and identities earlier than persons of European descent (Ferguson, Gever, Trinh, & West, 1990; Nance & Foeman, 2002). Even so, many children experience their early years from an unexamined cultural identity standpoint. Typically, young people lack an awareness of cultural differences and the central role that culture plays in everyday encounters. At some point, however, something triggers a move into the next stage (*cultural identity search*). Typically this shift can be caused by conflicting messages from family, friends, social organizations, or the media about race and ethnicity issues. Searching for our cultural identity involves an ongoing process of exploration, reflection, and evaluation. In other words, it involves thinking about our self-identity and how we fit into any number of different cultural groups. For some of us, this is completed in our young adult years. For others, it takes longer. The final stage, according to Phinney (1993), is *cultural identity achievement*. Within this final stage, we develop a clear, confident understanding and acceptance of ourselves. Subsequently, we internalize a strong cultural identity. Although this element is apparent in each of the racial identity development models we describe later in this chapter, one crucial element must be acknowledged: Our cultural identities are not static, fixed, or enduring. Instead, our identities are dynamic and subject to change as our field of lived experiences increases.

Identity formation, along these lines, is best seen as "becoming" rather than "being" (Sarup, 1996). The racial identity development models discussed here take on a linear, unidimensional form (R. L. Miller & Rotheram-Borus, 1994). Still, we must not oversimplify the complex ways that cultural identity is developed. Seldom does it occur in a neat, orderly fashion. Although some of us experience a straightforward progression of identity formation—moving from an unexamined state, to an identity search, and concluding with a clear sense of identity achievement—most eventually experience a "recycling" of stages based on new experiences (Helms, 1994). Because of this, the process of identity formation is more like a spiraling loop than a straight line.

As we alluded to earlier, Phinney's (1993) three general stages of cultural identity formation apply generically to all persons. Given the history of race in the United States (see Chapter 2), it should come as no surprise that the process racial/ethnic microcultural and macrocultural group members used to form their identities is similar, yet different. U.S. Americans of European descent create their identities within a dominant society that affirms the value of their culture. Persons of color within the United States, in contrast, must deal with social norms that define their life experiences as "sub-cultural." Because of this reality, microcultural and macrocultural group identity formation processes differ. People of color must form their racial identities within a larger society that does not necessarily value the same things. For example, think about how our society defines standards of beauty. Traditionally, beauty has been defined through European American standards in terms of skin color, hair texture, body shape, and facial features. How do you think identities are formed for individuals who do not match these standards? Without question, all persons are affected by these standards. However, you can see how the effects are different for people of color whose cultural standards contradict those present in the larger society.

Understanding Whiteness

The color of a person's skin holds social significance in the United States (Wander, Martin, & Nakayama, 1999). Historically, much of the research and self-reflection related to race and racism has focused on experiences of racial/ethnic microcultures. Because European Americans were in the majority, their culture was less visible than others (Hayman & Levit, 1997) who seemed deviant and in the minority. Being "White" was a sign of normalcy, importance, or privilege (in that it is viewed as the standard by which other racial categories are compared). This idea is not limited to race and ethnicity, though. Other macrocultures have also benefited from their majority status. Their experiences (e.g., heterosexuality, able-bodied, masculinity) have also remained unnamed and uninvestigated compared to those of specific microcultures.

Whiteness, by definition, is a "social construction which produces race privilege for white people by appearing 'neutral,' unlinked to racial politics, universal, and unmarked" (A. C. Rowe & Malhotra, 2006, p.168). Studies that explore Whiteness have increased tremendously in the past 10 years (P. C. Johnson, 1999). The interest in talking about Whiteness has been seen in academic fields such as sociology, English, education, women's studies, and communication. One of the major areas in which Whiteness has been placed at the center of analyses is in the work done by critical race theorists (see Chapter 6). Discussions of Whiteness have also appeared in the popular press (Stowe, 1996). We think it is important to address Whiteness here before our discussions on racial/ethnic identity development. Based on our experiences and those of our colleagues across the United States, we have come to realize that many European Americans do not see themselves as cultural beings. Because of their relative privilege, they are more likely to focus on the cultures of other racial/ethnic groups. Therefore, when asked about their cultural identity, most European Americans struggle with understanding their Whiteness as a cultural entity. Some students even felt silly or embarrassed identifying themselves as "White People." This is because Whiteness is an invisible social force that facilitates people of European descent as seeing themselves as "unraced" (A. N. Miller & Harris, 2005).

By naming and exploring European American culture, Whiteness studies play an important part in effective interracial communication research and practice (Rowe & Malhotra, 2006). First, studying Whiteness fosters an increased awareness of how race and racism shapes the lives of European Americans (Frankenburg, 1993). It helps all of us to view communication as a racialized process—meaning that our communication is structured by larger societal racial dynamics. Second, understanding Whiteness sharpens our awareness of how racial categorization is used to reinforce old hierarchies in which some races are more superior than others (see Chapter 2). It also helps us recognize how Whiteness signals dominance, normalcy, and privilege (rather than subordination, deviancy, and disadvantage) in the United States (Frankenberg, 1993). Finally, Whiteness studies also assign each person a role in race relations. No longer can European Americans sit by the sidelines in discussions of race and racism. Naming and understanding their Whiteness means they, as much as people of color, have a stake in issues related to race. In this regard, a critical attention to Whiteness, and working to productively negotiate the privileges that come with it, is part of a larger attempt to better inform race relations (J. T. Warren & Hytten, 2004).

In short, Whiteness studies enable us to advance our understanding of European American culture beyond that of a normalized and raceless category. Understanding Whiteness helps us recognize how race shapes European Americans' lives. As this growing body of research continues to develop, other important insights are also gained. For instance, Nakayama and Martin (1999) advance studies on Whiteness in innovative ways. In particular they study the role that communication plays in forming this aspect of social identity. Their edited book also points to an important aspect of this line of research: Understanding Whiteness requires us to see how it relates to other aspects of a person's cultural identity. In other words, Whiteness is not the only—or necessarily the most important—cultural marker we need to recognize. Instead, we must increase our understanding of how Whiteness intersects with other cultural elements (socioeconomic status, gender, sexual orientation, etc.) to inform a person's lived experiences (Frankenburg, 1993) (see Chapter 5). Next, we focus our attention on how the social identity of Whiteness is developed.

Macrocultural Identity Development Model

Ever since the work of Erik Erikson (1963), scholars have been interested in the concept of identity development. Earlier theoretical models did not focus explicitly on the experiences and processes of macrocultural group members. However, they were based on the lived experiences of being a European American in the United States. More recently, the focus of identity development models has moved from more generic stages to those specific to particular macrocultural and microcultural group experiences (see Box 4.4). Several majority identity development models (e.g., Hardiman, 1994; Helms, 1994) contain conceptually similar stages. For the purposes of a specific focus, we offer a brief description of Janet Helms's (1990, 1994) model. We chose her model because it is one of the most comprehensive.

❖ **Table 4.1** A Sampling of Racial Identity Development Models

Members of Microcultural Groups	Members of Macrocultural Groups	Biracial Persons
J. A. Banks, 1976 • Psychological captivity • Encapsulation • Identity clarification • Biethnicity • Multiethnicity	*Hardiman, 1994* • Unexamined identity • Acceptance • Resistance • Redefinition • Immersion/emersion • Autonomy	*J. H. Jacobs, 1992* • Pre-color constancy • Racial ambivalence • Biracial identity
B. W. Jackson and Hardiman, 1983 • Acceptance • Resistance • Redefinition • Internalization	*Helms, 1994* • Contact • Disintegration • Reintegration • Pseudo-independent • Integration	*Kich, 1992* • Awareness of differentness • Struggle for acceptance • Self-acceptance and assertion
Phinney, 1993 • Unexamined identity • Conformity • Resistance/separation • Integration		*Poston, 1990* • Personal identity • Choice of group categorization • Enmeshment/denial • Appreciation • Integration
Ponterotto and Pedersen, 1993 • Dissonance • Resistance/denial • Introspection • Synergetic articulation		

In order to increase our awareness of how European Americans formulate their racial/ethnic identities, Helms outlines six specific stages: contact, disintegration, reintegration, pseudo-independence, immersion/emersion, and autonomy. The first stage in Helms's model is **contact**. Within this stage, European Americans' self-perception does not include any element of being a member of the "White race." Instead, they assume that racial/ethnic differences are best understood as differences in individuals' personalities (as opposed to related cultural norms). Contact with people of color is limited and highly insubstantial. European American perceptions are guided by minimal knowledge of other racial/ethnic groups, which may result in behaviors that are naive, timid, and/or potentially offensive (Helms, 1990).

Disintegration is the second stage of Helms's model. Within this stage, European Americans acknowledge that prejudice, discrimination, and racism exist and are forced to view themselves as dominant group members. Typical reactions at this stage include experiencing overwhelming feelings of guilt and confusion, seeing oneself as less prejudiced than other European Americans, or proudly protecting microcultural group members from negative interactions with "White bigots." **Reintegration**, according to Helms, represents the last stage of the abandonment of racism phase of majority identity development. In this stage, European Americans tend to focus less on themselves in comparison to microcultural group members and more on themselves as a member of the "White race." They may deny any responsibility for the social problems experienced by people of color.

The fourth stage of majority group identity development is characterized by that of a **pseudo-independent**, a European American who unintentionally believes his or her culture is more advanced and civilized than others. Within this stage, individuals accept people of color as a whole and become interested in helping them become successful in society. Consciously or unconsciously, however, the underlying assumption is that "successful" means becoming more like European Americans (Helms, 1990). Distinguishing the fifth stage of Helms's model, **immersion/emersion**, from the fourth stage (pseudo-independence) can sometimes be difficult. In fact, movement from one stage to the next can be quite subtle. The basic difference is that European Americans in the pseudo-independence stage continue to blame racial/ethnic group members for their own problems. In comparison, those at the immersion/emersion stage recognize the contributions of European Americans in such matters. Most individuals, according to Helms (1994), do not advance to this stage of majority identity development.

The final stage of European American identity development is **autonomy**. According to Helms (1994), this is the "stage in which the person attempts to interact with the world and commune with himself or herself from a positive, White, non-racist perspective" (p. 87). European Americans at this sixth stage are committed to working toward what they see as a nonracist position. Many continually are involved in life experiences that will move them to this ideal. Within this framework, we must recognize autonomy as a lifelong process of discovery, recommitment, and social activism.

❖ **BOX 4.4**

Student Reflections

Basically, I feel for minorities. I go out of my way to help those who are racially different from myself and try to pay more attention to them than, say, my fellow White Americans. Because I think most minorities have a tough hill to climb just to get on the same playing field as most Whites. It sucks to say, but I view minorities as being disadvantaged, and I am quick to give them my sympathy. I think this is where my problem lies. Although some might not mind some sympathy now and then, some I'm sure don't need my sympathy and, frankly, don't want it. Fact is, though, I have few minority friends, if any. . . . Why is that so?

Microcultural Identity Development Model

As indicated by Table 4.1, various models describe the process of how microcultures (African Americans, Native Americans, Asian Americans, and Latino/a Americans) form their racial/ethnic identities (see also Cross, 1971, 1978). Each of these models overlaps considerably with other existing frameworks. In order to provide sufficient detail, we include additional research associated with other models (e.g., J. A. Banks, 1976; B. W. Jackson & Hardiman, 1983; Ponterotto & Pedersen, 1993).

According to Phinney (1993), the identity development process for U.S. racial/ ethnic microcultural group members involves four states: unexamined identity, conformity, resistance/separation, and integration. Note that a person does not typically arrive at the final stage and remain at that level for the rest of his or her life. Instead, people experience a recycling of stages as they engage in the process of dealing with life changes within their current sense of identity (B. W. Jackson & Hardiman, 1983). Because of this, the experience of identity formation is best understood as a series of continuous loops rather than a straight line. Phinney (1993) describes the first stage in this process as **unexamined identity**, a period of a microcultural group member's life with little or no exploration of racial/ethnic background. During this stage, individuals may have an extremely low awareness of their cultural heritage, often because of a lack of interest in particular cultural values, norms, language, and other elements.

The second stage (**conformity**) involves accepting and internalizing these dominant group perspectives. For some people of color, this stage may include accepting negative group stereotypes (B. W. Jackson & Hardiman, 1983), which results in an intense desire to try and adopt the values of European American culture (Phinney, 1993). Each racial/ethnic group has ingroup terms that describe those in the conformity stage (e.g., an African American who is labeled as an "oreo"). J. A. Banks (1976), in his research on minority identity development, uses a particular phrase to grasp this concept: "ethnic psychological captivity" (p. 191). He relates the process of internalizing negative beliefs about one's own racial/ethnic group to self-rejection and low self-esteem. Stage 3, **resistance and separation**, typically begins when individuals experience some tension when trying to understand themselves in the midst of ingroup and outgroup cultural perceptions. It is difficult to determine exactly when stage 2 dissolves and stage 3 begins. Much of this process depends on when (if) a person of color begins to think critically about macrocultural values and his or her own cultural standpoint. Once this process has started, however, the sense of resistance to Eurocentric perspectives appears to grow more intense. Oftentimes this leads a person to search for an increased understanding of racial/ethnic group histories. The result is the development of an extreme sense of pride based on the significant accomplishments of other racial/ethnic group members, more open challenges to racism, and a conscious attempt to separate oneself from European Americans.

Another important aspect of stage 3 is the initial transition that occurs between old identities (informed by outgroup cultural perspectives) and new ones (encouraged by a greater awareness of racial/ethnic pride). This process of identity transformation is continued in the fourth stage of microcultural identity development, **integration** (Phinney, 1993). The basic issue involves achieving a public racial/ethnic identity that is consistent with one's inner sense of self (B. W. Jackson & Hardiman, 1983). The ultimate outcome of this final stage of microcultural identity development is internalizing a confident and secure racial/ethnic identity. The next section deals specifically with how persons with more than one racial/ethnic heritage formulate their identities. Based on the descriptions provided earlier, you will be able to understand how biracial identity development models are similar to, yet different from, Phinney's (1993) microcultural identity development model.

❖ **BOX 4.5**

STUDENT REFLECTIONS

I have been told by others that I look Indian, Native American, Black, and biracial. My dad is Black and my mom is Irish and German, which makes me biracial. I see being both Black and White as having the best of both worlds; I'm not just one race but two. I think by being mixed I have different views and standpoints than others that are of just one race. I have had to grow up being both, trying to be my own person who is Black and who is White. I'm not trying to become someone who is Black or someone who is just White, but someone who is me. I get along with both races. I have more White friends, but that doesn't mean that I don't get along with or identify with the Black side of me. I see the world Black and White and not just one or the other.

Biracial Identity Development Model

For many years, biracial identity development was understood via frameworks developed for U.S. ethnic minorities. This makes sense, given the societal one-drop rule (Rockquemore & Laszloffy, 2005) described in Chapter 2. However, we can now understand why using existing majority and minority identity development models to understand biracial identity development is less than ideal. First, unlike microcultural and macrocultural based models, biracial identity has no clear-cut ultimate outcome (Nance & Foeman, 2002). Because their identities do not fit into simple categories, the last stage in identity formation may be ambiguous and tentative. For many biracial persons, identity development has no single end state (Rockquemore & Laszloffy, 2005). Second, existing models do not allow for several racial/ethnic identities. Biracial individuals typically have been forced to "choose" one over the other (Poston, 1990). In reality, these persons may identify with one group, both groups, an emergent group (multiracial community), or all three simultaneously (Orbe, 1999). For some biracial persons, self-identities may even change depending on the specific situational context (T. M. Harris, 2004). Third, research indicates that the biracial identity development takes on an even greater spiraling process when compared to the creation of monoracial identities (S. Alexander, 1994; Herring, 1994). Evidence shows that many biracial individuals repeat earlier stages as they mature (Nance & Foeman, 2002). This ongoing process is typically experienced with great intensity, awareness, and a sense of purpose (Herring, 1994). As such, multiracial identity continues to be studied by researchers in different fields (Spencer, 2006).

While a number of models of bi-/multiracial identity development exist, we focus on Poston's "new and positive model" (1990, p. 153) because it extends earlier models in productive ways. The first stage of identity development for multiracial people, according to Poston, is **personal identity**. Individuals at this initial stage are relatively young. Membership in any particular racial/ethnic group is secondary to the sense of self that is somewhat independent of his or her racial/ethnic heritage. In other words, children do not see themselves in racially specific terms. Instead, their identity is informed more by personality elements than cultural ones (Cross, 1978). Choice of **group categorization**, according to Poston, is the second stage in biracial identity development. At this stage, individuals gain an increased awareness of their race/ethnic heritage and are pushed to choose an identity. Typically, two likely choices are available at this stage: identity with one group or the other. Research on the lived experiences of biracial persons clearly indicates an external pressure for them to make a specific racial/ethnic choice (Funderburg, 1993). The choice made at this stage involves a number of interrelated factors, including demographics of home neighborhood, parental presence/style/influence, physical appearance, influence of peer groups, and support of social groups (Rockquemore & Brunsma, 2002).

The third stage is **enmeshment/denial**. Following the choices made in the previous phase, this stage is characterized by an emotional tension (e.g., confusion, guilt, or self-hatred) because claiming one identity does not fully express who they are. In many cases, a biracial person feels that his or her identity choice makes it difficult to identify with both parents. This conflict can result in feelings of disloyalty, abandonment, and/or guilt (Sebring, 1985). A sense of **appreciation** for one's multiple racial/ethnic background occurs at the fourth stage of biracial identity development. Poston describes individuals at this stage as attempting to learn more about all of the racial/ethnic cultures that make up who they are. But, although an appreciation of diverse cultures exists, biracial persons still primarily identify with one racial/ethnic group (as determined in stage 2: choice of group categorization). Within this stage, biracial persons recognize and value each aspect of their racial/ethnic identity (Poston, 1990). Through integration, individuals are able to carve out an identity that reflects their complete selves. This was not the case in earlier stages where their identities were necessarily more fragmented and incomplete. Here you can see how Poston's biracial identity development model is helpful in emphasizing the unique challenges that biracial people face, and outlines the process of how most persons formulate their identities in a healthy, productive fashion.

The different models described in the previous sections primarily present a linear formation of how identity develops along predetermined, ordered stages. While these models provide great insight into the general process, they are limited in that the realities of identity are not always easily captured in neatly formatted steps (Nance & Foeman, 2002). More recent theories reflect the idea that identity is constantly negotiated, and never really "achieved." The communication theory of identity, originated by Michael Hecht, is one theory that has great potential to provide insight into racial and ethnic identity negotiation.

Communication Theory of Identity

According to the communication theory of identity (CTI), identity is a naturally communicative and relational phenomenon (Hecht et al., 2003). Communication builds, sustains, and transforms identity. At the same time, identity is expressed through communication (Jung & Hecht, 2004). Identity is best understood as multi-dimensional and holistic in nature. As such, a major assumption of CTI is that identity is located in four interconnected layers: personal, enacted, relational, and communal (Hecht et al., 2003).

The theory originators assert that the **personal frame** of identity encompasses an individual's self-concept or self-definition. The personal level of identity is partially constructed from the messages received from relational others; however, the location is within the individual. The personal layer of identity provides clues as to how individuals view themselves in general as well as in specific contexts and situations.

The second frame of identity is the **enacted frame**. This frame is based on the idea that identities are communicatively manifested during social interactions. According to CTI, identities emerge through our interactions with others and are communicated either directly or indirectly through social roles, behaviors, and symbols (Hecht et al., 2003). This frame treats self as a performance and makes communication the location of identity (Hecht, Warren, Jung, & Krieger, 2005).

❖ **BOX 4.6**

STUDENT REFLECTIONS

When I was growing up, I developed a passion of sharing my Mexican heritage with others but was quickly shut down by many of my White friends. Some of whom would always accuse me of not being "Mexican enough," or say things like, "Oh, you're one of them that really looks like one of us." But as I entered high school, things began to change. I learned to not be ashamed of my heritage, but to embrace it and share it with others who could reciprocate their religions, traditions, and customs back with me.

The **relational frame**, the third location of identity, captures how identities emerge in reference to others (Hecht et al., 1993). According to CTI, identities are mutually constructed and negotiated through relationships (Hecht et al., 1993; Hecht et al., 2003). There are three aspects of this frame. First, individuals reflect upon themselves in terms of the people with whom they interact, which contributes to the ongoing alteration of their identity. Second, people gain their identities through relationships with others, for example, their friendships, romantic partners, or family members. Third, relationships themselves, such as couples, constitute units of identity (Hecht et al., 2005).

Finally, the **communal frame** points to a group of people or a particular community bonded by a collective memory as the locus of identity (Hecht et al., 2003). The community has its own identity and illustrates the joint identities of the individuals who associate with it (Golden, Niles, & Hecht, 2002). Thus, identities arise from group associations and social networks (Hecht et al., 2005). Labels, rituals, artifacts, and communicative practices are frequently used by a collective to assert and convey group identities and provide frames of reference for its members (Witteborn, 2004).

Although we have discussed each of these four frames separately, CTI explains that the frames are always interrelated and never separate (Marsiglia & Hecht, 1999). One's personal identity, for example, cannot be considered without the context of the relational, enacted, and communal layers (Hecht et al., 2005). Although the frames coexist and cooperate in the composition of a person's identity, they do not always work in accord; instead, they may contradict or compete with one another, revealing inevitable identity gaps (Jung & Hecht, 2004). For instance, a communal frame of identity for an ethnic group (e.g., Latino/as) may have certain things associated with it (e.g., being able to speak Spanish, eating certain foods, participating in certain celebrations). Latino/as who do not do these things may still identify as Latino/a (personal layer); however, a struggle may exist in terms of how they communicate (enacted layer) and relate to other Latino/as (relational layer) (Hecht et al., 2002). The ways in which the different frames influence, confirm, and contradict one another helps to capture the ongoing process of identity negotiation. Within the CTI framework, it is known as **interpenetration** (Jung & Hecht, 2004).

CTI has been used to explore racial and ethnic identity among various groups, including African Americans (Hecht et al., 2003), Arab women (Witteborn, 2004), and Jewish Americans (Faulkner, 2006; Golden et al., 2002; Marsiglia & Hecht, 1999). Golden and his colleagues, for instance, illustrated how Jewish Americans constantly create and negotiate their identities by revealing and concealing their Jewishness. This is accomplished through varying situational and contextual salience of either the personal, communal, relational, or enacted layer of identity. Similarly, Marsiglia and Hecht demonstrated how the interaction between the communal and personal gendered Jewish identity is expressed in core symbols, labels, and behaviors. Finally, adding another dimension to CTI studies, Faulkner (2006) studied how Jewish Americans who were gay/lesbian/bisexual/transgendered simultaneously negotiated different aspects of their identities. Faulkner's research demonstrates the value of studying multiple aspects of identity simultaneously—something that is explained in greater detail in Chapter 5.

Conclusion

This chapter described how individuals come to understand racial/ethnic perceptions of self and others. Much of the discussion focused on how a person comes to co-create his or her individual racial and/or ethnic identity. Specifically, we described in some detail the commonalities and differences of macrocultural, microcultural, and biracial identity development models. We also introduced the communication theory of identity that encourages us to understand how identity is located in different frames. Within all of these descriptions, we discussed how our own identities are inextricably linked with the ways that we perceive others.

We began this chapter with a statement from Tanno and Gonzalez (1998) that suggested the more attention the concept of cultural identity receives, the more complex it becomes. The information provided here is substantial in illustrating the importance of race/ethnicity in matters of identity negotiation. It is also largely incomplete, given that identity, and, subsequently, interracial communication, is informed by other elements of social categories. Chapter 5 will complete our coverage of the multifaceted, complex process of identity co-creation.

OPPORTUNITIES FOR EXTENDED LEARNING ❖

1. Create a chapter outline for a book that describes your racial/ethnic identity development. Create a title for each chapter that captures a significant event or time in your life that symbolizes an increased degree of awareness in terms of race/ethnicity. Chapter 1 should contain details of your first memories, and your last chapter should describe your current perceptions (the chapters in between will describe the process by which you got from there to here). Share and explain your outlines with the class.

2. The media contain a number of excellent examples of individuals at different stages of racial/ethnic identity development. Think about your favorite television show, movie, cartoon strip, or book. Who are the main characters? Think about what you have learned about them. Based on their communication about self and others, can you make an educated guess at which stage of racial identity development they are? Do you have any evidence that this has changed over time? Are there characters at different stages? How is their communication similar and/or different? If time permits, compare your judgments with others.

3. Root (1996) has created a "Bill of Rights for Racially Mixed People" that includes the following: "I have the right not to keep the races separate within me," "I have the right to identify myself differently than how strangers, parents, and my siblings identify me," "I have the right to identify myself differently in different situations," and "I have the right to change my identity over my lifetime." Break up into small groups and discuss your reactions to these "rights." Do you agree or disagree? Any that you might add to Root's list?

4. Using the frameworks presented here for macrocultural, microcultural, and biracial identity development, create a list of advantages and disadvantages for each stage. Although you might suspect that more disadvantages exist within earlier stages and more advantages in the latter ones, this is not necessarily the case. (For instance, European Americans in the early stages of identity development are oftentimes optimistic about the future of race relations and believe these problems *can* be solved.) Break into groups for a brainstorming session (e.g., advantages for microcultural development stages, disadvantages for microcultural development stages, etc.). Following group work, share with the entire class.

5. Spend some time exploring how Whiteness is experienced in different areas of the United States. For instance, do some research on how some European American groups in the Northeast (e.g., New York, Philadelphia, and Boston) emphasize their ethnic identities through celebrations (St. Patrick's Day parade) or other means ("Little Italy"). Do similar displays of ethnic pride occur for European Americans in other regions?

6. Go to the following Web site: http://magazine.interracialweb.com. This URL is home to an online magazine for and about interracial couples, multiracial persons, and their families. Look through the different resources provided on the Web site (blogs, articles, ecards, news stories, etc.) to gain insight into the issues of this growing community. Pay particular attention to the various ways in which personal and social issues are expressed. How do these things relate to the identity models and theories discussed in this chapter?

5

Recognizing Multiple Self-Identities and Other Identities

In order to comprehend the dynamics of any particular cultural phenomenon, you must see how it relates to other aspects of culture (Connell, 2005). In other words, understanding race must involve going beyond race. Within this chapter, we explain how all individuals have multidimensional identities. Thus far, we have focused on racial and ethnic identity, but it is important to recognize how all of us belong to a variety of other cultural groups that share common attitudes, values, and norms of relating to one another.

Refer back to the "Who Am I?" exercise that you completed in Chapter 4. Can you see how some of your responses are directly linked to your membership in one or more cultural groups? Some of these aspects of cultural identity receive a great deal of attention; others are less apparent but not necessarily less influential. Furthermore, some of these aspects remain relatively stable over time (race/ethnicity, gender), but others may change (age, socioeconomic status). The important thing to remember is that, like the authors of this text, you are a member of many different cultural groups that influence who you are and what you think and feel, as well as how you communicate with others. Recognizing the multiple aspects of your cultural identity promotes a deeper understanding of the complexities of interracial communication beyond simple racial/ethnic designations. Chapter 5 will to give you a conceptual framework to enhance your understanding of how other elements of cultural identity (abilities, age, gender, nationality, sexual orientation, spirituality, and socioeconomic status) affect interracial communication. Throughout this chapter, continue the self-reflective process initiated in Chapter 4 and you will begin to discern how race and ethnicity—and other cultural elements—become more or less significant in different contexts.

Acknowledging Multiple Cultural Identities

Cultural identities are central, dynamic, and multifaceted components of our understanding of self and others (A. Rodriguez, 2002). Once formed (at least if we could freeze time for that particular moment, before future points of negotiation), they provide an essential framework for organizing and interpreting our interactions with others. In addition, each aspect of our identity serves as a marker of who we are and, when acknowledged by others, affects how we are defined culturally. Research has provided consistent evidence that individuals categorize others based on attributes such as race, class, gender, and sexual orientation (Mallinson & Brewster, 2005). Our perceptions of others who are within groups marked by these cultural attributes influence our expectations that we have for social interactions (Waldinger & Lichter, 2003).

Mary Jane Collier and others have advanced a cultural identity theory (CIT) that provides a productive framework for acknowledging the existence and impact of complexities of cultural identity and interracial communication. The main ideas of the theory revolve around the central premise that each individual has multiple cultural identities that are formed through discourse with others (Collier, 2000, 2002; Collier & Thomas, 1988; Hecht et al., 1993). Consistent with most of the scholars whose work was referenced in Chapter 4, CIT is based within the perspective that "cultural identities are negotiated, co-created, reinforced, and challenged through communication" (Collier, 2000, p. 31). CIT also helps shed light on the various ways our cultural identities are defined in relation to one another. Recognizing the multiple types of identities that make up a person's self-concept avoids defining self and/or others as unidimensional beings. This process also assists in recognizing the diversity within cultural groups (Orbe, Allen, & Flores, 2006). In this regard, the theoretical framework serves as an excellent point of transition between the basic ideas presented in Chapter 4 and the focus here.

Two of the major ideas associated with CIT are avowal and ascription. **Avowal,** according to Collier (2002), refers to the perceived identity that a person or group enacts in a particular context. It consists of a more subjective identity, one that is typically viewed from the point of a specific individual (Collier, Thompson & Weber, 1996). **Ascription,** in comparison, is framed more from a collective position. It consists of an individual's perception of how others see his or her cultural identity. Although these two identity components can be described independently, they function together in inextricable ways (Moss & Faux, 2006). For instance, our self-identity is informed largely by our interactions with others, including our perceptions of how others perceive us. Others' perception of us—or at least our perceptions of their perceptions (ascription)—has a direct impact on how we come to see ourselves (avowal). In fact, membership within a cultural group typically occurs when a person self-identifies as a group member and then has that status confirmed by other members of the group (Carbaugh, 1990).

Another major aspect of CIT involves understanding the enduring/changing quality of cultural identity (A. Rodriguez, 2002). Typically passed down from one generation of group members to another, cultural identities are enduring in that historical group orientations inform present and future reality. Although certain aspects of a person's cultural knowledge can be readily attributed to the enduring quality of group membership (e.g., that which is based on religion), others are not so clear. Think for a moment about how you have accumulated other information about what it means to be a woman/man, member of a particular national/regional group, or member of a specific group based on sexual orientation. Although possibly less apparent, most of us can remember specific aspects of cultural identities based on sex, national/regional origin, and sexual orientation that were directly or indirectly communicated to us from others. Although our cultural identities possess an enduring quality, they simultaneously are also apt to change over time. Our cultural identities are dynamic and subject to constant examination, reexamination, and possibly alteration based on our interactions with others. This involves all aspects of our identity, including those more permanent (race/ethnicity and gender) as well as those more fluid (socioeconomic status and age). Most of us—especially students who have invested significant amounts of time, money, and energy in obtaining a college degree—foresee how this accomplishment might alter our self-identity in a number of ways (definitely age, possibly regional/geographical location, and hopefully socioeconomic!). However, even with a stable cultural marker such as race, our identities may also change over time. Just think about how an increased knowledge of self and others changes—if not your particular race/ethnicity—the ways you label, understand, and identify with that particular set of racial/ethnic lived experiences.

Furthermore, cultural identities comprise both context and relational levels of interpretation (Collier, 2002). This aspect of CIT recognizes that the meanings within interracial interactions are created not only by the content shared between interactants but also their relationship. Although much of communication effectiveness typically focuses on language usage (see Chapter 3), such an analysis cannot be removed from the relational context of the interaction. For instance, the mere adoption of ingroup or outgroup language creates meaning, as do efforts to emphasize one position over the other (Collier, 2002). Various aspects of *content* (language, jokes, self- and other labels) must be understood within the *context* of the participant's relationship (see Chapter 7). Take, for example, the use of *girl*. Among African American women, this term is used to refer to one another in a positive, affirming, and celebratory manner (Scott, 1996). In an interracial communication context, the use of *girl* by a European American woman to refer to an African American woman (e.g., "Hey, girl, how are you?") may generate a set of different meanings. The European American woman might perceive it as a way to establish rapport. The African American woman might perceive it as presumptions, offensive, and insulting in lieu of the sociohistorical context of the United States and absence of an established relationship (Orbe, Drummond, & Camara, 2002). In the context of an established, close relationship, *girl* may be used by both African American and European American women as a sign that racial differences may be transcended (B. J. Allen, 2004). Again, an effective interpretation of meaning involves both the content and relationship dimensions of the message.

A final aspect of CIT relates to the salience and intensity of particular cultural elements in any given interracial communication context (Moss & Faux, 2006). **Salience,** along these lines, "refers to the relative importance of one or two identities to others" (Collier, 2002, p. 305). Intensity is used as a marker that indicates the level of involvement and investment that a person has in a particular aspect of her or his identity (Collier, 2000). Both of these concepts are important because, as we described at the beginning of this chapter, people communicate within multiple cultural identities. In this chapter, we focus on taking a multidimensional approach to identity. This means acknowledging that in any given interaction, some aspects of cultural identity will be more salient than others. In this regard, interactions between people from two different racial and/or ethnic groups may be focused on a similar trait—thereby transcending racial/ethnic differences. For instance, in their collaborative research on their interracial friendship, Clark and Diggs (2002) describe how a common spiritual connection allowed them successfully to negotiate any tensions they experienced that were related to racial differences. Understanding how some cultural similarities, like those based within spirituality, can help individuals transcend racial differences is at the heart of this chapter.

Potentially Salient Aspects of Cultural Identity

Because our focus here is on interracial communication, it is not feasible to offer a detailed description of each aspect of culture that has the potential to impact any particular instance of interracial contact. Such a task appears especially difficult given the broad ways in which culture has been defined by most communication scholars. Instead, we have identified several specific elements of cultural identity that seem especially relevant to interracial communication in the United States. This conclusion, although not definitive, is the result of a thorough review of existing literature as well as our own research and lived experiences. Nevertheless, we acknowledge that additional elements of cultural identity may represent significant factors during interracial interactions (see Opportunities for Extended Learning, #3). As a means to illustrate the process by which multiple cultural identities are enacted, we focus on seven specific elements: abilities, age, gender, nationality, sexual orientation, spirituality, and socioeconomic status.

Think back to our discussions of societal privilege in Chapter 4. During that chapter we focused on the idea of White privilege and how it impacts identity emergence—either directly or indirectly—for both European Americans and people of color. Societal privilege, as discussed by McIntosh (1995a), is present whenever certain individuals are able to take advantage of unseen benefits simply based on their majority-group status. As such, societal privilege exists on many different dimensions, including those defined by the aspects of culture focused on in this chapter. Martin and Nakayama (1999) remind us that all individuals carry and communicate various types of privilege and disadvantage. In addition to White privilege, we hope that this chapter will make you increasingly aware of able-bodied privilege, male privilege, middle-/upper-class privilege, heterosexual privilege, Christian privilege, and so on. So, as you read through these descriptions, begin to think about the multidimensional nature of your identity and—depending on your majority/minority status for each—how it reflects a point of privilege or disadvantage.

❖ **BOX 5.1**

CASE STUDY

Consider the case scenario described here. Given this chapter's focus on acknowledging multiple cultural identities, what do you make of Professor Smith's efforts to make Michele more comfortable in her class?

Professor Smith teaches a number of undergraduate communication classes at a small liberal arts college whose student population is very "traditional"—largely European American students, 18 to 24 years of age. In one of the introductory communication classes she teaches, Professor Smith has noticed that one student, a thirty-something African American woman (Michele), seems isolated—both physically and psychologically—from the rest of the class. As the only person of color in class, she typically sits in the front corner of the room and keeps on her Sony Walkman until class starts. Although she is doing well in the course, Professor Smith is concerned because she does not speak at all in class.

One day during office hours, Michele stops by to ask Professor Smith a question about an upcoming paper. Seizing the opportunity to interact with Michele on a one-to-one basis for the first time, Professor Smith is surprised to see how personable and energetic she is in this more intimate setting. Thinking it would be good for her to meet other students in a more casual atmosphere, Professor Smith makes a suggestion:

Prof. Smith:	Have you been over to the student organization area yet?
Michele:	No, I haven't. . . . I have been real busy with school, and. . . .
Prof. Smith:	Well, why don't we take a walk over there right now? It will only take a couple of minutes, and I want to introduce you to some of my other students.
Michele:	I really need to leave campus, and start. . . .
Prof. Smith:	Oh, come on! It will just take a moment!

On the walk over, Professor Smith is proud of herself for taking the initiative to make Michele feel more at home on campus. When she brings Michele to the Multicultural Student Union's office, she is relieved to see some familiar faces. After introducing everyone, Professor Smith is surprised to see Michele become quiet and clearly ready to leave. Following an awkward silence, they leave and start walking past other student organization offices, including the Non-Traditional Student Union. Professor Smith tries to get Michele to attend a meeting, but Michele appears disinterested and somewhat annoyed.

Driving home that night, Professor Smith is troubled about Michele's lack of interest in getting to know other students, especially students with similar cultural backgrounds. In fact, she spends much of the weekend mentally replaying her interactions with Michele. Imagine her surprise (and relief) on Monday morning, when she finds the following e-mail message from Michele:

Prof. Smith:	Thanks for taking the time to introduce me around on Friday afternoon. I have been feeling a little uncomfortable on campus because it seems like all the students do is talk about partying, drinking, and having sex. This definitely is not my cup of tea; in fact, some of their attitudes are quite shocking! But guess what? At church on Sunday, I met two other people who just started taking classes on campus, and we intend to start a Christian Student Union soon. Having an opportunity for fellowship with other Christians on campus is just what I needed to feel more comfortable. Thanks again for your help. Michele (Communication 101)

In the sections to follow, each cultural aspect is described specifically in terms of its influence on communication processes. These descriptions (1) distinguish how each represents a cultural identity marker, (2) generate an understanding of its relationship to perceptions of communication, (3) illustrate how it relates to privilege/disadvantage, and (4) highlight the ways it intersects with racial/ethnic identity in the context of intraracial and interracial communication. As you read, reflect on how multiple cultural identities are negotiated in different contexts. Specifically, ask yourself the following questions: What is the salience and intensity of this cultural marker within my self-concept? How is this directly related to particular situational contexts and relationships with others? Are there any cultural elements that are enacted with more salience and intensity than those marked by race/ethnicity? If so, within what contexts and/or relationships?

Abilities

Abilities refer to the social effects of physical, emotional, or mental capabilities. When we discuss abilities, most often we refer to able-bodied persons and people with disabilities. According to the National Organization on Disability, there are approximately 54 million people with disabilities who live in the United States (W. Kim, 2006). This number includes people who we traditionally think about in terms of disability, including 2.7 million people who use a wheelchair, 1.8 million people who are unable to see, and 1 million people who are unable to hear. However, it also includes millions more who have limitations in cognitive functioning, physical impairments, and/or mental or emotional illness (W. Kim, 2006). Accordingly, we must be aware of various types of disabilities and the degree to which the disability affects one's everyday life (Cornett-DeVito & Worley, 2005).

Disability is a salient communicative issue (Harter, Scott, Novak, Leeman, & Morris, 2006). Research that conceptualizes persons with disabilities as a cultural group has resulted in a growing body of literature in and outside of the field of communication (D. O. Braithwaite & Thompson, 2000). Disability as culture views people with disabilities as forming distinct cultures or co-cultures; this underscores the empowering potential of disability as a cultural identity (Coopman, 2003). When discussing persons with disabilities as a cultural group, three points must be acknowledged. First, different frames serve to oppress persons with disabilities; these include labels such as "disabled," which is seen as "damaged" and "defective" (Harter et al., 2006). Historically, disability has been seen as a medical problem, an "impairment" that must be repaired (Coopman, 2003). Second, a person with a disability may identify with a community of other persons with disabilities generally or those with a particular disability (e.g., blind, deaf, or mobility-related disabilities). According to Waldrop and Stern (2003), almost half live with more than one type of disability. Third, like any other cultural group, differences in experiences (e.g., being born with a disability or having lived as a TAB—temporarily able-bodied person) affect the phases of identity development (Padden & Humphries, 1988), communication, and community life (Harter et al., 2006).

Persons with disabilities recognize that more often than not, able-bodied persons primarily see them as disabled first, and a person with other personality and cultural traits second (D. O. Braithwaite & Braithwaite, 2000; Chan, 1989). In most instances, a disability invokes a number of widely accepted stereotypes for people, including being "dependent, socially introverted, emotionally unstable, depressed, hypersensitive, and easily offended, especially with regard to their disability. In addition, disabled people are often presumed to differ from able-bodied people in moral character, social skills, and political orientation" (Coleman & DePaulo, 1991, p. 69). Based on these stereotypical images of persons with disabilities, many able-bodied persons' communication is characterized by one of two approaches (Chan, 1989). First, they try to ignore that any disability exists. This oftentimes results in ignoring people with disabilities completely. Second, able-bodied persons may become oversensitive to the disability and treat a person with a disability in an overly protective and/or patronizing manner. The best advice, provided by W. Kim (2006), is to first look at a person's abilities, then factor in what might need to be accommodated in terms of disabilities second.

According to the U.S. Census, people with disabilities are disproportionately people of color ("Why Do More Blacks Have Disabilities?" 2006). This point of analysis helps us to understand how different aspects of cultural identity work coexist. For instance, experts have long reported on the link between socioeconomic status and disability. Because people of color in the United States are more likely to have a lower socioeconomic status—and lack access to prevent and manage disabilities—it stands to reason why African Americans and Latino/as outnumber the number of European Americans with disabilities. The intersection of abilities and racial/ethnic identity provides some interesting case scenarios of interracial communication. Take, for example, the experiences of Sucheng Chan (1989), a person with a disability who is of Asian descent. Her experiences are especially interesting because in many East Asian cultures, a strong folk belief exists that sees a person's physical state in this life as a reflection of how morally or sinfully she or he lived in previous lives. Reactions to her decision to marry an able-bodied man outside her racial/ethnic group provide an insightful illustration of how race was more of an important factor for some (her father-in-law), and her disability was for others (mother-in-law, parents' friends).

Age

The United States has been described as an increasingly age-conscious society (McCann, Kellerman, Giles, Gallois, & Viladot, 2004) "where children want to be adults, adults want to be children, and those in their twenties and thirties are considered to be in the 'prime of their life'" (p. 89). Age remains a salient issue in a culture where people celebrate significant transition ages (e.g., 16, 21, 30, 40, 50 years old), have their social and relational roles (e.g., married or single) judged on the basis of age, and oftentimes report a fear of aging (McCann et al., 2004). Think about different age groups (senior citizens, Generation X, baby boomers). What images do you typically associate with each group? According to recent research (K. Anderson, Harwood, & Hummert, 2005), stereotypes related to age impact communication.

A significant amount of research has been done by communication scholars on the cultural aspects of different age groups (Hajek & Giles, 2002; McCann & Giles, 2002). Most of this work is based on the idea that the shared life histories of generations of U.S. Americans have resulted in a common culture of sorts, including common values, norms, languages, dress, and so on (Frey, 2004a; McCann & Giles, 2002). Take the case of *Generation X*. This term, used generally to describe those persons born between 1961 and 1981, reflects the facelessness and aimlessness of a group of U.S. Americans who have been criticized for having no distinct identity, cause, or ambition (Williams & Giles, 1998). Generation Xers are often regarded as losers, whiners, and/or slackers who are overly dependent on their parents. This group of young people feel patronized by older generation members who do not take them seriously, disapprove of their lifestyle choices, and force their values on them. Contrast the stereotypical characterizations of Generation Xers with those associated with senior citizens. Research (e.g., Radford, 1987) indicates that most perceptions of the elderly revolve around negative stereotypes: "greedy, lonely, afraid, incompetent, senile, sexless, inarticulate, forgetful, depressed, stubborn" (McKay, 2000, p. 184). Most of the images are reinforced by the media (Barker & Giles, 2003) and communicated through the large array of negative labels used in everyday talk to describe senior citizens (crone, old-timer, geezer, old fogey, hag, old fart) (Nuessel, 1982). The elderly are also the recipients of patronizing talk from young adults including simpler, lower, and more childlike talk (Cohen & Faulkner, 1986). Given the focus of this text, it is important to recognize that "elders" in different racial/ethnic groups are regarded at different levels of status.

It is important to recognize that age is a cultural phenomenon. The concept of age, and the perceptions related to different age cohorts, is culturally linked (Uotinen, 1998). This even includes what is defined as "young" and "old." Among Native American cultures, for example, determination of who is "old" does not solely relate to chronological age; evidence of particular social roles (e.g., being a grandparent or being unable to work) is equally as important. As such, someone can be considered "young" at 80 if economically and financially functional or "old" at 45 if sick or frail (Barker & Giles, 2003).

In individualistic, Western countries, aging is perceived negatively (Hajek & Giles, 2002). In comparison, in more collectivistic cultures, (e.g., Laos and Thailand) older people are highly respected because of the value of knowledge, wisdom, and sageness. Family-oriented Native Americans traditionally respect their elders for their knowledge and experience (D. K. Carson & Hand, 1999); as such, care of the elderly is the primary responsibility of relatives and a concern for the entire tribe (Barker & Giles, 2003). All of these things demonstrate the need to acknowledge racial, ethnic, and cultural influences on how individuals negotiate their lives. For instance, scholars have urged health care practitioners to consider race and ethnic identifications when creating health care policy, procedures, and public campaigns (Barker & Giles, 2003).

Gender

Of all of the aspects of cultural identity we have chosen to describe here, **gender** is the one most extensively researched by communication scholars. Julia T. Wood (1996, 1997b, 2005) is probably one of the most influential communication researchers who has approached gender communication studies using a cross-cultural perspective (Wood & Dindia, 1998). Scholars have achieved significant progress in identifying communication differences based on biological sex and psychological gender (Pearson & Davilla, 2001). More recently, research has focused on both the communication similarities and differences of men and women (e.g., Canary & Dindia, 1998).

❖ **BOX 5.2**

STUDENT REFLECTIONS

I'm a typical Midwesterner. I grew up in a pretty good sized town that had one major high school. We had some, but not a lot of, different races in our school. Like most schools, however, people pretty much stuck within their own cliques: jocks, band geeks, preppies, drama kids, brainiacs, druggies, etc. A few times someone might cross from one group to another, but not very often at all. The same went for race. . . . Sports were an exception, though. As an Asian, I was definitely a brainiac, but I also played soccer for 4 years—the only minority on the team. I really liked the fact that I could be friends with different groups of people at school. Playing soccer definitely allowed me to make friends that I normally wouldn't have, and I can be 100% sure in saying that my race didn't make a difference to my teammates. We practiced together, traveled together, and won and lost together.

Gender is avoidably involved with other aspects of social identity (Connell, 2005). In many instances, the interlocking nature of these two aspects of identity are so powerful that both are simultaneously enacted with high degrees of salience and intensity. Attempting to describe the impact of sex and race on interracial communication, in this regard, is not feasible unless we also pay attention to other elements of identity in specific interactions. Nevertheless, in some situational contexts, the commonality established through one aspect—let's focus on sex—may serve as a strong foundation for effective interracial communication. Traditionally, sports represent a context where men from different racial and ethnic groups come together for a common purpose (winning) (Connell, 2005). Following the advances made possible through programs that promote equal resources for women and men (e.g., Title IX programs), more women have also recently experienced the synergy, collective energies, and close relationships that come with competitive sports (e.g., WNBA, 1999 World Cup). Although criticized by some as simply another societal mechanism where the "politics of inequality" are played out (Messner, 1989), research does indicate that positive, long-lasting interracial relationships are initiated through participation in various sports.

Frustrated by issues of sexism within their own communications, some of these women turn to women's coalitions in order to fight various oppressions (P. G. Allen, 1986). The goal of many of these organizations is to focus on the common experiences of all women, transcending barriers based on racial/ethnic, class, and sexual orientation differences. However, according to women of color, addressing commonalties based on sex while ignoring differences of race between women represents a threat to the mobilization of women's collective power (Anzaldua, 1987; Cole, 1995; Horno-Delgado, Ortega, Scott, & Stembach, 1989). African American women report that their interpersonal interactions with European American women (even those perceived as well intentioned) reflect this focus on common experiences while ignoring salient racial differences. Attempts at solidarity, according to Marsha Houston (2004), come in phrases like "I never even notice that you're Black," "You're different than other

Blacks," and "I understand your experiences as a Black Woman because sexism is just as bad as racism" (pp. 123–124).

Although rallying around issues central to women can create a unified front, it should not be done by ignoring differences based on race/ethnicity. Effective interracial female relationships recognize the negative impacts of trying to downplay the importance of race. Instead, they consider the crucial role that racialized lived experiences play in how all individuals perceive self and others (Frankenberg, 1993). This point was illustrated in research on sexual harassment (J. Taylor & Richardson, 2006). They found that women must negotiate the double jeopardy of racism and sexism in organizations—something not always acknowledged by European Americans. In particular, they concluded that African American women and Latinas were the targets of "racialized sexual harassment" (p. 84), including being treated as an "exotic erotic" figure in the workplace.

Nationality

Traditionally, **nationality** has been used to refer to the nation in which one is born and holds citizenship. This simplistic definition, however, has grown increasingly complex given the large numbers of people who change their citizenship, have dual citizenships, or affiliate with multiple national cultures (Collier, 2002). For example, consider the lived experiences of Gust Yep (2002), who describes his "multicultural self" as follows:

> I am Asianlatinoamerican. Although I have never been to China, I am racially what my parents describe as "100% pure Chinese." During my formative years, we lived in Peru, South America, and later moved to the United States. . . . I am trilingual (English, Spanish, and Chinese). . . . I "look Asian American," yet at times my Latino culture is most prominent in some communication settings. I strongly identify with all three cultures, and they are more or less integrated into this complex entity that I label as "multicultural self." (p. 60)

Clearly, this example serves as a vivid illustration of the complexity that sometimes accompanies a person's nationality.

Some clarification may be necessary to distinguish nationality from other cultural identity elements such as race and ethnicity. Paying attention to these differences should shed some light on how complex cultural identity perceptions can be. Literature on the cultural experiences of one racial group, that of Asian/Pacific Islanders, serves as an excellent point of analysis. Designations of drastically diverse cultural groups into one label based on race is problematic because it ignores other cultural differences such as language and religion (Sodowsky, Kwan, & Pannu, 1995). For many non–Asian Americans, *race* serves as a primary cultural marker and *ethnic* differences remain less visible. Consider for a moment that Asian Americans can be Chinese, Japanese, Filipino, Korean, Indian, Cambodian, or Laotian (among other groups). Looking at *nationality* brings additional complexities into the negotiation of multiple cultural identities. Take, for instance, a Chinese person whose nationality may be most closely defined with the People's Republic of China, Taiwan, Hong Kong, or the United States. *Regional* differences (urban/rural, east/west/north/south) also come into play here. Imagine the differences of two Chinese Americans who were born and raised in different regions of the United States: one in Mississippi and the other in San Francisco's Chinatown (see Gong, 2004).

The idea of **transnationalism** captures the experience of today's immigrants who, instead of abandoning their old identities and assimilating, choose to simultaneously live in two (or more) cultures and construct bicultural identities; this often means integrating multiple, often diametrically distinct, cultures into one social world (Pedraza, 2006). Although immigrants have almost always maintained connections with their country of origin (Vertovec, 2001), their embeddedness in two cultures has been largely facilitated (although not caused) by the recent developments in modern transportation and communication technologies such as affordable telephone connections, fax, and the Internet (Cheng, 2005). The maintenance of close ties with the country of origin had been viewed as an early temporary stage in immigrant assimilation, which—if it did not end—was perceived as an exception to the rule (Baia, 1999). Moreover, immigrants' move to the host country as well as their occasional return to the homeland was usually viewed as permanent (Suárez-Orozco, 2000). However, recent research shows that individuals continue to identify with multiple nations.

Sexual Orientation

Sexual orientation refers to the direction of an individual's sexuality, often in relation to their own sex; heterosexual (straight), bisexual (bi), and homosexual (lesbian and gay) are common terms to reference sexual orientation. Most definitions of sexual orientation include (1) a psychological component that refers to the target of an individual's erotic desire, and (2) a behavioral component that focuses on the sex of the individual's sexual partner(s) (Shively, Jones, & DeCecco, 1984). The term sexual preference is sometimes used in place of sexual orientation; however, it implies an element of choice as opposed to the belief that sexual orientation is biologically predetermined and/or fixed early in life (Reiter, 1989).

Some scholars have reported that gays and lesbians are increasingly socially accepted in Western society (Seidman, Meeks, & Traschen, 1999). Yet others contend that they continue to live as minorities in a heterosexist world that harbors negative attitudes toward anyone not "straight" (Hajek & Giles, 2002). As such, heterosexist attitudes maintain a double standard related to sexual orientation: Heterosexuality is viewed as healthy when overtly shared, whereas homosexuality is not (Hajek & Giles, 2002). For instance, within the U.S. culture, heterosexual relationships are normalized, but same-sex relationships are not socially or legally sanctioned, nor recognized as viable or legitimate (Muraco, 2005). Within the context of friendships research has shown that sex and sexual orientation shape the norms and expectations of others' behavior (Muraco, 2005). Heterosexual persons, especially heterosexual men, evaluate behaviors more favorably when the other person is straight (Herek, 2000). When communicating with gay and lesbian people, negative attitudes are communicated through heterosexist talk and discriminatory nonverbal behaviors, like increased physical distance (Speer & Potter, 2000). While sometimes less visible than race, sexual orientation impacts our everyday communication (Lovaas & Jenkins, 2006).

Living the life of a cultural outsider in the United States provides gays and lesbians with a perspective shared with many other microcultures. For many individuals a basic assumption exists: A person who experiences oppression is more likely to identify with others who are also oppressed, regardless of the source of their oppression. Can the sting of confronting isms (racism, sexism, heterosexism) on a daily basis work toward creating a bond for these two racially diverse people? According to Brenda J. Allen (2004), it can and did in her close relationship with one of her colleagues, Anna. Both women have a great deal in common: baby boomers from the Midwest, raised with a similar socioeconomic status, and strong religious backgrounds. However, B. J. Allen (2004) attributes their strong friendship to sharing a similar marginalized position in society and concludes that "despite our similarities in personal style and background, Anna and I would probably not have become such good friends if she were straight" (p. 199).

Luna (1989), however, provides strong evidence that the discrimination gay communities face does not naturally lead to a greater vision of racial understanding and harmony. In fact, what appears prevalent in the gay male culture is a level of "gay racism" (Luna, 1989, p. 440) that parallels that which exists in the larger society. For instance, Ng (2004) describes how the sexual identities of Asian males are strongly informed by European American males. He argues that, within gay youth culture, the only role that gay Asian American men are expected to play is that of the submissive, exotic, and passive stereotype. In summary, race and ethnicity continue to exist as a key issue in many areas of gay culture. Alternatively, sexual orientation remains a salient issue among different racial and ethnic groups (E. P. Johnson & Henderson, 2005). Box 5.3 further illustrates this issue.

❖ BOX 5.3

LGBTQ AND JEWISH

Recently, Faulkner (2006) examined how individuals negotiate different aspects of their identities in various ways. Her research on LGBTQ (lesbian, gay, bisexual, transgendered, and queer-identifying) Jewish persons highlights the complex ways that the identity emergence process occurs. Below is a quote from her research:

Some . . . considered Jewish and gay as separate and non-competing categories where one identity was more salient to who they were. Some considered being Jewish as a secular, cultural designation that didn't influence being LGBTQ, often they did not think of being Jewish on a daily basis. Some saw a conflict between a religious Judaism and being LGBTQ as they worked to integrate them, whereas others absolutely integrated Jewish/LGBTQ as in a gay Havurot and couldn't separate the identities (p. 113).

- Can you see how, at times, difficulties can arise when people try to integrate different aspects of their identities?
- What examples can you think of where this would be an ongoing issue?

Spirituality

Spirituality generally refers to an individual's identification with and belief in a higher power. We prefer using the term spirituality rather than religion as a way to be more inclusive in our treatment of this aspect of cultural identity (Collier, 2000). Although religious and spiritual communities have not been studied extensively as cultural entities per se, group membership does represent an important aspect of cultural identity for many U.S. Americans. This is especially true for certain racial and ethnic groups, like African Americans, who traditionally relied on religious organizations to meet both spiritual and tangible needs such as health care, education, and financial assistance (Youngblood & Winn, 2004). As evidenced by recent polls, a resurgence in spirituality has caused an increased awareness of the central role of religion in the cultural values of many individuals. Examining various levels of spirituality in the context of interracial communication appears especially relevant, given that many people's perceptions of different racial/ethnic groups (as well as other cultural groups, such as women and gays and lesbians) are informed by such belief systems (see Chapter 10).

U.S. history demonstrates the central role of spiritual beliefs in the ways that different racial and ethnic groups have interacted. The call for a Manifest Destiny (see Chapter 2) was regarded as a "spiritual endeavor" and set the tone for how European Americans interacted with the people of color they found in North America (S. Brewer, 2006). Select biblical scriptures were often presented as evidence for the necessity and value of slavery and other oppressive measures against African Americans and other microcultures. The Ku Klux Klan, a self-defined religious organization, uses traditional Christian symbols like the cross as a means to illustrate their "spiritually inspired" actions (Ezekiel, 1997). Fighting back the advances and influences of groups that promised to kill the legacy of what it means to be a "real American" (by African Americans, Jews, Catholics, and so on), the KKK's ideology of White supremacy is grounded in "good old-fashioned Christian values." A similar sense of spirituality was intertwined with the messages of the nation of Islam, guided by the Honorable Elijah Muhammad, Malcolm X, and minister Louis Farrakhan. For many Black Muslims, defining all European Americans as "White devils"—along with other teachings from the nation of Islam—were regarded as spiritual Truths (McPhail, 1998b). These religious beliefs, and the various ways in which they maintain tremendous barriers to effective interracial communication, are still apparent today.

Interestingly enough, many individuals indicate it is their spirituality that promotes interracial understanding that transcends racial and ethnic differences (see, for example, Clark & Diggs, 2002). Historical accounts provide various examples of how interracial coalitions based within an overarching spiritual purpose generated positive relations across racial and ethnic lines. The Quakers and other religious groups within the abolitionist movement and the various religious communities involved in the civil rights movement are two such examples. For many individuals, the importance of their spirituality provides them with the common faith to interact, not as different racial or ethnic group members but as extensions of the same creator. Despite such beliefs, spiritual gatherings remain one of the most segregated aspects of society. Without question, spirituality seems to hold great potential for transcending racial/ethnic differences. Yet the "baggage" that comes with particular cultural systems oftentimes includes problematic perceptions, expectations, and behaviors that ultimately interrupt ideal relationships operating on purely spiritual levels (M. C. Gonzalez, 2002).

As such, spirituality can become a site of racial struggle. Such is the case with a significant number of Native Americans who attempt to mesh their cultural beliefs with those of established religions such as Catholicism (O'Hanlon, 2000). The reverse is also true, given how native spirituality has become increasingly of interest to Native and non-Native people alike. For many, tribal religions provide a sense of cultural authenticity for Native people and a religious novelty for others seeking personal spiritual quests (Deloria, 2003). This includes people

> who gradually rejected their everyday ways of life in favor of an "Indian" lifestyle, transforming their living environments, adjusting their schedules, and altering their personal relationships in order to live in accordance with how they perceived the native American spiritual traditions they were learning and practicing. (M. C. Gonzalez, 2002, p. 387)

Such interracial spiritual alliances appear like valuable opportunities to study interactions of race, spirituality, and other aspects of one's cultural identity (see Chapter 10).

❖ **BOX 5.4**

AUTHOR REFLECTIONS

I have quite a few memories about the role that socioeconomic status played in my self-concept and how I interacted with others. Growing up in a low-income housing project with subsidized rent meant that my family didn't have a lot, but neither did anyone else, so our lives seemed pretty "normal." This continued during elementary school when most of my classmates dressed like me, talked like me, and liked to do the same things as me (watching lots of TV, listening to music, and playing basketball, Kick-the-Can, Red Rover, and Cartoon Freeze Tag). Getting "free" or "reduced" lunch everyday at school was the norm, not the exception.

One of my realizations of class differences occurred in the seventh grade when I attended a citywide junior high school. During one of my first days of school, I vividly remember one of the teachers taking attendance and asking each student what elementary school he or she had attended. I couldn't help but notice that she seemed to treat students differently based on that information. Such treatment seemed to strengthen the boundaries between "us" (the poor kids) and "them" (the rich kids). Although some friendships were able to cross class divisions, these were relatively few and seemed to only play out in certain circumstances (e.g., during college-prep courses where a few of *us* were able to interact with more of *them* on a more equal level). Differences in dress, speech, and interests clearly facilitated a social/class division in our school. Bringing your lunch—and looking down on those of us who ate school lunches—was the preferred norm. The few of *them who paid* for their lunch received tickets that were a different color from those tickets that were *given to us* free or at a reduced rate. Distinguishing markers based on class were everywhere.

Socioeconomic status is a way of life, and does not necessarily change with your personal or family income. Thus, while my salary today is significantly higher than that of my parents, my life perspective in terms of class remains largely the same (regardless of whether I "pass" as a middle-class person or not) (see, for example, Moon & Rolison, 1998). For example, I rarely buy anything not on clearance—even sale prices are too expensive for me! I continually struggle with my three children (two teenagers!) who seem to have very expensive taste and always want to buy things on the spot without checking prices or waiting to buy it off-season. I keep telling them that my shopping is smart, but they are convinced it's because I'm cheap. My middle daughter has, in fact, started calling me "chmart" (a combination of the two!). Because of my early experiences growing up—something I wouldn't trade for the world!—socioeconomic status remains an important issue in most of my interactions with others. What are some of your salient cultural issues? How are they tied to specific life memories?

—MPO

Socioeconomic Status

In the social sciences, the examination of **socioeconomic status** (SES), or class, can be traced back to Karl Marx and Max Weber (Crompton, 1993). The field of communication has been slow to examine how SES impacts communication, although some significant work does exist (Houston & Wood, 1996; Moon & Rolison, 1998; Philipsen, 1975, 1976). One reason for this dearth of substantial research might be the lack of awareness and general silence about the role of SES in a country that values equal opportunity to achieve the "American dream" (Langston, 1995). Ehrenreich (1990) explains,

> Americans are notorious for their lack of class consciousness or even class awareness. We have a much greater consciousness of race and gender issues than we do of class. Race and gender are immediate—and they are irreversible. Class is different: The American myth is that we can escape (transcend) our class. We can work our way up and out of it.

An important consideration when examining class differences is recognizing that SES is not equated with economic standing. Income (how much you make) is different from wealth (what assets you have access to); particular perspectives on life are associated with wealth, something that is more stable over time (Lui, Robles, Leondar-Wright, Brewer, & Adamson, 2006). Are you familiar with the terms "old money" and "new money"? Typically, the latter term refers to individuals whose economic standing has drastically improved, yet their values, interests, attitudes, and behaviors have remained fairly constant. The term has been used by the upper class to distinguish themselves from others who have more recently achieved economic success, emphasizing that how much money you have does not automatically translate into a particular "class of people." Beyond current levels of income, class also entails assumptions concerning levels of economic security, the importance of family and kinship ties, interests and leisure time activities, and specific communication styles (Houston & Wood, 1996). According to some scholars, class is all-encompassing and influences every aspect of our lives. "Class is your understanding of the world and where you fit in; it's composed of ideas, behaviors, attitudes, values, and languages; class is how you think, feel, act, look, dress, talk, move, walk" (Langston, 1995, p. 101). In short, "We experience class at every level of our lives" (p. 102).

Classism is most commonly understood as a top-down practice whereby middle- and upper-class persons perpetuate discriminatory behaviors toward those of lower-class standing. One aspect of classism is the maintenance of separation, including conscious efforts of "affluent" groups to do whatever they can to avoid contact with the "less fortunate" (Ehrenreich, 1990). One result of the lack of any substantial interaction between different classes is stereotyping maintenance by all socioeconomic groups. More "enlightened" people from the middle- and upper-class segments of society stereotype the working class/underclass as ignorant, lazy, and hopelessly bigoted. It is important to recognize, though, that class prejudice (in the form of personal attitudes) functions at various levels of SES (Moon & Rolison, 1998). Wasteful, snobby, lazy, carefree, and prejudiced are some of the perceptions that members of a lower socioeconomic status have in regard to more affluent persons. Although the institutional power of individuals to enact these stereotypes into policy varies, the influence that they have on interpersonal contact remains strong for all SES groups.

Socioeconomic status remains a largely invisible issue within the United States (Liu et al., 2006). This is, in part, due to the reality that class standing is largely correlated with racial/ethnic identity and other cultural variables such as gender and family structure (Langston, 1995; Praeger, 1995). Therefore, many references to racial and ethnic groups are typically reflective of class distinctions more so than those solely based on racial/ethnic differences. At times, similar SES may provide common perspectives for certain members of diverse racial/ethnic groups, Lui et al. (2006) provide an in-depth, but highly accessible, analysis of the roots of the racial wealth divide in the United States that provides insightful descriptions of how each racial group (Native Americans, African Americans, Latino/as, Asian Americans, and European Americans) has, or has not, accumulated wealth. According to this comprehensive text, "for every dollar owned by the average white family in the United States, the average family of color has less than one dime" (p. 1).

Clearly, race intersects with socioeconomic status in meaningful ways. Looking at race and SES alone, however, does not give us a complete enough picture to predict the quality of interracial communication. Thus, any productive analysis of the potential for interracial communication effectiveness must not only account for race/ethnicity and SES, but also all of the other aspects of cultural identity described in this chapter. For example, consider recent communication research that studied the experiences of those individuals who were the first in their families to attend college (Orbe, 2003; Putman & Thompson, 2006). While having college-educated parents has an established correlation with socioeconomic status, their findings reveal that race, gender, age, and regionality were important aspects of their ability to succeed at college and maintain close ties at home. Studies on other issues, such as life expectancy, also demonstrate the importance of considering intersections of race, ethnicity, gender, and socioeconomic status (Neergaard, 2006).

❖ **BOX 5.5**

INTERSECTIONALITIES IN EVERYDAY LIFE

A recent research project studied the perceptions of restaurant servers in terms of how they perceived customers (Mallinson & Brewster, 2005). More specifically, the project revealed how servers were identified in "racetalk" and "regiontalk" in creating categories for customers who typically don't tip. Researchers conducted in-depth semi-structured interviews with servers working at two different well-known restaurant chains located in a small, rural southeastern city in the United States. Consistent across their data, servers identified two different categories of people who do not tip: "Blacks" and "Bubbas." The stereotype that African Americans do not tip is common; in fact, it was one of the initial points of discussion highlighted in the 2005 Academy Award–winning movie *Crash*. While this stereotype clearly does not hold true for all African Americans, the servers involved in the 2005 study did not note any intergroup differences in their "racetalk" about Black customers.

Servers also stereotyped lower class European Americans from "the country" as people who did not tip. The "racetalk" around this group, however, was negotiated around "regiontalk." All European Americans were not categorized as poor tippers in general, only those whom the servers described as "Bubbas," "White trash," "rednecks," and "hillbillies." In this regard, servers used the intersectionality of race, regionality, and class to define the group—something not done with African Americans. How did servers report being able to define "Bubbas"? They looked to the language that the customers used (e.g., "country accent"), particular styles of dress (e.g., "overalls," "John Deere hats," and "Dale Earnhardt shirts"), and the type of food that they ordered (e.g., hush puppies).

- Can you think of other everyday situations where stereotypes—either those solely based on race/ethnicity or intersections of race, class, gender, and other aspects of one's culture—are commonly held?
- What are the disadvantages of holding on to stereotypes?
- What specific things can one do to avoid the dangers of cultural stereotyping?

Intersections of Race/Ethnicity, Gender, and Socioeconomic Status

Take a minute to reflect on the descriptions of cultural influence provided in the previous section. It should become clear that interracial communication must be understood in the context of other cultural variables besides simply race/ethnicity. In order to achieve some level of organizational clarity, we chose to discuss each of the aspects of culture (abilities, age, gender, nationality, sexual orientation, spirituality, socioeconomic status) separately. But recognize that in reality these and other cultural markers are interlocking and inseparable. No one person is simply a member of one particular group. Instead, she or he simultaneously encompasses multiple cultural identities. The best vantage point to come to understand human communication is through an acknowledgment that each person experiences life as a complex individual whose cultural group identities function in concert with one another (Houston & Wood,

1996). **Intersectionality** refers to efforts that examine the combined impact of different cultural identities. Embracing this concept helps us generate deeper, more complex understanding of people's lives; it also assists in avoiding more superficial explanations of behavior based on one aspect of culture.

Gordon (1978) contends that, for many people of color, racial/ethnic identity develops during early socialization and continues to represent a core aspect of their identity throughout their lives. In the United States, this belief has often led to a narrow focus on racial identity that results in an oversimplification of how a person's cultural identity affects communication processes (Collier & Thomas, 1988). A more effective approach is to acknowledge, like Collier (2000, 2002) and her colleagues (Hecht et al., 1993) do, that cultural identities are ongoing and situational. Racial/ethnic identity may represent an enduring aspect of an individual's self-identity. Research indicates that this is more likely in situations where group identity is threatened, racial/ethnic comparisons are made, or a person is perceived as a prototype of his or her group (Orbe & Everett, 2006). More than likely, race/ethnicity is not the only enduring aspect of identity in all situations. In fact, people are constantly negotiating their identities (A. Rodriguez, 2002), and in some situations normally important cultural issues (like race/ethnicity) become less central to interaction. For instance, think about a recent *intra*racial small group discussion you have had (where all participants identified with the same racial/ethnic group). Within this context, do other cultural differences—based on sex, age, sexual orientation, and/or SES—typically become more visible at some point in the interaction? Research on race, sexuality, and communication (D. K. Drummond, 1997) supports the basic idea that other aspects of cultural identity emerge as more significant (at least temporarily) during intraracial conversations.

Most communication involves multiple cultural identities, with the exceptions reflecting one single identity to overwhelm all others (Hecht et al., 2003). Think about the previous statement for a moment. Can you generate any examples of communication that are *solely* the result of one aspect of your cultural identity? More than likely, any example you can come up with reflects an intersection of various cultural elements. For example, you may have heard the statement, "It's a Black thang. . . ," a phrase illustrating how certain behaviors are directly related to a particular racial experience. (The second part of the phrase, "you wouldn't understand," highlights the difficulty of outgroup members' understanding ingroup cultural norms, values, and/or ideas.) However, how many times is something described as a "Black thang," when in essence it refers to something more than simply race? In many cases, "it's a Black thang" might be better described as "a Black *urban* thing," "a Black *Generation X* thing," or "a Black *working-class* thing." These phrases help acknowledge that some African Americans may not share certain cultural experiences (because of region, age, or SES) and some non–African Americans may, because of similar cultural identities other than race/ethnicity.

One way to help us understand the interconnections of multiple cultural identities is by recognizing that persons typically form a "hierarchical organization of identity" (Hecht et al., 2003, p. 36). In other words, without assigning status to any one aspect of identity for all people, this idea assumes that certain sets of lived experiences result in moving specific identity elements to the core of a particular person's self-concept. Some

❖ **BOX 5.6**

STUDENT REFLECTIONS

The actual makeup of my race, like most African Americans, is pretty diverse. I like to call it gumbo! My great-grandmother on my mother's side was Irish and Cherokee Indian. Her husband was Black (and who knows what else). My great-grandfather on my father's side was African American, Mexican, and Blackfoot Indian; however, even this is unreliable information because of family secrets about marriage, paternity of children, and because the name "Blackfoot" was used to describe a number of tribes besides that of actual Blackfeet Indians. I know little about my exact family history due to death and family members who refuse to talk about those who have passed away. I identify most with being Black, but to add even more confusion, my racial experience specifically relies on being a light-skinned Black because I have experienced both detrimental and beneficial racism within and outside of my own race.

theorists see such multiple identity hierarchies as largely fluid, changing from one situation to another; others believe such organizations of key cultural identity markers are more enduring (Hecht et al., 2003). One way to incorporate the idea of hierarchical organizations of identity as both fluid and enduring—a basic property of cultural identity theory—is to envision a pyramid of sorts. Those more enduring aspects of an individual's self-identity exist at the top of the identity pyramid. Other more fluid cultural markers, whose salience and intensity vary depending on the particular situational context (Harris, 2004), are positioned at the bottom. This framework is productive in that it (1) embraces the interconnectedness of multiple cultural identities, (2) recognizes both the enduring and fluid nature of cultural markers, and (3) avoids the trap of building a rigid, definitive hierarchy of cultural identity for all U.S. Americans. This latter point is especially important given that some scholars (e.g., B. Smith, 1983) have criticized attempts to present a universal ordering of cultural experiences (e.g., "dealing with racism is worse than dealing with sexism, which is worse than. . . .").

❖ **BOX 5.7**

AUTHOR REFLECTIONS

I was talking with a staff member about a problem she was having. I gave her some advice on what she could do. After venting for a moment, she finally made a decision and said, "Well, I guess I'll just sit here like a tar baby and keep my mouth shut." My mind automatically went blank. Immediately, I thought *"Surely,* I didn't just hear her say *tar baby."* In all my life, I have *never* heard anyone use this incredibly derogatory and racist word! That was until that day. As she continued to talk about the problem, I felt as if a knife were slowly being pulled from my stomach. Although she was not calling me a tar baby and there was no racial overtone in what was said, I couldn't help but feel the sting left by her words. I blindingly walked out of the office with nothing to say. What *could* I say? Tar baby was a term adapted from African folktale to refer

(Continued)

(Continued)

to a sticky mess or situation. In the Disney film *Song of the South* (1946) Tar Baby is "a doll made of tar that traps Brer Rabbit when he beats it for not speaking to him" (Maloney, 2006). The term eventually evolved to refer to Black people and was glaringly negative in nature and tone.

How could someone say something so racist and offensive in the workplace? Did this mean she might one day slip and call someone this incredibly racist term? Because this happened in the workplace, I knew there would be consequences if I confronted her. I felt in my heart her intention was not to offend; rather, this was a reflection of the era in which she grew up. She could become defensive or angry, or she might even cry. Worst case scenario, our department chair could get wind of it and file a complaint, maybe causing her to lose her job, and I didn't want that. I knew if I said something, our working relationship would be changed, to my detriment, and could make for a very tense environment. In the end, I decided this was not a battle I was emotionally, mentally, or spiritually ready to tackle. I've been fighting for so long that I opted to let this one go. Regardless of your racial standpoint or identity, maybe you can help me by joining the fight. It will make for a better world in the end . . . at least I hope and pray so.

—TMH

Conclusion

Cultural identity, of which racial/ethnic identity is a part, is abstract, complex, multi-dimensional, and fluid. Developing a consciousness of the role that racial/ethnic differences play in the communication process is important. It should not be overemphasized, though, to the point of stereotyping each person based on his or her race/ethnicity. In other words, treating people as if they are solely defined by one facet of their cultural identity is problematic and arguably the best formula for *ineffective* interracial communication. Consider the following quote from Audre Lorde (1984):

> As a Black lesbian feminist comfortable with the many different ingredients of my identity, and a woman committed to racial and sexual freedom from oppression, I find I am constantly being encouraged to pluck out one aspect of myself and present this as the meaningful whole, eclipsing or denying the other parts of self. But this is a destructive and fragmenting way to live. My fullest concentration of energy is available to me only when I integrate all the parts of who I am, opening, allowing power from particular sources of my living to flow back and forth freely through all of my different selves, without the restrictions of externally imposed definitions. Only then can I bring myself and my energies as a whole to the service of those struggles which I embrace as part of my living. (p. 120)

As Lorde points out, interacting with others based on a single aspect of their identity denies them the opportunity to participate as complete cultural beings. Race remains a salient issue in the United States. But we should recognize the role that race/ethnicity plays in the communication process alongside other elements of a person's multiple cultural identity. Ultimately, the ability to recognize the multiple identities of self and others—and identify key elements of cultural difference of any given interaction—appears to be a fundamental component of interracial communication competence (Collier, 2002). In addition, paying attention to the multiple cultural identities of others and the various ways they influence communicative behaviors generates opportunities for enhanced self-identity development.

OPPORTUNITIES FOR EXTENDED LEARNING ❖

1. Create a case study that details a particular scenario in which multiple cultural identities directly influence intraracial or interracial communication (for an example, see Box 5.5). Ideally, these should be based on real-life experiences. Share your case study with the rest of the class/group and discuss the importance of recognizing multiple cultural identities in communication effectiveness.

2. Recent predictions of future demographic trends has resulted in an increased focus on growing influences of Latino/a culture. Use a popular Internet search engine to identify sources that describe various aspects of the cultural similarities and differences of La Raza. A keyword, like Latino, will return hundreds of cites. Therefore, you may want to use *La Raza* or *Latino culture*. Pay particular attention to the different labels used within these resources. How do they reflect the complexity of multiple cultural identities?

3. Create an identity pyramid that reflects the various components of your self-identity in the context of reading this book (as a student, scholar, practitioner, etc.). Then break off into dyads and share why certain elements are more salient than others. What other cultural elements did you include that were not specifically described in this chapter (i.e., profession, organizations, etc.)?

4. Use role-play scenarios to examine the impact of identity, culture, and communication. Within small groups, select one person to be the observer. Two persons will role-play a first encounter between two individuals who share one aspect of their cultural identity (this can be real or imagined, but both people need to agree on it). Within a period of 3 to 5 minutes, engage in a typical conversation. However, be sure to include self-disclosures that point to other aspects of your cultural identity (religion, sexual orientation, class, etc.). At the end of the conversation, ask the observer to share his or her perceptions of how the conversation changed, if it all, as other cultural markers were introduced.

5. A study done in the late 1980s reported that the most important issues of identity for college students were gender, religion, and ethnicity. School major and student status were of secondary importance, followed by hobbies and athletics (Garza & Herringer, 1987). After breaking into small groups, discuss your reactions to this study. As a whole, do you think these results hold true for college students today? Why or why not? Can you obtain a group consensus of the most salient cultural issues for students today? How might these vary from context to context? Lastly, discuss how this exercise helped clarify the idea of a hierarchical organizational identity.

6. Cyberspace communication that relies on textual messages has often been perceived as relatively free from racial and ethnic tensions because people can interact without recognizing the race of one another unless one chooses to do so (Bahk & Jandt, 2004). So, some people talk about it as a form of "color-blind" communication. Yet scholars (e.g., Kang, 2003) note that racial cues such as language, grammar, diction, and names continue to exist within online interactions. Consequently, people make assumptions and unconsciously activate racialized perceptions. What are your thoughts on this issue? What cues about a person's cultural identity, if any, exist when you communicate online? Do you think that cyberspace communication is a place where people can interact as individuals—with little, if no, attention to cultural differences?

Theoretical Approaches to Studying Interracial Communication

Theory. For most college students, this word triggers visions of abstract, dull, unnecessarily complex ideas that "academic types" use to intellectualize the world around them. Many believe that theories hold little practical value in terms of their everyday life experiences. Although these perceptions are not universally shared by all students, they do seem to hold true for significant numbers. We have collectively taught communication theories to thousands of undergraduate and graduate students at six different universities across the country, and we can also vividly remember our own perceptions as undergraduate students, being forced to study various theories that appeared to be the work of people who simply had too much time on their hands! As communication scholars (and emerging theorists), we now see theoretical frameworks differently. Theories are the mechanisms that allow us to understand communication phenomena in more complex ways. Without theories to guide our efforts, studying different aspects of interracial communication would be haphazard, disjointed, and random. Good communication theories expand our knowledge beyond superficial understanding. They also have practical value in enhancing communication effectiveness.

One of our challenges here is to help you make the connection between theory and practice. Begin to understand theoretical frameworks as lenses that assist us in seeing the world clearly. Using this metaphor can be a useful way to embrace the importance of theory, especially those of us who share common experiences at the eye doctor's office. Do you remember eye examinations where the doctor changed the lens and then asked you if the letters on the wall were clearer or not? Some lenses that were tried increased our vision slightly, whereas others made our vision more blurry. The key to this process is to continue trying on different combinations of lenses until 20/20 vision is achieved and the letters on the wall can be read with great clarity and confidence. Imagine the tremendous difference that corrective lenses make for those who have been experiencing life (sometimes unknowingly) without clear vision. Without a doubt, you see things in a different light!

According to Deetz (1992), "a theory is a way of seeing and thinking about the world. As such, it is better seen as the 'lens' one uses in observation rather than as the 'mirror' of nature" (p. 66). Theories are very much like lenses. They help us see communication phenomena in new, more vivid ways. This chapter introduces nine different theoretical frameworks that hold great promise for increasing our understanding of interracial communication. A general description of each theory or model is presented. Consistent with the lens metaphor used earlier, we acknowledge that some theories may be a better personal fit for you than others. The key is to identify and concentrate on those theories and models that facilitate the greatest understanding in terms of your life experiences. Ultimately, we hope that you are able to use multiple theories/lenses to view interracial communication. A great number of communication theories can be used to gain insight into the process of interracial communication. We have chosen nine specific frameworks that appear most relevant to how different racial/ethnic groups communicate in the United States. Before presenting these theories, however, let's look at the early work on interracial communication.

Interracial Communication Models

The earliest interracial communication models can be traced to the mid-1970s and linked to the increased attention to race relations in the United States at that time. During the 1960s and 1970s, people of color—most notably African Americans and Chicanos—gained national attention as they confronted historical, political, and social practices that were discriminatory and oppressive. Although most civil rights struggles continue today (Orbe, 2005), these historical acts of civil disobedience were instrumental in forcing a society to deal with a social ill traditionally ignored by most European Americans. As should have been the case, several communication scholars acknowledged the key role they could play in building productive relations among different racial/ethnic groups. For many scholars interracial communication represented an area of both great academic and practical relevance beyond most traditional work that focused on culture from an international perspective.

The earliest interracial communication model stemmed from the work of Molefi Kete Asante (previously known as Arthur L. Smith). His transracial communication model focused on describing the process by which individuals could "cross racial lines" to communicate effectively (A. Smith, 1973). However, Asante avoided traditional approaches of racial differences (based on genetics) that were prevalent in most research. Instead, he focused on interactions that were impacted by perceived racial identity distinctions on the part of one or more individuals. Interracial communication, then, included interactions when perceived racial differences were a critical feature. One of the important contributions of this model was increased attention to how each person's communication was reflective of a particular "ethnic perspective." For instance, the model was instrumental in illustrating the influence of individual worldviews—for both communicators—on how messages are created, articulated, and ultimately perceived. According to this model (A. Smith, 1973), the goal of transracial communication is the **normalization** of communication. Normalization was used to describe the process of identifying and moving toward a central threshold where both parties can find common ground to base their communication. To this end, ethnic differences could be transcended.

Andrea L. Rich (1974) and colleagues (Rich & Ogawa, 1972) created an interracial communication model that approached interracial communication differently than Asante's model. They believed that people of color could live within their respective communities relatively uninfluenced by the dominant structures of European Americans. This model focused on the process by which different non-White racial groups leave their own cultures and enter European American–dominated social structures. Specific attention was paid to the various ways that other cultural factors (socioeconomic status, skin color, degree of cultural differences) influenced the communication between European Americans and people of color. The interracial communication model was based on a number of assumptions. First, racial/ethnic minorities could never *totally* move within the realm of dominant European American society. Second, the model was based on the premise that European Americans controlled the amount of accessibility that people of color had in dominant societal structures. Third, the model assumed that European Americans could never become full-fledged members of other racial/ethnic cultures. From Rich's perspective (1974), this model dealt with the realities of race relations in the 1970s. Some might suggest that much has changed since that time.

The work of Jon A. Blubaugh and Dorthy L. Pennington (1976) differs from the interracial communication model in two distinct ways. First, their analysis of interracial communication is not limited to White–non-White communication. It can be used to understand European American–African American interactions, as well as those involving different racial/ethnic minorities (e.g., Asian American–Latino Americans, Native American–African Americans, etc.). Second, the cross difference model of communication recognizes that all racial/ethnic groups (including European Americans) share some aspects of a "common culture" affiliated with living in the United States. Furthermore, the model acknowledges the mutual influences of different racial/ethnic cultures on one another. The cross difference model focused on the importance of transcending racial differences while simultaneously understanding how such differences remain a part of one's culture. Blubaugh and Pennington (1976) believed that while cultural influences will still be apparent during interracial interactions, they must be diminished in order for communication to be effective. And although some racialized stereotyping and attitudes may arise from time to time, they no longer serve as a primary source of difference for the individuals. Blubaugh and Pennington specifically discuss six features of interracial communication that need to be addressed: racism, power relations, racial assumptions, language, nonverbal cues, and core beliefs and values. In short, the cross difference communication model advocates transcending (not erasing) racial differences so that persons can communicate on a "same-race (human race) basis" (Blubaugh & Pennington, 1976, p. 17).

Theorizing Interracial Communication

The past 30 to 35 years have yielded significant changes in terms of the political, social, legal, and economic structures that inform race relations in the United States. But a distinct voice among racial/ethnic microcultures asserts that "the more things have changed, the more they have stayed the same." A quick review of some of the statistical information on race seems to support this perspective. When compared to European Americans, African Americans, Latino/a Americans, and Native Americans are significantly overrepresented in disadvantaged categories across the board (economic status, education, housing, health, etc.) (Rudman, Ashmore, & Melvin, 2001). Consistent with the idea represented throughout this book, we do not assume an either/or positioning on this issue. Some advancement clearly has been made (e.g., increased levels of education and a growing middle class for different racial/ethnic groups). Nevertheless, a more critical review reveals that divisions between the haves and have-nots are still largely based on race.

For this reason, we believe early interracial communication models contain elements and approaches that are still pertinent to the 21st century. Still, they do not reflect some of the changing realities of the past three decades. The field of communication generally, and the area of intercultural/interracial communication specifically, offers a broad range of theoretical frameworks that provide insight into interactions and relationships among people of diverse racial and ethnic backgrounds. Most theories reflect a body of research that has primarily been applied to intercultural communication in international contexts. Others are situated specifically in terms of interracial communication, or other forms of co-cultural communication, in the United States.

The remainder of this chapter is divided into two sections. The first section covers theories (speech community theory, critical race theory, Afrocentricity, complicity theory, and co-cultural theory) that help us understand the communication of different racial/ethnic groups. As you read through this section, note how each theory provides insight into how racialized perspectives and locations (see Chapter 1) influence communication. Michael Hecht and his colleagues have produced a substantial amount of research on what we call "theorizing satisfying communication." This body of work serves as an effective transition between the first section and the second section, which highlights four theories (anxiety/uncertainty management theory, third-culture building, cross-cultural adaptation theory, and communication accommodation theory) that focus on the interracial communication process itself.

Understanding Different Forms of Racialized Communication

Speech Community Theory

Speech community theory, also known as the ethnography of communication and speech codes theory, is useful in explaining the misunderstandings that surface in communication between people of different social groups (Carbaugh, 1995; Hymes, 1974; Philipsen, 1996). According to Labov (1972), a **speech community** exists when a group of people understand goals and styles of communication in ways not shared by people outside of the group. In terms of interracial communication, speech community theory is useful for interactions with people with different language systems (e.g., a Spanish-speaking Cuban American and a Chinese-speaking Chinese American). It is also useful for those who use the same language (e.g., English) but whose racial groups have a different set of speech codes (e.g., a Native American and European American). A **speech code**, according to Philipsen (1996), refers to "a system of socially constructed symbols and meanings, premises, and rules, pertaining to communicative conduct" (p. 126). In other words, speech community theory focuses on how different cultural groups (including those defined by racial/ethnic differences) instill within their members distinct styles of communicating and interpreting the communication of others. Some instances of problematic interracial communication can be traced to a misunderstanding of the other person's speech code. Carbaugh (1999, 2002), for instance, presents an interesting analysis of how European Americans oftentimes misunderstand Native American speech codes, like those of the Blackfeet.

❖ BOX 6.1

CASE STUDY

In late 1996, the Oakland (CA) school board passed a resolution recognizing the important role that Ebonics (Black English) plays in the language development and academic achievement of young African Americans (Close, 1997). Their decision triggered a national debate on the value of Ebonics and its place in institutions of learning. Proponents pointed to evidence indicating that when teachers understood and respected Ebonics, they were able to use it effectively to teach standard English. Opponents to the resolution—across racial and ethnic lines—criticized it as discriminatory, misinformed, and counterproductive to long-term African American student success.

In terms of our discussion on interracial communication theoretical frameworks, the use of Ebonics serves as an excellent case study.

- From a communication perspective, what is Ebonics?
- What role does it play during interracial interactions?
- How does it impact ingroup and outgroup communication?
- How is its influence impacted by other variables?

As you read through the descriptions of various theories and models contained in this chapter, think about these questions:

- How does each framework provide a different way of looking at this communication phenomenon?
- How does Afrocentricity, for instance, regard Ebonics as compared to models of third-culture building?
- Try to take the perspective of each theory. How can Ebonics be understood through each framework? The variety of images might surprise you!

Speech community theory is grounded in four assumptions (Philipsen, 1996). First, members of cultural communities create shared meaning among themselves. These communities are oftentimes defined by differences in language and geography, as well as other less visible boundaries. Whenever there is a distinctive culture, there is typically a distinctive speech code. Second, communicators in any cultural group must coordinate their actions. Even though it may not be apparent to nonmembers, each speech code is guided by some order or system. Milburn (2002), for instance, found that within a Puerto Rican community center, individuals created speech codes that bridged "American norms and Puerto Rican practices" (p. 303). Third, meanings and actions are particular to individual groups. During interracial interactions, attempts to understand another person's communication by using your own cultural norms may be ineffective. Fourth, each cultural community has a set of distinct resources for assigning meaning to its actions. Not only are patterns of communication different among some racial/ethnic groups, but each group may also have its own set of meanings with which to understand its own codes. In other words, every attempt possible should be made to understand speech codes within their cultural context.

Within the field of communication, this theoretical framework has proven instrumental in understanding how people from different cultural groups follow different sets of communication rules. Much of the work was based in ethnographic research that discovered how groups create shared meaning through unique cultural norms (e.g., Carbaugh, 1995; Philipsen, 1975). Despite some existing criticisms (for a summary, see Philipsen, Coutu, & Covarrubias, 2005), speech community theory continues to provide significant insight. More recent work has extended ethnography, traditionally a humanistic methodology, to a more scientific perspective. This includes using knowledge of speech codes to predict and control the communication of others in order to facilitate more effective communication (Philipsen, 1997). Remember, however, that understanding that speech is structured via different cultural groups is not to say it is absolutely determined (Philipsen, 1992). In other words, attempts to predict another person's communication based on knowledge of her or his speech community must recognize that a speech code represents a pattern, not an absolute. Speech community theory, then, offers a valuable perspective to understanding the communication styles of different racial/ethnic groups when we acknowledge that variations of understanding, accepting, and using speech codes exist within and across groups.

Critical Race Theory

Compared to all of the theories presented in this chapter, critical race theory represents a framework that was developed outside the field of communication (Calvert, 1997). Its origins can be traced back to the late 1970s and early 1980s (K. Crenshaw, Gotanda, Peller, & Thomas, 1995). Specifically, critical race theory was developed by civil rights activists who were seeing many of the gains achieved during the 1960s disappearing (Matsuda, Lawrence, Delgado, & Crenshaw, 1993). The earliest work in this area was done by scholars in critical legal studies. Their efforts generally challenged dominant values of equal opportunity and justice for all by highlighting the realities of race. Recently, communication scholars have drawn on this emerging theoretical approach to inform their research on race, ethnicity, and communication. This has included research on racial science (K. H. Wilson, 1999), hate speech (Cornwell, Orbe, & Warren, 1999; Downing, 1999), and recent anti-immigration measures (Hasian & Delgado, 1998).

The essence of critical race theory can be best captured by identifying several core elements (Matsuda et al., 1993). First, it recognizes that racism is an integral part of the United States. Instead of debating whether racism can ever be totally eliminated, critical race theorists work to challenge existing structures that reinforce racial oppression. Second, critical race theory rejects dominant legal and social claims of neutrality, objectivity, and color blindness. It embraces the subjectivity that comes with a particular field of experience. As part of the rejection of neutrality, critical race theorists describe their work as explicitly political. The third core element rejects a historical approach to studying race. Instead, this theoretical approach insists on looking at interracial communication from within a contextual/historical context. From this perspective, the current state of race relations in the United States is directly linked to earlier events. Attempting to understand interracial communication in the 21st century, then, is only possible through an awareness of the history of interracial contact in the United States (see Chapter 2).

Fourth, critical race theory recognizes the importance of experiential knowledge that comes from various microcultural standpoints. In other words, it (like Afrocentricity, discussed later) values insight grounded in the experiences of those racial and ethnic groups that have historically been marginalized. The fifth core element relates to the interdisciplinary and eclectic nature of critical race theory. The ideas of this theory are borrowed from several traditions, including Marxism, feminism, critical/cultural studies, and postmodernism. Finally, critical race theory actively works toward the elimination of racial oppression. But although the focus is on racial oppression, the ways that racism is closely tied to other forms of oppression based on gender, class, and sexual orientation is acknowledged. And although critical race theorists have focused on legal remedies, they also understand that racism cannot be solved by creating additional laws (Hasian & Delgado, 1998).

As described by Matsuda et al. (1993), the work of critical race theorists is both pragmatic and idealized. Specifically, their scholarship attempts to address the immediate needs of those who are oppressed. In doing so, they strive to work toward the ideals of equal opportunity and justice that the United States was founded on. New forms of critical race scholarship have emerged, including the use of personal histories, stories, dreams, poems, and fiction (Matsuda et al., 1993). These nontraditional approaches to scholarship have been used effectively to examine the relationships among labels, knowledge, power, and reality (see Chapter 3). In addition, critical race theory has been used to gain insight into the ways that "neutral" discussions of race often implicitly reinforce existing racial/ethnic dynamics (Hasian & Delgado, 1998). In terms of interracial communication, this emerging body of work contributes to a more complex understanding of how race affects our everyday communication.

Afrocentricity

Without question, Molefi Kete Asante is the foremost scholar associated with Afrocentricity (also known as African-centered scholarship). His work has provided much of the framework for personal, social, educational, and theoretical/methodological development (Asante, 1988, 1998a), and other scholars from various disciplines have also contributed important ideas. In its most basic form, Afrocentricity places Africans and the interest of Africa at the center of research and practice. According to Austin (2006), Afrocentricism is a concept used in two ways. First, it refers to a paradigm that makes African in general, and the ancient Nile Valley civilizations of Egypt and Nubia in particular, central to African Americans. Second, it describes an approach to African American experiences that reflects cultural pride and identification.

❖ **BOX 6.2**

STUDENT REFLECTIONS

My name itself is reflection of my Blackness. My mom didn't make up my name, like most Black mothers are known for; she heard it on television and thought that it was unique. My last name is a slave name that I have inherited. My great-great-great grandmother was a slave who was impregnated by her slave master on a plantation in Alabama. That is all I know about my history. I never really thought about how much I didn't know my history until my coach asked people on the team where their family came from. People responded with "Dutch," "Germany," "Ireland," "Jamaica," etc. When he asked me I had no response, but "Alabama." When I said that everyone laughed, but it is the sad truth. I am a living example of what slavery has done to Blacks in America; I don't know where I come from. . . . I recently realized that I have had to learn so much about the White culture, but they haven't had to learn about mine. My high school U.S. history book was huge with small words, while my African American history book was very small with large letters. . . . I love being Black and I wouldn't want to be anything else. I love how we talk loud and dramatic, I love how we show love through food, I love our deep connection to God, and I love how we sometimes are a connected community. I just love the skin I am in and those who share it. I am a Black American woman and I plan to continue to share, enjoy, and reflect on my Blackness. It is me and I am it.

Do you see how this idea is consistent with standpoint and critical race theories? Such a move is especially important given that for many years communication research on persons of African descent was completed within European frameworks (Asante, 1998a). Afrocentricity has provided a powerful critique of the problems with communication research that is solely situated in traditional Western thought (McPhail, 1998a). Asante (1998a) contends that critics who label the theoretical framework as anti-European and divisive are misinterpreting his positions (see also Phillips, 1993). Afrocentricity is not meant to be placed above other perspectives. Instead, it should exist alongside other cultural/historical standpoints. In this regard, Afrocentric thought provides an alternative to traditional frameworks when exploring the perspectives of people of African descent. Afrocentricity is not the opposite of Eurocentrism. In fact, some scholars (e.g., McPhail, 1998a) have found a complementary foundation between the two based on how both approaches implicate one another. In short, "The Afrocentric idea is one way of revealing the multicultural essence of our effort to understand the human experience" (Woodyard, 1995, p. 43). Other approaches, like an Asiacentric perspective (P. Wong, Manvi, & Wong, 1995), also offer valuable frameworks for studying interracial communication from non-European standpoints.

What exactly is an Afrocentric theoretical framework? First, it involves the development of a theoretical perspective that reflects African ways of knowing and interpreting the world (Ribeau, 2004). Afrocentricity assumes that people of African descent, despite some diverse lived experiences, share a common set of experiences, struggles, and origins. The African Diaspora provides a common cultural base that reflects a key set of values: harmony with nature, humaneness, rhythm, and communalism in terms of how wealth is produced, owned, and distributed. Second, Afrocentricity seeks agency and action through collective consciousness (Asante, 1988). In other words, Afrocentricity serves as a mechanism to embracing African ideals at the center of intellectual/personal life. It relies on the self-conscious actions of individuals with direct attention to the way they relate to one another. Note that being African American does not make you Afrocentric (Asante, 1998a). In fact, non–African Americans who embrace the principles of Afrocentricity can produce Afrocentric research (Asante, 1991; Brummett, 1994).

One of the major components of Afrocentricity—as it relates to interracial communication—is that it represents an intellectual framework that sees people of African descent as participants (rather than subjects/objects) in their human existence. It also recognizes that features of the human condition (feeling, knowing, and acting) are interrelated and should not be viewed as separate (i.e., viewing emotion as irrational and less valuable than reason). According to F. P. Delgado (1998b), Afrocentricity is important because it embraces an "alternative set of realities, experiences, and identities" (p. 423) for research attempting to view interracial communication from a non-Western perspective. From the beginning, U.S. history has been pluralistic. Given this, interpretations of human existence (communication) from any one cultural standpoint are unproductive. Spellers's (2002) research on African American women's negotiation of hair within the workplace is an excellent example of this.

Afrocentric forms of communication can be seen within the college classroom (Duncan, 2002). Students may have professors who facilitate Afrocentric styles of learning. These individuals, according to Kenyatta (1998), emphasize freedom, variation, creativity, flexibility, uniqueness, experience, humanistic understanding, and an evolving people-focused approach to learning. In comparison, Eurocentric styles of teaching emphasize rules, standardization, conformity, rigid order, normality, mechanical understanding, and a constant thing-focused approach to learning. As some of you have probably noted from past experiences, not all African American professors adapt an Afrocentric style of teaching (Austin, 2006).

In short, Afrocentricity proves a valuable lens in that it promotes a culturally centered analysis of interracial communication. In addition, all analyses of race and communication are situated within a particular cultural standpoint, complete with ideological assumptions. As such, Afrocentricity offers a theoretical framework that draws attention to existing problems with scholarship that solely reflects one group's cultural experiences.

Complicity Theory

Mark McPhail, in 1994, published *The Rhetoric of Racism* (McPhail, 1994b). Within this book, he outlines the key concepts associated with complicity theory—ideas that were clarified and extended in *The Rhetoric of Racism Revisited,* published in 2002. According to McPhail, complicity theory extends some of the ideas central to Afrocentricity by challenging the underlying assumptions that see African Americans and European Americans as naturally different. Studying complicity theory is significant for two reasons. First, unlike most of the other theories in Chapter 6, it represents a theory that was created specifically to study issues of race, language, and communication (as opposed to those that study culture more generally). Second, complicity theory challenges our basic understanding of race, in particular as it relates to racial differences. In this regard, it reflects an important shift or, in the least, a paradigm extension (McPhail, 2002).

Complicity theory is grounded in two key ideas. We describe each of them here as a means to introduce you to the foundation of the theory. First, at the core of racism is a language system that divides and ranks human beings in black-and-white terms (McPhail, 1994b). According to McPhail (1991), what has been created is a "language of negative difference" (p. 2) that affects social reality. In other words, racism and the concept of race are interrelated; to challenge racism you must challenge the language that we use regarding race. This is important because race designations are made and maintained with no recognition of commonality and interdependence (Hatch, 2003). The results are social practices that perpetuate the principle of negative difference in human interaction (McPhail, 1991). In other words, racism is not merely a problem of "Blacks" and "Whites," it is a consequence of understanding the world through black-and-white terms (McPhail, 2002).

A second key idea central to complicity theory is that dominance and marginality are not fixed states (McPhail, 1996b). The theory challenges the idea that racism is a social practice of domination that can be reduced to a "relationship between oppressors and the oppressed, between victimizers and victims, between white people with power and black people without it" (McPhail, 1996b, p. viii). According to complicity theory, racism reflects the Western predisposition to produce essentialist classifications and categories—separate, distinct, general groups (McPhail, 1994a). What it fails to take into consideration is how racism exists within a social system that also marginalizes people based on gender, class, age, sexual orientation, and the like (McPhail, 1994a). Acknowledging this helps individuals to recognize how positions of dominance and marginality are multidimensional and complex. In this regard, complicity theory advocates for efforts that avoid overgeneralizations based on a single cultural factor (this practice is known as **essentialism**).

As a means to advance the ideas central to complicity theory, McPhail introduces three key concepts: complicity, coherence, and implicature. By definition, **complicity** simply means "an agreement to disagree" (McPhail, 1991, p. 2). In the context of McPhail's work, complicity involves using language that highlights differences instead of commonalities, and emphasizes division at the expense of unity (McPhail, 1994a). In addition, complicity occurs when individuals fail to resist discourse that privileges some groups over others (Fine, 1991). According to complicity theory, productive race relations can never occur when complicity is the norm. Instead, we must move from complicity to coherence.

Coherence is a concept that emphasizes interconnectedness and commonalty (McPhail, 2002) in attempts to facilitate "harmonic discourse" (Fine, 1991, p. 271). It avoids a focus on the negative differences and critiques existing frameworks that depict human beings in terms of separate and distinct races (McPhail, 1998a). While complicity hinges on the idea of negative difference as oppositional forces, coherence sees difference as complementary (McPhail, 1996b). Accordingly, coherence defines and constructs reality in a way that does not privilege one position at the expense of another (McPhail, 1991). As such, it challenges the status quo from which racism functions (T. O. Patton, 2004). The final key concept, **implicature**, involves a basic acceptance of the belief that we are all implicated in each others' lives (McPhail, 2002). Implicature is more than having empathy for others; it includes the idea that "human beings are linguistically, materially, psychologically, and spiritually interrelated and interdependent" (Dace & McPhail, 2002). In other words, implicature is grounded in the idea that we are all connected; what affects one of us, affects all of us.

Complicity theory has been used by various communication scholars to critique existing representations of race. This has included critiques of movies by Spike Lee (McPhail, 1996a), speeches by Louis Farrakhan (McPhail, 1998b), and interactions on U.S. college campuses (T. O. Patton, 2004)—all of which have been described as grounded in complicity. Other scholars have pointed to complicity theory as a helpful framework to transform the current state of race relations into more liberating dialogues (R. L. Jackson, 2000) where true racial reconciliation can occur (Hatch, 2003). In many ways, the core ideas of this textbook reflect key principles associated with complicity theory.

Co-Cultural Theory

Co-cultural communication refers to a particular form of intercultural communication research that centers on issues of societal power and dominance within the United States (e.g., Folb, 1997). Co-cultural communication theory, as described by Orbe (1998a, 1998c), helps us understand the ways that persons who are traditionally marginalized in society communicate in their everyday lives. Grounded in muted group (Kramarae, 1981) and standpoint theories (D. E. Smith, 1987), co-cultural theory focuses on the lived experiences of a variety of "nondominant" or **co-cultural groups**. Subsequently, it represents a relevant framework for studying the experiences of people of color, women, people with disabilities, and gays, lesbians, and bisexuals (Fox, Giles, Orbe, & Bourhis, 2000; Orbe, 1996). In terms of interracial communication, it can be used (like Afrocentricity) to understand interracial communication from the perspectives of racial and ethnic microcultural group members. In its most basic form, co-cultural theory lends insight into how members of microcultures negotiate their underrepresented status with others (both a part of macrocultures and microcultures) in different situational contexts (Orbe, 1997; 1998c).

Co-cultural theory is based on the idea that, because of their marginalized societal positioning, people of color have to develop certain communication orientations in order to survive and/or succeed in the United States (Orbe & Spellers, 2005). However, it is important to recognize the vast diversity within and among different racial and ethnic groups. Therefore, the adoption and maintenance of certain orientations—as well as the rationale behind such decisions—varies greatly. Six interrelated factors (field of experience, perceived costs and rewards, ability, preferred outcomes, communication approach, and situational context) reportedly influence such decisions. **Field of experience** relates to the sum of lived experiences for people of color. Through a lifelong series of experiences, individuals learn how to communicate with others. They also come to realize the consequences of certain forms of communication. Based on her or his unique field of experience—which is simultaneously similar to, yet different from, others'—an individual comes to recognize **perceived costs and rewards** are associated with different communication practices. In some instances the advantages and disadvantages are clear. However, in others, they are less straightforward and more complex.

❖ **BOX 6.3**

AUTHOR REFLECTIONS

In the spring of 1992, I was a graduate student in my last quarter of course work. During a graduate seminar on qualitative research methodologies, I worked with a colleague and friend, T. Ford-Ahmed, on a project about how African American graduate students deal with racial prejudice at predominantly European American college campuses (Ford-Ahmed & Orbe, 1992). With the humblest of beginnings, that project launched a series of research projects that has contributed to the development of co-cultural communication theory (Orbe, 1998a).

Within this personal reflection I wanted to present an idea inherent within co-cultural theory that probably was not apparent in the description included in this chapter. One of the assumptions of the theory is that co-cultural groups (e.g., people of color, women, people with disabilities, gays, lesbians, and bisexuals) deal with oppression (racism, sexism, ableism, heterosexism) in similar ways. In other words, traditionally marginalized group members draw from common communication tactics regardless of the type of oppression they are faced with. Evidence from personal experience, as well as that gained from more scholarly endeavors, indicates that the types of strategies used vary significantly within and between different co-cultural groups depending on the particular standpoint of the particular person.

This idea is tied to a personal philosophy that I've adopted over the years. I believe that people who come to understand the oppression(s) they face are more likely to understand their role in oppressing others. Differences in terms of how racism, sexism, ageism, heterosexism, and so on are played out clearly exist. However, I see them in strikingly similar terms in the way that they are tied to power, control, and dominance. Understanding the direct and indirect influences that power has in interracial communication is a crucial element of ultimate effectiveness. We all possess varying levels of power. Simultaneously recognizing the similarities and differences across life experiences can facilitate the process of naming privilege and power in productive ways. I hope that co-cultural work provides such a theoretical/practical framework.

—MPO

A third factor influential to interracial communication is the **ability** to enact certain strategies that work to establish and maintain a specific communication orientation. Consistent with communication accommodation theory (discussed later), co-cultural theory understands that people of color have varying levels of success in using certain strategies (e.g., "passing" or networking with other people of color). Much depends on the specific dynamics inherent in any given **situational context**. This includes where the interaction takes place, other parties who are present, and the particular circumstances that facilitate the interaction. It should be apparent that situational context, like the other five factors, intersects in highly complex ways to influence interracial interactions (Orbe & Spellers, 2005).

The final two factors are **communication approach** and **preferred outcome**. Communication approach refers to the specific "voice" used by racial/ethnic microcultural group members in the United States. Is the communication approach aggressive, assertive, or more nonassertive? Preferred outcome relates to the ultimate goal that the person of color has for the interaction: (1) Is he or she aiming to fit in and not bring any unnecessary attention to racial differences (assimilation)? (2) Or is the goal to recognize racial and ethnic differences and work with others to ensure that these differences do not translate into unequal treatment (accommodation)? (3) Or still yet, is the goal to limit interaction with European Americans and create affirming communities exclusively of people of color (separation)?

Note that no one approach or preferred outcome is most (or universally) desirable (Orbe & Spellers, 2005). Much depends on how the other factors influence the person's perceptions. The stated objective of co-cultural theory, then, is not to predict the behaviors of people of color. Instead, it is to understand the complex factors that influence how they communicate in a society that traditionally has treated them as cultural outsiders (Orbe, 1998c). Identifying how these factors are apparent in specific tactics and communicative stances is an important step in this process.

Theorizing Satisfying Communication

The work of Michael Hecht and colleagues has been instrumental in providing models for satisfying communication from the perspectives of U.S. racial and ethnic microcultural group members (Hecht & Ribeau, 1984; Hecht, Ribeau, & Alberts, 1989). Particularly, they have engaged in ongoing research that has looked at how African Americans and Mexican Americans characterize satisfying intraracial and interracial (primarily focusing on interactions with European Americans) communication (Hecht, Jackson, & Ribeau, 2003; Hecht, Ribeau, & Sedano, 1990; Ribeau, Baldwin, & Hecht, 1997). Some of the early work in this line of research focused on identifying satisfying conversational themes among African Americans and Mexican Americans. In terms of interracial communication, Hecht and his colleagues have provided great insight into specific issues that people of color find most important for effective, satisfying communication.

In research that tapped into a Mexican American perspective to interracial communication (focusing on interactions with European Americans), five specific themes were found (Hecht & Ribeau, 1984; Hecht et al., 1990). These themes are not assumed to be complete, but are offered as a contribution to workable frameworks for effective interracial communication. They capture "how things operate"—what is important/unimportant, acceptable/unacceptable, and effective/ineffective from the perspective of Mexican Americans. The first theme relates to **worldview**. Sharing common experiences and interests is seen as crucial to communication satisfaction. **Acceptance** is the second theme. Interracial interactions that were regarded as satisfying involved a perception that one's ideas and culture were accepted, confirmed, and respected. The third theme, **negative stereotyping**, is a main source for dissatisfying communication. Being categorized solely in terms of your ethnicity (as opposed to being seen as a unique person first) creates barriers between persons. **Relational solidarity**, the fourth theme, relates to the positive value attributed to developing close interracial relationships. According to Mexican Americans, the most satisfying communication was seen as part of a process of an ongoing, potentially intimate relationship with a European American. **Expressiveness** is the fifth, and final, theme. Interracial communication was characterized as satisfying when a comfortable climate was developed by both parties. In other words, individuals could express themselves openly, honestly, and fully without a fear of rejection, judgment, or retaliation.

In parallel research on an African American perspective of interracial communication (again primarily with European Americans), similar themes were identified (Hecht et al., 1989; Ribeau, et al., 1997). These included issues such as the rigid use of negative stereotyping, acceptance, emotional expressiveness, authenticity, understanding, goal attainment (achieving desired outcomes), and power dynamics (not feeling controlled or manipulated). In order to generate some practical guidelines from their research, Hecht and his colleagues used their data to identify a series of improvement strategies for enhancing effective interracial communication. Some of these are summarized here:

1. Engage in interracial communication with an open mind; do not dismiss others' points of view without sufficient consideration.

2. Identify a common threshold of language that is accessible to both parties (e.g., avoid cultural slang that might be unfamiliar to the other person).

3. Be genuine in how you present yourself and views of others.

4. Practice other orientation. In other words, attempt to involve the other person as you locate common ground. This will enhance understanding.

5. Do not be afraid to assert your point of view; discussing disagreements and confronting problematic issues can be beneficial to building long-term relationships.

6. Take advantage of teachable moments where learning about other cultures can occur naturally.

Understanding Interracial Communication Processes

We began by describing some theories that help us understand the importance of recognizing intraracial communication processes, as well as those that center the perspectives of people of color. Then we used the work by Hecht and his colleagues to gain insight into what particular racial/ethnic group members define as satisfying interracial communication. Now we move to another cluster of interracial communication theories—those that focus specifically on what happens when members of different racial and ethnic groups interact.

Anxiety/Uncertainty Management (AUM) Theory

Anxiety/uncertainty management (AUM) theory largely has been used in a number of intercultural communication contexts (Gudykunst, 1988, 1993, 1995). It also serves as a valuable framework for interethnic and interracial interactions (Gudykunst & Hammer, 1988). AUM theory focuses on interactions between cultural ingroup members and "strangers," defined as persons who are outside their primary cultural communities. The work of Gudykunst and his colleagues is based on one central idea: An increase in our abilities to (1) manage our anxiety about interacting with others who are from different racial/ethnic groups and (2) accurately predict and explain their behaviors will work to increase communication effectiveness (Gudykunst, 1995). Effective communication, then, refers to the process of minimizing misunderstandings and involves certain levels of self-consciousness and cultural competencies (Howell, 1982).

The central idea of AUM theory is that anxiety and uncertainty are the basic causes of communication failure in intergroup interactions (Gudykunst, 2005). Although these two elements are closely related, they are different in a few crucial ways. **Anxiety** is an emotion triggered by anticipation of things yet to come. Gudykunst (1995) defines it as "the feeling of being uneasy, tense, worried, or apprehensive about what might happen" (p. 13). **Uncertainty** is best understood as cognition. It includes doubts of one's abilities to predict the outcomes of interracial interactions. All communication encounters involve varying levels of anxiety and uncertainty. AUM theory suggests that minimal levels of these two elements can be productive in that they motivate us to keep focused on being effective communicators. However, levels of anxiety and uncertainty are closely tied to the degree of perceived cultural difference among individuals. More simply put, the greater the perceived racial/ethnic differences, the more prevalent role that anxiety and uncertainty will play. As alluded to earlier, AUM theory is built on the idea that higher levels are the major cause of communication ineffectiveness.

❖ BOX 6.4

STUDENT REFLECTIONS

I guess one could say that my first experience with being around all African Americans was when I worked at a concession stand. Now, I do not like to judge everyone of a race based on one group of people; however, it is hard not to with the situation I was in. These people in this city were rude, loud, and just plain disobedient. During pool hours, none of the people followed any of the pool rules. When they came to the concession stand, they were extremely rude and made my job difficult. From that time forward, I have had an image of African Americans all being like these people in this city. I guess that I do have stereotypes because of the experiences I have had growing up. That isn't to say that I am rude or outwardly mean to any of these people. I do not think that Asians can drive, but at the same time, a lot of White old people cannot drive either.

According to the AUM theory, three variables contribute to the prevalence of anxiety and uncertainty during interracial communication (Gudykunst, 2005). One of these variables involves motivational factors. How important is interracial communication success in any given context? How do these efforts work toward achieving certain needs, gaining valuable information, and other desired outcomes? Knowledge factors represent a second variable. Examples include expectations and awareness of other racial/ethnic groups, understanding different perspectives, and information gained through shared networks. Knowledge also involves a recognition of the similarities and differences of racial/ethnic groups. The third variable, skills, refers to factors that allow individuals to put knowledge bases into practice. They include the ability to practice empathy (not sympathy), tolerate ambiguity, and accommodate new behaviors.

An article by Gudykunst (1995) used three factors, and how they inform varying levels of anxiety and uncertainty, to generate a total of 94 axioms (self-evident truths) concerning intercultural communication effectiveness. We have applied these directly to the context of interracial communication and have included a sampling here. As you can see, AUM theory focuses on increasing abilities to predict behavior to develop interracial communication competence.

1. An increase in our need to develop a sense of belonging with others who are racially/ethnically different will produce an increase in our anxiety. (motivation)

2. An increase in the perceived similarities between racial/ethnic groups will increase the likelihood for effective management of anxiety and uncertainty. (knowledge)

3. An increase in our ability to empathize with others from different racial and ethnic groups will produce an increase in our ability to predict their behaviors accurately. (skill)

As evidenced by existing studies (Gudykunst & Hammer, 1988), AUM theory is a useful framework for studying interracial interactions. Recent publications (e.g., Gudykunst, 2005) provide comprehensive explanations of the theory and its utility for contemporary research.

Third-Culture Building

The idea of **third-culture building** can be seen within Asante's model of transracial communication. Remember that the model includes movement of two people, communicating from particular ethnic perspectives, toward a common threshold. Third-culture building models are based on the idea that through communication, diverse individuals work together to create a shared, mutually acceptable culture that incorporates individuals' cultures in ways that facilitate a unique, third culture (Uchida, 1997). Third-culture building models are important for two reasons. First, the focus is on interaction between individuals and how that shapes culture (Uchida, 1997). Historically, intercultural communication research has focused on outcomes; third-culture building models realign the focus on process—something that is at the heart of communication. Second, models of third-culture building regard culture as something that is constantly being developed and maintained through interaction. In this regard, culture is not seen as something static or preexisting. Instead, culture is defined as a construct that is dynamic, emergent, and constantly negotiated (Uchida, 1997).

According to Starosta and Olorunnisola (1993), the process of third-culture building involves five phases that occur in a cyclical order (see also G. M. Chen & Starosta, 1998). The first phase is **intrapersonal interpersonal communication**. Beginning at a point when individuals are aware of other racial/ethnic groups, this phase is characterized by a curiosity about others. It can also involve a desire to work with others in order to maximize mutual benefits. Motivations for contact with others grows to the point of initial contact, which reflects the second phase, **interpersonal intercultural communication**. This phase begins at the stage of inquiry when the person who initiated the contact seeks out information about others in different racial/ethnic groups. Ultimately this interaction becomes more reciprocal with both parties exchanging information about self and others. This phase is characteristic of mutual adjustment, especially in terms of identifying common goals for benefits of working together.

The third phase is **rhetorical intercultural communication**. Here both persons increase their consciousness as to how the other person's culture influences current (and future) interactions. In order for third-culture building to continue through this phase, individuals must develop a conscious awareness of cultural similarities and differences, as well as a willingness to fight the negative influences of ethnocentric judgments. Through ongoing communication, the emergence of a third culture, one that draws from the best of both independent cultural worlds, occurs. Over time, the patterns of interaction associated with this new culture become integrated into everyday communication. **Metacultural communication** represents the fourth phase of third-culture development. Within this phase, individuals continue to work through the complexities of the new emergent culture, including co-created roles, norms, and mores. Through this process, third-culture practices are readjusted, reinforced, and fine-tuned. Over time, a mutual assimilation of all parties occurs that results in a unique culture that becomes more permanent. The fifth phase, **intracultural communication**, involves a movement away from one's primary culture toward identification with the newly created culture. Here the development of the third culture accompanies a newly created identity for both individuals. Following this final phase, the model begins a new cycle (returning to phase 1 again).

Several communication scholars have used third-culture building models to study the interactions between racially and ethnically diverse individuals (e.g., Metzger & Springston's 1992 analysis of Native American and European American treaty rights debate in Wisconsin). Of particular interest to us is the work of Uchida (1997) who extended earlier third-culture building models in her research on diversity within women's support groups. Her research is significant in that she raises three important issues. First, Uchida (1997) argues that culture building is a continuous process that involves multiple layers of cultural negotiation. The result of this process are numerous emergent cultures, none of which necessarily reflect a singular "third" culture. As such, she advocates for using "culture building" instead of "third-culture building."

Second, Uchida (1997) argues for the necessity to refrain from focusing on one aspect of culture building. Consistent with the concept of intersectionality discussed in Chapter 5, she stresses the fact that one aspect of the culture building process (e.g., race) necessarily involves negotiations of other salient issues like those related to gender, class, age, and the like. Finally, Uchida advocates for examinations of culture building that are understood within a larger context of power structures, various layers of privilege and penalty, and societal values systems—something that addresses existing criticism (Casmir, 1993; Shuter, 1998).

Cross-Cultural Adaptation Theory

Cross-cultural adaptation theory, largely based on the work of Young Yun Kim (2001, 2005), has been applied primarily to intercultural interactions stemming from international travel. According to Kim (2005), **cross-cultural adaptation** focuses on the process of change that occurs over time when individuals whose primary socialization is one culture come into continuous, prolonged contact with a new and unfamiliar culture. Given Rich's (1974) conceptualization of interracial communication, it appears a valuable mechanism to understanding the adaptation process that some racial/ethnic group members experience when communicating with others outside their communities. This is especially true for racial/ethnic group members whose early life experiences involve little contact with members outside their particular group. Think about Latino/a or African American students who are raised in predominantly ethnic communities and then go to public state universities. Or European Americans who, because of humanitarian or religious convictions, decide to dedicate their lives to working within communities where they are the clear minority. How do these persons adapt to these instances of prolonged interracial contact? Cross-cultural adaptation theory represents one window into the central role that identity and communication play in answering this question.

Cross-cultural adaptation is based on the idea that humans have a natural drive to adapt and grow (Y. Y. Kim, 2005). While we become enculturated with specific norms, values, and beliefs early on in life, entrance into an unfamiliar culture increases our awareness of self and others. Facing new situations can trigger both stress and adaptation responses and ultimately cause us to grow as individuals. Because it is neither reasonable nor practical to expect any large population to significantly modify its own cultural habits, cultural newcomers must adapt. Part of that process involves learning and acquiring the elements of the new culture (**acculturation**) and possibly unlearning some of the old cultural habits (**deculturation**) (Y. Y. Kim, 2005). Because cross-cultural adaptation usually requires both acculturation and deculturation, individuals may experience varying levels of stress. This is especially true during initial encounters. According to cross-cultural adaptation theory, such experiences help individuals develop a new sense of their cultural identities.

Cross-cultural adaptation is a complex and dynamic process that occurs through communication via a number of channels (interpersonal, small group, mass media). Successfully adapting to a new culture involves an intercultural transformation of sorts that includes three specific outcomes. First, a functional fitness is achieved whereby an individual develops skills to communicate and build satisfying relationships with the host culture (Y. Y. Kim, 2001). Second, these communication skills have a direct impact on the psychological health of the cultural newcomer. Not being able to manage the internal responses (mental adjustment) and external demands (physical adjustment) in the new culture is directly tied to poor psychological adjustment. Third, the "self-shock"

(Zaharna, 1989) of new cultural experiences generates a new emergent intercultural identity. Unlike third-culture building, however, only the identity of the cultural newcomer is transformed. She or he develops an increased self-consciousness of multiple identities that may result in feelings that come from being on the borders (margins) of both cultures.

Several factors influence the abilities of individuals to enter different racial/ethnic communities and adapt successfully to new cultures. One is the preconceived expectations that the newcomer has of the racial/ethnic communities. Another is the level of preparation that has been accomplished through attempts to learn cultural histories, norms, and values. Preparation also involves an emotional state of "motivational readiness" whereby individuals strongly desire successful adaptation. Finally, research (e.g., Y. Y. Kim, 2005) indicates that certain personality traits—being open, resilient, flexible, resourceful, and willing to take risks—also are connected to effective cross-cultural adaptation. In addition, attention to certain aspects to the host culture must also be taken into account. How accessible and receptive is the culture to those who are identified as racially or ethnically different? What levels of racial pride exist and how are ingroup/outgroup distinctions enforced? What are the tolerance levels for attitudes, beliefs, values, and behaviors that do not conform to cultural norms? As described earlier, cross-cultural adaptation is a dynamic and complex process, especially given the constant evolution of cultures over time. Effective moves from one culture to another reflect an increased attention to these issues.

Communication Accommodation Theory (CAT)

CAT was first presented as a "speech" accommodation theory by Howard Giles and colleagues in the early to mid-1970s (Giles, 1973, 1977; Giles, Taylor, & Bourhis, 1973). It was initially a theoretical framework that focused on language and linguistic elements, but has developed into an insightful lens through which all aspects of communication between different racial/ethnic groups can be understood. Specifically, CAT explains the ways that individuals adjust their communication during intergroup interactions (C. A. Shepard, Giles, & Le Poire, 2001). Accommodation can be seen in almost all communication behaviors, including accent, rate, loudness, vocabulary, grammar, and gestures. In addition, it has important consequences in terms of self- and other identity, ingroup/outgroup distinctions, and communication effectiveness.

Following the foundations of social identity theory (Tajfel, 1978), CAT maintains that individuals derive a significant portion of their identity from groups to which they belong. As we discussed in Chapter 5, remember that different aspects of a person's identity may be more important in different contexts (Gallois, Ogay, & Giles, 2005). During interactions where racial/ethnic differences are significant, CAT can be used to understand how a person's communication will be used to emphasize or downplay those aspects of group identity. In other words, CAT focuses on how verbal and nonverbal communication is used to achieve the desired level of social distance (immediate or distant) between ingroup and outgroup members.

Two major aspects of CAT are how convergence and divergence are present during intergroup interactions (Gallois et al., 2005). **Convergence** is defined as a strategy that individuals use to adapt their communication to become more like the other person. Convergence, like divergence, can be partial or complete. People may converge for different reasons, including a desire to again acceptance, social integration, or as a means for effective communication (Gallois, Giles, Jones, Cargile, & Ota, 1995; Giles, 1973). In all intergroup interactions, and especially in the context of interracial communication, it is important to note that convergence may be toward a person's actual communication *or* a preconceived stereotype of how the racial/ethnic group members communicate. According to Tajfel and Turner (1979), persons react to others, not necessarily as individuals, but as representatives of different racial/ethnic groups. Can you see how some attempts at convergence may be quite offensive and work to construct barriers to effective interracial communication? Clearly, convergence is not the best strategy for all case scenarios. The success of convergence in intergroup interactions depends on a number of factors, including a person's ability to converge effectively and how his or her efforts are perceived by the other person.

❖ **BOX 6.5**

CODE SWITCHING

Looking at specific racial and ethnic group members who are involved in code switching is an excellent way to see the practical implications of convergence. **Code switching**, also described as style switching (Seymour & Seymour, 1979) or language mobility (Sachdev & Bourhis, 1990), refers to a communication strategy used by individuals who have mastered the speech codes from two different cultural communities. During interactions with others, these individuals discern which system of communication is more appropriate in the specific situation and adapt accordingly. Research (Hecht et al., 1989) reports that interracial interactions where no code switching occurs is more likely to be ineffective. According to Collier (1988), European Americans are less willing (and possibly less able) than African Americans to adopt outgroup speech codes. What is your reaction to this statement? Do you agree? Why or why not?

This research has some interesting implications for interracial communication in a variety of contexts. The following questions are provided as a means to understand the possible practical implications of intergroup convergence. Think about how they might be used to guide specific behaviors.

- What factors must be taken into account when using code switching during everyday interracial interaction?
- What are some of the consequences—positive/negative, anticipated/unanticipated, individual/group—of the switching?
- Are these consequences the same for all persons generally, or do they vary from group to group?
- Is it possible to create some practical guidelines for code switching and interracial communication?

Divergence refers to the ways in which communicators stress verbal and nonverbal differences between themselves and others. Divergence is an active process that emphasizes communication differences; it is not doing nothing about different communication styles. Convergence is typically the result of internal scripts and occurs on a largely unconscious level. In comparison, persons are oftentimes more aware of divergence in interracial interactions. In many cases, divergence is used by racial/ethnic microcultural group members as a means to maintain their identity, cultural pride, and distinctiveness (Gallois et al., 2005). But it is important to understand that divergence (as well as convergence) can be mutual or nonmutual. In other words, one person or both persons can use divergence to emphasize the social distance between racial/ethnic groups.

In summary, Giles et al. (1987) record a number of scientific propositions that reflect the basic ideas of CAT. Read through the following statements. Do they make sense to you based on your interracial communications experiences?

People will attempt to converge communication behaviors when they desire social approval and a shared identity base.

People will attempt to diverge when they desire to communicate a contrasting self-image and define the interaction in intergroup ways.

People are more likely to evaluate convergence positively when they perceive the other person's efforts to be well intentioned and based on actual communication style (not stereotypes).

These propositions represent just a few that Giles and his colleagues have generated. In this light, general CAT research seems to offer some valuable practical guidelines for interracial communication effectiveness. Of course, as articulated throughout this book, much depends on the particular individuals and their cultural identities, as well as the specific context of the interaction (for an advanced model, see Gallois et al., 2005). Generally speaking, the most satisfying interracial interactions typically involve a delicate balance of convergence (as an indication of a willingness to communicate effectively) and divergence (as a means to acknowledge the importance of racial/ethnic group identification) *for both persons.*

Conclusion

Almost 30 years ago, Pennington (1979) reported that the state of interracial communication research and theory was in its infancy. Her call for increased productivity focusing on the "deep structures" (p. 392) and different worldviews that inform interracial interactions does not appear to have gone unnoticed. More recent research and theory appears to face additional challenges, especially in terms of its focus on difference and application to everyday practice (Houston, 2002). In addition, interracial communication research must continue to explore the value of alternative methods and theories (Hecht et al., 2003). As illustrated within the broad range of frameworks described in this chapter, substantial options are available to theorists and practitioners who are interested in validating, critiquing, and/or extending research. However, other challenges still exist.

First, theoretical frameworks must create a delicate balance between providing insights into the general cultural norms of each racial/ethnic group and acknowledging the great diversity within each group. Second, interracial communication theoretical frameworks must assume an action-sensitive approach to theory development and practical application. Houston (2000), for instance, argues that a change in research and theory priorities is needed in academia. She calls for a new purpose of research where theory development is put into practice and used for the improvement of life. In a country where race relations continue to be highly adverse, communication scholars have a unique opportunity—and responsibility—to utilize theories in the discipline to improve effectiveness of everyday interracial interaction. Responding to this challenge, Part II extends theory into practice within a number of specific interracial communication contexts.

OPPORTUNITIES FOR EXTENDED LEARNING ❖

1. Select one theory and conduct a more thorough analysis of its usefulness to interracial communication. Start by locating and reading the references that we cite. Then reflect on the strengths and weaknesses of the theory. This will allow you to identify certain criticisms of each theory (something that we did not do because of space limitations). During your analysis, ask yourself other questions such as: What are the basic assumptions and main ideas of the theory? How does the theory help guide future research? How can it be applied to everyday interactions?

2. Think about your favorite television shows and movies. How would you characterize the portrayal of interracial communication within these media forms? What attitudes, values, and behaviors promote effective communication among different racial and ethnic groups? What about interactions that are less productive? How does the work by Hecht and others assist in identifying specific themes of satisfying and dissatisfying communication? Check your perceptions with other ingroup and outgroup members.

3. The following is a productive avenue to move theory from the conceptual to the practical. Break the class into several groups, and assign each group a particular theoretical framework. The objective of each group is to create a 3-hour cultural diversity training program that focuses on race relations. Group members must decide on the following details for the program: (1) Who is the target audience? (2) What structure will it follow? (3) What aspects of the theory will be used, and how will they be incorporated into the training? and (4) What types of experiential learning will be included? Time permitting, share your race relations training modules with the class.

4. According to speech community theory, each distinctive cultural group has a distinct speech code. Select one cultural group of which you are a member, and brainstorm its communication rules, norms, and values. How easy or difficult is this process? Then break up into groups and share speech codes. During this interaction, take special note of similarities and differences across groups. Also, discuss any different rules that were recorded by others for the same cultural group.

5. Use the Internet to search for articles that highlight model programs of cross-racial collaboration. These can be related to college campuses, professional organizations, different religious denominations, community-based organizations, and so on. (For a general search, using the keywords *multiracial organizations*, *interracial unity*, or *cross-racial alliances* will provide a more focused search.) Review the key aspects of these

programs in terms of their success. How can different theoretical frameworks assist in understanding the effectiveness of these real-life success stories?

6. Gudykunst and his colleagues believe that anxiety and uncertainty are the primary sources of miscommunication for interracial interactions. Spend 10 to 15 minutes of class time brainstorming all of the different forms of interracial communication that are likely to cause unproductive anxiety and uncertainty. Then take the necessary steps to process this information. How are these things closely related? What are some possible strategies to overcome high levels of anxiety and uncertainty?

PART II

Interracial Communication in Specific Contexts

7

Interracial Friendships

As suggested by the title of our book, we have divided our textbook into two parts. Part I (Chapters 1–6) has been dedicated to exploring race as a social construct (theory), specifically deconstructing its evolution and emergence into a phenomenon that shapes our identities and understandings of human interaction in the presence of racial difference. We learned that race as a concept was introduced as a means for marginalizing and oppressing certain ethnic groups. This racial hierarchy and systemic oppression was part of a political agenda designed to preserve the position of power occupied by European Americans. For racial/ethnic groups, this limited their access to resources and opportunities that would remedy this economic, political, and occupational inequity, which moved the politics of race from the political to the social arenas of life.

Part II (Chapters 7–12) provides a context within which to better understand this transition. Specifically, these chapters are designed to further our understanding of these man-made differences by presenting real world scenarios that apply theories and concepts about race to specific kinds of interracial interactions and everyday activities. In these chapters, we will learn how racial oppression and the history of race relations have played a critical role in how our interpersonal and interracial relationships are shaped. These scenarios and contexts will afford us the opportunity to understand and reflect on how we manage our attitudes, beliefs, and values when we are faced with racial differences. In short we challenge the reader (ourselves included) to move "from theory into practice"—applying our book knowledge to our actual, real interpersonal interactions—and use our own lives and experiences as a site for eradicating racism . . . one relationship at a time. By examining the current state and perceptions of interracial friendships, we aim to establish a knowledge base on this topic and identify the perceptual and communicative barriers that prevent these relationships from occurring.

The Significance of Interracial Friendships

Research has shown that human interaction and relational intimacy are essential for our survival. No matter how archaic the phrase "no man is an island" may sound, it really speaks to a basic human necessity—relationship. Sometimes we all need our personal space to decompress, but in the end, we all need the company of others in order to live a healthy, normal life. While we all need these relationships, it is imperative that we have the proper tools necessary for establishing and preserving these relationships. In general, we are first introduced to relationship in our family unit. As children we learn the rights and wrongs, the dos and don'ts that shape our world and interpersonal interactions. This learning process is both informal and formal, with the informal lessons being learned through observations and formal lessons learned through actual communication between parent(s) and child, with further learning occurring when social rules and norms are violated. Our familial relationships allow us to learn communication as a transactional process between interactants and to develop the skills that facilitate positive communicative interactions.

Another relational context that provides a tremendous opportunity for relational learning and growth is **friendship**. Unlike our familial relationships, into which we are born, we have the freedom to choose our friendships and use a variety of criteria to determine with whom we will establish some of our most intimate relationships. Our relationships with family last for a lifetime and provide us with unconditional love and support, whereas our friendships are established by choice and are voluntary in nature. Both relationship types are very rewarding and offer intimacy and connection to its partners in very distinct ways. One characteristic that makes friendship relationships different from family relationships, however, is that friendship relationships can be initiated and terminated for a variety of reasons and do not have the expectation that the relationship will last a lifetime. This means that friends must work to maintain the relationship and assure each other that the relationship is mutually satisfying. Eventually, the friends develop a pattern of communication that is comfortable for them and create a means of continued interaction that facilitates the preservation of the relationship and relational intimacy.

In general, our friendship relationships should offer support, intimacy, and connection that are most likely not found in other relationships. Take a moment to reflect on your friendships. Is there a marked difference between each relationship? Are there some qualities about one friend or relationship that cannot be found in others? How hard would you say you and your friends work at keeping the relationship alive? Do either of you need regular contact with each other, or is it okay to go a few weeks without talking, knowing that you can pick up where you left off without missing a beat? Taking this scenario a step further, how many of those relationships would you say are with a person from a different race? Do these interracial friendships differ at all from your same-race friendships? If so, why do you think that is? Hopefully, as you contemplated your answers to these questions you began to think of two things: (1) the importance of friendship and (2) what it might mean if we do not have a racially diverse friendship network. While several mitigating factors might not have afforded you the opportunity to interact, let alone develop, friendships with people who have membership in racial groups different from your own, it is our hope that you will give more thought to this relational phenomenon and what it means in terms of race relations. Please do not misinterpret our position. We are not advocating the initiation and development of interpersonal friendships for the sole purpose of **racial reconciliation** (the process of healing the racial tensions and bridging the racial divide that exist between the races); rather, we challenge everyone to self-reflect on how they/we have been socialized to perceive racial differences and how that process might have directly impacted our decision to (or fear of doing so) have close, personal relationships with people who are racially different from ourselves.

As we will discuss further in this chapter, the **contact hypothesis** (Allport, 1958) is a theory that has attempted to help us better understand this very phenomenon. In short, the theory asserts that increased interactions with racially different others will reduce prejudiced thoughts and beliefs in optimal conditions. While this may be true in theory, in practice, this may not be the most appropriate way by which to change one's belief system (Dixon, Durheim, & Tredoux, 2005). I don't believe scholars are arguing that interracial friendships be entered into with the purpose of deconstructing our preexisting belief systems. Rather, they suggest that these interracial interactions function to challenge us to reflect internally on our stereotypical beliefs about racially different others with whom we have had little to no contact.

Unlike our relationships with family members, our friendship relationships provide us with the unique opportunity to choose with whom we would like to interact and establish an emotional bond. Through our friendships, we learn things about ourselves that we might not learn from our family members. More importantly, these friendships equip us with the interpersonal skills we need to better and effectively communicate with people outside of our friendship network. We understand how personality and cultural differences shape our individual identities and experiences, which undoubtedly have an impact on how we interact with people in other situations and contexts. Because of our experiences with our friends, we become wiser and more attuned to our intimacy needs and become more discriminating in our friendship choices, choosing to preserve those relationships where we feel accepted, supported, and validated and dissolving those that do not (Collier, 1996; Goldsmith, 2004; Hamm, Brown, & Heck, 2005; Jaasma, 2002; Korgen, Mahon, & Wang, 2003; Welner, 2006). It doesn't take a rocket scientist to reach this conclusion, but we all desire to be in healthy relationships that make us feel good about ourselves, have a high level of trust and commitment, and challenge us to become competent communicators.

According to LeCroy (1988) friendship can be defined as "a mutual involvement between two people that is characterized by affection, satisfaction, enjoyment, openness, respect, and a sense of feeling important to the other." These criteria for friendship are created subconsciously in childhood wherein individuals are drawn to each other for very basic reasons. Because we spend most of our time in environments and contexts with racially similar individuals (Forbes, 1997; Halualani, et al., 2004; Hamm et al., 2005; Hean & Dickinson, 1995), it is no surprise that our friendships are established within the confines of those interactions. Past research has shown that this relational patterning and socializing occurs at a very young age (Fink & Wild, 1995; Graham & Cohen, 1997; Lawhon, 1997; Lundy, Field, McBride, Field, & Largie, 1998). What are missing from this process are the opportunities and/or personal encouragement from others to foster friendships across racial lines.

❖ BOX 7.1

AUTHOR REFLECTIONS

Reflecting on my friendships, I think I've done a pretty good job of choosing to have close, personal relationships with a wide variety of people who have come into my life for a variety of reasons. Those true relationships that remind me of how blessed I am to have such wonderful people in my life illustrate the beauty of having diverse friends who aren't necessarily just like me. Many of my friends and I share common values and beliefs, and in most cases, we also share identities as Christians; however, there are those relationships where we have differences, which I think is of equal importance. The differences may be in our race or culture, but it is our similarities and appreciation of each other as individuals (who happen to have membership in a certain racial group) that make our friendship all the more valuable. I have certain friends from both racial groups with whom we share the same sense of humor, similar life experiences, and core values that override our racial differences or similarities.

My current friendship network primarily involves other African American women and some European Americans. I truly wish I had closer friendships and more frequent interactions with racially/ethnically different others. I attribute these lacks to the lack of diversity at my institution (see Banton's six orders of contact) and the limited contact among most people in suburbia who hole themselves up in their homes when the garage doors go down. I remain hopeful that this will not always be the case. As our nation continues to become racially and ethnically diverse, it is only natural that interracial interactions and friendships will follow suit—I look forward to the change.

—TMH

Friendships established in early childhood are definitely different from those we have later in life. Although we have the tendency to become friends with people who are in close physical proximity to us (e.g., workplace, neighborhood, church, and school), those relationships become more complex as we transition from adolescence into adulthood, per se. The criteria we use as we get older become more involved and discriminating (read detailed) than when we were in elementary school. Lending someone a crayon may have facilitated relational efficacy in elementary school but doesn't really cut it when we're in middle or high school. A new set of criteria are introduced that reflect our value system and what we believe are important for establishing a good friendship relationship. While it may hold true that friendships developed in our youth are primarily with people of the same sex and race as our own, the same can be said of those relationships we have later in life. Even though other relational issues may determine what a "true friend" is, human interactions and relationships continue to be established with people from our same racial group (Goldsmith, 2004).

Interracial friendships are very much like same-race friendships, the primary (and obvious) difference being that the friends have membership in two different racial groups. This racial difference creates for each friend a qualitatively different lived experience that might directly impact the friendship. For example, Milagros (Hispanic American) is having a difficult time communicating with her English professor (European American) and feels she is receiving unfair treatment because of her ethnicity. Candace (European American) is in the same class and doesn't agree with Milagros's assessment of what is going on. After several attempts to share her frustrations with her friend, Milagros resolves to confide in Bei (Chinese American) who seems to understand and empathize with her. Despite the fact that her friend "doesn't get it," Milagros recognizes that they each have different racial standpoints that allow them to interpret their experiences differently. Eventually, Candace comes to the realization that their professor *is* treating certain students differently. She apologizes to Milagros for not understanding and explains that she's never had to think of things from a **racial perspective**, and because of their friendship, she is more sensitive to and aware of the possibility that racism and discrimination do still exist. This is also the first interracial friendship Candace has ever had, so she didn't necessarily have the communication skills that would prepare her for this dimension of their relationship.

Barriers to Interracial Friendships

As anyone can guess, interracial friendships face a set of barriers that are absent from same-race friendships. One of the dominating barriers is the stereotypes that friends might have of each other prior to the relationship's initiation. Few studies have been conducted that actually measure these stereotypes within this relational context; however, other research does indicate that we live in a society where racial differences are oftentimes perceived as a negative factor in the development of interracial relationships (Diggs & Clark, 2002; Glascock, 2003; Houston, 1997; Hughes & Tuch, 2003; Leonard & Locke, 1993; S. Wright, Aron, McLaughlin-Volpe, & Ropp, 1997). In their various studies, these and other researchers continue to demonstrate that societal prejudices and stereotypes remain a constant in the minds of many people in society. By extension, our beliefs about racial difference are informed by these ways of thinking and ultimately influence our perceptions of each other as well as whether or not we choose to interact with or even have relationships with members of an outgroup.

Of the aforementioned studies, the Leonard and Locke (1993) study specifically aims to determine the extent to which such unhealthy assessments and judgments hinder the development of interracial friendships. In their study involving evaluations of an outgroup by European Americans and African Americans, Leonard and Locke (1993) found evidence proving this to be true, thereby supporting the assumption that interracial communication is difficult to facilitate and maintain. In short, they found that both groups harbored negative stereotypes of each other that would make interracial communication impossible, which would most definitely preclude any possibility of any positive interracial interactions and relationships. Similarly, in their autoethnography where they chose to discuss the intricacies of their interracial friendship, communication scholars Rhunette Diggs and Karen Clark (2002) demonstrate how friends from diverse racial backgrounds must have some level of commitment to their relationship in order for the relationship to work. In order for each partner to feel safe and comfortable with themselves and their differences, Diggs and Clark urge the friends to communicate with each other while also having conversations with their same-race friends (intraracial communication) about the possible difficulties their relationship might be having. More importantly, they also suggest that the interracial friends make it a top priority to come back to each other and discuss those issues in order to maintain a healthy friendship relationship.

A second barrier that may hinder the development of interracial friendships is *mistrust* by one or both relational partners (Houston, 1997; Kohatsu et al., 2000). In an effort to further explore the relationship between stereotyping and interracial friendship, communication scholar Marsha Houston (1997) examined these issues in her essay on dialogues between African American women and European American women. Her analysis suggests that although all interracial friendships do not experience stress, the history of race relations has led to a long-standing mistrust and suspicion between racial/ethnic groups. Furthermore, Houston suggests that hesitation or uncertainty about race relations can be largely attributed to mutual negative stereotyping. In this case, both African American and European American women, as well as other racial/ethnic groups and men, have false perceptions of each other that ultimately create barriers to effective, improved interracial communication.

A third barrier we would like to introduce is the issue of *intentionality* versus *emotionality*. A theme underlying many of the behaviors we have discussed and will discuss in this chapter deal with the intended meaning and motivations behind behaviors that can potentially be viewed as racist and harmful. For the purpose of our discussions of race, **intentionality** refers to the degree to which a certain behavior is viewed by an offended party as purposeful in causing hurt or harm. Through confrontation and honest communication, the offender and offended party can identify the offending behavior and discuss (a) whether or not the offender intended to offend and (b) the consequences this behavior had for (un)intended parties. Such dialogue can also be used to identify and recognize the **emotionality** or emotional component of an interracial interaction gone bad. Intentions aside, emotionality refers to the negative emotions or feelings a party experiences as a result of experiencing firsthand, hearing, or observing the behavior she or he deems offensive. As we suggest, relational partners, friends, colleagues, or others must commit themselves to engaging in frank discussions about verbal infractions that can potentially widen the divide between racial groups.

History and Interracial Friendships

Within recent years, there has been an increased interest in how interracial friendships function (Antonio, 2004; Carlson, Wilson, & Hargrave, 2003; Collier, 1996; Jaasma, 2002; Welner, 2006; Wright et al., 1997). Whether they occur in middle school or college, interracial friendships are increasing in number and are a reflection of the changing demographics in our country. Same-race relationships remain a common relational dyad and should serve as a template for interracial dyads. Although relational partners bring their racialized experiences to the relationship, they don't necessarily have to determine the entire course of the relationship. We live in a country where the government played a very active role in shaping race relations and purposely separated its citizens by race, making it illegal for European Americans and African Americans to share many of the basic rights we currently enjoy. This legal segregation of racial groups was a deterrent to any and all interracial interactions that those in power feared would taint the "pure blood" of European Americans. These efforts stem from concerted efforts to preserve a racial hierarchy and maintain an unequal power distribution that placed European Americans at the top of the social structure.

❖ **BOX 7.2**

AUTHOR REFLECTIONS

Friends are an important part of a person's life, and my life is no exception. Over the years, I have relied on my closest friends for encouragement, unconditional support, "tough love," and more uncontrollable laughter than should be allowed by law. These are the individuals who have always "had my back"—especially during tough times (e.g., the deaths of both parents and the challenges of graduate school). My friends have also provided me physical things in times of need; for example, during high school my best friend and her family "adopted" me and gave me a place to live when I moved out of my parents' house. When I reflect on my lifetime friendships, I can't help but appreciate all of the blessings that have come my way. . . . I also recognize how I've benefited from close friends from diverse racial and ethnic backgrounds.

After leading discussions on interracial friendships with students, I am convinced that the presence, or lack, of having a diverse set of friendships is heavily related to the environment in which you were raised. According to Banton's six orders of contact, positive interracial contact is only possible through acculturation and integration. Fortunately for me, being raised in a culturally diverse neighborhood encouraged friendships where any racial differences were transcended through the identification of other similarities (e.g., faith, music, sports, etc.). Students who were raised in environments with little diversity—and reflective of little, or unsubstantial, interracial conflict—were less likely to have friends from other races. Many have found that college presents the perfect opportunity to create friendships beyond current social circles. In my case, college allowed me to get to know people of different socioeconomic levels, and in doing so, eliminate negative stereotypes that I had. Hopefully, our interactions also helped them overcome some stereotypical beliefs. My hope, and prayer, is that you also extend your personal network of friends while in college.

—MPO

Systemic forms of oppression such as colonization, slavery, and racial segregation conveyed a clear message to the United States and the world that a racial social order was in play and would remain that way. The obvious resentment of racial groups, particularly African Americans, precipitated the legal separation of the races with the inception of the Jim Crow laws. These laws mandated that European Americans and other racial groups literally be separated from one another in both public and private spheres. Water fountains, restaurants, bathrooms, and other public facilities were decorated with signs labeled "For Whites Only" and "For Blacks Only," thereby presenting physical markers of the racial lines that divided the country, its people, and the government. Not only were public spaces racially demarcated, but so were interpersonal relationships between racial groups, and if anyone even gave the *appearance* of violating any of the laws or social rules, they were subjected to imprisonment, beatings, and social isolation, and in extreme cases murder and/or lynchings. Although interracial marriages were outlawed, interracial friendships were also frowned upon, thereby discouraging any and all interactions that seemed to blur the color lines and alter the racial hierarchy.

It wasn't until 1954 that the laws separating the racial groups were dismantled. *Brown v. Board of Education* (Sigelman, Bledsoe, & Combs, 1996) was the landmark U.S. Supreme Court case that desegregated all public educational institutions (e.g., elementary schools, high schools, and colleges and universities) throughout the nation. In theory, the playing field was being leveled. Up to this point, children of color, specifically African American students, were prohibited from receiving the same type of schooling as their European American cohorts. Their textbooks, curriculum, and buildings were of lesser quality, which had an adverse affect on the quality of education the students were receiving. By overturning the Jim Crow laws, the U.S. government was attempting to put an end to racial segregation in our education system. This shift in the political and social landscape would offer new educational and economic opportunities for African Americans, with interracial contact a by-product of this newfound "equal opportunity" (Sigelman et al, 1996). It is also important to note that this change also facilitated increased interracial interactions in the public and private spheres (M. Wilson & Russell, 1996), which were most likely discouraged. In this constrained environment, however, those relationships that did emerge were strained, discouraged, and stigmatized.

Case Study: Some of My Best Friends

We have posed a few questions in this chapter that ask you to reflect on the racial composition of your friendships, as we have. Using a similar approach, English professor Emily Bernard posed the same question to her colleagues. In her published book entitled *Some of My Best Friends* (2004), Bernard presents to the reader a collection of essays and writings from a variety of noted writers from diverse racial and ethnic backgrounds. The purpose of their essays is to address the complexities involved in interracial friendships. The racial composition of the relational dyads include Latino and White, Black and Asian, and Black and Jewish, among others, and provide the reader with examples of experiences with race the writers have had in their personal lives. From their individual perspectives, each writer is giving voice to experiences relative to being in a friendship with a person from a different race. What's most interesting about this book is the candid manner in which the writers share the joys, pains, and frustrations that come with allowing themselves to become emotionally vulnerable with someone whose experiences, beliefs, and ways of thinking and doing things are different from their own.

Bernard (2004) was inspired to edit this book because of her fascination with how friendships function. Her racialized experiences most likely informed her own interracial friendships, which she probably assumed were not the result of a phenomenon unique to her. It is quite possible that Bernard's standpoint as an African American woman created experiences that were similar to her other friends from the same racial group. While their experiences in no way are identical, there is a strong likelihood that they share some commonalities. Bernard should be commended for her efforts to explore an unknown territory that many people are too quick to dismiss as insignificant or inconsequential. We are at a time in history where people are under the misconception that racism is a thing of the past. For those who have never had to think about their race, they might not consider it a big deal in general, let alone when it concerns the friendships they choose to establish. This could be a potential problem for them. Their lack of awareness could manifest itself in the relationship as a barrier to true communication and intimacy between the friends. On the other hand, a friend who has had encounters with racism and chooses not to share those distressful experiences with a close friend from a different race is also creating barriers to their relationship. Friendship is supposed to be a safe space where each relational partner can share their most intimate secrets or feel comfortable enough to express him- or herself without fear of judgment or contamination. In an ideal situation, the friends would *really* confide their true feelings in each other as well as their understandings of race issues that are directly or indirectly related to the friendship. When the relational dynamics do not facilitate an adequate amount of intimacy, the partners will experience what Bernard (2004) calls "**friend divorces**." This is the decision made by one or both friends to dissolve the relationship. This may be attributed to issues or stresses plaguing the relationship that are just too difficult to bear.

If you reflect back on your past relationships, you can probably remember a friendship that just didn't work out. For whatever reason, either you or your friend decided it was best to not continue the relationship. Regardless of the whys or hows behind the decision, you probably felt a great deal of pain, hurt, and disappointment. Well, in the case of interracial friendships, the pain can be doubly worse. Not only might the person experience feelings of rejection as a "person," per se, but he or she could very well feel the friend no longer wants to be in the relationship because the friend "just doesn't get it," it's too much work, or the person talks about race way too much. For either person, the decision to end an interracial friendship only perpetuates the cycle of racial separation or segregation in the social sphere of our daily lives. As with any other relationship, the interracial friendship takes just as much work and is equally as rewarding as a same-race friendship, if not more so. The racial differences create experiences for each friend that the other may not fully understand, yet the similarities or common ground shared should be important and strong enough to push the friends to commit themselves to a form of relational intimacy that can only make them better, well-rounded, and culturally sensitive people.

Six Orders of Contact

As you think about your interracial interactions, how have you been socialized to communicate (or not) with other racial/ethnic group members? Has your family or society socialized you to believe that such interactions are healthy and normal, or were you discouraged from having any type of interracial contact at all? Whatever your experience has been, it is our hope that you have become sensitized to how cultural group membership (e.g., dominant culture, U.S. nationality) influences our attitudes toward and beliefs about interracial contact.

Banton (1967) developed six orders of interracial contact to describe how two racial/ethnic groups positively or negatively manage this unique communicative experience. As you will see, four of these orders discourage, and two orders encourage, an appreciation of racial/ethnic difference in varying degrees.

The four orders fostering negative or no interracial contact include peripheral contact, institutionalized contact, pluralism, and assimilation. **Peripheral contact** refers to a minimal amount of contact between racial/ethnic groups that is transient (e.g., in classrooms, grocery shopping, riding the bus). In this framework, limited interracial interaction is expected and maintained by individuals. **Institutionalized contact** refers to contact occurring between independent nations. As we noted in previous chapters, this type of contact is manifested through colonialism (subordination) or paternalism (sharply defined roles and status). More importantly, the dominant group maintains social distance through regulation (e.g., antimiscegenation laws) and repeated demonstrations of power. **Pluralism** occurs when racial/ethnic differences reflect variation in expected behavior and there is minimum social interaction. In general, racial/ethnic groups are coexisting without much effort put into interracial contact, which could potentially be mutually beneficial. The final order that fails to value racial/ethnic difference is **assimilation** or amalgamation. Banton describes this order as an unavoidable consequence resulting from integration via interracial marriage. Others have operationalized assimilation as a people adopting the dominant group's attitudes and beliefs while forsaking those of their primary racial/ethnic group. For the purposes of this text, the latter definition is used to describe the tensions associated with interracial contact.

❖ BOX 7.3

STUDENT REFLECTION

A few years ago I attended a party at the Abby West Apartments. My girlfriend and her roommates had befriended the superintendent, who happens to be a Black male. His name is Martin or "Big Nasty." It was his 30th birthday, and he was throwing a big bash at the pool and having a lot of his friends attend. She had made a huge happy birthday poster/banner with his name on it along with many other fun sayings that were aesthetic to the eye. When we got to the pool, we realized we were the only White people among approximately 60–80 Black people. My friend Rachel took the banner up to Big Nasty and a few other people standing around him to show it off. Immediately she received some comments pertaining to her place at this party and why was she here. Big Nasty overheard these comments and immediately asked those other people to leave. He didn't want anyone making us feel uncomfortable.

So, after they were asked to leave, one of the guys we came with went up to the DJ booth and asked for the microphone. He stood in front of an all-Black crowd and started rapping. He was actually pretty good and the crowd loved him. They were all dancing and after that we were having the best time ever. We all got along and not another word was said about our different cultures. I really respect the way Big Nasty handled the situation and basically stood up for what he believed in and wasn't going to let anyone feel out of place. He also stood up for us by not allowing discrimination to occur and not let those few ruin his party and ruin our good time. He invited us and wanted us to feel welcome. I didn't act in any ways [*sic*] because it wasn't my place and I did feel a little out of place. But I don't think that I would've wanted anything else to happen. I think overall it was a very good experience and it is nice to see that people of different cultures can not only befriend each other but also stick up for one another in a situation that needed to be confronted.

The two orders that foster more positive interracial contact are *acculturation* and *integration* (Banton, 1967). These two processes are more effective in resolving tensions related to interracial contact by valuing difference and accommodating for this difference in one way or another. Acculturation occurs when racial/ethnic group members learn about a culture (dominant group) that is different from the one they are born into (racial/ethnic group). In this case, people learn to live in both worlds while maintaining their racial/ethnic heritage and identity. In the case of integration, however, racial distinctions are given minor consideration and interracial interactions are maximized. More importantly, friendships and social relationships are fostered that provide individuals with choices that allow them to move across racial/ethnic lines. Ideally, both orders of interracial contact would greatly contribute to effective interracial communication. Unfortunately, various barriers prevent this utopian state of race relations from occurring. In order to achieve this complex, yet attainable, goal of positive interracial communication, we must first consider what barriers prevent this process from occurring.

Understanding the Contact Hypothesis

The contact hypothesis, also referred to as the mutual intergroup differentiation model, was developed by Allport (1958) who hypothesized that increased interaction between ingroup and outgroup members will reduce prejudice. This framework was not used to dismantle the Jim Crow laws of years gone by but can be utilized to address the aftereffect of such a dramatic change in society. As N. Miller (2002) notes, the contact hypothesis functions under the assumption held by "social interventionists" (Miller, 2002) that being in the presence of people from other outgroup members will lead to a change in the way they think about racial and ethnic differences. The most natural relationship to emerge from these interactions is friendship, and it is our goal to use this theory to better understand how to foster positive race relations within the context of interracial friendships.

According to Miller (2002), there are four key concepts that inform the contact hypothesis and how we perceive racial differences. The first concept is **salience** and refers to the attention individuals place on their intergroup differences. Individuals are highlighting the racial categories to which they belong, thus increasing the salience of those differences. **Decategorization**, the second concept, is different and refers to "an awareness of individual distinctiveness," which involves a person redirecting his or her interest from a person's outgroup status to more individuating information. In short, the person is "evaluated on [his or her] own merit" (p. 394). This concept suggests that an individual is faced with "counterstereotypical information about the outgroup"; however, it is not guaranteed that the individual's bias is removed. She or he may perceive the person as an anomaly, or an exception to the rule. The third concept, **personalization**, occurs when "(1) one responds to others in terms of their relationship to self (commonalities are found) and (2) one self-discloses positive information they otherwise would not know. Individuating information is processed. Anxiety and discomfort are often times experienced (affective impact)" (Miller, 2002, p. 397). The fourth and final concept is **typicality** and involves a "pleasant interaction among ingroup and outgroup members [that] can be effective in reducing intergroup bias only if the outgroup members typify their group" (p. 398). If individuals adhere to this approach to interracial interactions, they perceive the outgroup members to "fit the stereotype of their book," and if they don't, "they will be perceived as an exception and intergroup attributional bias will remain intact" (Miller, 2002, p. 398).

Regardless of our orientation toward racial identity, we have been socialized to think of racial differences as being a significant way of categorizing people, which ultimately shapes how we interact and communicate with each other. For some, differences are framed as something to be avoided, either out of fear, uncertainty, or resistance. For others, those same differences are perceived as an unavoidable human quality that exists, is "just there," and has no impact on human interaction. The final orientation involves a recognition and appreciation of racial differences that fosters positive interracial communication between an ingroup and outgroup member; while their differences are acknowledged, individuals are able to identify those moments when race does matter and those times when it does not. The latter orientation is obviously the ideal approach we should use in our interracial interactions, but there are those times when interactants reach an impasse. For one reason or another, our different orientations because of our race, gender, class, or sexual identity, among others, cause us to see each other in a different way, which may result in miscommunication.

This theory hypothesizes that these differences that sometimes create barriers in our interracial interactions can be overcome by frequent, regular intergroup (or interpersonal) contact between individuals from differing racial and ethnic groups. Studies designed to test the theory have found that a change in interaction pattern or environment does create opportunities for interracial communication; however, the more salient issue or problem concerns the quality of these interactions. Before we explore the criticisms or pitfalls of this theory, we will first establish a brief overview of its history and evolution and how the contact theory has changed to become an appropriate framework for exploring how these interactions can facilitate positive interracial communication and friendships. In the following paragraphs, we will provide a summary of the general assumptions posed by prominent scholars who have used the contact hypothesis as a theoretical umbrella under which they have posed their own questions about intergroup relations.

T. F. Pettigrew's (1998) approach to intergroup contact has directed attention toward the personal and intimate nature of these and future interactions. This is referred to as the "generalization of benefit" and obviously refers to the overall benefits that result from interracial communication. The three levels of contact are not posed as sequential in nature or dependent on each other to move a person toward optimal communication with racially different others. Rather, they are presented in no specific order and describe three types of contact that demonstrate varying degrees of intimacy or familiarity an ingroup member has with people outside of their racial group. The first level of contact is most likely to happen and involves multiple interactions with one individual in other new contact settings. An example of this is Seneca (African American) who has had very little interaction with Native Americans (also referred to as First Nations People) until she met Linda in her communication theory class. The stereotypes or inaccurate beliefs she had about Native Americans were dispelled as she got to know Linda in class and in other social settings.

The second level of contact differs from the first level in that a person has several interactions with other people who share the same social category as the original person. In this case, Seneca has a variety of personal interactions with Linda as well as other people of Native American ethnicity, thus providing her with several reference points concerning interracial interactions with people from this group. The last and final contact is least likely to happen and involves continued interaction with a variety of people from multiple, other outgroup categories. T. F. Pettigrew (1998) suggests that these occurrences are infrequent because most people do not typically have a multiracial friendship network, thus making this the least likely scenario describing typical interracial interactions and friendships. Nevertheless, in order for a person to seriously understand the nature of their friendship relationships, they must reflect on the interracial interactions they have had and how diverse and numerous they have (or have not) been thus far in their life. Doing so will challenge them to gain introspection concerning the extent to which their own and/or societal perceptions of racial difference and interracial interactions have influenced their friendship selection process.

In a similar vein, M. B. Brewer and Miller (1984) describe these similar contact experiences in the following ways. Category-based responding occurs when an entire outgroup is perceived as being monolithic or "relatively undifferentiated, tightly bounded, and distinct from the ingroup (differentiated)"; the self is seen as prototypical of the ingroup. Prior to her friendship with Linda, Seneca thought that all First Nations People were alike. The **differentiated model** transitions a person from this way of thinking to seeing some distinctions between ingroup and outgroup members. This level of contact presents members as being atypical, thus allowing a person to see variability within the group. The final level of contact is personalized interaction, which can be described as observations and perceptions of similarities between the self and outgroup members and higher levels of dissimilarity between self and ingroup members. This can also be described as decategorized interaction wherein a comparison is made between self and other, thereby facilitating the opportunity for reduced prejudice and stereotyping.

❖ **BOX 7.4**

STUDENT REFLECTION

As we wrap up the semester, I have begun to realize a lot of things about myself. [Through] working on the diversity workshop . . . not only did I learn a lot about numerous countries, I learned a lot about my teammates. After we gave our presentation, we all said that we would go to dinner so that we could all get to know each other a lot better. I was quite surprised about the bonds that I had formed with all of these ladies that it made me do a lot of thinking. What is very surprising to me is that they are all White! Spending so much time with all of my White team members these last couple of weeks has made me see them as people, and not as races. The biggest problem that I had with my White friends in the past was gossip. I used to work with a White girl and through us working together, we became really close friends. She would always compliment me on my hard work and she would be the first to tell me how cute I looked each day. Then one day, my manager tells me that she needs to speak with me. I was nervous but I knew that I hadn't done anything wrong.

My manager tells me that I needed to make sure that I was not accidentally ringing up people's sales as my own sale. . . . It was a nice way of saying, "quit stealing people's sales." I asked her where she got the idea that I was stealing sales from, and to my surprise, she said that one of my coworkers had come to tell her. [It was] the one person in the store that I thought was a good friend of mine. That experience completely changed my views of White people. I have come a long way since that day, and I am very happy that I have let that pain and anger go. When Jessica told me about the situation with her dad, it completely took me back to this particular day. I felt betrayed! Well after you (Dr. Harris) told me what you did about Jessica caring about the friendship, it completely changed my mind about her. . . . I think that I have reopened the door to letting her back in. Jessica is a great friend and I am glad that I met her. She has made me rethink my opinion about some White people!

Yet another articulation of the contact hypothesis is Hewstone and Brown's (1986) **mutual intergroup differentiation model.** Consistent with the theory, they argue that "positive contact w/individual outgroup should result in positive behavior and reactions toward individuals but not the entire group because the person is perceived as being 'atypical'; therefore, interventions must be made at the intergroup not interpersonal level." Consistent with other critical approaches to the theory, Hewstone and Brown highlight the fact that intergroup interactions will not always result in a change in attitudes toward racial/ethnic difference. Instead, the outgroup member is perceived as an "anomaly" or someone who is not representative of their racial group. Because they do not conform to that person's preconceived notions of what it means to be a member of that racial group, interactions with this outgroup member, albeit positive, fail to challenge those preexisting beliefs or assumptions.

The final interpretation or modification of the contact hypothesis is the **common intergroup identity model** (Gaertner & Dovidio, 2000). This model presupposes the following:

> Bias toward outgroup members is reduced by changing a person's perceptions of an inter-group context from one that involves members of different groups to one that involves members of a single common or superordinate group. Former outgroup members are recategorized as ingroup members within a superordinate category that they respectively share with one another. (Gaertner & Dovidio, 2000, p. 394).

As the name of the model suggests, an ingroup member begins to recognize the common ground or similarities they share with the outgroup member. Instead of allowing racial differences to function as barriers to their interactions, the ingroup member, through frequent interracial interactions, is reconceptualizing the way they perceive this person and the racial group. Their racial identity is then foreshadowed by the identities that are common between them.

Consider the following scenario. Neal (European American) was very disturbed by the September 11, 2001, terrorist attacks on the United States (as were/are millions of others). Prior to this moment in history, he had limited knowledge of Middle Eastern culture or the Muslim faith, although he is friends with Saliq from college (they are in the same political science class). After the attacks, his perceptions were informed by the heinous act of a few members of this racial/ethnic group. Neal was very angry and confused and began to have misgivings about Middle Easterners in general. His feelings surfaced when he and Saliq got into a heated debate about politics. Neal "slipped" and made a racial slur against Saliq and his ethnicity, and suffice it to say, Saliq, in turn, became angry and highly offended by his friend's behavior. A few days after the mêlée, Neal shared with his father the incident and how angry he was toward his Middle Eastern friend. Noting this visceral and inappropriate response to a seemingly innocent interaction, Neal's father expressed concern to his son that he obviously had an unhealthy attitude toward an entire racial/ethnic group because of the September 11 attacks and had misdirected his frustrations and unleashed them on his friend, an innocent bystander. Once he got through the denial, Neal finally acknowledged his attitude and realized that his feelings about the terrorist attacks were legitimate; however, he had been in error in choosing his friend as a target for venting those frustrations merely because of his friend's racial/ethnic group membership. Neal made concessions to his friend, asked for forgiveness, and made every attempt to restore their relationship. Fortunately, Saliq and Neal found their way back to the common ground that forged their relationship in the first place: family values, major, political science, and friendship.

Educational Institutions as Sites for Interracial Alliances

Elementary schools, high schools, and, more recently, colleges are sites where interracial friendships (also referred to as interracial alliances) have the opportunity to develop (Collier, 1988; Goldsmith, 2004; Kohatsu et al., 2000; Stearns, 2004). It is during these stages of identity development that individuals are becoming aware of how complex this process of growth is and how critical a role their relationships with others play in facilitating this knowledge and understanding. According to Goldsmith (2004), intergroup relations and racial compositions of high schools (as well as other educational contexts) are two factors that influence "interracial friendliness" and "interracial conflict." It is in these contexts that individuals have an increased likelihood of interacting with racially different others. Considering the conclusion for U.S. Census 2000 data predicting a significant shift in our racial landscape in the very near future (by the year 2050; Bergman, 2004), it is imperative that we use the findings from such studies as guidelines or signposts for equipping ourselves and future generations for positive race relations in these educational contexts as well as other social settings.

In their study of interracial contact among Asian Americans, Kohatsu et al. (2000) found that despite the fact that the student participants were members of a culturally diverse environment, there were still societal boundaries that dictate how racial groups should (or should not) interact with each other. They specifically found that Asian American and African American students at this particular school had "low to moderate levels of intergroup contact" (p. 339), which is very problematic. The findings are surprising, yet demonstrate that social boundaries regarding interracial communication exist. More specifically, the results reveal that these "restrictions" on interactions between these two racial groups can potentially have "an adverse effect on meaningful racial contact" (Kohatsu et al., 2000). Though not addressed in their study, there is the possibility that the Asian American and African American students were socialized by their respective interpersonal networks, society, and the media to perceive each other as so dissimilar that their outgroup member status is foregrounded as a deterrent to interactions between them. Ideally, being in close proxemics to one another in such a natural, real-world setting should facilitate a plethora of opportunities for interracial communication; however, as this study suggests, being *physically* close to racially different others doesn't necessarily decrease or reduce the *social* or *psychological distance* that exists.

Within the last 10 years, racial diversity in educational institutions has become a growing area of interest for lawmakers, educators, social scientists, and communities with a vested interest in the education of our current future generations (Stearns, 2004; Welner, 2006). Whether the strategy is to make race-conscious student assignments to school districts (Welner, 2006) or to create opportunities for increased intergroup interactions (Carlson et al., 2003), providing students from all racial groups with equal educational opportunities is the primary concern of most schools and invested parties. According to Welner (2006), "this is also an effort to 'avoid a segregated educational environment,'" which should result in "reduced negative racial stereotypes among young children of all racial and ethnic backgrounds" (p. 352). After thorough research on race–school assignments for K–12 in the United States, Welner discovered several benefits that come with a racially diverse school. If they are open to them, students who are enrolled in such schools receive the following benefits:

1. Development of interracial friendships

2. Greater civic engagement

3. Greater likelihood of residing in integrated neighborhoods and of maintaining regular interracial contacts

4. Increased likelihood of working in an integrated environment and of having positive experiences in the integrated workplace

5. More positive intergroup attitudes in general

6. The potential for a "critical mass" enabling students to learn racial tolerance by building cross-racial relationships

As the list suggests, being in a school environment that is full of racially and ethnically diverse students creates an environment full of learning possibilities that are not restricted to classroom instruction. Interactions with students, faculty, and administrators with outgroup membership status have the potential to be enriched. Through these interpersonal encounters, members of this institutional environment may even begin to rethink their biases and prejudices regarding racial difference, which might spill over into other areas of their lives.

This is what Welner (2006) refers to as societal benefits, which have the potential to reduce segregation and to break the cycle of racial segregation, whether it is imposed legally or socially. Welner further describes this as a "lifelong and even intergenerational, self-perpetuating process of segregation that institutionalizes inequality" (p. 352). In other words, we as a society must be more proactive in our efforts to remove most, if not all, semblances, of racial segregation from our institutions. One form of separation by race is what Tatum (1997) identifies as self-segregation, which typically occurs when students of color are in the minority in a given social context (e.g., school). Because of their experiences with being one of a few (if any) students of color at their school, they will oftentimes seek each other out as a form of social support not offered by their interactions and/or relationships with students of the majority group. So, sitting at a cafeteria table or being involved in student organizations targeted to their own racial/ethnic group is a form of retreat from the larger institution and the isolation they experience because of their marginalized status. Some may argue that self-segregation is a form of racism; however, we must consider the fact that this a phenomenon that occurs when certain individuals are numerically in the minority, have daily experiences that remind them of their racial identity, and rarely have people of the dominant group demonstrate interest in them as individuals beyond the color of their skin. Thus, it stands to reason that students of color seek solace, comfort, and intimacy with each other, thereby allowing their racial affiliations to serve as a respite from their daily lives.

Intraracial or same-race relationships are, in general, healthy and good for a person's psyche; however, having a relationship with outgroup members is also equally beneficial. In fact, as Carlson et al. (2003) suggest, these interracial friendships can occur in racially diverse contexts, but the racial composition of the student body is the one ingredient that can really determine if these relationships will take place at all. They are essentially positing that the more diverse an environment (possibly with equal numbers of people from each racial/ethnic group), the increased likelihood of interracial contact and, ultimately, interracial relationships. Carlson et al. (2003) found this to be true in their study of Hispanic students and intergroup relations. They learned that although cross-race or interracial friendships "were a significant predictor of other-group orientation, this variable contributed little variance compared with both school racial composition and perceived comfort of close friends with cross-race social interaction" (p. 215). Hispanic girls were noted has having a significantly high number of interracial friendships, were very comfortable with interracial interactions, and scored high on scales measuring other-group orientation.

We learn from this study that Hispanic female students felt comfortable enough in their multiracial or multiethnic respective schools to communicate and have relationships with students from other racial/ethnic backgrounds, specifically European American and African American students. Jaasma's (2002) research on "interethnic encounters" yielded very helpful data that can aid in our understanding of actual communication behaviors individuals use to negotiate and manage their interracial friendships. Analysis of 906 interviews with sixth graders revealed a total of 19 responses to interethnic relationships. Students were asked to describe a positive and a negative experience with interethnic (interracial) friendship.

The eight categories of **positive responses** included the following: (1) Becoming Friends—friends perceived their ethnic differences as positive qualities; (2) Shared Activities—friends play and talk together; (3) Going Places—friends participate together in an activity that takes place in a specific location (e.g., skating at the skating rink); (4) Sharing Culture—friends exchange knowledge about each other's ethnicity (or culture) (e.g., "learning each other's language, sharing ethnic food, and learning about religions and holidays" [p. 161]); (5) Cooperating—"getting along with each other, helping each other, especially with school work" (p. 161); (6) Sticking Up For—coming to a friend's defense by protecting him or her or intervening when people verbally (or physically) attack the friend; (7) Romancing—developing an interest in or an actual romantic relationship with a racially/ethnically different friend of the opposite sex; and (8) Nothing Happened—a positive interethnic or interracial experience did not happen.

The positive responses to their friendships demonstrate a concerted effort on the part of both friends to ensure that the relationship is mutually beneficial. These responses involve the friends engaging in regular communication with one another and exchanging ideas, thoughts, and experiences, as well as defending their friend (and quite possibly the relationship) from those external to the relationship itself. They even report actual activities that facilitate their interaction, which also serve to create opportunities for increased relational intimacy and connection. In contrast, the students also reported a variety of strategies they have used to respond to the negative interracial friendship experiences that stood out for one reason or another. These 11 categories of **negative responses** are as follows: (1) Because I'm Different—being excluded from play because of their ethnicity; (2) Can't Understand—the friend's inability to understand language differences; (3) Fighting—the use of physical aggression in response to "differences or slurs, problems with playing, dislike for each other, and disagreements in what was said" (p. 157); (4) Verbal Aggression—an argument or verbal attack triggered by the friends' ethnic differences; and (5) Indirect Aggression—passive/aggressive strategies to alienate. The remaining six responses occurred in the presence of a third person from a different ethnic background: (6) Getting Mad; (7) Stealing; (8) Embarrassing Events—the friend created an event that purposely caused her or him to be embarrassed; (9) Getting in Trouble—found themselves in a troublesome situation with a student from another ethnicity; (10) Loss—an existing friendship or the opportunity for another friendship relationship was lost; and (11) Nothing Bad.

The fact that there were more negative than positive responses should not be inferred or interpreted to mean that interracial friendships are doomed from the outset. Instead, these findings and responses should highlight for us how important it is for friends to, first, have a high level of commitment to the relationship. Regardless of their racial identity, friends who are pretty compatible, trust each other, and enjoy each other's company should figure out a way to deal with the difficulties that come with establishing a close and intimate relationship. Second, they should not let their racial or ethnic differences become a barrier or stumbling block to the friendship. While it is important for each friend to demonstrate sensitivity within the relationship, they should be sure that the stressors associated with having membership in a certain racial group or having little to no awareness of their own racial identity do not prevent the relationship from being maintained. Instead, the friends should commit themselves to engaging in open and honest discussions about these problems, which should reduce the frequency of miscommunications or arguments that are a barrier. This can be alleviated by each friend maintaining intraracial friendship, a third important point for friends to be aware of. As Diggs time and Clark (2002) note, these intraracial relationships can serve as a buffer to the interracial friendship. Having relationships with others from one's racial/ethnic group can function to validate one's racialized experiences (affirmation) and reduce stress caused by racism, prejudice, or discrimination, all of which relieve pressure and frustration that emerge from the friend from another race or ethnicity who honestly cannot empathize with their friend.

Just as a friend of color will experience a myriad of emotions because of societal oppression (e.g., racism, discrimination, and prejudice), the friend from the dominant group will experience feelings of frustration because of an inability to relate to his or her friend's standpoint. The friend may be experiencing racial awareness for the first time and is finding it difficult to conceptualize how and why a person is discriminated against or has negative feelings toward a certain racial group. The friend of color may have legitimate reasons for having those feelings; however, the friend from the outgroup can try to be supportive (e.g., letting the friend vent) and nonjudgmental as the friend tries to process her or his encounters with racism. Interracial friends will undoubtedly experience problems and stress that are independent of race, and it will be very important for them to recognize this reality. Doing so will make it possible for them to identify when those racial moments do occur and how to best help each other resolve them without creating undue stress or pressure on the friendship. Creating such a supportive climate will also help the friends deal with conflict between them that does deal with race. If one of them makes a racially insensitive comment or appears to minimize the salience of a racial moment, it is imperative that they each have the communication skills and knowledge necessary to resolve the conflict while preserving the relationship.

Effective Communication Strategies

As we have already discussed, there are a plethora of benefits to having a friendship with a person who belongs to a racial/ethnic group different from our own. While we are not advocating the initiation, development, and maintenance of an interracial friendship for the sole reason of becoming more racially aware, we encourage you to remove the blinders that have served as barriers to being friends with someone outside of your race. There is no handbook; we hope we have challenged you to self-reflect and broaden your horizons when it comes to issues of difference. So, you can begin by asking yourself why you may or may not have a racially diverse friendship network. If you do, that's great! If not, then you might want to begin to think seriously about (1) to what degree your own attitudes toward race and ethnicity are shaping your beliefs about interracial friendships, (2) if and how they have influenced your opportunities to have friendships with people from different races, and (3) whether you have had the opportunity to have such relationships. In either case, it is our hope that we have at least planted a seed for thought concerning racial difference. We challenge you to consider the following suggestions for breaking down the barriers that might be preventing you from having the most rewarding relationships of your life!

In their essay on interracial friendship, Houston and Wood (1996) offer ideas that might help us to initiate, develop, and maintain relationships with people who are different from us racially. First and foremost, we must come to the realization that we may not completely understand the other person. Because people often have different meanings for the "same" behaviors (Houston & Wood, 1996), we should assume our definitions for terms are going to be the same. Instead, we should perceive these communicative exchanges as opportunities to learn about communication styles that are unique to diverse racial/ethnic groups.

Another guideline for effective interracial communication is to avoid imposing our standards on other racial/ethnic groups. Houston and Wood (1996) use the media as an example of how individuals use their cultural standards to determine the value of other social groups. In the United States, we are socialized to perceive European behaviors and attitudes as the norm; therefore, when we encounter individuals from racial/ethnic and cultural groups, we impose these standards on them. For example, Lozano's (1997) research on cultural uses of space and body reveals that in the United States, people are socialized to maintain a great deal of physical space when they are in public settings. However, for Latino/a Americans, particularly in Miami, Florida, space use has "transformed cultural practices." In other words, a cultural style of body expressivity is used that may not adhere to U.S. expectations of behavioral norms.

We should also have a commitment to "respect[ing] how others interpret experience" (Houston & Wood, 1996, p. 54). If a Korean American friend comes to you and shares that he has experienced racism in one of his classes, do not invalidate his experience. Your friendship will be enhanced if you empathize with him and understand this dimension of his (racial/ethnic) identity. Additionally, we should provide support and engage in active listening that communicates respect and acknowledgment. Houston and Wood (1996) believe that friends from different races and classes should avoid silencing or denying the other's experiences from their standpoints (see Chapter 5). They also suggest that we acknowledge but not totalize our differences.

Although acknowledging differences can be productive, we shouldn't overemphasize them. A Latina woman is of a different race than an African American woman, but each of them is more than just her race. . . . To avoid ignoring or totalizing differences, we can recognize and learn from ethnic and class diversity that is part—but only part—of who we are. (Houston & Wood, 1996, pp. 53, 54)

Conclusion

The history of race relations in the United States was born from a system where racial differences have been foregrounded as incredibly problematic. Systemic forms of oppression such as desegregation in education, residential areas, and the workplace, among others, were introduced and designed to separate racial groups and perpetuate a racial hierarchy that has permeated our interpersonal relationships. It wasn't until *Brown v. Board of Education* that racism was struck a serious blow. The legal barriers designed to preserve racial purity (see Chapter 8) were dismantled and created opportunities for people to examine their attitudes toward and beliefs about racism and racial differences. Interactions between European Americans and African Americans were strained, hostile, and tense, which made it incredibly difficult for the playing field to be leveled. At the very least, the possibility of effective race relations was seen as a virtual impossibility.

Our public and private spaces as such as public schools, colleges and universities, the workplace, and residential neighborhoods are becoming increasingly diverse, racially, ethnically, and culturally. This diversity is undoubtedly creating circumstances and situations where people from these different ingroups and outgroups will be interacting and communicating with each other to achieve a common goal. Whether they are in a class together, are working on the same ad team, or are next door neighbors, it is imperative that each person have the knowledge and interpersonal skills necessary if effective interracial communication is to occur. As Korgen, Mahon, and Wang (2003) note, universities that have been successful in diversifying their student bodies must also be equipped to aid those students in adjusting to the change in the racial landscape of the institution.

One approach has been to require that students take at least one multicultural course in partial fulfillment of graduation requirements. Enrolling in such a class is believed to increase student racial awareness and sensitivity to racial and ethnic differences. While such efforts are essential and imperative, it is our interpersonal interactions and relationships that can really serve as a context for achieving the goal of improving race relations (Antonio, 2004). Through the informal and natural evolution of an interracial friendship, we are able to gain a better understanding of not only racial/ethnic groups different from our own, but how we as individuals think about race, not to mention how we communicate and develop relationships with others. It is not until we examine ourselves and our relationships that we will begin to bridge the racial divide that continues to plague our interpersonal networks and society at large.

❖

TIP: THEORY INTO PRACTICE

There is no handbook to offer guidelines or rules on how to navigate through an interracial relationship; therefore, we present the following tips as a starting point. Regardless of your racial standpoint, each person in an interracial friendship must choose to work toward healthy communication with one another.

- If you do not have any interracial friendships, reflect on the reasons you believe this to be so. If given the opportunity, would you have a friendship with a person from another race? Why or why not?
- If you do have at least one or more interracial friendships, how you would say they compare to your same-race friendships? Are there many differences between them?
- Think about the various topics or issues you can talk about with your friends. Is there anything discussed in one relational friendship dyad that may or may not be discussed in the other? Why or why not? Reflect on whether your racial differences or experiences are contributing to this.
- Be willing to communicate openly about the topic of race and your racial differences within the relationship.
- Challenge yourself to leave your comfort zone and develop an interracial friendship.
- Are you and your friend from a different racial/ethnic group able to self-disclose freely? What barriers, if any, are preventing this communication from occurring? If you can speak openly, then describe how the two of you have created a supportive climate in which to do so.
- Do not use (exploit) interracial friendships for the sole purpose of understanding racial/ethnic differences. Your actions will be perceived as insincere and offensive.
- Be willing to be educated and to educate each other about racial difference when opportunities for learning present themselves.
- Determine an effective way to maintain *racial equilibrium* in the relationship, where you are able to discuss issues of race but purpose not to allow them to overburden the relationship.
- Do not assume that you or your friend will be a spokesperson for your racial/ethnic group.
- Be sensitive to the validity and reality of a friend's experiences with racism and prejudice.
- Engage in honest communication if, and when, racial differences become problematic. Choose to benefit from this conflict/learning opportunity.

OPPORTUNITIES FOR EXTENDED LEARNING   ❖

1. Do an Internet search of the phrase "interracial friendship." As you view several sites, compare and contrast how nonacademic/nonscientific Web sites and social networking sites are devoted to understanding how these relationships function. Then, view articles from another search on the keywords *contact hypothesis*. From the articles, determine what factors are suggested as promoting relational intimacy. Make a list of similarities and differences these relationships have in comparison to intraracial friendships.

What topics and relational issues may be discussed or avoided? Consider how this might compare to intraracial friendships.

2. Generate a list of your best/closest friends. List descriptors (e.g., honest, funny, caring) for each friend that best describes the qualities you most appreciate about them and your friendship. In examining your list, consider whether or not those relationships are racially/ethnically diverse. Explore what role family, friends, and society might play in socializing you about the relationship selection process. This activity provides you with the opportunity to be self-reflective of your friendship experiences and to further understand what qualities constitute "true friendship."

3. In groups of five, have the students create a template for identifying barriers they believe exist and prevent interracial friendships from occurring. The discussion should involve any racist behaviors. Using the racial tirades as an example, the student groups should provide exemplars of behaviors that have racial (blatant) overtones and (subtle) undertones. Please refer to the concepts intentionality versus emotionality in Chapter 7. The list should include familiar and unfamiliar phrases or terms that serve as verbal markers of such behavior.

4. Think about how friendships and race are portrayed in the media. For example, the movie industry has produced a series of interracial buddy films, *Rush Hour* (1 and 2) and *Lethal Weapon* (1–4), starring men of color. In small groups, compare and contrast how the media represent the communication styles, content issues (e.g., being masculine and/or racialized in law enforcement), styles of humor, and identity issues relative to the racial/ethnic audience members targeted. Considering gender, generate a list of comparable movies depicting interracial friendships involving women from differing racial groups and how their relationship, communication styles, and racial identities are portrayed.

5. In class and in small groups of five people, create an Action Plan for the development of interracial friendships. This Action Plan is a list of guidelines an individual can follow or use to be proactive in bringing about change in "the real world." Develop a list of realistic goals or strategies a person can use to diversify his or her interpersonal network.

6. Assemble a group of friends who are interested in being part of a book club. (The book club could be long term.) Hopefully book club members will be from diverse races and ethnicities. Read the book "*Some of My Best Friends: Writings on Interracial Friendship*" by Emily Bernard (2004) and plan a series of meetings to discuss the book. At each meeting, plan to have open and honest dialogue about the book's content, its influence on your thinking about interracial and same-race friendships, and similar and different barriers these two kinds of relationships face.

Interracial Romantic Relationships

As we have discussed in earlier chapters, race relations in the United States are grounded in a history of colonization by Europeans, which was the foundation for racial and gender oppression of racial/ethnic groups because they were perceived as intellectually and physically inferior. This inhumane way of thinking served the primary function of preserving a racial hierarchy that currently remains a part of our moral fabric as a nation. Although racist behaviors as well as oppressive ideologies that perpetuate the vicious cycle of racism, prejudice, and stereotyping have begun to take on more subtle forms, it is not until something unexpected happens or we have a "crash moment" (like the ones in the movie *Crash*) that our attention is directed toward race, prejudice, and discrimination.

As we continue our journey toward racial healing, we must remind ourselves of the origin of racism (see Chapters 1 and 2), which we have already done. Chapters 7 through 12 challenge each one of us, regardless of our racial and gender identities, to become more self-reflective about our thoughts on racial difference and how those ideals inform our perceptions of each other and subsequently affect our interracial interactions. In Chapter 7, we took a more general approach and discussed how interracial friendships are established and identified specific barriers that some suggest cause these relationships to dissolve or never even develop. In this chapter, we undertake the task of exploring the unique nature of interracial romantic relationships. We explore the causes, patterns, and trends of interracial marriage in the United States (Docan, 2003; Dovidio, Kawakami, & Gaertner, 2002; Lehmiller & Agnew, 2006; Root, 2002), and debunk myths typically associated with interracial romantic relationships (IRRs) and the individuals who become involved in them. We hope to offer insight into how history, socialization through interpersonal networks (e.g., family, friends), and societal expectations or norms concerning interpersonal communication shape some of our most intimate relationships that cross the proverbial color line.

Current Trends in Interracial Romantic Relationships

Whether it is shared racial group membership, gender, education, status, or personal interests, our interpersonal networks are typically developed among people with whom we have a lot in common (S. M. Lee & Edmonston, 2005). As such, when we consider different types of interracial relationships, societal norms seem to change and perpetuate a racial hierarchy that deems a person less valuable the more different from us they are perceived to be. However, according to Wellner (2005), attitudes toward interracial dating are becoming more liberal, which he attributes to the increasing racial diversity in our nation. The increasing likelihood of IRRs may be challenging to some people because it forces them to face and then disregard the liberal ideologies they purport to espouse when someone close becomes romantically involved with a person of a different race.

According to data from the Population Reference Bureau (Wellner, 2005), the patterns of IRRs will assuredly increase as the racial and ethnic diversity of the U.S. population continues to rise, which may be due to increased interracial interactions in the workplace, neighborhoods, and universities. U.S. Census data state that there are, in fact, an increased number of interracial romantic relationships (Lee & Edmonston, 2005; Lobe, 2005). Interracial romantic relationships grew from 1% to more than 5% in 2000 (of 57 million couples). In short, there were 300,000 interracial couples in 1970, and within a 30-year span, the numbers grew to 3 million. Lobe (2005) suggests that

> that trend, which shows no sign of slacking, suggests that the United States is shifting increasingly from a salad bowl—where racial groups maintain their separate identities and resist marrying outside their groups—to an updated "melting pot" where they are far more open to relations, including marriage, with people of a difference race. And interracial marriage means more bi- or even multiracial children. (p. 32)

The racial compositions of these interracial marriages have also experienced change. Historically, interracial unions have been primarily between Whites and non-Whites, which remains a constant in current trends in interracial marriage (Lobe, 2005). The data reveal the following patterns (Lobe, 2005): (1) The lowest intermarriage rates occur between Whites and Blacks, and the highest rates occur among American Indians, Hawaiians, and multiple-race people; (2) Black women are less likely to marry interracially than are Black men, Asian women are more likely to do so than Asian men, and men and women representing other racial groups "are equally likely to intermarry" (Lobe, 2005, p. 32); (3) "younger and better-educated people in the U.S. are more likely to intermarry than older and less-educated citizens"; and (4) Asians and Hispanics born in the United States and Whites and Blacks who reside in the United States but were born in foreign countries are more likely to marry interracially than Asians born in foreign countries and Whites and Blacks born in the United States.

In order to understand this phenomenon, we have consulted Lee and Edmonston's (2005) exhaustive analysis of the Public Use Microdata Sample (PUMS) files from the 1970, 1980, 1990, and 2000 censuses. Data reveal that interracial marriages are on the rise but remain the exception and not the norm. They are the exception because individuals are socialized to adhere to social norms that govern marriage, which Lee and

Edmonston (2005) note "play critical roles in preserving the racial or ethnic status quo in racially or ethnically stratified societies" (p. 4). By choosing not to cross racial boundaries in their personal lives, people are maintaining racial boundaries.

It can be inferred from the data that there has been an attitude change in society toward racial differences, which must take place as romantic relationships across racial boundaries become more commonplace. In fact, a 2003 Gallup Poll revealed that 86% of Blacks, 79% of Hispanics, and 66% of Whites reported they would be accepting of a child or grandchild that chose to marry interracially. It was also learned that 77% of Whites had no objections to Blacks and Whites dating, "which is a marked decrease from a 1990 poll where two out of every three whites said they would oppose any relative marrying a Black person" (Lobe, 2005, p. 32).

According to S. M. Lee and Edmonston (2005), immigration has played a critical role in the rising rate of intermarriages, and as Table 8.1 indicates, Native Americans (they use the term American Indians), Hawaiians, and Asian Americans have a propensity to marry interracially more frequently than do African Americans, "suggesting that social norms against white–black marriages were much stronger than marriages among other groups" (p. 11). Their analysis also reveals that intermarriage is more likely to occur among smaller populations, hence the larger a demographic, the decreased possibility that its members will marry outside of the group. This supports previous research indicating that homogamous relationships occur at a higher rate than heterogamous relationships. If you are in close proxemics to people who are similar to you, then chances are the possibility of meeting and marrying someone of your same racial group is greater.

The History of Interracial Romantic Relationships

Despite current census data that interracial marriages are increasing in number, this was not always the case in our country. Laws were created for the sole purpose of preventing marriages from occurring between Whites and non-Whites. Though interracial marriages between people from different races/ethnicities (miscegenation) were indeed occurring, legislation made it illegal for intermarriages to take place for Whites who wanted to marry outside of their race. For example, Arizona, California, Idaho, Mississippi, Missouri, Utah, and Wyoming (Spickard, 1989) adopted **antimiscegenation laws** forbidding marriages between European Americans and Mongolians; other states outlawed European Americans from marrying American Indians (Georgia, Louisiana, North Carolina), Chinese (Montana, Nevada, Oregon), Japanese (Montana, Nevada), Croatians (North Carolina), Indians, and Malayans (Nevada, South Dakota, and Wyoming) (Spickard, 1989).

In order to maintain physical distinctions between racial/ethnic groups, European Americans imposed slavery, internment camps, and, more recently, Jim Crow laws to separate the races in public (e.g., restaurants, rest rooms, and schools) and private contexts. This unfounded fear of racial blending came from the belief that the "influx of swarthy 'new' immigrants might breach their region's color line, producing untold horrors" (T. F. Pettigrew, Fredrickson, Knobel, Glazer, & Ueda, 1982, p. 79). Although all "race mixing" was perceived as a threat, intermixing between African Americans

❖ **Table 8.1** U.S. Interracial Marriage Rates by Race and Gender, 1970–2000 (Number of marriages per one million people)

Race	1970			1980			1990			2000		
	Total	Men	Women	Total	Men	Women	Total	Men	Women	Total	Men	Women
White	0.4	0.4	0.3	1.0	1.1	1.0	1.5	1.6	1.4	2.7	2.9	2.6
Black	1.1	1.5	0.8	2.4	3.6	1.2	4.1	5.8	2.3	7.0	9.7	4.1
American Indian	37.6	35.9	39.1	53.1	52.7	53.6	59.7	58.7	60.6	56.7	55.7	57.6
Asian	19.9	14.2	24.9	21.1	13.1	27.7	17.7	10.8	23.7	16.0	9.5	21.6
Hawaiian	50.1	45.6	53.8	58.0	56.0	59.8	50.7	50.1	51.4	45.6	45.5	45.8
Other race	—	—	—	15.8	16.6	14.9	15.7	16.5	14.9	17.7	17.1	1.2
Multiple race	—	—	—	—	—	—	—	—	—	56.0	55.4	56.6

NOTE: Dashes indicate no information available. From "New Marriages, New Families: U.S. Racial and Hispanic Intermarriage," by S. M. Lee & B. Edmonston, 2005, *Population Bulletin, 60*(2), p. 12, Washington, DC: The Population Reference Bureau. Used with permission.

and European Americans was the most disturbing type of union (Yancey, 2002). Foeman and Nance (1999) attribute this reaction to the fact that these two groups "represent what many identify as opposites along the race continuum" (p. 540). Therefore, the closer your skin color was to European American skin, the less threatening interracial marriage would be. In any event, commitment to maintaining racial purity fueled the opposition to race mixing in general.

Until 1910, interethnic marriages among European Americans were more common than interracial marriages because of antimiscegenation laws (Davidson & Schneider, 1992; Pagnini & Morgan, 1990). Although interethnic marriages are still commonplace, it is the rise in interracial marriages that many have difficulty accepting. Prior to the *Loving v. Virginia Supreme Court* case, there were violent consequences for interracial married couples. Irrespective of race, spouses, children, family members, and friends were beaten, murdered, or run out of town because of their relationships. These brutalities sent a clear message to the world that dire consequences awaited those who chose to be "race traitors" and marry interracially. Thirty-nine years have passed; however, interracial romantic relationships continue to be stereotyped as taboo. All too often, people either wonder to themselves or ask the couple why they chose to enter that kind of relationship, which I am certain they would not ask of a same-race relationship. Therefore, we must purpose to change our thinking and correct ourselves and others if we even question why a couple has chosen to be in an IRR.

In the 1967 landmark case of *Loving v. Virginia Supreme Court*, the tide was turned against antimiscegenation (Davidson & Schneider, 1992; Ely, 1998; Myra, 1994; M. B. Tucker & Mitchell-Kernan, 1995; "Woman Who Changed Laws," 1992). In 1958, Virginia residents Richard (European American) and Mildred (African American) Loving decided to marry legally in Washington, DC, because their home state actively practiced the 1924 antimiscegenation laws. After residing in Virginia for a year, the Lovings were arrested and prosecuted in 1959 and sentenced to a one-year prison sentence for violating state antimiscegenation laws. The Virginia sheriff forced the couple from their home because of their "ungodly relationship" ("Woman Who Changed Laws," 1992). A suspended sentence required them to not return to the state for 25 years. Four years later, the Lovings retained an American Civil Liberties Union lawyer ("Why Interracial Marriages Are Increasing," 1996) to fight the unconstitutionality of their extradition from Virginia. In June 1967, the Lovings won a legal victory that would change the state of marital law in the United States forever. The Supreme Court ruled unanimously to remove antimiscegenation laws. This legal action forced Virginia and 15 other states to eradicate their laws as well, making interracial/interethnic marriages legal.

Recent research has shown that, unlike friendships, IRRs continue to experience a significant amount of scrutiny that potentially affects whether or not the relationship will ever be maintained. It is quite possible that cross-sex, interracial friendships perceived as potentially evolving into IRRs might experience the same kind of pressure. External pressure might be exerted onto the couple by family, friends, and strangers to avoid involvement in a historically taboo relationship (T. M. Harris & Kalbfleisch, 2000; Kalmijn, 1998), which ultimately hinders the development of a romantic relationship. In the end, people may be forced to choose between their families and relational partners because of racism. While this may not be the case for all IRRs, it is a fact that our interpersonal networks play a critical role in the important decisions we make in our lives. When it comes to IRRs, however, these relationships seem to have a significant impact on whether a person chooses to become romantically involved with a person of a different race.

Mental Models of Interracial Romantic Relationships

Even though the racial lines in society are not as clearly demarcated as they used to be with signs that read "For Whites Only," there are still social norms that tell us the races *just shouldn't mix,* especially when it comes to romantic relationships. As was demonstrated in the previous section, laws were enacted to prevent interracial unions from occurring but were later abolished because people's attitudes toward them were changing (or at least we can hope that was the case). Despite this change in legislation, interracial couples were ostracized, taunted, alienated, and in some extreme cases disowned by family members, friends, and society because they chose to cross the color line when it came to matters of the heart. It cannot be assumed, however, that all interracial couples have been mistreated by their families. In fact, there are probably stories that have not yet been told of supportive interpersonal networks (e.g., family) that created a safe place where an IRR could flourish and grow like a same-race relationship. Nevertheless, we must first understand what mental models are being used to frame IRRs. Such understanding will assist us in re-thinking romantic relationships that occur between racially different people.

❖ **BOX 8.1**

PERSONAL REFLECTION

During a class session several years ago, a European American female shared how her family was putting pressure on her to end the relationship with her then-boyfriend, who happened to be African American. Her family was convinced the relationship was not good for her, fearing she'd "end up just like Nicole Simpson." A few weeks later the student stopped coming to class and I never saw her again. She called the following semester to apologize for not staying in the class. Because she continued to date the African American guy, her father refused to pay her summer tuition, even though he told her it had been taken care of. Her father had been lying to her, and she didn't find out until the bursar's office notified her that her class schedule was dropped.

Years later a European American female graduate student shared with the class that her mother knew a young European American female whose mother drafted a contract stating that if her daughter promised to altogether stop dating African American men (forever), she and her father would renovate her new home, "free of charge." Suffice it to say, the woman refused to sign the contract and has further distanced herself from her parents.

(continued)

(continued)

> I'd like to think that these incidents are isolated, but it's very likely that such thinking would be faulty. Sadly, stories like these give life to the research (Harris & Kalbfleisch, 2000) showing that there is extreme pressure placed on people by social forces (Kalmijn, 1998) to not date or marry interracially. What I question is, is there *really* no cost or charge when we conform to societal or familial expectations concerning issues of race and dating or marriage? Are people willing to cut off family relationships or friendships because of personal biases and prejudices? The answer appears to be a glaring "yes."
>
> —TMH

Let's play a word association game. When you hear "interracial dating," what's the first word that comes to mind? You may have heard the phrase "jungle fever," which is a term commonly associated with IRRs. The term originated with Spike Lee's film *Jungle Fever* (1991) and provides a visual representation of the tensions imposed on romantic relationships between people from two different races and cultures, with the issue of extramarital relations aside (Foeman & Nance, 2002; Paulin, 1997). While the term may appear innocent in nature, it has very negative connotations, which may be a reflection of societal attitudes toward IRRs, particularly between African Americans and European Americans. According to Paulin (1997), the title and film

> [reiterate] dominant representations of interracial relationships [as evidenced by] . . . the underlying discourse of contamination implied by the clichéd title. However, the title is never deconstructed, and, thus, *Jungle Fever* effectively reinscribes the notion that interracial love is the result of irrational, racialized, heated passion—which manifests itself in a sickness—confirming the dominant belief that interracial sexual relations are wrong or immoral. (p. 168)

Similarly, Yancey (2003) posits that jungle fever is a stereotype suggesting that individuals who enter interracial relationships do so out of a desire to experience sex with someone of a different race, hence ignoring any possibility of an emotional, intimate connection.

Although no research exists measuring if it either shaped or reflected societal attitudes toward IRRs, there is the possibility that *Jungle Fever* did in fact capture the tensions associated with IRRs between African Americans and European Americans. The only qualitative study that explores societal attitudes toward this particular relationship was conducted by Childs (2005) who wanted to deconstruct the "myth of the angry Black woman." There is this myth that African American women are resentful of European American women who are dating and/or married to African American women. Through in-depth interviews with African American women, Childs (2005) learned that these relationships represent a form of rejection. In light of the shortage of marriageable African American men due to incarceration, drug abuse, and homicide, African American women interpret these relational choices by African American men as a rejection of their racialized and gendered bodies, thus leaving them doubtful of ever being in a loving, committed, romantic relationship.

Our mental models of IRRs as they currently stand are problematic. These mental models are created and shaped by legislation and personal biases imposed on individual choices in the mate selection process. It is our hope that by reflecting on the role our society and interpersonal networks play in shaping our attitudes, we can create new mental models of what our understanding of IRRs should be.

Theories on Interracial Romantic Relationships

Acknowledging the racially exclusive nature of most theories about romantic relationships (Heaton & Albrecht, 1996; Kalmijn, 1993; Schoen & Wooldredge, 1989; Van den Berghe, 1960), social scientists have introduced three theories or concepts to explain why some IRRs do or do not exist. Despite limited research in general about these so-called taboo relationships, the following theories provide a solid, more inclusive foundation for understanding interracial relationships. Instead of being presented as deviant relationships that violate society's relational norms, the theories present these unions as natural relationships that evolve for various reasons. Note that the motivating factors vary from person to person and, in general, are not a means for exoticizing the other racial/ethnic group. Conversely, the relationship is the result of mutual attraction, increased interracial interactions, and geographic location, among other factors.

Structural Theory

Currently, two theories articulate why individuals might become involved in IRRs. Kouri and Lasswell (1993) used the structural theory and the racial motivation theory to better understand these motivations. The **structural theory** suggests that demographics (e.g., socioeconomic status, education, occupation, residence) and mutual attraction contribute to the initiation, development, and maintenance of an interracial marriage, whereas the racial motivation theory believes that interracial marriages occur *because* of racial difference, whereby at least one partner finds the racially different other more appealing because of her or his race.

The first approach within structural theory is **endogamy**, which occurs when people marry within their group. This approach would include a person who prefers a marital partner from the same racial/ethnic background. The second approach, **homogamy**, is a slightly different approach and refers to a person's preference for a mate who is the same or close in racial/ethnic background, social status, educational background, and/or religion. Because of their similar backgrounds and interests, relational partners are more likely to develop a romantic relationship. If a person is using either an endogamous or homogamous approach to relationships, she or he is practicing a form of group closure because the person prefers to marry within the group (Kalmijn, 1998). Additionally, the person prefers a marital partner who is from the same racial/ethnic background, social status, educational background, and/or religion.

Racial Motivation Theory

In contrast, **hypergamy** describes an interest in or willingness to marry someone of a different status. These theories are distinct from traditional exchange theories because they account for partner attributes and qualities not traditionally deemed pertinent to relationship initiation, involvement, and/or satisfaction. One theory that has received very little attention or application in social scientific research is the **racial motivation theory**. According to this perspective, a person becomes involved in an interracial relationship or marriage *because* of racial difference. One or both partners are dating or married because they find the racially different other more appealing because of her or his race. Though rarely used, this theory may very well explain instances when partners exoticize each other, which speaks to the integrity of those relationships where race is only a part of what each partner perceives as an attractive partner attribute.

Spaights and Dixon (1984) propose this behavior is grounded in curiosity about myths of sexual prowess and promiscuity, rebellion against family, display of a liberal attitude, or interest in a cultural experience. They also believe some African Americans use interracial relationships to rebel against an oppressive society, for financial gain, or to attain social status, which may still be true today. In short, Spaights and Dixon promote the belief that all relationships between African Americans and European Americans are anomalies and doomed to fail. Although their essay does address the reality of some misperceptions of why individuals become involved in interracial romantic relationships, Spaights and Dixon fail to acknowledge the fact that interracial relationships are as likely as same-race relationships to be healthy experiences without one or both partners objectifying each other.

The racial motivation theory may reflect the true motivations of some (but not all) people involved in interracial romantic relationships. Overall, these theories about IRRs reflect the reality of the mate selection process. Such factors as education, interracial contact, group size, chance encounters, geographic location, and preference (Blau, Blum, & Schwartz, 1982; Heaton & Albrecht, 1996; Qian, 1998) directly influence a person's decision to adopt a hypergamous approach to dating.

Social Forces that Influence Interracial Romantic Relationships

In order to understand more clearly why and how interracial relationships are initiated, developed, and maintained, we must understand the social forces (Kalmijn, 1998) that lead to the decision to date or marry interracially. Upon entering a romantic relationship, we look for certain qualities and characteristics in a prospective mate. Naturally we are looking for someone who can contribute to the relationship. We consider how we will benefit or grow from this emotional attachment to another human being. No matter what background we come from, we are socialized to adopt a homogamous approach to mate selection. Theorists who study trends in interracial marriage have found **three social forces** that influence marriage patterns: (1) preferences for marriage candidates, (2) social group influence on mate selection process, and (3) constraints in the marriage market (Kalmijn, 1998). While all three social forces are important, we will focus on the first and second, as there is a significant body of research that explains their influence on how we choose our romantic partners.

In general, interracial marriages (and other romantic relationships) depend on opportunities for social relationships between racial/ethnic groups (Blau, Blum, &

Schwartz, 1982; Foeman & Nance, 1999; Kalmijn, 1998; Powers & Ellison, 1995). Thus, it is reasonable to assume that a person's environment and interpersonal network have a direct impact on his or her decision to date or marry interracially. In order to fully appreciate the complexities associated with IRRs, we must understand the variables that influence how a person might reach the decision to become involved in a socially taboo relationship. This knowledge will also enlighten us as to how choice and socialization work together, or separately, as individuals choose to be either homogamous or hypergamous in their mate selection process.

Preferences for Marriage Candidates

In his extensive research on interracial relationships, Kalmijn (1998) suggests three social forces that inform our partner choices. The first social force is **preferences for marriage candidates**, which refers to the resources romantic partners offer each other. Have you ever been set up on a blind date by a close friend? Prior to the actual date, your friend probably considered what qualities you find attractive in another person. Education, physical attractiveness, and a sense of humor are examples of qualities you may have communicated to your friend that you find most appealing. Our decision to date or marry someone is partially based on the *socioeconomic resources* he or she can bring to the relationship. Past research indicates that socioeconomic resources are primarily expectations of males held by both males and females. This includes "resources that produce economic well-being and status . . . [which] is shared by the family members" (Kalmijn, 1998, p. 399; for additional information, see also Jacobs & Furstenberg, 1986; Stevens, Owens & Schaefer, 1990).

Cultural resources relates to how important the individual feels it is that both relational partners share similar cultural or racial/ethnic backgrounds (Byrne, 1971; Kalmijn, 1998). The underlying implications regarding the importance of shared racial/ethnic identity stress that partners should have similar values and opinions. This shared similarity will prove attractive for each partner and allow them to share conversations, activities, and mutual understanding central to and independent of their racial/ethnic differences. According to preferences and homogamy, a person's educational attainment is directly related to the qualities he or she is looking for in a mate. Therefore, interracial marriage may become an option when people have more in common with those from a different racial/ethnic group than their own. For example, a microcultural group member with a doctorate may desire a same-race mate with similar interests, but may have difficulty meeting someone. The racial/ethnic identity of the potential mate may have less significance because that person places emphasis on interests, similarities, and education. This does not, however, imply a lack of commitment to maintaining the importance of one's racial/ethnic identity.

Social Group Influence

The second type of social force that influences partner choice is the social group. According to this approach, third parties have an incentive to keep new generations from marrying interracially (Kalmijn, 1998; Mills, Daly, Longmore & Kilbride, 1995). Therefore, they employ strategies that will prevent group members from marrying someone who is not a member of the ingroup. In the case of interracial marriages, a history of opposition from external forces has worked to destroy the initiation, development, and maintenance of romantic relationships between people from different racial/ethnic groups. If people believe intermixing between the races should not occur, it is quite possible they are basing this on the belief that the internal cohesion and homogeneity of the group is being threatened (e.g., "watering down of the races").

The first type of social influence is **group identification**. According to Gordon (1964), people's desire to preserve the social history of their racial/ethnic group directly influences their efforts to prevent interracial marriages from occurring. A common retort to people considering interracial marriage is, "What will people say, or think?" This statement implies that the family heritage will be threatened as a result of the interracial marriage. In her research on Vietnamese dating trends and patterns, Nguyen (1998) found that racial/ethnic identity is important to most families. Therefore, Vietnamese men and women are socialized to believe that intraracial dating (dating within one's own race) is a Vietnamese tradition. If both partners are from the same racial/ethnic group, they are likely to have a shared belief and communication system. This exploratory study found that participants' experiences with interracial and intraracial dating are influenced by Vietnamese and U.S. American values on the opinions and attitudes of participants toward interracial dating between Vietnamese and European Americans. Overall, Nguyen (1998) found that the more acculturated a Vietnamese person is, the more likely she or he is to date interracially in spite of cultural and familial expectations.

The second type of social influence, **group sanctions**, refers to institutions that traditionally oppose marriage between people from different racial/ethnic backgrounds. The role of these group members is to impose some sanction against those individuals who may potentially become involved in an interracial romantic relationship. The two institutions of *parents* and *state* are cited as offering such sanctions to family members. In the case of family, parents can communicate opposition to their children in a number of ways. According to Kalmijn (1998), parents can sabotage the relationship by one of the following methods:

1. Meeting with potential partners to discourage interest in the relationship.

2. Taking on the role of matchmaker and selecting mates with whom they feel their child will be better suited.

3. Offering advice and opinions to their child to discourage interest in the relationship and the relational partner.

4. Withdrawing emotional and relational support to the child as a form of punishment for involvement in an interracial relationship.

❖ **BOX 8.2**

AUTHOR REFLECTION

I, somewhat jokingly, tell people that I was an "equal opportunity dater"—open to dating women from all different racial and ethnic groups. The truth is that I really didn't have lots of women interested in me in high school . . . so I wasn't exactly in a position to be overly picky. Growing up and attending schools with significant amounts of diversity, it probably wasn't surprising that I dated European American, African American, and Puerto Rican women. I met my wife in 1983 when I was in the second year of my undergraduate studies at Ohio University; she was in her first year. It sounds like a cliché, but the truth is that I knew that I was going to marry her the first time we met (yes, she is that amazing!).

While both my wife and I have multiracial backgrounds, and both have European ancestry, people see us as an interracial couple. This makes sense given that my wife has always identified as an African American woman, and I have negotiated my European and Spanish/Filipino background. Yet, when it comes to our marriage, race is seldom the issue that causes the most disagreement. We both are similar in terms of age, ability, nationality, and spirituality, but are different when it comes to gender, regionality, and socioeconomic status. When I think about the issues that we continue to negotiate even after 15+ years of marriage, it seems like socioeconomic status is the most salient. As you might recall from my personal reflection in Chapter 5, I was raised in low-income housing projects; my wife, on the other hand, was raised in a solidly middle-class neighborhood. This background has cultivated different views on money, spending, and saving—things that sometimes cause disagreements. And while socioeconomic status is at the core of this issue, I can't help but see how our gender identities (she's more feminine and I am more masculine) and regional backgrounds (she's was born and raised in the Midwest, and I in the Northeast) influence our ability to communicate effectively with one another.

It is important to note that all relationships are multidimensional—all couples have both similarities and differences that must be recognized. While interracial relationships may still get the most attention, other intercultural pairings can be just as challenging. What are your views of relationships that are interfaith? Intergenerational? International? Interability? Can you see how racial difference isn't always the most salient issue in relationships?

—MPO

The current list of family-oriented sanctions is by no means exhaustive. Nevertheless, it illustrates the kinds of negative reactions parents, and some family members, can have when they learn a family member has decided to date and/or marry interracially. Another institution that has been cited as imposing sanctions against marriages between people from different backgrounds is the church. In their research on interfaith marriages (Jiobu, 1988; R. A. Johnson, 1980; Kennedy, 1944; Lazerwitz, 1995; McCutcheon, 1988), social scientists have found that religious worldviews often prescribe homogamous or endogamous marriages for its members, which is similar to research findings on perceptions of interracial marriages. For those churches espousing this ideology, there is the belief that interfaith marriages decrease the number of church members and the very lifeblood of that faith. By increasing its membership through marriage, that faith would become a part of the family's history whereby children and future generations would continue in that particular faith. Social scientists have also found that interfaith marriages were often perceived as potential factors contributing to the rise in interracial marriages. Although very little data is available to support this observation, there are other social groups that have directly prohibited interracial marriages from occurring.

Case Study

According to research, there are several myths and misconceptions about IRRs. We have already discussed the social forces that oftentimes exert a significant amount of pressure on relational partners who are from different racial groups. Listed below are several myths researchers have explored and offer evidence to the contrary.

Myth 1: Individuals involved in IRRs have "non-normative" (read "abnormal") sexual attitudes (Yancey, 2003).

Fact: There are no differences between same-race and interracial relationships in the way of sexual intimacy, thus debunking the myth that individuals involved in interracial sexuality have permissive sexual attitudes.

Myth 2: People involved in IRRs have lower self-esteem and poorer relationship quality (commitment, satisfaction, realistic expectations, the level to which expectations were met, and partner preferences) than people in same-race/ethnicity relationships (Gurung & Duong, 1999).

Fact: Findings suggest no differences between these groups. In fact, those involved in such relationships most likely have high self-esteem and confidence, which may be necessary to defy societal norms and date outside of their racial/ethnic group.

Myth 3: Partners in interracial relationships are less satisfied with their relationship than same-race partners (Troy, Lewis-Smith, & Laurenceau, 2006).

Fact: Interracial romantic relationship partners have significantly higher levels of relationship satisfaction compared to those in intraracial relationships. (Troy et al., 2006)

Myth 4: IRRs experience more conflict and have less relationship quality than same-race relationships. (Troy et al., 2006)

Fact: No differences were found or reported between the two groups.

Creating New Mental Models

Interracial Relationship Development Model

In order to illustrate the need for a new mental model of IRRs, we will use a film and Foeman and Nance's (2002) interracial relational development model to explore how prejudice and bias put people in the difficult position of deciding whether to remain romantically involved with a person of another race. By using the film *Something New* (Hamri, 2005), we hope to stimulate your thoughts and challenge you to become more reflective about your own beliefs about and perceptions of IRRs. We hope this exercise will be helpful in general as we move toward a more positive attitude toward such relationships.

In the spring of 2006, director Sanaa Hamri introduced to the world a revisionist's perception and visual representation of IRRs in the film *Something New*. Hamri presented to audiences a fictionalized, yet very "real," account of a professional African American woman's journey to finding true love. Sanaa Lathan portrays financial analyst Kenya McQueen, a thirty-something, single, attractive, successful African American woman whose relational options for marriage are virtually nonexistent. Upon meeting handsome landscape architect Brian, played by actor Simon Baker, Kenya finds herself rethinking the mental model of marriage she adopted when she was a little girl. As her story and journey unfold, the audience witnesses Kenya becoming vulnerable, letting down her guard, and becoming open to the possibility of crossing the color line—all in the name of love. Kenya's experience is best understood through Foeman and Nance's (2002) model of interracial relationship development. In the following sections, we will explain the model and reference various scenes from the film we suggest illuminate the process in which Kenya engages to find true happiness in the relationship of her dreams. Unlike its cinematic predecessor *Jungle Fever*, the title *Something New* connotes a reconceptualization of love, beyond racial differences and social stigma.

Before the relationship can even begin, it is apparent that Kenya has a mental model of how her ideal mate, or Ideal Black Male (IBM), should look, and being Black is an obvious criterion. Immediately upon meeting Brian, Kenya is using this mental model and her personal checklist to eliminate Brian as a possible marriage (or dating) candidate. There are four social forces that influence the mate selection process: (1) *cultural resources*—how important the individual feels it is that both relational partners share similar cultural or racial/ethnic backgrounds; (2) *preferences for marriage candidates*—the resources partners offer each other; (3) *socioeconomic resources*; and (4) *social group influence*—a third party's incentive to keep new generations from marrying interracially; strategies are employed that will prevent group members from marrying an outgroup member. Kenya allows cultural resources, preferences for marriage candidates, and social group influence to deter her from entering an IRR. Kenya abandons all possibilities of an interracial romantic relationship. She assumes the cultural resources are too important to not consider in a romantic relationship; therefore, she resolves that her relationship with Brian will be "just business."

Foeman and Nance's (2002) model of interracial relationship development is a theoretical framework designed to facilitate understanding of how relational partners negotiate their individual racial identities and their identity as a romantic unit. The four stages of the model include (1) Racial Awareness, (2) Coping, (3) Identity Emergence, and (4) Maintenance, each of which will be discussed in greater detail below. The model has been used to understand or describe how Black/White IRRs come into being and could very well be used to understand the relational development of other interracial pairings. Nevertheless, Foeman and Nance (2002) suggest that

African Americans involved in IRRs deal with pressures that their European American partner most likely does not face, such as being labeled a "sell out" or "interloper," and "may experience guilt for imposing his or her burden of race on the White partner" (p. 241). In contrast, the

> negative implications of an interracial relationship may be more vague to the White partner. . . . Whites are more likely to experience the world as a fair or safe place. The result may be that the White partner encourages the Black partner to relax about race and may view the Black partner as paranoid. (p. 242)

In the second scene in the film ("Never Married"), the audience is introduced to a visual representation of the structural theory. Although no formal introduction of this theory is made, the main character Kenya and her close girlfriends engage in dialogue about relationships that is reflective of this theory and the socialization process many experience concerning mate selection. The women are "celebrating" Valentine's Day and become distressingly aware of the unavailability of marriageable Black men. Her friends reprimand Kenya for "the list" she has of all the qualities she's looking for in a man (e.g., "a good brotha," with a "good job," "taller than me, college educated, and not crazy. No kids, good teeth . . ."), and they all resolve to release themselves from "this preconceived notion of what we think we want." These women are using the structural theory to determine which men they believe are potential candidates. Structural theory suggests that demographics (e.g., socioeconomic status, education, occupation, residence) and mutual attraction contribute to the initiation, development, and maintenance of an interracial marriage (Kalmijn, 1993). The first approach within structural theory is *endogamy*, which occurs when people marry within their group. This approach would include a person who prefers a marital partner from the same racial/ethnic background. A slightly different approach is *homogamy*, which describes a person's preference for a mate who is close in social status. If a person is using either an *endogamous* or *homogamous* approach to relationships, he or she is practicing a form of group closure because the person prefers to marry within the group (Kalmijn, 1993). As her story unfolds, the audience learns that Kenya is such a person, which is a fairly common ideology. It becomes apparent that she has been indoctrinated to believe she should be romantically involved with Black men who have the same educational background and social status (i.e., upper-middle class) as her. To create opportunities for love that seem to be denied to them, Kenya and her girlfriends decide to "let go, let flow."

Stage 1: Racial Awareness

At this point in the film (Scene 4: "No Pressure"), Brian and Kenya appear to "formally" enter Stage 1 of the interracial relationship development model—attraction. According to Foeman and Nance (2002), this stage involves partners becoming aware of a mutual attraction and the possibility for an intimate involvement. Attraction is defined as both an interpersonal and cultural experience where partners must (1) address social frames—is the attraction grounded in a complex racial past (i.e., jungle fever) and (2) "come out of the closet"—rather than remaining covert, the partner(s) chooses to inform outsiders (family members and friends) about the relationship (p. 239). Brian nonverbally addresses Kenya's concerns and hesitancy and explicitly uses strategies to assure her that his intentions are pure. In this scene, Brian recognizes the extreme level of discomfort Kenya has with their racial differences, and consistent with Foeman and Nance's (2002) model, Brian makes it clear his loyalties are with her and demonstrates an "increased sensitivity to the function of race" in Kenya's life.

It's a preference, not prejudice. As Brian and Kenya begin to explore their mutual attraction, they have an honest, frank discussion about interracial dating. Although not addressed directly, Brian and Kenya are demonstrating how important it is for partners to acknowledge and have open communication about racial difference and, to some degree, the myths and misconceptions associated with IRRs. In addition, these characters debunk the myth that "people involved in mixed ethnic relationships (MEDs) have low self-esteem and poor relationship quality (commitment, satisfaction, realistic expectations, the level to which expectations were met, and partner preferences) than individuals involved in same-race/ethnicity relationships" (Gurung & Duong, 1999, p. 652–653; see Troy, Lewis-Smith, & Laurenceau, 2006). Kenya and Brian are clearly well-adjusted and have a genuine attraction to each other.

Stage 2: Coping

Kenya and Brian allow their relationship to quickly transform into a romantic one when they realize their growing attraction for each other. They are now in the **coping** stage (Stage 2) of the model. Foeman and Nance (2002) describe this stage as the couple "pulling together . . . [and] away from others" (p. 244). Concerned with the criticism and lack of support from their other close relational networks, the couple uses active behaviors where they "[develop] reactive and proactive strategies and learn to *insulate* [themselves] . . . or to *negotiate* . . . potentially threatening situations as necessary" (p. 245). Kenya and Brian spend very little time together when their relationship escalates into a full-scale romance after an innocent hiking date. After a passionate kiss in the wilderness, and despite Kenya's declaration that the relationship cannot go any further, Kenya and Brian become physically intimate, thus transitioning the nature of their relationship. Kenya brings the relationship "out of the closet" when she informs her friends about Brian.

Stage 3: Identity Emergence

In Scene 9 ("A Little Color"), Kenya and Brian enter stage 2—identity **emergence**. As Foeman and Nance (2002) explain, the couple has "solidified their relationship and present themselves as a couple to outsiders." In this scene, Brian and Kenya are on a double date with her friend Cheryl and boyfriend Walter (Mike Epps). In this stage, "a defensive posture" is taken and "[t]he couple stands ready to protect itself. But while safety is important, healthy relationship life demands more than simple defense from a racially charged culture. . . . [It] requires that restrictive and inaccurate descriptions of interracial couples be *rethought* . . . or *reframed.*" Brian is the one who must defend the relationship when Walter confronts him about his "intentions" or motivations for being involved with Kenya. Walter believes he is in the relationship *because* of their racial differences, which is an example of the racial motivation theory or a curiosity about myths of sexual prowess and promiscuity (Yancey, 2002). Despite the allegations, Brian attempts to make it clear that this is in fact a real relationship and rejects Walter's allegation that he has "jungle fever."

Although their "coming out" was somewhat difficult, Kenya and Brian become closer. Kenya vents to Brian about the racial issues she is experiencing at the firm. Instead of dismissing her claims of racism, Brian tries to empathize and be supportive of the obvious difficulties Kenya is facing because of her minority position. Kenya, on the other hand, is facing a significant amount of opposition from her brother and mother, who openly express their support of a homogamous perspective on dating and marriage relationships. In fact, brother Nelson imposes this belief on Kenya when, in Scene 12 ("Party Crasher"), he introduces her to what he believes to be her "IBM." Kenya has no interest in meeting Mark (Blair Underwood), but does so any way.

❖ BOX 8.3

STUDENT REFLECTION

My best friend of 10 years is in an interracial relationship. She and her man went on vacation over spring break to Savannah for St. Patrick's Day. When they were seen together, something happened that she and I were shocked about. She is a Black woman and he is White. This is a combination that most do not expect to see. They are perfect together, and I have never seen two people so happy with one another. They apparently went down to River Street [in Savannah, GA] . . . and got picked out to be ridiculed for their relationship. A Black man came up to her and put his arm around her when her boyfriend was standing right next to her holding her hand. He said, "Hey baby, I am sorry you must not have realized there were real men out there, so you had to settle for this piece." She said she was shocked. First, she was mad for his addressing her man as a "piece," and secondly, how dare someone question her judgment.

They have been together for almost five years and have never been harassed in this way. Her boyfriend, not a small guy, continued to confront the man and, according to [my friend], "beat his face in." I do not think violence was the best way to deal with this situation, but he got his point across. Kelly then went on to stand over the guy while he was lying in the street and say, "Now, a real man, no matter what his color, doesn't judge and can take care of his woman. Can you say that about yourself? CHUMP!" I was shocked by what she said! I do not believe violence is the best way to deal with these types of racist interactions, but the guy got the point.

I think that this is another example of why people hate interracial relationships. No matter how much two people love each other, social stigmas will always be present and cause stress. I know they will be together forever, but I wish there was some way, other than pounding a guy, to make people understand how they feel. We have spent so long trying to make people realize that color doesn't matter, why is it that fighting is the only way to prove anything?

I told her I was sad that her boyfriend [Keith] felt like he had to do that. Then I told her about some of the things we had been talking about in class. She wishes that everyone in the world could have a glimpse into our interracial class. She loves that people like us are trying to understand all sides and realize that color really doesn't matter. She knows this and hopes that classes like this can continue to broaden people's views. It made me feel so good to be able to share with [my friend] what I have been learning.

Relational Regression. Their relationship becomes strained when their racial and cultural differences cause tension between Brian and Kenya. Scene 13 ("Put On Hold") demonstrates for the audience how extreme pressure from external forces can cause relational partners in an IRR to internalize the negativity imposed upon them by others and allow the relationship to be more complex than necessary or to altogether fail. Kenya and Brian have an argument about their experiences with race and are having difficulty understanding each other's viewpoint. Realizing they are at an impasse, the couple decides to dissolve the relationship, concluding that "maybe this isn't gonna work."

Abandoning all efforts to preserve their identity as a couple is indicative of Kenya and Brian's inability to develop coping strategies that allow them to deal with the external stressors that are draining their relationship and Kenya outside of the relationship. Each is being accused of being racially insensitive, and this problem *must* be addressed if any IRR is to reach the fourth and final stage. At this point in the film, the audience is led to believe that IRRs just do not work. This belief is fueled by the dissolution of the relationship, quite obviously, and when Kenya appears to readopt her ideal of the IBM.

After putting her theory of the IBM to test by dating an African American man who has all the qualities she was initially looking for in a relationship, Kenya realizes that their "common ground" and cultural resources are not enough to establish and maintain a mature, loving relationship. In Scene 16, she realizes they have "No Fizzle, No Magic." Kenya actually becomes unhinged by two critical events: (1) an awkward moment at Leah's wedding when she and Mark run into Brian and ex-girlfriend Penelope and (2) a stressful and uncomfortable evening with Mark, her parents, and brother (Scene 17: "Putting On a Show"). The wedding incident stirs up her feelings for Brian, which Kenya tries to convince herself and her friends no longer exist.

It is not until Scene 18 ("Daddy Knows Best") that Kenya begins to think more seriously about the barrier she has allowed to prevent her from having the kind of relationship she has been seeking. After having a heart-to-heart conversation with her Dad about her feelings, Kenya becomes empowered by her father's obvious approval and support of IRRs and treks off to find Brian.

Stage 4: Maintenance

The audience is unclear about if and how Kenya and Brian can overcome the problems and barriers that attempted to derail their relationship. According to Foeman and Nance (2002), the final stage, **maintenance**, requires that the couple "see their vision [of the relationship] through for a lifetime. Their communication can become a natural part of how they present themselves and how others speak about them" (p. 248). Kenya and Brian transition into this stage in Scene 19 ("Belle of the Ball") when Kenya boldly professes her love to Brian and her willingness to commit to a relationship with him. As their ensuing dialogue suggests, Brian and Kenya have successfully transitioned into stage four. They are dedicated to a lifetime commitment of making sure their relationship lasts, and take their relationship to a deeper level of commitment by having a wedding in Kenya's beautifully landscaped backyard.

Conclusion

By using the film *Something New* (2006) as a text, we have demonstrated how IRRs are unnecessarily framed by society as being more complex and difficult to maintain and manage than same-race romantic relationships (Troy et al., 2006). We have used Foeman and Nance's (2002) model of interracial relationship development to describe what we believe is a fairly accurate relational account of an IRR between an African American woman and a European American man. Through Kenya and Brian, we gain an understanding of the dynamics of their relationship and how it is essential for romantic partners in interracial (and interethnic) relationships to develop strategies to deal with external forces that oftentimes plague these relationships (Donovan, 2004; Dovidio et al., 2002). Such factors as family and societal disapproval, language barriers, logistics, cultural barriers and traditions, and children (Donovan, 2004) exert so much pressure on the relationship and the respective partners that they are forced to decide whether to put forth the effort necessary to preserve and maintain the relationship.

As was the case with Kenya, she had to rethink her mental model of marriage, much to the chagrin of her family and some members of the African American community. While those in her interpersonal network eventually came to support her IRR, Kenya was forced to battle some inner demons (e.g., prejudice, homogamy) that caused her to believe love with someone of a different race could not work. She also chose to resist the external pressures to dissolve the relationship altogether. Because our mental models of racial difference as a society cause us to prejudge racially different others (Dovidio et al., 2002), it is imperative that we create new models or ways of thinking about race and IRRs. In essence, through an increased understanding of the inner workings of IRRs, we as a society make progress toward stabilizing, maintaining, and establishing an "understanding [of] the nature of interracial interaction," which Dovidio et al. (2002) state is critical to understanding race relations. Although it may be presumptuous to suggest we do so through the fictional characters in a movie, we hope that we have challenged everyone to be self-reflective about their attitudes toward and beliefs about IRRs.

❖ BOX 8.4

STUDENT REFLECTIONS

I love hanging out with one of [my boyfriend's] best friends, Ram, who is Indian. Ram and I got to spend a good amount of time together this weekend, and through our time together, I feel like I learned many things about Indian culture. My boyfriend and many of his good friends, including Ram, are in the Air Force ROTC at Tech. Many of the other AFROTC members joke with Ram about being Indian. I think they tease him because they know Ram is a good sport, and Ram even makes fun of himself.

On Saturday, the AFROTC had Dining Out [and a party afterward]. At the party, Ram and I spent a lot of time together talking about Indian culture. He was telling me about a White girl that he brought to the party named Sarah. Ram was telling me that according to his Indian culture, he does not feel like dating her is appropriate. He said that his father does not really care who he dates, but his mother wants him to preferably date an Indian girl. Also, in Indian culture, many times they have arranged marriages, so Ram is not used to dating a girl just for fun. He is more concerned with dating for marriage. It was really hard for me to understand the concept of dating solely for marriage because American culture has a different perspective on dating than Indian culture. He is having a hard time deciding whether to keep dating Sarah even though they have only been dating for a month. He says that so far he does not see himself marrying her. After our talk, Ram still was not sure if he should continue dating Sarah or break off their relationship. Everything we discussed got me thinking more and more about the interracial relationship between the two of them.

If it was difficult for me to understand Ram's attitudes on dating due to my Americanization, I am sure that it would certainly be hard for Sarah to understand too. We are used to a culture that promotes dating for fun, starting at young ages. Indian culture, however, encourages young people to either let their parents select their spouse or to simply date to find their own spouse. These differences in cultures are going to put strains on their relationship. While I want them to continue dating, I think it is going to take huge efforts on both of their parts to make the relationship work. Even though their parents might disapprove and even though they might have different ideas about dating for fun and marriage, I still think that their relationship could work out.

Whether it is society, family, friends, or our own fears of racial and cultural difference, partners in interracial relationships experience pressures that do not surface in same-race relationships (Kalmijn, 1998). Both partners must determine the degree to which they will allow these external forces to impede the development and maintenance of their romantic relationship. People often have little hope that interracial relationships can withstand these pressures; however, research indicates that they can survive as long as the partners are committed to doing so. The partners must first engage in *racial awareness*, which challenges them to face the harsh reality of racism and its potential effect on the relationship and the psychosocial health of both relational partners. As they remain committed to the relationship, the partners must also negotiate between themselves and as individuals within the relationship how they will *cope* with external pressures of the relationship. Will they allow their differences to overshadow their commitment to each other? Or will they appreciate and value their difference and work to have a relationship that is beneficial for both of them? From there, the partners are able to experience *identity emergence* where they define who they are as a relational unit independent of what others may say about them. Finally, they must be aware of and actually engage in *(ongoing) relationship maintenance*.

As history and personal experiences tell us, racism is an inherent part of U.S. history. Therefore, interracial romantic partners are not immune to the racist, prejudiced, or discriminatory behaviors and attitudes of others. In order to preserve and nurture the relationship, both parties must be committed to fostering a communication pattern that meets the needs of each individual partner. After reading this chapter, we hope you have come to think more positively about interracial romantic relationships. Much like same-race partners, interracial partners enter relationships out of a basic human need for emotional intimacy with another person. They desire a relationship with someone who has life goals, attitudes, beliefs, and values similar to their own. So the next time you see an interracial couple and you think to yourself, "Why are *they* together?" ask yourself if you would ask the same question of a same-race couple. The answer goes beyond the physical differences that seem to separate the partners from each other. We must rethink our own and others' perceptions of the cross-race mate selection process. With the increasing racial diversity we are experiencing in the United States, we should avoid asking the "whys" and understand the "why nots" of interracial romantic relationships.

TIP: THEORY INTO PRACTICE

Do you want to be supportive of romantic relationships that involve people from different racial/ethnic groups? Do you wonder how you can communicate this to friends, colleagues, family members, or others who are interested in initiating or maintaining these relationships? Here are a few tips to guide you:

- Support these couples just as you would support others in comparable relationships (initial dating stages, bonding, marriage, termination, etc.). Do not focus on their racial/ethnic differences, but don't ignore them either.
- Acknowledge the many benefits of the relationship, as well as some of the possible unique challenges the couple may face.
- Do not automatically assume that race is the defining factor for these relationships. (Other similarities/differences in age, spirituality, socioeconomic status may be more important than racial/ethnic difference.)
- Confront existing myths (about self and others) that suggest all interracial romantic relationships are based on sexual stereotypes and/or power plays.
- Do not prejudge individuals who prefer same-race or other-race partners. Instead, get to know these persons so you can better understand these preferences in the context of their life experiences.
- If possible and/or appropriate, cultivate a relationship with the couple so you come to know them as romantic partners who happen to be from different racial/ethnic groups (as opposed to simply "an interracial couple").
- Be open and honest about your support for all types of positive, affirming relationships (even when others might criticize or dehumanize interracial relationships).

OPPORTUNITIES FOR EXTENDED LEARNING ❖

1. As an out of class assignment, have each student or pair of students conduct an informal poll among their family and friends. The list of questions to be asked should be generated in class and should prompt them to ask what social rules exist concerning what racial pairings are "more appropriate" than others. Questions should also ask them to discuss how these rules are learned and what rules they believe should replace the rules that discourage IRRs.

2. In class, view the movie *The Pelican Brief*. Divide the class into groups. Focusing on the main characters portrayed by Julia Roberts and Denzel Washington, ask the students to describe their relationship and what observable nonverbal and verbal behaviors communicated to the audience the nature of their

relationship. After these responses are recorded, then ask the groups to discuss why they believe the producers of the movie changed the script to reflect a nonromantic relationship between the characters. (Note: In several prescreenings of the film, audiences had a negative response [shouting back at the screen] to Julia and Denzel kissing, which led to a change in the script.)

3. Using Yancey's (2003) study entitled "A Preliminary Examination of Differential Sexual Attitudes Among Individuals Involved in Interracial Relationships: Testing 'Jungle Fever,'" discuss the myths associated with IRRs. Have the students generate an action plan for debunking these myths and creating a new mental model of these relationships. Explore the following questions: Why were these myths created in the first place? Are the myths different for each racial/ethnic group? If so, how and why are they different? Is there any relationship between the myths and the history of race in the United States? What role does slavery or other forms of societal oppression play in perpetuating these myths?

4. Using blank index cards, write down actual firsthand or secondhand comments others (or you) have made about IRRs. After collecting the cards, your instructor will share the anonymous comments with the class in an effort to understand (on a small scale) current attitudes toward the topic. The class should be encouraged to discuss the origins of these beliefs and what can be done to deconstruct them.

5. Each group is to examine the following racial compositions and provide pros and cons for being involved in such relationships. Assign a different sex to each racial partner to determine if gender influences the pros and cons in any way. After reviewing the list, discuss the roles that family and society play in our perceptions of these relationships. Why are some relationships more (or less) socially acceptable or problematic than others? What role does communication play in constructing these attitudes toward interracial romantic relationships?
   a. European American/Asian American
   b. Asian American/African American
   c. European American/African American
   d. Native American/African American
   e. Latina or Latino/African American
   f. European American/Native American
   g. Latina or Latino/European American

6. Using the Internet, find and make a list of interracial dating Web sites, or Web sites designed for individuals with specific interest in dating someone from a different race. Review several of the profiles, using an equal number of men and women from different racial groups, and make a general observation of what motivations the Web site members appear to offer regarding their interest in dating interracially. If time permits, do the same for Web sites targeted toward individuals interested in same-race relationships. (Be sure to diversify your racial groups represented here.) Which of the three theories can be used to explain each person's interest? What kinds of rules appear to exist concerning interracial dating? What are some general trends noted within the different Web sites? Are they pretty much the same or very different from each other? How so?

Interracial Communication in the Context of Organizations

Thus far, we have investigated interracial relationships, which involve partners actively choosing to become emotionally intimate with someone who is racially/ ethnically different. We will now shift our attention to what happens when an organization or company is directly impacted by racial/ethnic diversity and is no longer monoracial. In order to accommodate this change, businesses and organizations alike must themselves change if they are to create an environment that will ultimately be supportive of its ingroup and outgroup members. Because many people have had limited interracial interactions (and contact), we must all become sensitive to how our behaviors positively and negatively impact our interracial communication (Freidman & Davidson, 2001; Grimes, 2002; Linnehan, Chrobot-Mason, & Konrad, 2006). By becoming more aware of how an organization (1) functions and (2) adapts to change in its environment, we can work toward improving how we interact and communicate in the workplace with people who are racially/ethnically diverse.

This chapter is a brief overview of organizational communication. More specifically, we examine what happens when we are given opportunities to develop positive interracial relationships within an organizational context. In particular, we direct our attention to how interracial interactions and relationships are managed within organizations. In order to understand the importance of interracial communication in our organizations, we explore organizational theory, organizational communication, organizational culture, and organizational context. As you are reading this chapter, we challenge you to think critically about the direction our organizations are taking in the 21st century. Instead of divorcing ourselves from the reality of racism, we must now commit to making a difference in the way we interact with coworkers and others from racial/ethnic groups other than our own.

Within the last few years, racial relations in the United States have become incredibly intense with the increasing number of Mexican illegal immigrants crossing our national borders. Myriad explanations have been given to articulate why U.S. citizens are angry, frustrated, and hostile regarding the change in demographics; however, the consensus among many is that privileges and rights afforded to citizens born in the United States are being usurped by individuals who are illegally residing in this country. Our country was essentially founded on the American dream. No matter their social location, everyone is believed to have the right to pursue the dream of having a home, family, career, economic resources, and material possessions of their choosing. However, when those dreams and natural born rights are perceived to be threatened, people will seemingly do whatever they can to protect what is rightfully theirs. At least this appears to be the case with illegal immigrants in the United States.

Coverage in virtually all media outlets of the illegal immigrant issue and ensuing protests framed it as a serious issue (and rightly so) that will not likely go away in the very near future. The crux of the problem is economic in terms of employment opportunities, housing, and the American dream. An underlying theme of the argument against illegal immigration is that Hispanics and other racial/ethnic minority groups and people of lower economic status are competing for economic resources (e.g., jobs) that are far and few between (Jacoby, 2006). Although they have the same basic human needs, the issue has been complicated by issues of race and ethnicity and, for some, ethnocentric ways of thinking. Regardless of your attitude about racial and ethnic diversity, it is an impending reality for the United States for which we must be prepared. It just so happens that the issue of illegal immigration provides a context within which we must examine how prepared we are as a country to deal with what has yet to come. A recent study conducted by the Pew Hispanic Center found that "7.2 million illegal immigrants hold jobs in the United States, making up 4.9 percent of the overall labor force" and "[u]ndocumented workers make up 24 percent of farm workers and hold 14 percent of construction jobs" (Associated Press, 2006). As these and other statistics demonstrate, the racial landscape is currently changing and will continue to do so regardless of how the government chooses to address the issue of immigration. Therefore, our organizations and institutions must become proactive in preparing their people for pending changes in the way we think about racial differences and communicate between racial groups.

Organizational Communication

In the spring of 2006, a series of protests were held throughout the country by undocumented (illegal) immigrants protesting their treatment in the United States. The national protest was called "A Day Without Immigrants" (Ferre et al., 2006) and "asked those opposing tighter restrictions on immigration—namely immigrants themselves—to flex their economic muscle by boycotting all aspects of commerce, including going to work and school" (Ferre et al., 2006). They assembled themselves in the streets of New York, Washington, Atlanta, Las Vegas, Miami, Chicago, Los Angeles and San Francisco, Denver, Phoenix, New Orleans, and Milwaukee, among others, by the thousands to protest "legislation passed by the U.S. House that would make it a felony to be in the United States illegally. It also would impose new penalties on employers who hire illegal immigrants, require churches to check the legal status of parishioners before helping them and erect fences along one third of the U.S.–Mexican border" (Associated Press, 2006). Many demonstrators and supporters alike were of the opinion that lawmakers were "unfairly targeting immigrants who provide a major labor pool for America's economy" and orchestrated the protest as a "visible demonstration of political clout for supporters of the nation's estimated 11–12 million undocumented immigrants" (Associated Press, 2006).

As of March 25, 2006, according to the Associated Press, there were approximately 11 million illegal immigrants in the United States. Because the immigrants are not citizens of the country, policymakers and much of the public have varied opinions about how to address this issue of citizenship. The Senate proposed to "allow illegal immigrants to obtain legal status, and eventually citizenship, by working for six years, paying a fine, undergoing a background check and learning English," which supporters perceived as "earned citizenship," and "opponents denounce it as 'amnesty'" (Associated Press, 2006). This seemingly sudden influx of racial/ethnic diversity has created a hotbed of strife and contention that exacerbated race relations in a unique yet familiar way.

Whether people want to accept it or not, the issue of illegal immigration is going to significantly impact the way we communicate in the workplace. Although this is something for which organizations should already be prepared, they are not, and neither is society as a whole. This is why we challenge you in this chapter to extend your thinking about what an organization is and how racial/ethnic identities influence its culture. We present ways to consider how our interracial interactions in the workplace can improve race relations and promote a larger organizational agenda in a healthy, productive manner.

Scholars provide a number of definitions for what constitutes organizational communication. Organizational communication is an interdisciplinary area of interest (K. Miller, 1999; Reardon, 1996) and has its foundations in management. Organizational communication involves "exchanging messages to stimulate meaning within and between organizations and their environments" (Infante, Rancer, & Womack, 1990). K. Miller (1999) has identified seven concepts associated with the terms *organization* and *communication* that provide a basic understanding of organizational communication. An **organization** can be described as (1) a social collectivity (a group of people) (2) where coordinated activities (3) achieve both individual and collective goals. These activities provide (4) a structure that enables organizational members to deal effectively with each other (5) within the larger organizational environment. In terms of communication, it is a process that is (6) transactional (which involves two or more people interacting within that environment) and (7) symbolic (communication transactions represent or stand for other things on some level of abstraction) (K. Miller, 1999). As these facets demonstrate, a great deal of negotiation takes place on the part of individuals as they become part of an organization. In order to maximize our organizational experiences, we must consider how our organizational, individual, and racial/ethnic identities are affected by our membership in that organizational culture.

Let's use a fictional company to understand how these concepts facilitate our understanding of organizational communication. You are working for an advertising agency that has approximately 30 employees (social collectivity) who have weekly meetings (coordinated activities) to update everyone about the progress made on various ad campaigns (collective goals). Each member has prior advertising and PR experience and is very much interested in their organizational roles and how society benefits from the products being sold through advertisements (individual goals). Being aware of their roles and the organizational goals allows members to acknowledge the chain of command (structure) and how this hierarchy functions. In essence, this knowledge allows the members to see the big picture of what the organization is all about (organizational environment). In order to maintain this organizational culture, the members exchange ideas and thoughts (transactional process) that relate specifically to the organization and its goals (symbolic).

An organizational member must think about the degree to which her individual identity will be influenced by the organization. For example, have you ever had a good friend change after she joined a social group? Maybe she only wanted to hang around with her new friends and found very little time for her old friends. Or, in the case of a job, a person must determine the extent to which she will allow her life as a PR specialist to consume her personal life. In any event, she must learn how to balance her organizational and individual identities in order to have success within the organization and a healthy psyche. The same is also the case for racial/ethnic identity. Just as the young woman must negotiate her identities, so must an organizational member who comes from an underrepresented racial/ethnic group.

❖ **BOX 9.1**

PERSONAL REFLECTION

Because of our *social locations* (e.g., race, class, gender, professional status), my African American friends and I are constantly faced with "isms" that our European American colleagues rarely (if ever) face. These experiences, or **defining moments**, with racism and sexism help develop our inner strength to face adversities in spite of our circumstances. Prejudiced and racist thinking is more frequently evidenced in the perpetrators' nonverbal behaviors. (Is that some subconscious way to veil their hidden racism?)

I recently had the honor of writing an essay on race and pedagogy (classroom instruction) in higher education. In my essay, I discuss how our multiple identities, for African American female faculty members (and members of other marginalized racial groups), are frequently placed at odds when we are confronted by competing societal definitions of one's race and gender. Since graduating from my doctoral program a few years ago, I have found myself in the uncomfortable position of repeatedly defining and defending my professional identity because of my race and/or gender. In short, I oftentimes have to continually request that I be addressed as *Doctor* Harris when occupying space in the academy, which is something with which I am confident my European American male colleagues don't have to contend.

My experience is neither conclusive nor generalizable, but sheds light on an experience that may contribute to the difficulties associated with recruiting and retaining faculty of color at predominantly White institutions (PWIs).

—TMH

Some organizational members may feel their racial/ethnic identities become less important as they climb the ladder of success. Let's assume an Asian American woman has become quite successful in telecommunications. Prior to her entry into the business world, Mae was committed to understanding and learning about her race/ethnicity. She attended cultural events, learned Japanese, and valued family. As she navigated her way from sales to management, Mae attempted to maintain a sense of who she was and where she came from. Unfortunately, as she began to rise in the company, her time turned from learning about her roots to learning how to advance in her career. Eventually, her family observed this change and questioned Mae's lack of commitment to her race/ethnicity. Not only did she begin to spend much of her time attending gala corporate functions, Mae began to purposely date European American men she thought would fit into her "new world." This transformation is referred to as assimilation, which involves a slow progression from one's own race/ethnicity to that of the majority group (Frankenberg, 1993). During this process, a person may begin to devalue personal racial/ethnic group membership as he or she strives to become a part of mainstream society.

Understanding Organizational Theories

Organizational communication is very different from interpersonal communication in its origin and intent. Most organizational scholars agree that analysis of the relationship between communication and organizational activities originated with Max Weber (1947), Henry Fayol (1916), and Frederick Taylor (1911). With the passage of time, however theorists began to acknowledge the importance of human relations occurring in the workplace. Before we address this very important change in the critical thinking processes of scholars in this area of research, we briefly discuss several theories that illustrate the significance of human (and race) relations within the organizational context.

In the late 1800s to early 1900s, Taylor, Weber, and Fayol developed theories that investigated the relationship between organizational culture and productivity. Classical management theory includes three subtheories that reflect the divergent principles of each theorist: scientific management theory, administrative management theory, and bureaucracy (P. Y. Byers, 1997). **Scientific management theory** originated with Taylor, who placed great significance on how work was accomplished. After observing workers who were shoveling iron ore in a steel mill, Taylor deduced that a prescriptive approach to the workplace is the best method for achieving the task, which in turn maximizes efficiency. Six principles guide this organizational theory (Taylor, 1911):

1. There is "one best way" to perform a task or job.

2. Employees should be scientifically selected and improved (based on skills and expertise to increase productivity).

3. Workers are monetarily motivated.

4. Management plans the work and laborers follow through with the plan (cooperation vs. individuality).

5. Clearly defined rules, regulations, and roles (creates harmony within the organization).

6. Loafing should be eliminated.

Taylor's theory places great importance on cooperation on the part of organizational members. According to this theory, communication between worker and employer enables the employer to direct and control the worker's behaviors, thus facilitating work standardization and planning.

In 1916, Fayol created the **administrative management theory**, which "discusses the organizational hierarchy and the flow of communication within that hierarchy" (P. Y. Byers, 1997). In essence, strict chains of communication among organizational members were an essential part of the organization. The style of communication within this theory is vertical in nature. If peers wanted to communicate with each other, they had to receive permission from their supervisors. Principles under the administrative management theory were somewhat similar to scientific management theory, but differed in several ways: (1) managers should use control, (2) subordinates should yield to superiors' authority to control, (3) centralization of power with administration, and (4) employee tenure is more likely when employees do their job correctly and accomplish assigned tasks (see Fayol, 1916). Although space limits our discussion of all 20 principles involved in the theory, the overarching theme is that horizontal communication (between peers) is very limited, thus doing very little to further the role of communication within organizations (P. Y. Byers, 1997).

The final theory that falls under the umbrella of classical management theory is Weber's **bureaucracy theory**. Organizations described as bureaucratic are viewed as very formal, inflexible, and insensitive to the needs of its workers (Weber, 1947). Eight qualities define a bureaucratic organization:

1. Formalized rules, regulations, and procedures achieve organizational tasks.

2. Role specialization simplifies workers' activities.

3. Formal hierarchy helps direct employees' interpersonal relationships toward the goal of the organizations (e.g., title, expertise).

4. Technical competence and an ability to perform his or her task is the sole basis on which an individual should be hired and maintained.

5. Organizational tasks are more important than the individuals performing them.

6. Interpersonal relationships should remain impersonal and professional in order to accomplish organizational goals.

7. Clearly defined job descriptions provide all members of the organization with a formal outline of their duties and job responsibilities.

8. Organizations should have logical, clear cut, and predictable rules and regulations to help promote order and to facilitate accomplishing organizational goals.

P. Y. Byers (1997) notes that this approach to organizational communication is self-defeating. Organizations adhering to a bureaucratic approach (e.g., government, large organizations, and universities) may potentially develop a plethora of rules, regulations, policies, and procedures that stifle their growth and progress.

In essence, the classical management perspective advocates standardization, wherein there is a "formal and rational flow of tasks and communication, structure, and social control" (P. Y. Byers, 1997, p. 24). In other words, if the organization is to succeed and fulfill its goals, there must be some sense of structure regarding how members communicate and how those in positions of power maintain control. Additionally, the worker is perceived as being only interested in making money, and communication is used by workers only as a means for achieving organizational goals.

TIP: THEORY INTO PRACTICE

In 1998, the President's Initiative on Race developed some criteria that were important in creating effective race relations programs and organizations (see A. Smith & Ahuja, 1999). If you are currently in, or thinking about creating, an organized effort to promote more effective interracial communication, ask yourself the following questions:

- Do the participants reflect the full racial/ethnic diversity of the community? If not, how can the group become more inclusive to others who are underrepresented?
- Do programs encourage participants to examine conscious and unconscious attitudes about race?
- Do your efforts explicitly educate others about the importance of historical and contemporary facts regarding race, racism, and culture?
- Are opportunities for peer-to-peer collaboration created and encouraged?
- What is done to make those institutional leaders (outside the group) aware and/or supportive of your goals?
- Are unique perspectives of different groups—racial/ethnic, gender, spiritual, age, sexual orientation, and so on—also taken into account?
- Do efforts move beyond awareness-raising to specific action plans that address systemic change?
- How are your efforts, at both the micro- and macrolevel, evaluated?
- How does your organization/program adapt to the dynamic needs of the communities it is a part of?

In order to resolve this disregard for individual needs, organizations must become more focused on their employees' individual and social relationships, which are becoming more paramount to organizational communication research (P. Y. Byers, 1997). Instead of perceiving the human experience as external to the organization, organization members and theorists alike have come to see all members as humans in need of positive interpersonal communication in the workplace. This change was introduced to preserve some classical features of organizations while providing individuals with the tools necessary for managing relationships that exist within systems based on hierarchy and authority. After conducting test after test on human relations and the workplace, researchers learned that worker productivity was positively related to additional attention from others. Reportedly, this attention made the workers feel valued and important.

Further theorizing has advanced **human relations theory** and its goal of improving all interpersonal—including interracial—relationships among employees in the workplace. Four activities can be applied specifically to positive interracial communication. Management development activities involve management serving as role models for employees and being committed to human relations beliefs. Employee relations activities are coordinated to provide employees with the information that promotes job satisfaction, motivation, and interracial cooperation. Labor relations activities attempt to meet the needs of labor and management while also maintaining effective two-way communication between them. The final activity involves public or community relations, where employees enter an organization with preexisting attitudes. As a result, it is important that the organization acknowledge the influence of an individual's environment on her job-related behaviors.

The human relations theory best lends itself to our understanding of organizational communication by taking into consideration the multiple identities of its organizational members (see Chapter 5). Although the organizational goals remain a priority, people in positions of authority are sensitized to the identities shaped by race, gender, class, occupational, and other lived experiences. This becomes even more important when we consider the importance of interracial communication within the context of organizations.

❖ BOX 9.2

AUTHOR REFLECTION

In addition to my responsibilities as a university professor, I also am involved in various collaborations with corporate, educational, healthcare, and community-based organizations. Most often, I work with these organizations to provide diversity training for their members. Through this work, I attempt to utilize my expertise to enhance the ways in which people communicate in diverse settings. As you might expect, my focus is on having individuals understand the role that culture—race, ethnicity, age, gender, nationality, spirituality, ability, and sexual orientation—plays in communication. Working with these organizations provides a great opportunity to apply different theories and concepts to real-world contexts; it also allows me to stay current in terms of what's happening outside the walls of academia.

Working with various organizations on diversity-related issues is important work. However, it is filled with a number of challenges. First, some organizations only engage in diversity training as a form of "window dressing." Sessions are typically not substantial (in terms of time, content, and quality) and done as a means to an end. A second, related, challenge exists when the sessions are conducted without a visible commitment from organizational leadership. This results in a lack of incentive for participants to get involved, and situates the issue as outside of the central mission of the organization (e.g., an add-on feature of less importance). Third, organizations want diversity training that provides easy answers to complex issues. In other words, they want a laundry list of "dos and don'ts"—something that facilitates cultural stereotypes and

(Continued)

(Continued)

a false sense of security. A fourth challenge occurs when the organization only wants to focus on one aspect of diversity (e.g., race) without recognizing the need to address all aspects of diversity. This, as you will remember, goes against the idea of intersectionality explained in Chapter 5. Fifth, and finally, a challenge for providing effective diversity training exists when the focus is on eliminating personal biases. While this may be an important place to begin engaging participants, it does little to address institutional forms of oppression that are often-times embedded within the organization itself.

Over the years, I have worked with some organizations whose efforts to provide diversity training to its organizational members were thwarted by some of the challenges identified here. Others have fearlessly confronted these issues and remain committed to addressing the tough issues related to race and ethnicity. These are individuals who understand that the future of the United States will only make the ability to communicate with diverse groups more important. Taking an entire course on interracial communication is a productive step to enhance your abilities. Hopefully, following graduation, you will join an organization that will provide additional opportunities for professional development in this area.

—MPO

Organizational Culture

Because our nation is becoming increasingly diverse, it is of utmost importance that we begin to think critically about how both our personal and professional relationships can benefit from such change. Furthermore, we must ask ourselves questions that challenge us to reexamine how we think about racial/ethnic diversity and its effect on our private and public lives. In order to engage you in this thinking exercise, consider the following questions:

How do people respond when there is considerable change in the racial demographic of their organization?

Does the competitive nature of an organization become exacerbated when team members are from different racial/ethnic groups?

As organizations commit to racial diversity and require cooperation from their employees, do their organizational members of color experience increased feelings of isolation?

Do dominant group members become frustrated when they are required to attend diversity workshops?

Will racial diversity foster honest and true communication between organizational members from different racial/ethnic backgrounds?

How will these changing and new interracial relationships affect the organizational culture and its goals?

As these questions demonstrate, racial diversity in the workplace will definitely have an impact on communication between organizational members and will undoubtedly influence the organizational structure as the members know it (Blake-Beard, Murrell, & Thomas, 2006). While our personal relationships outside of work are established and initiated by choice, those relationships we create in the workplace are not. Workplace relationships in general are established based primarily on the innate needs of the organization and, more recently, on the needs of its people. Because organizational members are assembled to fulfill that need (e.g., submitting a business proposal, working in small groups, doing a class project), the forced interaction inevitably fosters interpersonal relationships. Choice is not an option; therefore, individuals are expected to develop positive working relationships with each other. When this expectation is met with resistance, however, it affects the overall dynamic and goals of the organization.

When people come together to either create a new or become part of an existing organization, very little consideration is given to establishing a solid foundation on which to build organizational identities and goals. Before members determine what the organization will do, they must first conceptualize what an organizational culture is. Schein (1985) provides the following definition. An **organizational culture** involves

> a pattern of basic assumptions—invented, discovered, or developed by a given group as it learns to cope with its problems of external adaptation and internal integration—that has worked well enough to be considered valid and, therefore, to be taught to new members as the correct way to perceive, think, and feel in relation to those problems. (p. 9)

External adaptation has to do with the influence of the environment on the goals of the organization, whereas internal integration has to do with changes made within the organization. Members are adapting their ways of thinking and behaving to those that closely resemble those of the organization. In essence, the culture reflects or represents the values, beliefs, and expectations shared by its members (Lahiry, 1994). As an extension, members are pressured to conform to shared codes, and their behaviors are shaped by the culture.

Racializing the Organizational Context

In Chapter 5, we discussed how important it is to be aware of the multiple self- and other identities embedded in our societal structure. Race is fluid and multiple in its production of meaning within an individual (Cagney, Wallace, & Browning, n.d.; Smalls, 1998). In other words, our racial/ethnic identities become more or less salient as we go from one social context to another. In Chapter 10, we discuss the interracial conflict that can occur when the races intermingle; therefore, we will limit our discussion in this chapter on these potential problems.

As a nation, we have traditionally thought about race within the context of our personal relationships without giving much thought to organizations. Recently, efforts have been made to sensitize corporate America, community-based organizations, and the business world to the significance of race. In essence, these efforts are made to consider the degree to which the organizational context influences the organizational communication. In general, communication within an organization can be complex because of the differing work habits of the employees and management. Therefore, we must pay close attention to the importance of context in managing organizational culture and identity (see Weick, 1979). Three contexts inform us of how we communicate with each other and adapt to the culture.

The **physical context** refers to the physical environment where the communication takes place (e.g., boss's office, employee lounge). **Social context** refers to the type of relationship that exists between the communicators, and **chronological context** refers to the role of time in influencing the interaction (e.g., morning vs. afternoon meetings). Through our orientation to the organizational culture, we understand the rules that guide our behaviors across these contexts. For example, if a meeting of all staff is called, you know it will be in the conference room (physical context) at 7:30 a.m. (chronological context) and very formal in nature (social context). In contrast, if you are meeting with your coworker, you may choose to have a casual (yet productive) meeting at a restaurant over lunch. In both cases, the culture and process of communication determine the appropriate behaviors.

Historically, these have been general concerns with which many monoracial organizations have been faced. Now they must consider how these contexts will be influenced by racial/ethnic diversity. As we have noted, the U.S. population is becoming increasingly racially diverse, which will affect our relationships in both our private and public lives (see Chapters 1 and 10). In our public lives, our relationships within organizations will experience a change that some may find difficult to cope with. Individuals who have only dealt with status, power, and interpersonal differences are now faced with the impact of racial/ethnic differences on their professional relationships. In the past, they may have only worked with people who looked just like them. Now they are challenged to work alongside racial group members with whom they have had limited interactions. In any event, a degree of uncertainty is experienced as the face of the organization continues to change.

Some people were solely concerned with power and status differentials, but they are now faced with racial/ethnic difference and its impact on the organizational experience. Organization members must now consider how the organization will adapt itself and its members to the impending racial/ethnic diversity. As these issues are considered, we must remember to value racial/ethnic difference as we work toward achieving our goals. Yes, it is imperative that organizations celebrate their newfound diversity; however, it becomes even more important that they not lose sight of their own short-term and long-term goals. If organizational members are perceived and treated as having only one identity (racial/ethnic), then they are devalued as organizational citizens. According to this line of thinking, organizational members of color are totalized (see Houston & Wood, 1996), thus trivializing the importance of racial/ethnic diversity in corporate America. Racial/ethnic diversity can bring new, rich ideas to an organization that has traditionally been unidimensional. Therefore, the organization and its members should not become so consumed by race that their mission and purpose fall by the wayside. Yes, it is important to acknowledge and celebrate racial/ethnic diversity. But organizations must be sure their goals and attempts to diversify the organizational body work together to improve their mission. In the following section we discuss the influence of race/ethnicity on profit and nonprofit organizations.

General Organizational Principles

L. Alexander (1998) applauded President Clinton for creating an organization committed to addressing the nation's state of race relations; however, he contends that the focus should be on "what pulls us together instead of what pulls us apart." He further states that the common set of principles (e.g., equal opportunity, individual rights, self-government) traditionally used in the United States to address social inequalities should be central to the race initiative many people have come to support. Yes, there must be some acknowledgment and discussion about "why we are the way we are" as a nation. If we fail to understand what the problem is and how to resolve it, then we will continue to have racist, sexist, and prejudiced ideologies permeating the very core of the nation's thought processes. Therefore, we must discuss how each sector of the American public is dealing with racial diversity and race relations within that specific context. This self-reflexive approach to race consciousness and organizational communication can only lead to increased knowledge and understanding of the degree to which our racial identities influence race relations on a micro- and macrolevel.

In every facet of American society, we will in one way or another experience the increasing racial/ethnic diversity that is projected to take place in the 21st century (see Chapter 1; Helms et al., 2003; Y. Y. Kim, 1995; K. M. Thomas & Davis, 2006; R. R. Thomas, 2006). Corporations and communities alike are now being forced to examine what image they are going to project to society as a whole (Etzioni, 1996). Traditionally, we have all been expected to conform to the melting pot metaphor where racial/ethnic differences are removed from this collective identity. This ultimately creates a blended identity with no distinctions between, or acknowledgments of, racial/ethnic diversity. Rejecting this assimilationist approach to diversity, others have chosen the rainbow metaphor that acknowledges various people of different colors and the significance of working/living next to one another.

Case Study: University Summit on Race

Your professor has nominated you to serve on a coordinating committee that is responsible for coordinating a race summit to be held on campus in the next year. This is the first time such a conference will be offered to the university and surrounding community, and conference organizers are concerned that there will not be enough involvement from students and faculty and residents in the city to achieve the goal of community outreach and collaboration. University officials have strongly advised the coordinating committee to include more racially/ethnically diverse groups in the summit. Unfortunately, a few community-based

---

❖ **BOX 9.3**

STUDENT REFLECTION

At my old job, I worked as a server. We had bussers there. All but one of the bussers were African American. Many of the bussers lived in the Athens-Clark County public housing system [and] . . . would ride the city bus to work. Many times they would call a friend to pick them up or I would take them home. The first time I drove my friend(s) home, I pulled [over] . . . to stop and let my friend out. [He said] "This is no place for a White kid after dark." So the next day, I said, "Look, I know what you mean, and I'm not trying to be a hero, but I'm driving you home, man. C'mon."

Well, immediately following my leaving the neighborhood, I was pulled over by Athens' finest. The White cop insisted that I had just bought drugs. Now I give him a lot of leeway, because, well, I have been with people who have bought drugs here before, and because I know some of my friends sell drugs in here. I proceeded to tell him that I drove my friend home from work. He proceeded to tell me no White kid drives a Black guy home from work into the projects and that I should quit lying. I said roughly, "Look, dude, I'm really not in the mood for you right now. I don't have anything on me. I just had a really long night, and I have to use the restroom, so if you want to search my &*^$#* and get this over with so I can go home, then please do so. If not, I need to be on my way." Not to be outdone, he proceeded to lecture me on how to speak respectfully to an officer (which under normal circumstances I do), then let me go by saying I should not come around here anymore.

I was pissed. I was racially profiled (like Blacks are all the time) by a White cop. His motivations were based on stereotypes, and he would not accept that he was wrong. Not only that but all of the public housing saw me get pulled over so now when I come back I am going to have to deal with the suspicion that I am in cahoots with the police.

---

groups have voiced hesitancy in being involved in the program, stating that the summit will be like other university-led initiatives on public discourse about race. Once the summit is over, everyone will return to their respective communities and all plans to keep the dialogue will be abandoned, which will make it even more difficult to hold the summit the following year. As a committee, how do you think you and the members can fulfill your duties and address the concerns expressed by the community? Can you really design a race summit that will have an impact on both communities once the summit is over?

According to P. Y. Byers (1997), there are seven steps to be followed for achieving group and organizational goals:

1. Define the *problem.*

2. Determine *goals and objectives* (for advertising).

3. Analyze *target audience.*

4. Determine *media* to be used to reach audience.

5. *Create a message plan* (theme, slogan, keywords, and visuals).

6. Determine your *budget* (costs and extra revenue generated).

7. *Devise evaluation measures* to assess success of the plan (advertising).

In a racialized organizational context, these steps are critical to those organizations purposely making efforts to include their members from a variety of racial/ethnic backgrounds. As the steps demonstrate, the committee members must actively work toward including people who have too often been excluded from the decision-making processes that occur within organizations. As you think about your present and future involvement in organizations, consider how racial/ethnic identity can positively influence the group experience. By exchanging ideas and thoughts about how to fulfill their goals, organizations and their members can establish an inclusive culture that values and appreciates racial/ethnic differences.

Practicing Diversity Management

As leading scholars in diversity management research, Kecia Thomas and colleague Jimmy L. Davis (2006) do an excellent job of describing the issues organizations face in the midst of racial diversity in the workplace. In the following section, we will use an essay by Thomas and Davis to underscore the importance of managing diversity in an ever-changing organizational culture. (For greater discussion of competition and interethnic conflict, see Chapter 10.) Despite the apparent need, organizations remain unprepared for such change. The organizations themselves and their members are oftentimes ill-equipped to deal with the racial differences that are taking place within the organizational culture. As such it is imperative that the organization itself make a concerted effort to measure its performance in the areas of diversity and organizational success.

In their essay, K. M. Thomas and Davis (2006) argue that diversity management must first begin with the leadership, or leaders who "value and [are] commit[ted] to a diverse and inclusive workplace" (p. 73). The leaders must engage in communication behaviors grounded in a belief system that is reflective and supportive of a diverse working environment, which facilitates the leader being situated as a diversity change agent. The behaviors include (1) **goal setting**—the establishment of diversity goals that can be measured by "establish[ing] relationships with minority communities in and outside of the organization, increase the number of mentoring relationships available to female and minority employees, or raise retention rates of high-potential and minority managers" (p. 74); (2) **framing**—communication from leaders to organizational members about diversity that "positively frame[s] it as a strategic learning opportunity for the organization . . . an opportunity to learn about new practices and markets that can improve and expand the business" (p. 74); (3) **accountability**—when the leader ensures that "human resource practices and decisions, such as those related to selection, promotion, and compensation, consider diversity goals and values" (p. 74); and (4) **readiness**—"refers to leaders' understanding of the complexities of diversity in the organization and society . . . engag[ing] in self-exploration and, as a result, understand[ing] how privilege and ethnocentrism operate within their organizations and lives" (p. 75). As each of these behaviors suggests, leadership requires that the leaders not only create an organizational culture and environment that is supportive of racial diversity, but serve as exemplars who espouse positive mental models of workplace diversity.

By developing recruitment strategies that are purposely diversified and target non-White segments of the labor pool, organizations can successfully work toward achieving their goal of an inclusive working environment. According to K. M. Thomas and Davis (2006), research has shown that recruitment advertisements are one way of doing this. Results show that "female and minority job seekers are more attracted to demographic diversity among those in recruitment advertisements than to a portrayal of a homogeneous, white workforce" (p. 75), whereas White males looking for jobs were indifferent toward both kinds of advertisements. K. M. Thomas and Davis (2006) argue that based on these findings, "organizations can aggressively promote diversity in recruitment campaigns, including advertisements, to attract minority and female job seekers without losing white male job seekers" (p. 76). Leaders can also change their approaches to recruitment by using various forms of communication (e.g., Monster.com, online mailing lists, and one-on-one referrals) to access members of marginalized racial groups that will become a prominent part of the emerging workforce.

Another important factor in diversity management is diversity training and multicultural competence (K. M. Thomas & Davis, 2006). "Most organizations provide some form of diversity training, yet may still become defendants in discrimination-related litigation" (p. 77), which is highly problematic. Regardless of the impetus for diversity training (e.g., moral imperative, legal and social pressure, business necessity), the ultimate goal of racial and cultural sensitivity can be reached through "training objectives [that] provide knowledge, enhance self-awareness, change behavior, develop skills" or are used as "a tool for larger organizational change . . . [via] personal growth or skills-based training" (p. 77). In short, diversity training and workshops function as a form of intervention that ultimately prepares the organization and its members for change in the racial demographic. More pointedly, organizational members are equipped, as much as they can be, with the skills and knowledge necessary for communicating effectively and productively across racial lines, while achieving the goals of the organization.

In the midst of this change, K. M. Thomas and Davis (2006) advise us to be mindful of what they call the **glass escalator**, a new phenomenon we will face in years to come. The metaphor we are all most familiar with is the **glass ceiling**, which is used to describe the invisible barriers that prevent women and people of color from advancing in the workplace, despite their qualifications or achievements. Historically, these marginalized groups have been looked over for promotions while White men are promoted at a much faster rate (K. M. Thomas and Davis, 2006); however, in the not-so-distant future, this pattern will change. As the "new" minority group, White men will remain a privileged segment of the population and acquire upward mobility as they did when they held most of the societal power. In any event,

> companies must make sure that they are not discriminating against women and minorities and that their practices are favorable to *all* groups [italics added]. . . . The glass ceiling cannot be broken until leaders are convinced of its existence, and then they must understand

the realities of being a member of a minority group in the workplace. For this to occur, some CEOs' perceptions must change. (K. M. Thomas & Davis, 2006, p. 78)

Case Study

In their essay on diversity management, K. M. Thomas and Davis (2006) talk about human resource development strategies and use Xerox and IBM as examples of two organizations that have been successful in preparing themselves to deal with diversity. Three strategies that facilitate this preparation are important and can be used by other organizations, even student organizations, that desire to be ready for a diverse demographic.

The first strategy involves developing "communication structures [that allow] top leadership to hear underrepresented workers' voices" (p. 78), which might include formal coaching or mentoring of junior minority group members by senior members. Through a formal mentoring relationship, junior female engineers being mentored by senior executives in Xerox's Mentor Up Program were able to receive "career advice, expanded networks, and advocacy," while senior executives "learn[ed] about the experiences of the female engineers in their organizations and the conflicts they confront that can stifle their careers" (p. 79). The mentoring program and information learned from the mentoring pairs benefited Xerox by the learning gained by the mentor and protégé, which will most likely have a positive effect on the organization on an individual and macrolevel.

The second strategy requires that the leaders in the organization "monitor all selection materials and procedures" (p. 79). This would involve the organization determining how racially sensitive and inclusive its efforts and strategies are in recruiting possible organization members from diverse racial and ethnic backgrounds. By closely monitoring this process, the leader and other authority figures may be able to identify holes and problems in their recruitment tools. K. M. Thomas and Davis (2006) suggest, for example, that organizations target other organizations and institutions composed primarily of the racial/ethnic group from which they are trying to recruit. They describe this as organizations "using different, nondiscriminatory selection methods."

The third strategy involves the organization monitoring "diversity results from an organization's promotion policies" (p. 79). Most organizations with a true commitment to diversity will develop goals, objectives, and policies that articulate for the organization and its members how diversity will be achieved. IBM managers use this strategy in the form of a "5-minute drill" at meetings where each of them is expected to make "explicit efforts . . . to discuss management talent at all levels, making sure minorities and females are discussed along with white males" (p. 79) as viable candidates for promotion within the company.

Employing one or more of these strategies can only contribute to the successful management of organizational diversity. Coupled with strong leadership and a high level of commitment by its members, an organization that is proactive in creating a supportive and productive environment for all of its organizational members and its members of color in particular can potentially become a model for diversity management in the 21st century.

As we examine the saliency of race within corporate America, we must discuss how European American males are dealing with racial/ethnic diversity (Sanchez-Burks, Nisbett, &Ybarra, 2000). Can you imagine what it is like to be qualified for a job and have someone who is part of a historically disadvantaged racial/ethnic group be hired for the position instead of you? Although you are in support of diversity, you are also concerned with how this is displacing others who are equally qualified for the same positions. According to Gates (1993), European American males account for the following percentages of various sectors of our public sites: 39.2% of the population, 82.5% of the Forbes 400 (people worth $265+ million), 77% of Congress, 92% of state governors, 70% of tenured college faculty, approximately 90% of daily newspaper editors, and 77% of TV news directors (p. 49). Therefore, we can see why racial/ethnic diversity is often perceived as a threat to European American males' positions of power in the United States. Galen (1994) describes this emotional-laden issue as follows:

> But in such companies as AT&T, DuPont, and Motorola, where diversity is becoming more than a buzzword, the emotional landscape for white males is changing. There, white men must compete against people they may not have taken seriously as rivals—mainly women, blacks, Hispanics, and Asians. White males may also say that the diversity programs often make them feel threatened or attacked. (p. 51)

European American males are being forced to deal with this sobering new reality (K. M. Thomas & Davis, 2006) because of the restructuring taking place in corporate America. This phenomenon is commonly referred to as "white male backlash" or reverse discrimination (Rowan, 1995). The issue taken to task is merit, or who is best qualified for the job, which becomes even more problematic when you have candidates who are of similar merit. Reverse discrimination is cited as the reason for the European American male not being hired, when in actuality this move is an effort to remedy (by law) past discriminations in the workplace (Galen, 1994).

❖ BOX 9.4

STUDENT REFLECTION

I understand that there are many "illegal immigrants" in this country that "hurt" the economy when they send their money back home to their families and don't spend their money on U.S. goods, but people have to make a living somehow. An even bigger problem arises when you look at families that have been here for years that have had children in the country. What do we want to do? Send parents away from their legal biological children? I think if laws on this subject are going to be passed, they should take more into account when they are viewing families as "illegal." This is more than just a legal issue, it is also a humanitarian issue and laws can't just be passed at the snap of a finger ruining millions of people's lives.

Many people do not like the number of immigrants who are currently in the country because they take away jobs from Americans. Immigrants get jobs over Americans because they have proven to be extremely hard workers and don't cause as many problems. For instance, my uncle builds houses and has employed many Hispanic workers. He explained how much better workers Hispanic individuals are than their American counterparts. He even said that he pays them more than he would any American because they care so much about their work and put in three times the time and effort that they deserve and earn everything they make. My uncle explained how the Americans he has employed are filled with bad excuses of coming to work and many times have drinking and drug problems. He told me that people should look more to the reasons Americans are not getting jobs before they look at who it is taking the jobs away from them. Possibly, my uncle holds stereotypes on the types of people he has hired, but he told me that he has never had any problems with Hispanic workers and has rarely had an American worker stick around long enough to remember them. He respects the Hispanic culture and wishes that Americans would take a closer look at why their jobs are being taken away and possibly learn a little on the ways people maintain and keep jobs in his field.

If you look at the big picture, if all of the immigrants in the country were sent back to the countries they came from, the United States economy would suffer in a BIG way. Maybe we should take a harder look at what immigrants do to help this country before we decide it is important to ship them all back home unjustly and unfairly.

The company and individuals in positions of authority are faced with a moral dilemma. They are expected to diversify the workforce yet are blamed for past discriminations. One strategy K. M. Thomas and Davis (2006) suggest that can address these concerns is to "conduct an organizational diversity climate assessment that also can serve as a needs assessment" (p. 78). Regularly updating the data can "help leaders develop needs-based diversity initiatives that those responsible for their implementation are more likely to accept" and "[provide] the organization an opportunity to benchmark best practices within departments or functions that could have utility organization-wide" (p. 78). Although there is not one solution to this problem, we must engage in open, honest discussion about the communication climates that exist within organizations and how racial/ethnic diversity is a positive quality for any and all organizations to possess.

Case Study

In the 21st century, it is very likely that you will be interacting with racially/ethnically different others. To be prepared for interracial and interethnic interactions, Brilhart and Galanes (1995) suggest that we use behaviors that facilitate effective interracial communication. Although these behaviors are specific to intercultural communication, they are appropriate for interracial interactions. Because our racial/ethnic identities are central to how we define ourselves, we must be sensitive to how they influence our communicative experiences.

According to their observations (Brilhart & Galances, 1995), effective interracial communication is possible if we (1) *acknowledge* that every discussion is intercultural (racial/ethnic differences are present), (2) *recognize and accept* our differences (affirmation of each other), (3) *understand* that behaviors may be attributed to culture, (4) *engage in* open dialogue about observed differences, and (5) *be willing* to adapt to difference. These suggestions are very appropriate because they challenge you to leave your comfort zone. More importantly, you are challenged to think about how you *really* interact with racially/ethnically different others. Remember, someone may be thinking about you in the same way and may be unsure how to interact with you. Communication is an interaction that involves what we say as well as who we are.

An approach that has been used in organizations that can be applied to a racialized organizational environment is employee empowerment (Butcher, 2006). Empowerment involves an individual or group having power, authority, or influence over events and outcomes important to them. Within corporate America, individuals are operating with a shared system of meaning; therefore, the notion of empowerment for the benefit of the individual is subverted. The social collective is valued more so than individuals, which makes it difficult for anyone to feel valued by the organizational culture. These feelings become even stronger when a person's multiple identities inform his or her understanding in terms of organizational experiences.

Let's take the example of a Korean American woman. If she does not feel valued as a member, she could potentially feel even more unappreciated because her identities as a Korean American and a woman are often ignored. What is even worse is that she may be expected to take on the role of spokesperson for *all* Korean Americans in corporate America (what a great responsibility!). Therefore, the onus of responsibility lies with the manager, who, as a leader, is responsible for engaging organizational members in open communication about work-related issues (K. M. Thomas & Davis, 2006) as well as racial/ethnic diversity as it affects the employees from diverse racial/ethnic groups and those in the majority. Because corporate America is being continually educated on the urgency of racial/ethnic diversity in the workplace, it is of utmost importance that managers make a concerted effort to foster a positive social climate conducive to effective communication that crosses racial borders. More importantly, the interpersonal communication skills and relationships developed between racially/ethnically different organizational members must become, and remain, a top priority, as we continue into the 21st century.

Conclusion

This chapter examined the significance of race within an organizational context. We found through case studies and research that although efforts are being made to prepare corporate America, educational systems, and communities for racial diversity in traditionally European American contexts, people from all sides of this racial/ethnic divide have feelings of apprehension and discomfort. The good news, however, is that people are taking the initiative to improve race relations on both a micro- and macrolevel. In corporate America, we see that administrators and employees alike are struggling with this change in the environment. Although microcultural racial/ethnic group members face barriers to advancement, administrators are actively dealing with this glass ceiling and its effect on the overall well-being of its new organizational members. In our educational systems, students, faculty, and administrators are developing and creating programs and organizations that value the multiple identities of *all* students. Instead of making these students tokens, organizational members collectively celebrate racial/ethnic diversity through learning opportunities in and outside of the classroom. As an extension, some community-based organizations are working to improve race relations by establishing a common ground (e.g., religious beliefs) that can be used toward racial reconciliation.

These different types of organizations are important if we are to increase our race consciousness in the 21st century. By using diversity training programs as a method for increased racial sensitivity, we can use the organizational site as a context for promoting more effective interracial communication in the form of diversity management. We are a nation that is becoming increasingly diverse, both racially and ethnically; therefore, we must use our membership in different organizations to become social agents of change.

OPPORTUNITIES FOR EXTENDED LEARNING ❖

1. Make a list of four or five companies you believe produce quality products and have a fairly good reputation in the business world. Do an Internet search and create a profile or portfolio for each of the companies. As you gather data, identify core goals and values, as well as whether each company has a diversity management program in place. Provide a critique of how the company has measured its success in reaching the outlined goals (in general and those related to racial/ethnic diversity) and actually diversifying its organizational members.

2. Using the Internet, do a search for current cases of workplace discrimination. In reviewing those cases, identify what forms of discrimination (e.g., sexism, racism, heterosexism) are occurring. How are the companies choosing to address this inappropriate workplace behavior? If the case has been settled, how did the company reorganize or redefine itself afterward? Were any programs set into place to ensure that future instances of discrimination would not take place?

3. Using the Internet, provide the legal and popular definitions of affirmative action. Compare and contrast how these definitions create dissonance for people who are either in support or opposition of "leveling the playing field." According to the legal definition, does this mean that people who are less qualified for a position are going to be hired instead of qualified people? Discuss as a class how affirmative action is still needed to provide people, including women, people of color, and physically challenged people, with equal access to opportunities that have traditionally been denied to them.

4. After reading R. Thomas, Jr.'s (2006) article "Diversity Management: An Essential Craft for Leaders" in *Leader to Leader*, create your own "Top 10 Tips for a *Really* Diverse University Campus." In your own words, generate a list of 10 strategies that students, administrators, faculty, and staff at a university can use as a template for realistically creating a diverse university campus. The list should involve strategies that will create a climate that discourages hostile communication, fosters emotional and psychological support, and encourages interracial relationships between a variety of racial and ethnic groups on the university campus. Type your list and bring them to class. The lists will be collected from students and shared in class to facilitate discussion about this topic. The discussion should include an assessment of how realistic, appropriate, and effective each strategy is. Be ready to provide suggestions for how the strategies can be modified in order to reach the aforementioned goals.

5. Using 10 interview questions, pair up with someone to conduct in-depth interviews with men and women of local businesses and organizations facing racial/ethnic diversity. Questions should gauge their attitudes toward and beliefs about diversity and its effect on the organizational culture (e.g., "How would you define diversity?" "How do you think your organization will be affected by diversity? Do you anticipate a change in the racial composition of the employees?") Compare the responses and share them with the class. Discuss what, if

any, types of positive or negative attitudes surfaced among the participants. Address how power/status, race/ethnicity, and sex of participants may have influenced opinions about racial/ethnic diversity.

6. Recall an occasion when you attended a public presentation and were in the minority (e.g., the only Latina, only male). List the feelings you had about being in that situation, hearing the speech, and the speaker's (in)ability to connect with you as an audience member. On another list, write down suggestions for that speaker that would have made his or her speech more effective in a racialized environment.

10

Interracial Conflict

onflict is an inevitable part of the human experience (Roloff, 1987). Consequently, people in relationships find themselves in conflict on a regular basis (Guerrero & La Valley, 2006). When in conflict, individuals often demonstrate preferences for certain communication styles, something that is oftentimes learned within various cultural contexts (Kitayama, Markus, Matsumoto, & Norasakkunkit, 1997). For instance, according to Collier (1991), an individual's racial and ethnic background, coupled with social interactions with family and friends, impacts how they are taught to deal with conflict. In short, race, ethnicity, and culture are frames through which we view, experience, and perceive conflict (Ribeau, 1995). Given the history of race relations described in Chapter 2, conflict, power, and inequality are present in current-day interactions. Because of this, interracial and interethnic communication is commonly seen as a site of struggle (Moss & Faux, 2006).

Communication scholars have studied social conflicts for the past 30-plus years (Putnam, 2006). This chapter draws from this research with a particular focus on interracial and interethnic conflict. According to Ting-Toomey (2000), conflict is "the perceived and/or actual incompatibility of values, expectations, processes, or outcomes between two or more parties . . . over substantive and/or relational issues" (p. 388). We adopt this definition and apply it specifically to individuals from different racial and ethnic groups within the United States. Consistent with the focus of the book, we differentiate between *interracial conflict* (conflict between members of different races, i.e., African African/Asian American) and *interethnic conflict* (conflict between members of different ethnic groups, i.e., Cuban Americans/Puerto Rican Americans). This chapter is designed to provide students with a background on the sources of conflict, as well as different conflict styles. Following these descriptions, we discuss some of the limitations of existing research and offer some practical examples on how some groups have created interracial unity within their organizations.

Research on intercultural conflict generally, and interracial and interethnic conflict specifically, is a rapidly growing area of study (Orbe & Everett, 2006). The vast majority of research on culture and conflict, however, has focused on comparison studies of conflict styles among people from different countries (M.-S. Kim & Leung, 2000). The same could be said for research on interracial or interethnic conflict (Houston, 2002). At times, it is the different cultural styles of individuals, and not necessarily the content of the conflict itself, that creates problems within the conflict episode (Ting-Toomey, 1988). Other times, the focus of the conflict could be over personal, social, or professional issues; oftentimes racial and ethnic differences complicate the conflict. Before discussing different conflict styles, we begin by describing how interracial and interethnic conflict is oftentimes the result of existing context issues.

Contextual Sources of Conflict

Interracial/ethnic conflict is a dynamic process; any one episode is typically the result of multiple sources of conflict (H. Waters, 1992). In other words, conflict can simultaneously involve personal and cultural issues. In order to provide insight into how conflict often becomes racialized, we describe various sources of interracial/ethnic conflict.

Present-Day Social Inequality

As covered in Chapter 2, ingroup/outgroup tensions have existed since the origins of the United States. These historical tensions continue today, and a present-day social inequality between groups serves as a contextual source of interracial and interethnic conflict (Stephan & Stephan, 2001). In a capitalist society, such as the United States, people oftentimes find themselves competing for limited resources. Social inequalities—in terms of health, housing, employment, income, and education—exist and become a key source of frustration because people are not able to participate on a "level playing field." What is especially frustrating for marginalized groups (most often people of

---

❖ **BOX 10.1**

STUDENT REFLECTIONS

Growing up in what I would say were two different extremes really shaped my feelings and opinions on racial issues. Until I was 7 years old, I lived in a neighborhood where there were Mexicans, Puerto Ricans, African Americans, and Caucasians all in one block. Then, my father decided to move our family to a safer city, to get us out of the bad neighborhood we were living in. This is where my life, and views on race and issues surrounding it, changed drastically. I didn't understand why there were no kids that looked like me, or even more, why all the kids at my school were the same. I was no longer in a multicultural setting. Instead, I was getting asked why I talked the way I did, or what certain slang words that I used meant. As a child, I didn't understand. As I got older I realized that the color of my skin, my last name, and even the way I talked, was going to impact the rest of my life. I would frequently have a racial slur thrown at me, even by those people who called themselves my friends. I have been called everything from the N-word, to dirty Mexican, and the one that for some reason bothers me the most, White girl. Although I would like to think that most people don't look at you and automatically see the color of your skin, more and more, I feel that they do. But, I am also glad that people recognize me as a Latina, because I am proud of my background and feel that it is a very important part of who I am.

color) are recent attempts to ignore that social inequality exists and advocate for colorblind communication (Tierney & Jackson, 2002).

Despite the attempts to mend a history of oppression and discrimination, the U.S. population continues to be divided in terms of "haves" and "have-nots"—a division that oftentimes occurs largely along racial lines. For example, according to Rudman, Ashmore, and Melvin (2001), African Americans continue to suffer from oppression in employment, housing, and health care. African Americans do not have equal opportunity in the area of the justice system or police protection, and although they have equal access to public education, the quality of education is highly unequal (Rudman et al., 2001). In research on face-to-face interactions between Korean immigrant retailers and African American customers, Bailey (2000) concluded that social inequality in the United States shapes the local context in which interracial encounters occur. Specifically, he found that social inequality fueled social assumptions that storekeepers and customers brought to the stores, the result of which were interracial episodes grounded in misunderstanding and mistrust.

Similar social inequalities are at the root of tensions between African Americans and Latino/as. Historically, African Americans and Latino/as oftentimes found themselves in communities of color, and/or alternatively in contexts where they are in the distinct minority (Rios, 2003). Solidarity between Latino/as and African Americans is well documented (Rowe & Ramos, 2003). In some instances, however, both groups find themselves in conflict over limited resources or struggles with social standing. The forms of this type of interracial conflict vary depending on historical context and geographical location (Rowe & Ramos, 2003). For example, in the Northeast, tensions between African Americans and Puerto Rican Americans have centered on bilingual education and competition for jobs and political clout. Similar tensions have existed between Cuban Americans and African Americans in southern Florida. In the Southwest and California, tensions have emerged amid debates about legalizing immigration. Given all of this, it is important to note that some scholars, like Ryoo (2005), described these widely publicized tensions as exaggerated.

Ingroup/Outgroup Tensions

Within a historical context of domination, slavery, colonization, and military conquests, it is no surprise that ingroup/outgroup tensions exist among European Americans and different racial and ethnic groups (Dovidio, Gaertner, et al., 2002). The long history of mistreatment, discrimination, and racism has fostered a general sense of mistrust and suspicion of European Americans among some communities of color (Akiba & Miller, 2004). At times, individual knowledge of the history of mistreatment of one group at the hands of another increases the negativity between racial and ethnic groups—something that can trigger conflict (Gallois, 2003). In addition, community conflict is often generated by an influx of new racial and ethnic groups (Oliver & Wong, 2003) who are perceived by residents as a threat (M. H. Ross, 2000). Within this context, the majority group may feel that their economic and social privilege is threatened; such, reportedly, has been the case for some European Americans and African Americans who have felt threatened by the economic power of Asian Americans (Oliver & Wong, 2003). The end result is increased ingroup/outgroup tension, which typically results in increased communication apprehension during interracial interactions (Toale & McCroskey, 2001).

Historically, much of the literature on race, ethnicity, and conflict has focused on tensions between European Americans and different racial/ethnic groups. However, according to Shah and Thornton (1994), one of the most tense relationships between different racial and ethnic groups exists between African Americans and Latino/as. Because of the political inroads that have been gained by the Latin community, and the new Latin immigrants taking low-paying jobs, African Americans believe that Latino/a success has come at their expense (D. M. Rowe & Ramos, 2003). Latino/as counter the African American's argument stating that African Americans are insensitive to Latino/a needs and that African Americans do not want to share their resources with other minorities (Shah & Thornton, 1994).

❖ **BOX 10.2**

MIGRATION TRENDS AND RACIAL AND ETHNIC TENSIONS

For centuries, the South has been defined by the color line and the struggle for accommodation between African Americans and European Americans (Calafell, 2004). In the first half of the 20th century, hundreds of thousands of African Americans migrated to the north and Midwest (Frey, 1998). In the last 10 years, a reverse migration has occurred with African Americans returning to Georgia, North Carolina, and Florida in record numbers (Frey, 2001, 2004b). However, the arrival of hundreds of thousands of Latino/a immigrants in the past 5–10 years has changed the dynamics of race in many towns across the South (Swarns, 2006). These demographic shifts have resulted in some tensions between Latino/as and African Americans who compete fiercely for working-class jobs and government resources. An effect of this, according to some Latino/as, is hostility, insults, and ethnic slurs from African Americans (Swarns, 2006). Growing anti-immigration sentiment has been understood by some as covertly reflective of racial and ethnic tension (Domke, McCoy, & Torres, 2003).

- What other examples of interracial and interethnic tensions exist that relate to recent patterns of migration and/or immigration?
- Can you also identify examples of unique interracial unity that has also occurred as a result of population shifts?

Another form of ingroup/outgroup tension reportedly exists between some Korean Americans and African Americans in urban areas across the United States. According to Jo (1992), the tension began when Korean Americans moved into the African American communities and established residences and businesses in the area. African Americans accuse Korean Americans of overcharging, rudeness, taking over African American businesses, and siphoning money out of the community without putting it back in (Jo, 1992). Korean Americans argue that the African Americans are wrong, and that the misunderstanding comes from conflicting cultures and miscommunication. For instance, Jo (1992) explained that the reason Korean Americans are less likely to exchange pleasantries is because of their unfamiliarity of the English language, not rudeness. Also, Korean Americans are less likely to hire African Americans in their stores because they cannot afford to pay well, so they employ their own families who will work for a lot less than the average employee. In the end, Cho

(1995) argued that Korean Americans, like their African American counterparts, face ingroup/outgroup tensions with different racial and ethnic groups on varying levels (e.g., Korean American/European American).

Perceptual Differences

Members of different racial and ethnic groups define and perceive conflict differently (Hecht et al., 2003). From a person of color's standpoint, it is not always clear if the conflict is a function of race or some other issue (e.g., personality differences). In addition, when conflict arises, people of color are left wondering if the conflict was malicious (reflective of racial bias) or more indicative of naiveté, miscommunication, or misperceptions (H. Waters, 1992). European Americans, in comparison, often misunderstand the degree of offense that oftentimes accompanies unintentional, subtle forms of racially biased statements and questions (K. T. Warren, Orbe, & Greer-Williams, 2003). Perceptual differences also exist in terms of expectations. What is appropriate when engaging in conflict? The answer to this question can be quite different when asked of different racial and ethnic groups. If individuals do not recognize that "appropriate" behavior can be relative oftentimes results in a polarized conflict situation where trust and respect are lacking (Buttny & Williams, 2000). Such situations only work to further distort perceptions of other groups (Ting-Toomey & Oetzel, 2001).

Communicating styles and values can be misinterpreted by individuals who are not a part of the same race (Houston & Wood, 1996). For example, certain common practices that are valued within the African American community (e.g., verbal dueling) can be misperceived as attacking by members of other racial groups (Kochman, 1990). Another example involves instances when European Americans view African American styles of communicating as rude and African Americans see European American styles as cold and unfeeling (Houston & Wood, 1996). Generally speaking, African Americans have a tendency to be more expressive with their feelings, while European Americans tend to be more reserved and believe that feelings should be more contained (Speicher, 1995). Accordingly, when interracial encounters do occur in the context of differing interests, values, and norms, there is a sense of psychological distance, which inhibits the ability for different races to reach common goals (Orbe & Everett, 2006).

❖ **BOX 10.3**

PERCEPTUAL DIFFERENCES OF CONFLICT

Reality-based television has, in many ways, come to dominate television. MTV's *The Real World* was one of the first shows to show "seven strangers, picked to live in a house, and have their lives taped to show what happens when people stop being polite and start being real." The success of this show, as well as all reality-based television, was connected to the amount of conflict between cast members. Researchers Kiesha Warren, Mark Orbe, and Nancy Greer-Williams (2003) used a clip from one of the early reality-based television programs, MTV's *The Real World*, to study the perceptions of individuals from different cultural groups.

(Continued)

(Continued)

Specifically, they presented a video clip from the first season of the show (New York) to diverse groups of people (African Americans, European Americans, and Latino/as). The clip showed an argument between Julie, an 18-year-old European American woman from Alabama, and Kevin, a 24-year-old African American man from New Jersey. Participants in the study were then asked to discuss their perceptions of what happened, who was at fault, and what could have been done to avoid the conflict.

The results were extremely interesting, especially in how they relate to the perception differences between cultural groups. In fact, although everyone saw the same video clip, the perception patterns were clearly different for each of the three groups examined. African American women saw *race* as the main factor in the conflict. Specifically they pointed to the potential role that interracial sexual attraction and racial stereotyping played in Julie and Kevin's argument. In comparison, European American women saw *gender* as the distinguishing marker in the conflict. Their perceptions focused on how a man, Kevin, attempted to aggressively use his body and voice to intimidate Julie.

European American men saw the conflict as a result of *personal* differences. Race and gender were only addressed in limited ways. Instead, the focus of the discussion was on how Kevin and Julie's personalities were at the root of the conflict. And what about African American men? Many defined the conflict as one where race played an issue; however, they also saw how *other factors*—like age, socioeconomic status, and upbringing—came into play as well.

Interestingly, Latino/as consistently described the conflict in terms of being simultaneously about personality, gender, and race differences. Within a person's comments, for instance, she or he would begin by talking about the conflict as a personality conflict, but then conclude by pointing out the ways in which the interaction was also layered with racial and gender (mis)perceptions.

Stereotyping/Lack of Exposure

Although the United States is attempting to move toward a nation that is racially integrated, most races tend to live apart rather than together (Maly, 2005). Racial segregation in neighborhood communities, worship centers, educational institutions, and social organizations increases the chance for misunderstanding (Y. Y. Kim, 1994). One of the primary reasons for this is that racial segregation increases the likelihood that stereotypes and false generalizations will make interracial/-ethnic interactions potentially volatile (Oliver & Wong, 2003). In the least, it results in greater caution on the part of diverse individuals (Orbe & Everett, 2006). At worst, it creates an increased sense of relational inequality that makes effective intercultural encounters difficult (Gallois, 2003).

Y. Y. Kim (1994) recognized stereotyping, and a lack of interest in communicating with other racial and ethnic groups, as a source for conflict. When different races are trying to uplift their own race while other races hold stereotypes against them, it can cause serious conflict between the two groups (Habke & Sept, 1993). For example, according to Oliver and Wong (2003), in some contexts Asian Americans are likely to view Latino/as as having a lack of intelligence and being welfare dependent. Alternatively, Blacks and Latino/as both may view Asian Americans as difficult to get along with. Both stereotypes, given the competition for limited resources, typically result in conflicts between these racial and ethnic groups (H. Lee & Rogan, 1991). In addition, Romer, Jamieson, Riegner, and Rouson (1997) noted that ethnic tension may also be ongoing because many Latino/as still have negative feelings and hold negative stereotypes toward African Americans. Interestingly, **metastereotypes**—the perceptions that racial and ethnic groups have concerning the stereotypes that others have for them—appear to be more prevalent than the actual stereotypes themselves (Sigelman & Tuch, 1997). Therefore, the perceptions of outgroup stereotypes by racial and ethnic group members may actually exacerbate tensions that are not as salient as assumed (Stephan & Stephan, 2001).

Media also play a role in accelerating stereotypical images of racialized others (e.g., Orbe, Warren, & Cornwell, 2001), especially when they have little or no contact with individuals from that particular race (Bramlett-Solomon & Hernandez, 2003). Shah and Thornton (1994) found that African American and Latino/a communities were represented as inner city, Black ghettos, and Hispanic districts, and positioned as isolated from other communities. The neighborhoods of African Americans, for example, were portrayed in the media as neighborhoods of destruction and danger (Shah & Thornton, 1994). By naming the neighborhoods in this manner, it created a psychological distance from the European American community. Not surprisingly, journalists who report to mainly European American audiences frame minority stories as interracial conflicts to make the stories more newsworthy (Romer, Jamieson, & de Coteau, 1998). When negative images are constantly placed in the media, individuals who have not had contact with the different racial and ethnic groups may either have their stereotypes that they hold against these ethnic groups reinforced, or new stereotypes and negative feelings may emerge (Oliver & Wong, 2003). In either case, the result is a public image that perpetuates interracial and interethnic conflict as the norm (Viswanath & Arora, 2000).

Conflict Styles

Racial/Ethnic Conflict Styles

As stated earlier, intercultural conflict researchers have primarily focused on the conflict styles of U.S. and non-U.S. cultures (Ting-Toomey et al., 2000). This body of research has largely used traditional conflict frameworks and measures of individualism/ collectivism as a means to identify patterns of conflict strategies (M.-S. Kim & Leung, 2000). In similar ways, interpersonal conflict researchers in the United States have tended to use similar concepts to inform their research on race, ethnicity, and conflict. The result has been research that stems from individualistic/low-context and collectivistic/high-context value systems regarding communication generally, and conflict specifically.

Individualism refers to the cultural values that emphasize the individual identity, rights, and needs over the collective identity, rights, and needs of the larger group. Communication in these cultures is generally more self-focused, ego-based, and self-expressive. **Collectivism** refers to cultural values that emphasize a group identity over an individual identity. Group obligations and needs take precedence over individual wishes and desires. In other words, collectivistic cultures emphasize a "We-Identity" more so than an "I-Identity." Communication in these cultures typically adheres to group norms and is evaluated in the context of others' behaviors. Another dimension used in traditional cross-cultural research looks at the importance of context. In **high-context** cultures, differences can exist between what is meant and what is actually said. Communication in high-context cultures, like Japan, involves many subtle nonverbal nuances and forms of indirect negotiation. In this regard, collectivistic cultures are highly sensitive to the effect of their words on others, and weigh what they say very carefully. The role that context serves in low-context cultures is different. In **low-context** cultures, persons are expected to say what they mean. The norm is not to rely on contextual clues for communicating meaning but to strive for literal meaning. As you might imagine, effective communication, then, involves direct statements, linear speaking patterns, and overt forms of expression.

According to Ting-Toomey et al. (2000), the assumption is that European Americans are individualistic/low context, while Latino/a, Asian, and African Americans are collectivistic/high context (see Table 10.1). Following this assumption, research has explored how these cultural values affect the ways in which these racial and ethnic groups engage in conflict. Trubisky, Ting-Toomey, and Lin (1991) found evidence that during conflict with acquaintances, Asians tend to use higher degrees of obliging and avoiding conflict styles than European Americans. Asians also tend to use a third party more often than other racial groups (Leung, Au, Fernandez-Dols, & Iwawaki, 1992). In comparison, European Americans tend to use upfront, solution-oriented styles, such as integrating and compromising, in dealing with conflict problems (Leung et al., 1992). Mexican Americans, according to Kagan, Knight, and Martinez-Romero (1982) and Garcia (1996), utilize avoiding conflict styles as a means to preserve relational harmony when conflict arises among close Mexican American friends. Research on African Americans has concluded that they tend to use more emotionally expressive and involving modes of conflict (Ting-Toomey, 1986).

While this line of research reflects the dominant frame of traditional research on race/ethnicity and conflict, research has begun to advance conceptual assumptions beyond a simple individualistic–collectivistic dichotomy. In Chapter 5, we discussed the concept of intersectionality, an idea that points to the importance of studying race and ethnicity alongside other aspects of cultural identity. As early as the mid-1980s, research on conflict styles began to consider intragroup differences, like those related to gender. For example, Ting-Toomey (1986) found that African American women tend to use more emotionally expressive conflict styles than African American men, European American men, and European American women. Other research has utilized **self-construals**—one's self-perception as being either independent or interdependent of larger group influences—to also explore additional factors predicting conflict style patterns. In a study of Latino/as and European Americans, self-construals were a better predicator of conflict styles than racial/ethnic background (Oetzel, 1998). While some have criticized the limited nature of self-construals (M.-S. Kim & Leung, 2000), it represents an advance in research beyond unilateral assumptions among race, ethnicity, and conflict styles.

Much of the research that we have drawn from thus far has come from social scientific studies that treat race, ethnicity, and culture as variables. Additional research, however, has used culturally based qualitative research designs to generate insight into conflict styles that were difficult to obtain through recall data via written surveys. For

❖ **Table 10.1** Core Cultural Differences in Conflict

Individualistic/Low-Context Cultures	Collectivistic/High-Context Cultures
Issue orientation • Conflict is necessary to work out major differences and problems • Conflict is functional when it provides a way to address problems • Focus should be on specific issues; relational issues should be handled separately	*Relational/face orientation* • Conflict viewed as damaging to social status and relational harmony • Conflict reflects a lack of self-discipline and emotional immaturity • Topical issues and relational issues are intertwined and must be dealt with together
Goal orientation • Focus is on achieving specific goals with an eye on the future • Conflict episodes must be isolated and addressed accordingly • Conflict management should follow a preset schedule with clear agenda items	*Process orientation* • Focus on the process and how it relates to the past, present, and future • Conflict management has no clear beginning and end • Conflict management is a delicate, subtle process that has no predetermined schedule
Use of formal mediator • Preference for formally trained mediator • Mediator should be impartial and not know any parties involved • Mediator should only focus on the issue(s) at hand	*Use of informal mediator* • Preference for informal mediator, usually a well-respected elder • Mediator should know all parties involved • Mediator should attend to past events to help understand current conflict
Tangible power resources • Power is reflected in the ability to reward and/or punish others • Struggles to gain more power happen both overtly and covertly • Power is asserted through threats, direct requests, and aggressive defense strategies	*Intangible power resources* • Power is reflected in gains or losses in reputation, prestige, or status • Fewer struggles to gain more power exist; if they do, they happen covertly • Power is displayed subtly through indirect requests, tag questions, and inferences
Direct/competitive communication • Communicators have a responsibility to be open, direct, and clear • Emphasis on verbal offense and defense to justify one's position • Uses communication strategies that reflect a win/win competition between parties	*Indirect/integrating communication* • Communicators have a responsibility to pick up on the hidden meaning and intentions of others • Relies on ambiguous, indirect verbal and nonverbal messages • Uses communication strategies that reflect a win/win negotiation between parties

example, ethnographic studies involving various Native American nations have pointed to the importance of recognizing varying cultural values and the ways they impact conflict behaviors (Sanchez, 2001). Such qualitative research has been invaluable in recognizing that past interpretations of other racial and ethnic group behavior often missed the mark in terms of the rationale for using certain conflict strategies. For example, Basso (1990) reported that, in times of conflict or negotiation, non-Native Americans oftentimes can misinterpret the silence of Native Americans—like that which occurs within the Western Apache culture—as disinterest, a reluctance to speak, or lack of personal warmth. What cultural outsiders fail to recognize in this context is that silence itself carries multiple meanings (see also C. Braithwaite, 1990).

Gaining the perspectives of traditionally marginalized racial and ethnic groups—outside of comparisons with European Americans—represents an important advance in existing conflict research. As such, additional research has focused on accessing ingroup racial and ethnic assumptions of communication behaviors. Of particular note is the work of Hecht and colleagues on African American (e.g., Hecht, Ribeau, & Alberts, 1989) and Mexican American (e.g., Hecht, Ribeau, & Sedano, 1990) perspectives on interethnic communication. This research does not focus solely on conflict, but instead on what each racial/ethnic group regards as satisfying interaction, a framework that is useful when looking at conflict (Ribeau, 1995). While this line of research appears especially useful in advancing existing understanding of how different racial and ethnic groups understand conflict, most of the research has compared different racial and ethnic groups (Houston, 2002).

Racial/Ethnic Comparisons

From the outset of scholarship in the area of race, ethnicity, and conflict, researchers have compared the conflict styles of different groups (Donahue, 1985). For instance, in his seminal research on Black and White styles in conflict, Kochman (1981) focused on direct comparisons: the "Black mode of conflicts is high-keyed, animated, interpersonal and confrontational; the white mode of conflict is relatively low-keyed, dispassionate, impersonal, and non-challenging" (Kochman, 1981, p. 18). Contrasting African American and European American conflict styles was adopted by other interracial and interethnic communication research (e.g., Hecht, Larkey, & Johnson, 1992; Ting-Toomey, 1986) and continues to frame current discussions (e.g., Hecht, Jackson, & Ribeau, 2003).

Such research has provided insight into various points of particular comparison. For example, Martin, Hecht, and Larkey (1994) explored the concepts of realism and honesty among different groups. African Americans view realism as telling it like it is whether you are being positive or negative. In comparison, European Americans' idea of realism is slightly different. European Americans use the term honesty in the place of realism (Martin et al., 1994). Honesty can be honest but unrealistic, and can become problematic when disclosing positives and negatives. For example, if an African American is too honest to a European American, the European American may get offended; similarly, if a European American is not "real" with an African American, it can produce the same results (Martin et al., 1994).

This line of research has generated additional racial comparisons between African Americans and European Americans within particular situational contexts, like organizations. Shuter and Turner (1997), for example, focused on the different perceptions of organizational conflict between African American and European American women. While both groups perceived their own attempts to reduce conflict as most effective, each enacted different strategies toward the same objective. African American women, interested in getting the conflict out on the table so it could be readily addressed and moved beyond, reported that a direct approach to conflict is most effective. In comparison, European American women used more of an avoidance strategy and felt fear or anxiety when having to approach conflict directly (Shuter & Turner, 1997).

In a study conducted by Collier (1991), three ethnic groups (Mexican, African, and European Americans) were examined to analyze conflict differences within friendships. Participants were asked to describe their definitions of friendship and conflict, and whether they felt that their friends handled conflict effectively or ineffectively in a recalled interaction. Collier found that the different races defined conflict differently. The European American males defined conflict as a difference of opinion, an attack on a person's beliefs and opinions, an unresolved situation, and an inability to compromise; African American men saw conflict as a disagreement, different views, and misunderstandings; Mexican Americans described conflict in a more relational manner. The study also examined how each racial/ethnic group perceived competent communication during conflict episodes. European Americans valued taking responsibility for behaviors, directness, equality, rational decision making, concern for others, and shared control. African Americans believed that information should be given, opinions should be credible, criticism is not appropriate, and assertiveness is important. Mexican American answers were similar to those of European Americans in terms of being concerned about the other person, but unlike European Americans, Mexican Americans believed that in some situations confrontation was appropriate (Collier, 1991).

The research of Ting-Toomey et al. (2000), which compared the conflict styles of multiple racial and ethnic groups (Latino/a, African, Asian, and European Americans), is significant for three reasons. First, it studied conflict styles of all racial and ethnic groups without placing any one at the center of the study. Second, it did not assume that racial/ethnic identity was the most salient factor related to conflict style. Instead, it examined the relationship between ethnic identity salience (how important is ethnicity to an individual), larger U.S. cultural identity (how important is belonging to a larger national culture), and conflict management styles in the four different racial/ethnic groups. Third, the research focused on acquaintance relationships, a relational context where racial/ethnic conflict styles are more likely because third-culture norms have not yet been established.

According to Ting-Toomey et al. (2000), strong identification with one's racial/ethnic group increases the likelihood of culturally oriented conflict behaviors. African Americans were found to strongly identify with their own racial/ethnic group. Interestingly, Latino/a and Asian Americans identified both with their racial/ethnic group and U.S. culture. European Americans, as discussed in the section on Whiteness included in Chapter 4, identified primarily with the larger U.S. culture. Some of Ting-Toomey et al.'s (2000) findings reaffirmed earlier research (e.g., Asian Americans use more avoiding than European Americans, and Latino/as use more third-party conflict styles than African Americans). However, the study made significant contributions to existing research on race, ethnicity, and conflict by providing insight into the complex ways that multiple aspects of a person's identity influence conflict styles.

Thinking Critically About Existing Research

As illustrated through our summary in the previous section, existing research on interracial and interethnic conflict has established a strong base of foundational knowledge. One of the objectives of this book is to encourage students to be active consumers of knowledge—this includes thinking critically about what you read. All research has limitations, and by identifying them, we hope to help students advance beyond simplistic explanations of complex ideas (see the ideas of complicity theory, covered in Chapter 6). Within this section, we highlight four of the most salient limitations of research on race, ethnicity, and conflict.

❖ BOX 10.4

AUTHOR REFLECTIONS

People are always surprised when I tell them that my intentions for earning a Ph.D. were so that I could teach communication classes, preferably at a community college. When I started my doctoral work, my goal was to do "just enough" research to complete the degree and secure a college teaching position. This made sense given that my goal was to focus on teaching; however, to be honest, I was also not interested in research because I did not feel as if I had anything to contribute. Up to that point, the research that I had read did not "speak" to me or my experiences.

Something happened during my first year of my doctoral program, however, that changed all that. I started reading research in communication and related fields on different racial and ethnic groups. While the topics—interracial dating, biracial identity development, racial stereotypes, African American nonverbal communication—were interesting, I found the research highly problematic. From my perspective, the social scientific research did not do anything more than promote cultural stereotypes of all racial and ethnic groups. In one graduate seminar on nonverbal communication, I vividly remember talking about this issue in class. As is usually the case, I shared my criticisms with a passion and forcefulness that was perceived by some as unproductive, defensive, and overly critical. My graduate professor listened intently to my comments, validated my concerns, and then asked me: "So, what are you going to do about it? Keep reading research that you find problematic or make the commitment to advance the research?" At that point in my doctoral program, I did not have the confidence or the expertise to think that I could make significant contributions to the field of communication. However, that one scenario planted a seed that would ultimately serve as the primary motivator for conducting research on various topics related to race, culture, and communication.

- What research have you read in this text that you find problematic?
- How might you use a class project, independent study, or graduate school to help advance different research?

—MPO

The first limitation of existing research is the way in which it has generated and perpetuated cultural generalizations. According to M.-S. Kim and Leung (2000), research on racial and ethnic conflict styles pays little, if any, attention to intragroup differences. A good example of this can be seen within the work of Kochman (1981). His often-cited book, *Black and White Styles in Conflict*, has served as the foundation reference for research on African Americans and European Americans. While his findings are applied generally across contexts, he specified the particular circumstances of Blacks and Whites whom he describes in his work: "Middle-class whites, the white group I have been writing about, and Blacks whose social networks exist almost entirely within the Black community" (p. 165). Research often fails to recognize that conflict is experienced differently by racial/ethnic group members based on factors such as class, gender, age, and spirituality; in this regard it practices essentialism.

Another way that existing research has worked to facilitate cultural generalizations is through a failure to acknowledge ethnic differences among large, diverse racial groups. Earlier we discussed the value of recent research by Ting-Toomey et al. (2000) who sought to explore the saliency of other factors beyond racial/ethnic identity. While they found correlations between larger national (United States) identity and conflict styles among different cultural groups, the study remains limited because it fails to consider the differences within these cultural groups. The study, for example, grouped all Asian Americans (Chinese Americans, Filipino Americans, Korean Americans, and Asian Indians) together without considering any intragroup differences. Assuming that all members of one racial group (e.g., Asian) share common cultural values (e.g., individualism/ collectivism) is dangerous (Miyahara, Kim, Shin, & Yoon, 1998).

Much of the existing research on interracial/ethnic conflict is limited in that European Americans have been studied as the normative group. That is, the norms and rules of European Americans have been the focus of study while other racial and ethnic groups have been neglected (Ting-Toomey et al., 2000). As such, the vast majority of research reviewed earlier situates interracial/ethnic conflict around the experiences of the dominant group (e.g., European American–African American conflict, European American–Latino/a conflict, and so on). Focusing on European American styles of conflict has also facilitated a Eurocentric view of other group norms for engaging in conflict. For example, M.-S. Kim and Leung (2000) have critiqued widely accepted conflict management styles that define avoidance style as reflecting a low concern for self and other. They argued that a Eurocentric bias failed to understand that the strategy, when enacted by Asians, was positively related to one's desire to preserve relational harmony (high concern for self and other). Similar insights have been offered regarding the use of silence by Native Americans—not as avoidance but as a means to communicate uncertainty, ambiguity, or a respect for the unknown power of others (C. Braithwaite, 1990).

Another limitation of existing research is related to a focus on racial and ethnic difference, and a lack of attention to similarities (Houston, 2002). The assumption of, and focus on, racial/ethnic differences can be traced to the work of Blumenbach (1865/1973). As described in Chapter 2, his typology was the first to incorporate a hierarchical ordering into classifications of race. Existing research on race, ethnicity, and conflict, for the most part, reflects Blumenbach's social hierarchy in several different ways. First, it continues to place European-based conflict styles in a superior position.

Second, it has focused on attending to the differences among racial and ethnic groups as distinct, separate entities. Third, and finally, interracial/ethnic conflict research has embraced the assumption that groups placed the furthest away from one another on the social hierarchy will experience the greatest amount of conflict. Giving privilege to racial and ethnic differences, while ignoring ways in which individuals are similar in other ways, "presents an incomplete picture" (Collier, 1996, p. 334) of the ways in which people communicate.

The fourth, and final, limitation described here relates to how research on race, ethnicity, and communication has focused on microlevel practices. While these lines of research have produced multiple studies providing significant insight, they have been criticized as doing so through an "evaded analysis of how interpersonal practices connect to larger cultural, historical, and political systems" (Houston, 2002, p. 31). Communication generally, and the ways in which individuals engage in conflict specifically, is an essential aspect of one's culture. Yet simply focusing on communication micropractices without recognizing how they are shaped by larger macrolevel frameworks does little to advance understanding of these particular forms of communication (Ribeau, 1995). Contemporary scholars, in fact, have called for research that attends to historical power structures within society (Stephan & Stephan, 2001) that inform present-day hostile cultural distances between different racial and ethnic groups (Gallois, 2003).

We began this chapter by discussing how communication scholars have long studied conflict that occurs between different racial and ethnic groups. This research is important but, as discussed within this section, it is hampered by several limitations. One additional point must also be made: Why the focus on interracial and interethnic conflict, and not interracial and interethnic unity? Houston (2002) describes the history of race and communication research as a "story of difference." We would extend her insights by adding that interracial/-ethnic communication research as been a "story of conflict." In order to paint a more complete picture, we highlight one example of interracial/-ethnic unity within the next section.

A Case Study in Interracial Unity

There is a difference between being a multiracial organization and being a multicultural organization (Bowers, 2006). The first can be achieved by simply adding more racial and ethnic diversity to a homogeneous group; however, without sufficient attention to negotiating cultural similarities and differences, sustained conflict is inevitable. A **multicultural organization**, in comparison, makes internal, structural changes to infuse diverse perspectives—based on race, ethnicity, gender, socioeconomic status, age, and so on—within its everyday functions. Based on this distinction, it should be clear that creating a multiracial group is easier than cultivating a multicultural one. In order to highlight the necessary commitment, dedication, and focus needed to create and sustain a truly multicultural organization among various racial and ethnic people, we turn to the Baha'i Faith, a spiritual community that has had racial unity as a core value since its inception.

❖ **BOX 10.5**

INTERRACIAL UNITY, SPORT TEAMS, AND THE ALMIGHTY WIN

Remember the Titans is probably the most well-known movie highlighting the ways in which a common goal (winning/gaining respect/working together as a team) can serve as a strong motivation for achieving interracial unity. In fact, over the years, a number of feature films have highlighted the ways in which athletic teams have overcome the negative aspects associated with different forms of cultural diversity (based on racial, ethnic, national, or class differences). Given the dominant movie format, it should come as no surprise that the end result is a unified team that wins against another team that is less diverse but heavily favored.

While interracial unity does occur within sport teams around the United States, communication researchers have found that race continues to be a salient issue. For instance, Andrew Billings and colleagues (Billings, 2004; Billings & Eastman, 2002; Denham, Billings, & Halone, 2002) have explored how athletes are described by sportscasters. The results of their research were that comments about successful African American athletes focused on their body size, natural athleticism, and strength. In comparison, successful European American athletes were described in terms of their intelligence, work ethic, and commitment to training. Given these research findings, can you see how they might explain the large number of professional African American athletes, but the relatively small number of African American head coaches?

The Baha'i Faith

Most major world religions are several hundreds, or even thousands, of years old. In comparison, the Baha'i Faith is the only world religion to emerge in the modern age. In fact, it began as a small, local religious movement in Persia (now Iran) less than 200 years ago (Hartz, 2002). According to recent estimates, there are currently 6 million people worldwide who follow the Baha'i Faith. Drawing from multiple religions, races, ethnic backgrounds, nationalities, and creeds in the world, it is also probably the most diverse religious group. In fact, according to organizational documents, the Baha'i Faith represents more than 2,100 different racial, ethnic, and tribal groups across 182 countries. Although Baha'is celebrate their diversity, they understand that they must be firmly united in order to achieve their goals.

In particular, Baha'is have established spiritual communities in 236 countries; the largest communities are in South Asia (the largest population living in India), Africa, and Latin America (Hartz, 2002). Within the United States, there are close to 150,000 Baha'is participating in 1,200 spiritual assemblies (Garlington, 2005). The U.S. American Baha'i community dates back to the late 1800s and grew significantly during the 20th century, playing a significant role in the civil rights movements. Some of the more long-standing Baha'i communities were located in Kenosha, Wisconsin; Chicago, Illinois; Baltimore, Maryland; Sacramento, California; and Atlanta, Georgia (Garlington, 2005).

Interestingly, the Baha'i Faith, unlike most other religions, has no clergy. Instead, there is a great deal of responsibility on the individual to read the scriptures for themselves and apply lessons from them to their lives. In this regard, the emphasis is on personal development—both in terms of physical and spiritual needs. According to Hartz (2002), Baha'is are guided by several key guidelines, including:

- Each person must independently seek truth for him- or herself.
- All divine religions are one. Everyone worships the same God.
- Human progress does not occur through material things alone. Genuine progress comes from spirituality.
- Science and reason are in harmony with religion.
- The whole human race is one. All human beings are equally the children of God. People must wipe out all prejudices: religious, racial, political, national, and class.
- Extremes of wealth and poverty must be abolished.
- Women are the equals of men and are to have equality of rights, particularly of educational opportunity.
- All children must receive a basic education.
- There should be a single world federation with a single economy and a single language. (p. 18)

Of particular interest to interracial communication students (and scholars) is the principle that affirms the human race and promotes active elimination of prejudice. At the core of the Baha'i Faith is the **unity of harmony**—a concept that emphasizes transcending all divisions of race, nation, gender, caste, and social class. In this regard, the Baha'i Faith serves as a valuable case study in interracial harmony.

In a recent analysis, Vance (2002/2003) examined the ways in which diverse racial and ethnic persons practicing the Baha'i Faith work harmoniously together to create a sense of community. The result of her work was a model of intergroup unity comprising four different "categories." First, Vance points to the existence of social structures inherent to the Baha'i Faith that centralize "unity in diversity" as a core concept. In particular, she references key principles (Oneness of Religion, Spiritual Nature of Human, and The Writings) as providing a larger foundation within which diverse persons can come together to transcend individual differences. In other words, while racial, ethnic, and cultural differences provide diverse perspectives, they are seen as secondary to human spirituality. Within this context, Vance describes the second category, **internal states** as the human nature influence within the process of intergroup unity. Internal states include individual, personal, and cultural differences that can hinder group cohesiveness. As such, the process toward interracial harmony involves negotiating deeply ingrained differences against the ideals of oneness. It is important to note that, within Vance's model, differences are seen as acceptable and desirable.

The third aspect of the model of intergroup unity is known as **external bridges**. Vance (2002/2003) describes this as the place where the work of unity is accomplished. External bridges are comprised of communication practices that Baha'is use as connectors to unite themselves with the larger world. At the core of this process is **decentering**—efforts at "extending outside of one's own culture to apprehend the others' viewpoints" (p. 78).

The fourth, and final, aspect of the model features **multicultural communication** as a means toward group unity. Reflective of building a third culture (see Chapter 6), this aspect reflects the process by which Baha'is align different communicative behaviors toward a culture that focuses on the good of the whole. Within this context, individuals continue to work on embracing diverse perspectives and eliminating prejudices. Consultation, as described by Vance, is at the heart of the process but not the end objective:

Unity begins with consultation but needs to result in action, such as relationship formation. "Indeed, [individuals] deem working in groups toward a common goal as an activity conducive to unity. In the community depicted by [Baha'is], everyone must participate because truth lies among the group, not in any one individual" (p. 78).

The process through which intergroup unity is sought after has great potential for all multiracial organizations, not simply those grounded in spirituality. In fact, many organizations—community, governmental, corporate, and educational—have consulted Baha'i organizations to tap into their experiences in promoting racial harmony.

❖ **BOX 10.6**

TEN COMMANDMENTS FOR RACIAL AND ETHNIC HARMONY

While racial unity has been at the core of the Baha'i Faith since its inception, such is not the case for most other religions in the United States. In fact, most have been segregated since Colonial times—something that largely continues in contemporary times. However, a number of churches have adopted platforms that place racial reconciliation as a top priority. A recent book (Bowers, 2006) on multicultural congregations offers 10 commandments toward that goal:

Commandment 1: Thou Shall Not Deny Difference

Commandment 2: Thou Shall Not Categorize by Cultural Grouping

Commandment 3: Thou Shall Not Practice Ethnocentrism

Commandment 4: Thou Shall Resolve Conflict by Maintaining Honor

Commandment 5: Thou Shall Practice Empathy

Commandment 6: Thou Shall Ask Questions

Commandment 7: Thou Shall Foremost Preserve the Relationship

Commandment 8: Thou Shall Practice "Gracism" (Distinct from favoritism, gracism reaches across difference to lend assistance and extra grace.)

Commandment 9: Thou Shall Not Judge Others

Commandment 10: Thou Shall Not Hoard Power

What are your reactions to each of these guidelines? What do you think each means in terms of facilitating interracial unity? What are the connections between these commandments and some of the key concepts discussed in this book? How, if at all, might they be applied to other types of multiracial organizations beyond those focusing on spirituality?

❖ **BOX 10.7**

AUTHOR REFLECTIONS

In October of 2001, I experienced one of the most tense, horrific experiences of my professional career. A former interracial communication class student invited me to be a guest speaker for the Inter-Fraternity Council (IFC). Around 1,000 male and female pledges were required to attend a monthly educational workshop, and I was asked to speak about interracial communication. I was totally unprepared with how the students responded to my message. Despite my mild-mannered, conversational approach to such a sensitive topic, the students were incredibly hostile, which may have been due, in part, to their anger surrounding the terrorist attacks on September 11th. Throughout my talk, students were mumbling inappropriate comments under their breath (even though I could hear them) and demonstrating a great deal of resistance and anger toward me.

The student who invited me apologized on stage in front of the crowd for what happened, as did a few IFC organization members. In fact, two students acted as "messengers" for their friends who were too ashamed and humiliated to apologize to me themselves. I graciously accepted their apologies. While my students were angry, they were offended and hurt that someone would speak to their professor that way, not to mention display such racist and prejudiced beliefs about Middle Eastern, African American, and other racial/ethnic groups.

The students learned that racism is alive and well; they also learned how to actively address the issue of racism. After several of them, along with some IFC members, made formal complaints to the Office of Greek Life, all organizations were sanctioned by having one of their socials taken away from them for the semester and were later required to attend a series on racial awareness, which was a significant price to pay for their actions.

—TMH

Conclusion

When you think about interracial communication, do you naturally picture scenarios that involve some sort of disagreement or conflict? The mass media—in the form of newspapers, television programs, movies, television, and so on—seems to focus more on conflict because that is what sells. This chapter was designed to cover the fundamental ideas related to interracial conflict. In particular, we introduced the reader to existing research in this area, including that which described various sources of conflict (present-day social inequality, ingroup/outgroup tensions, perceptual differences, and stereotypes due to lack of exposure) and divergent conflict styles. While this body of literature is valuable, it has several limitations. We concluded the chapter with some attention to interracial unity—an area of research that, compared to interracial conflict, is minuscule.

Throughout this chapter, we have tried to illustrate several key ideas related to interracial conflict. First, present-day interracial conflict occurs in a context that is tied to the past. Issues of trust, respect, and competition sometimes exacerbate minor issues to more significant ones. Second, not all conflict that occurs between people from different racial and ethnic backgrounds is defined as interracial. In some instances, the conflict can be based on personal, or other cultural, aspects (e.g., gender, age, socioeconomic status). Third, given the limitations of existing research, more attention is needed in studying interracial unity. Opportunities, in this regard, exist in a number of contexts, including companies, student organizations, sports, worship centers, and community organizations.

OPPORTUNITIES FOR EXTENDED LEARNING ❖

1. Select two scenarios to describe: one that illustrates an instance of interracial conflict and one an instance of interracial unity. Within your descriptions, be sure to respond to the following questions: What was the particular setting? Who was present? What was the core issue that defined the conflict/sense of unity? What types of communication were present? Once you've generated your descriptions, break up into small groups and try to identify common trends for examples of interracial conflict and interracial unity.

2. Use an Internet database to learn more about how different racial and ethnic group perceptions can contribute to interracial conflict. For instance, you might research the various reactions to the aftermath of Hurricane Katrina. Try and locate comments from Mayor Ray Nagin, President Bush, former first lady Barbara Bush, rap star/activist Kayne West, among others. Analyze these comments to see how they reflect different sources of conflict described in this chapter. You might also want to check the following book: *There Is No Such Thing As a Natural Disaster: Race, Class, & Katrina* (Squires & Hartman, 2006).

3. The Association for Conflict Resolution is the largest national organization designed to promote peaceful, effective conflict resolution. Visit their Web site at http://www.acrnet.org/ and learn about some of the conflict resolution efforts across the world. Pay particular attention to how the Web site addresses issues of race and ethnicity. Is race invisible, marginalized, or central to how the organization engages in conflict resolution?

4. At times, certain political issues like ballots to eliminate affirmative action programs are explicitly related to race and ethnicity. Other political issues, like immigration (Merrill, 2006), rental laws (J. B. Miller, 2003), and voting procedures (Connaughton, 2004) have more implicit ramifications for different racial and ethnic groups. Select a local, state, or national issue and research it in terms of how it impacts different groups. Be sure to gain diverse perspectives from a variety of sources (e.g., community newspapers). Then compare and contrast your initial perceptions of the issue with those that you were able to gain from various sources.

5. Review the different theories covered in Chapter 6. Which one of the theories do you think does the best job at explaining why some interracial interactions end in conflict and others do not? What particular concepts, models, and processes are included in the theories that specifically address the sources of conflict described in this chapter?

11

Race/Ethnicity, Interracial Communication, and the Mass Media

How often do you watch television, read the newspaper, listen to the radio, use the Internet, or use your PDA to get the most recent information on current events or some other topic of interest? Whether we want to admit it or not, we all rely on the media to help shape our opinions, attitudes, and beliefs on a variety of social issues that interest or affect us. Although using the media may seem very straightforward in terms of being informed or entertained, the consequences can be far reaching. The perceptions that we develop of ourselves, others, and the world are grounded in representations of reality vis-à-vis mass media images. This chapter begins by discussing the importance of the mass media and then follows with specific descriptions of how racial/ethnic groups are typically represented in various media outlets. Once this foundation has been established, we present the implications and consequences that these mass media images have in terms of interracial communication.

The Importance of the Mass Media

As demonstrated throughout this book, many elements influence how we think about race/ethnicity in the United States, and the pervasiveness of the media, however, places it as a central influence on how we come to create, maintain, and/or transform our perceptions of race. In a society where formal racial barriers have been eradicated for several decades, a racial division continues to be perpetuated in the media. Whether it is in the newsroom, film, music television, situation comedies, or radio, the images of racial/ethnic groups (or lack thereof) presented in the media contribute to the ideologies that preserve the status quo of racism and discrimination in the United States. If we look more closely, we can even see how the media have a direct influence on interpersonal/interracial interactions (T. M. Harris, 2001; T. M. Harris & Donmoyer, 2000; D. Kellner, 1995; Omi, 1989). Because the media informs us about issues salient to our local, national, and international communities, our perceptions of each other are shaped and influenced by misinformation that only works to maintain the racial divide.

The visual images and verbal words spoken oftentimes function to shape our understanding of the information we are seeking from the media, which sometimes creates problems when we use it to guide our interactions across racial lines. More specifically, mass media venues are used as primary sources of information for many people (Bednarski, 2003; Christian & Lapinski, 2003; Mastro & Stern, 2003; Means Coleman, 2003; Merskin, 2001). Because we live in a largely segregated society, then, it is very likely that preliminary information received about those who are racially and ethnically different will come from some form of mass communication. The media may be used as an escape from or confirmation of reality. However, the images that we come to know through mass media exposure are often perceived as representative of certain racial, ethnic, or cultural groups (Pal, 2005; Park, Gabbadon, & Chernin, 2006; Rivadeneyra & Ward, 2005; C. F. Sun, 2003). These (mis)representations can make interracial communication difficult because they may create false perceptions of others. In many cases, these media images can evolve into barriers and stereotypes (D. Brown, 2006; Christian & Lapinski, 2003; Entman, 1994; R. Taylor, 2000; Watson, 2005; Wu, 2002) that hinder positive interracial interactions from occurring.

Studying mass communication is important to developing a deeper understanding of the connection between mass media images and interracial interaction. First, mass media images *reflect* societal values and ideas about race/ethnicity. Second, these images also *reinforce* or *shape* widely shared ideals in terms of what is defined as normal. Increasing our critical awareness of these images, like those that appear in popular culture, enhances our understanding of how our society negotiates race (Artz, 1998; D. Brown, 2006; Park et al., 2006). Finally, it is important to understand how the media serve as gatekeepers to information about race/ethnicity. By selectively regulating what we see, the media influence how we ultimately come to understand issues related to race. Acknowledging these things allows us to see how the media influence everyday interracial communication.

Mass Media Representations of Racialized Others

The United States is becoming an increasingly diverse racial and ethnic society (see Chapter 1). Research suggests that racial and ethnic microcultures (specifically, studies have focused on Latino/a and African Americans) watch more television and go to the movies more often than European Americans (Tirodkar & Jain, 2003). However, representations of "racialized others"—those racial/ethnic group members who are identified by their nondominant racial status in the United States—have a marginal presence in the U.S. media. People of color are largely underrepresented in all dominant mass media outlets, and in some areas, some racial/ethnic groups (e.g., Middle Easterners) are largely invisible. When images of microcultures do appear, more often than not they are placed in stereotypical roles. In order to clarify these statements for you, we review how each microculture has been represented in television and film. As you read through these descriptions, think about how each set of representations reflects general patterns of (1) invisibility, (2) underrepresentation, (3) stereotypical depictions, and (4) misrepresentations.

European Americans

One group that has a pervasive presence in the media is European Americans. We include them in our discussion because they are a racial group with ethnic diversity (see Chapter 3) that oftentimes is unacknowledged, unexplored, or unknown by its members for various reasons; however, due to space limitations, we will briefly discuss three different ethnic groups and how they are depicted in the media. As we note in earlier chapters, European Americans are a very diverse group and are represented in the media through a variety of different images. We must first note that, in general, European Americans are

> separated through color-coded iconography, such as by means of their eye, hair and skin color and/or their clothing wear. Good whites are mostly visually depicted as being lighter, while bad whites are mainly portrayed as looking darker, in reference to some or all of the prior factors. (R. Dyer, 1997)

Typically, this racial group is categorized by phenotypic features we have been socialized to view as the standard of what is normal and beautiful; however, when their images or members do not conform to this standard, then negative connotations are associated with the group being represented.

Most often, European Americans are portrayed as white-collar suburbanites who are typically middle class or wealthy. In addition to being blonde, blue eyed, and porcelain skinned, these characters are valued more than their darker counterparts. In such shows as *The O.C., Boston Legal,* and *Gilmore Girls,* the European American characters frequently also possess negative qualities, such as intellectual inferiority, sexual promiscuity, and dishonesty. Shows like this depict all European Americans as fitting a norm or ideal that many do not. *Desperate Housewives* is a very popular television show that typifies this normative depiction. The characters are of upper-middle- to middle-class status, materialistic, greedy, self-absorbed, and unscrupulous. Careful examination of these characters and television programs demonstrates that racial group membership is something oftentimes unacknowledged until the characters are in the presence of the racialized other.

There are several ethnic groups who are depicted on television as possessing qualities that are oftentimes perpetuating stereotypes that are problematic in nature. According to the 2000 U.S. Census, Italian Americans are the fifth largest ethnic group in the United States and are "stereotyped as either being blue collar workers or involved in organized crime" (Order Sons of Italy in America, 2003). Shows such as *The Sopranos* influence audiences to believe that "Men are uneducated, dishonest, and/or violent; women are elderly, overweight housewives and grandmothers wearing black dresses, housecoats, or aprons" (Order Sons of Italy in America, 2003), and both men and women are portrayed as being hot-tempered. In the show *The Nanny,* Jewish women are depicted as sassy, self-deprecating, loud, gaudy, and obnoxious (Antler, 2004), further perpetuating the "Jewish-American Princess" stereotype. "This particular stereotype is built on the perception that the daughters of well-to-do Jewish families (or at least a number of them) have identifiable superficial, perhaps somewhat spoiled, 'young princess' attitudes" (University of Waterloo, 2000). This is also evidenced in the character Janice on *Friends.* The presence of this recurring character among the regulars was visibly an unwelcome and detested interaction, which is disturbing. Although virtually every television show has some element of comedic relief, it is oftentimes at the expense of the racialized (or ethnic) other.

A third ethnic group in the racial category of European American is Irish Americans. This racial ethnic group has been virtually invisible in popular culture, except between 1998 and 1999 when there were five television shows (*Costello, The Turks, Trinity, To Have and to Hold,* and *Love and Money*) depicting Irish culture in the United States. Negra (2001) suggests that these television shows positioned "Irishness as a representational lexicon compatible with family values" or a close familial network. According to Kitman (1998), this identity and familial values are often portrayed as "working class, salt-of-the-earth stereotypes, with long-suffering mothers, fathers with poor communication skills and large families whose members work for 'the finest' in neighborhoods like South Boston and New York's Hell's Kitchen" yet are alcoholics. While scholars have not identified controlling images associated with this and other racial groups, Negra (2001) recognizes that Irishness does not "carry the burdens of alterity borne to Latino and African Americans" (p. 237).

African Americans

Images of African Americans in the mass media have attracted significantly more attention than those of other racial and ethnic U.S. minorities. While the majority of research has focused on images within television and film (e.g., Berry, 1992; Bogle, 1994; Evoleocha & Ugbah, 1989), mass media images of Africans Americans in a number of contexts have also been critiqued including those in cartoons (McLean, 1998), newspapers (Byrd, 1997; Martindale, 1997), magazine advertising (Seiter, 1990), and pornography (Mayall & Russell, 1995). Mass-marketed images featuring racially charged humor can be traced to the late 1700s when stereotypical caricatures of African slaves appeared in theater presentations (Means Coleman, 2003; M. M. Moore, 1980). European American performers, and later African American ones as well, entertained the nation by wearing blackface, exaggerating African American behaviors, and creating racist stereotypes that continue to exist in the mass media (Means Coleman, 2000; Bogle, 1994).

These controlling images (Collins, 1990) permeate every aspect of the media and include representations of African American males as a Sambo (lazy, jolly, content with life), coon (foolish, idiotic), Uncle Tom (quiet, respectful, goal is to please White man), and buck (strong, athletic, and sexually powerful). African American female portrayals include those of mammies (asexual, nurturing caregiver) or sapphires (sexually enticing). Both female and male pickaninnies (dirty, unkempt animal-like children) and mulattos (African Americans light enough to deceive European Americans to think they were White) are also prevalent.

From the 1970s to the 1980s, there was an increasing number of shows featuring African Americans that debuted and later aired in reruns (Gandy & Matabane, 1989). Included in this large influx were shows like *Sanford & Son, Good Times, The Jeffersons, What's Happening, Different Strokes, 227,* and *Amen.* These shows remained highly popular with African American audiences, but were continually criticized by researchers as simply reinventing traditional stereotypes in a contemporary context (MacDonald, 1992). This set a precedent for African American images in the mass media: They most often are relegated to comedic roles (T. M. Harris, 1997), also referred to as neominstrelsy (Means Coleman, 2000). Some of these characters also embodied the Jezebel, Mammy, matriarch, buffoon, and minstrel or Stepin Fetchit stereotypes (Collins, 1990), which perpetuate the myth that African Americans are unscrupulous, lack morals, and are only capable of entertaining others through comedy.

This is evidenced in the critically acclaimed drama *Frank's Place* (CBS, 1987–1988). In short, this well-written and well-acted drama defied television programming norms by introducing a drama with a predominantly African American cast. Due to the network programmers' failure to find a fixed time slot, which prevented it from securing a strong fan base, the show was cancelled. The cancellation may also be attributed to the fact that audiences expected a traditional comedy rather than a show with serious content (Campbell, 1999). *Frank's Place* deviated from traditional representations of African Americans, yet failed to provide a "safe or unthreatening context" to deal with the issues of class *and* race. This alternative format led to the demise of a promising drama that broke the expectation that racial/ethnic groups should be confined to sitcoms. As of September 1, 2006, there are currently fewer than five television programs with a predominantly African American cast. Not surprisingly, they are situation comedies— *Girlfriends, The Game, All of Us,* and *Everybody Hates Chris.*

❖ **BOX 11.1**

AUTHOR REFLECTION

Whenever you sit down to watch television, how often does the issue of race come up? Do you ever wonder why the programs you watch rarely have a racially diverse cast, and when they do, those characters seem to perpetuate a stereotype or appear assimilated into mainstream society? Do the other characters appear to make racist, prejudiced, or stereotypical comments that are potentially offensive? These are questions I challenge you to think about the next time you watch television or a movie or even read the newspaper. People of color face these questions on a daily basis as they/we use the media to be entertained, educated, or informed about current events. It is very disheartening when we fail to see ourselves represented in television programming or wherever, and when we are, the images are sometimes so distorted that we might even prefer not to have any images out there at all if that's how people are going to think we are.

For example, the show *The Flavor of Love,* to varying degrees, embodies the Jezebel and the buffoon stereotype (Collins, 1990). Sadly, these images aren't going to go away; therefore, we all have to be proactive in *not* supporting programs that further marginalize *any* group that doesn't fit into what we are socialized to believe is "normal." It may be as small as changing your viewing habits or talking with others about the impact these images have on how we see ourselves and each other, but at least it's a step in the right direction—one TV program at a time. So, what shows are you watching? Do you feel guilty or have concerns for how groups are being portrayed? What can you do to make a difference?

—TMH

Asian Americans

The diverse group of U.S. citizens described within the umbrella term **Asian Americans** occupy diverse walks of life. Asian Americans were and are perceived as a homogenous group of people whose ethnicity is Chinese, Korean, or Japanese. This worldview of an ethnically diverse people is problematic and restricting. Controlling images of Asian Americans (Shah, 2003) emerged from efforts by Whites to oppress racial groups deemed inferior and to reduce them to caricatures of how dominant society perceived their racial and gendered identities (Shah, 2003). This was due to an unfounded fear of threatened Asian expansion (**Yellow Peril**) (Shah, 2003). Due to space limitations, we recommend work by Sing (1989) for further explication of the history of Asians in the media.

General cultural stereotypes are assumptions that Asian Americans in general are (1) the model minority, (2) perpetual foreigners, (3) inherently predatory (immigrants who never give back), (4) restricted to clichéd occupations (e.g., restaurant workers, laundry workers, martial artists, etc.), and (5) inherently comical or sinister (Shah 2003; C. F. Sun, 2003; Wu, 2002). Four controlling images depicting Asian American identity include Charlie Chan, Fu Manchu, Dragon Lady, and China Doll (C. F. Sun, 2003; Wu, 2002). Charlie Chan and Fu Manchu are emasculated stereotypes portraying Asian men as eunuchs or asexual (C. F. Sun, 2003, p. 658). **Charlie Chan**, a detective character, (C. F. Sun, 2003) was "effeminate, wimpy," "dainty" (p. 658), and "a mysterious man, possessing awesome powers of deduction" (Sun, 2003, p. 658), yet was deferential to Whites, "non-threatening, and revealed his 'Asian wisdom' in snippets of 'fortune-cookie.'" Conversely, there is the **Fu Manchu** character who is "a cruel, cunning, diabolical representative of the 'yellow peril'" (C. F. Sun, 2003, p. 658).

Asian American women are portrayed as being hypersexual, which is the opposite of "asexual" Asian men (C. F. Sun, 2003). The **Lotus Blossom** (China Doll, Geisha Girl, Shy Polynesian beauty) is "a sexual-romantic object, utterly feminine, delicate and welcome respites from their often loud, independent American counterparts" (C. F. Sun, 2003, p. 659). The Dragon Lady is the direct opposite of the Lotus Blossom (Shah, 2003). She is "cunning, manipulative, and evil," "aggressive," and "exudes exotic danger" (C. F. Sun, 2003, p. 659), "but with added characteristics of being sexually alluring and sophisticated and determined to seduce and corrupt white men" (Shah, 2003, p. 9).

Shows with at least one recurring character of Asian descent include, but are not limited to, *The Courtship of Eddie's Father, Happy Days, Quincy, M.E., All American Girl, Ally McBeal, Mad TV, Half & Half, Lost,* and *Grey's Anatomy.* Long-held stereotypes of Asian American women are perpetuated by the characters Ling Woo (Ally McBeal) and Miss Swan (Mad TV). Attorney Ling was "tough, rude, candid, aggressive, sharp tongued, and manipulative" (C. F. Sun, 2003, p. 661) and hypersexualized. She was a feminist and in stark contrast with past portrayals of Asian women. While some Asian Americans believed Ling was a stereotype breaker (Nakako, 1999), she still perpetuated the Dragon Lady stereotype (Chihara, 2000), especially when she "growl[ed] like an animal, breathing fire at Ally, walking into the office to the music of Wicked Witch of the West in *The Wizard of Oz*" (C. F. Sun, 2003, p. 661). Conversely, the character Miss Swan is the perpetual foreigner who speaks in broken, childlike English, appearing to never shed her status as a foreigner in the United States.

All American Girl is a television show from the 1990s that attempted to introduce audiences to an Asian American family. For the first time in television history, producers attempted to "showcase an Asian American [Korean] family" (Shah, 2003) and cast only one Korean actor (Cho). All others were either Japanese or Chinese American. This perpetuated the assumption that Asians are interchangeable (Shah 2003; see Orbe, Seymour, & Kang, 1998) and must assimilate to mainstream (White) culture in order to "fit in." The controlling images of Asian Americans distort what it means to belong to this very heterogeneous ethnic group. *Lost* and *Grey's Anatomy* have strong and visible Asian American characters who are part of the regular cast. As D. Brown (2006) notes, these shows and characters are complex and have great appeal across racial and ethnic groups; however, we should be "concerned that the Asian American characters on television [are] portrayed in high status occupations, perpetuating the 'model minority' stereotype."

Native Americans (First Nations People)

Like Asian Americans, Native Americans have largely been invisible in terms of their representation in film and television. "Native Americans are rarely portrayed in movies and television," and are shown wearing stereotypical attire (i.e., headdress) (Kilman, 2005), or armed with antiquated artillery (i.e., bow and arrow), ready to fulfill the all-too-familiar image of the "noble" savage. These images perpetuate a negative image of racial/ethnic identity for First Nations people and instill the belief that being Native American is a "thing of the past." We are led to accept as truth that Native Americans either do not exist or are too small in number to be fairly represented. No matter what period of time in which a story is being told, "contemporary portrayals [of First Nations people] are typically presented in an historic context" (Merskin, 1998, p. 335). Check this statement with your life experiences. How many different Native American characters, in either films or on television, can you recall? Chances are you struggled to name very many, beyond stereotypical depictions of Native Americans in television programming that featured the U.S. frontier (e.g., *F-Troop*). This reality reflects the vast invisibility of Native culture in every aspect of the mass media. When Native American characters have appeared in film and television, like many of the other microcultures in the United States, they have been limited to roles that are largely stereotypical and marginal to the main plot.

Historically, Native American life has been portrayed negatively in the mass media. On television, Native American characters are typically depicted as vicious, cruel, lazy, and incompetent (in terms of keeping a job or surviving away from reservations) (Tan, Fujioka, & Lucht, 1997). In film, these portrayals have consistently involved characters who are bloodthirsty savages, barbaric drunkards, or uncivilized (free) spirits (Dwyer, 1993; Morris & Stuckey, 1998). In many instances, these characters were created and performed by non-Native people who knew little about Native culture outside of larger societal stereotypes.

Because of this, many of the images of Native Americans that appeared in the mass media were actually outrageous *mis*representations of Native culture and language. *Taza, Son of Cochise*, for instance, was released in 1954. Throughout the film, the "Indian" characters do not speak in any one of the many Native American languages. Instead, they speak gibberish. In a couple of scenes "Indian" characters actually are seen speaking Spanish (Dwyer, 1993)! Similar forms of misrepresentation appeared throughout the 1970s, including the film *Billy Two Hats* (1974). In this film, Native Americans were depicted by Israeli actors whose language and culture overshadowed any attempt to portray Native American life accurately (Dwyer, 1993). This depiction is a visual representation of a linguistic image accepted as an accurate symbol of First Nations people (Meek, 2006). They are restricted to an image of being a homogenous group of people lacking any distinctive qualities (e.g., tribes) or heterogeneity. The most pervasive and troubling image is the "conventionalized imagery [that] depicts Indians as wild, savage, heathen, silent, noble, childlike, uncivilized, premodern, immature, ignorant, bloodthirsty, and historical or timeless, all in juxtaposition to the white civilized, mature, modern (usually) Christian American man" (Meek, 2006, p. 119). Other stereotypes include being drunkards, gamblers, and wards of the government. Unless these images change, we as a society will continue to perceive these images as accurate representations of the original inhabitants of the United States.

We would also like to note that U.S. companies exploit the images of American Indians for product promotion to "build an association with an idealized and romanticized notion of the past" (Merksin, 2001, p. 160). Products such as Land O'Lakes butter, Sue Bee honey, Big Chief sugar, and Crazy Horse malt liquor have stereotypic caricatures on them that are supposed to reflect Native American ethnicity, which are "dehumanizing, one dimension images based on a tragic past" (p. 167).

Middle Eastern Americans

Prior to September 11, Middle Easterners were viewed as an age-old homogenous ethnic group with similar racial, physical features and a belief system in opposition to the Christian belief system of most Americans (Weston, 2003). Depictions were typically negative and racist and became even more so after the attacks. We became even more familiar, unfortunately, with the term "racial profiling." The media were becoming "psychologically and socially toxic" (Watson, 2005).

Middle Easterners were a relatively invisible and unknown racial/ethnic group to most Americans; however, all of that changed on the morning of September 11, 2001.

The cultural memory of every U.S. citizen was changed forever (Christian & Lapinski, 2003). Three thousand Americans lost their lives as a result of terrorist attacks in New York City, the U.S. capital, and Pennsylvania, and it was the first time in our country's history that we were faced with the reality of war on the homeland.

Most people became fearful of future attacks and struck an offensive posture, which ultimately had a negative impact on race relations among and between racial groups. Americans were "no longer absolutely secure in the belief that they were safe" (Pal, 2005, p. 119). Racial profiling targeting Middle Eastern–"looking" individuals perpetuated the existing racial divide and articulated for the world the complexities associated with life in a world consumed with race. "Americans who looked Middle Eastern were harassed, assaulted and their property vandalized in a wave of misplaced retaliation" (Weston, 2003, p. 92).

❖ BOX 11.2

AUTHOR REFLECTION

I have a "nonscholarly" confession to make: I have always loved to watch television. While my viewing has fluctuated over time, I currently average at least 4 hours of television viewing a day. This may sound like a huge amount of time for a university professor actively involved in teaching, research, and community service who is also a faithful parent of one teenager and two preteens. The good news is that a significant amount of my television viewing is tied to one of my research areas: representations of diversity within the media.

My current research interests have focused on reality-based television. More specifically, I'm interested in those shows that feature different forms of interracial and intraracial conflict (something that seems to be a hallmark of many reality shows). For instance, I am currently working with a doctoral student on analyzing the 2006–2007 season of *Survivor*. In particular we are interested in examining representations before, during, and after the contestants were divided into four "ethnic tribes" (African American, Asian American, European American, and Latina/o). I am also interested in comparing and contrasting similar shows with a specific focus on representations of race/ethnicity. For instance, as someone who has seen both seasons of VH1's *Flavor of Love*, I am intrigued with how this show's depiction of female competition compares against other similar shows (e.g., *The Bachelor*), especially the ways in which "Blackness" and "Whiteness" intersect with representations of sexuality.

- What types of media are you most interested in?
- What can you learn from analyzing the ways in which race and ethnicity are represented?

—MPO

The months and years following the attacks led to repeated media coverage of this American tragedy. Televisions, newspapers, and the Internet were bombarded with detailed stories of the Middle Eastern attackers and their religious beliefs. A clear message was being sent that all people who were dark skinned (read Middle Eastern), "foreign," or practiced the Muslim faith were a clear and present danger. Since

September 11, very few television shows exist with Middle Eastern actors or characters, including *JAG* and *24* (Watson, 2005). The central theme is their glorification of the military and war. The most troubling depiction many believed would inflame the stereotypes associated with Middle Easterners was on the show *24*. The 2005–2006 season was "replete with scenes of torture administered to various suspected terrorists or their associates by U.S. government operatives" (Watson, 2005). It was criticized for casting Iranian-born actress Shohreh Aghdashloo as a "stay-at-home terrorist mom . . . and wife of a terrorist" (Watson, 2005). The character murdered her son's American girlfriend. She was depicted as having no conscience, heartless, inferring that being Middle Eastern was synonymous with being a terrorist. Aghdashloo appeared on *The View* to discourage viewer protests. She felt the show accurately depicted terrorists who happened to be Muslims. The show's cowriter and producer Robert Cochran said "we have a legitimate interest in telling stories that are grounded in reality, at least to a considerable extent grounded in reality" (Watson, 2005). All season, *24* received criticism for its role in depicting immigrant families as members of terror cells ready to attack U.S. suburbs and the nation.

Latino/a Americans

During the 1970s and 1980s, Latino/a representation in television and film lagged far behind African Americans (Gandy & Matabane, 1989). Like Asian Americans and Native Americans, Latino/as have been nearly absent in prime-time television (Lichter, Lichter, Rothman, & Amundson, 1987). The invisibility of this growing segment of the U.S. population is further maintained through non-Latino/a depictions of Latino/a culture (Hadley-Garcia, 1990). For the most part, "Latino representation in Hollywood is not keeping pace with the explosion of the U.S. Hispanic population, and depictions of Latinos in television and film too often reinforce stereotypes" (Stevens, 2004). Television shows are believed to be reliable in their depiction of the real world, but this is rarely done when it comes to casting characters (Méndez-Méndez & Alvario, 2002). The advocacy group Children Now reports that Latino/as make up over 12.5% of the U.S. population, but only 2% of television characters are Latino/a (Stevens, 2004), which does not include those Latino/as who are portraying White (nonethnic) characters.

Much like other racial groups, Latino/a Americans have been subjugated and oppressed as immigrants "invading" U.S. culture. Recent immigration issues notwithstanding, the most prevailing stereotypes of Latino American males are the glorified drug dealer, the "Latin Lover," the "greaser," and the "bandito" (Márquez, 2004). Latina women are depicted as deviant, "frilly señoritas," or "volcanic temptresses," and Latino families in general are "unintelligent," "passive," "deviant," and "dependent" Márquez (2004). In this regard, Valdivia (1998) sees mass media images of Latinas as similar to African American women (e.g., welfare mother) but also different. Some of her work has analyzed the different roles that Rosie Perez has played in several films (e.g., *Do the Right Thing, Fearless, White Men Can't Jump,* and *It Could Happen to You*). Her conclusions are that Latinas are portrayed uniquely in terms of their stereotypical accents, loud personalities communicated both verbally and nonverbally (e.g., dress), and out-of-control sexuality (most often represented through sexually suggestive dancing). Valdivia's conclusions are made even more problematic given that most images of Latino/a culture are of men, further limiting the chance for a greater range of Latina images.

These depictions may be rare but "the roles that do exist have that much more impact" (Rebensdorf, 2001). Images of Latino/a Americans do not reflect the "Latino explosion" in U.S. culture and ultimately reinforce the stereotypes that should be countered (Stevens, 2004). These images may be neither fully positive nor fully negative (Rivadeneyra, 2006); however, their rarity makes it more problematic that these images are so restricting. Traditionally, when they do appear in television or in films, people of Latin descent are limited to stereotypical roles most always associated with lower status occupations (Atkin, 1992). Latinos are portrayed as inner-city criminals—usually Puerto Rican or Mexican American—who are violent and/or drug addicted (Rios, 1997; Siegel, 1995).

With such limited opportunities, it is nearly impossible for mass media images to capture the complexities of the diverse racial and ethnic groups that fall under the label of Latino/a. However, although still largely underrepresented on television, a mid-1990s analysis indicated that the number of negative portrayals of Latino/as has declined (National Council of La Raza, 1997). Some researchers (e.g., Delgado, 1998a) see Latino/a mass media images following earlier patterns set by African Americans. Notable television programs featuring or including a Latino/a American character include but are not limited to *Chico and the Man*, CBS-rejected *American Family, Luis, The Ortegas, NYPD Blue, Will & Grace, Popstar, George Lopez, Kingpin, The West Wing, Brothers Garcia, Taina, Dora the Explorer, Freda, Desperate Housewives, CSI: Miami,* and *Ugly Betty*. Latino/a American culture has had tremendous appeal in popular culture, yet members of the different ethnic groups within the Latino/a community remain marginalized in prime-time television programming (Márquez, 2004; Mastro & Behm-Morawitz, 2005). The most promising television program that can potentially debunk these controlling images is *Ugly Betty*, whose lead character defies conventional wisdom regarding televisual success. Although Betty doesn't conform to the Eurocentric standard of beauty, her resistance to do so reframes the Latina as a strong, independent woman of integrity.

❖

TIP: THEORY INTO PRACTICE

The next time you sit down to watch television, read a newspaper, or are in the movie theater, there are a few things we would like you to consider as you absorb the images before you. In general, most people use the media in ways that are personally beneficial. In some cases, there is a desire for some to see themselves or their racial group represented accurately. Unfortunately, certain images either perpetuate racial stereotypes or fail to represent some racial groups at all. Nevertheless, we would like to pose to you the following points to ponder.

- Identify and recognize the myths and stereotypes perpetuated in the media about different racial/ethnic groups.

- Do research on how different racial communities have actively made the media more conscious of and responsible for their stereotypic portrayals of racial/ethnic groups.
- Broaden your viewing preference and support television programs and networks (e.g., Black Entertainment Television [BET], Univision) that target different racial groups.
- Engage in open and honest dialogue with friends and peers from different racial/ethnic groups about racial/ethnic representation in the media.
- Engage in open and honest dialogue with your same-race friends about the way your own and other racial/ethnic groups are represented in the media.
- Be open to films, newspapers, music, and so on, targeted to racial/ethnic groups other than your own.
- Recognize that racial/ethnic stereotypes do exist and are often offensive to certain groups of people.
- Rethink the types of stereotypes you have about racial/ethnic groups.
- Rethink how you perceive racial/ethnic groups based on messages and images communicated in the media.
- Become more acquainted with magazines, films, and television programs targeted to certain racial/ethnic groups.

Racialized Television Viewing Habits

As you can see, television, as well as other forms of media, plays a major role in the lives of most U.S. Americans. We have presented some information about the representation of racial/ethnic images on television. However, we turn now to another television phenomenon worth some attention: the viewing habits of different racial/ethnic groups.

In terms of television viewing, two clear patterns emerge when comparing different racial/ethnic groups. First, Latino/a and African Americans watch considerably more television than their European American counterparts (Perkins, 1996; L. R. Tucker, 1997). Although this behavior may be more reflective of socioeconomic differences rather than simply race/ethnicity, the differences are noteworthy. For instance, in a study conducted from October 1993 to January 1994, African Americans were found to watch television 74.9 hours a week compared to 49.9 hours for non–African Americans (Perkins, 1996). The largest differences occurred during late night programming when African Americans were found to watch 90% more TV!

The second pattern regarding racialized television viewing habits includes the specific types of programs that attract specific racial groups. Like most other research on race, studies found glaring differences in European American and African American viewing habits, which is much more notable than differences among other racial/ethnic group comparisons that exist but do not receive much scholarly attention. For instance, three studies completed at different times throughout the 1990s reveal the weak correlations between the Top 10 prime-time shows when comparing African American and European American viewers. For the 1993–1994 season, not one show appeared on both lists ("African-Americans' Viewing Habits," 1994). *Home*

Improvement, the top-rated program among European Americans, barely made the Top 30 list for African Americans. Other popular shows for European American viewers, like *Seinfeld* (no. 3) and *Frasier* (no. 6), did not even crack the Top 90 most watched shows for African American viewers. *Living Single*, the top-rated show among African Americans, ranked 69th among all audiences (Farhi, 1997).

This trend was repeated in a study conducted on the 1996–1997 season. One show, ABC's *Monday Night Football*, managed to appear in the Top 10 programs for both European American and African American viewers' list (Dorsey, 1997). However, the differences between racialized viewing habits remained apparent. Ten of the fifteen most watched programs for African American households had predominantly African American casts. Overall, their top three shows—*Living Single, New York Undercover*, and *Martin* (all of which appeared on Fox)—had dismal numbers among European Americans viewers (ranking numbers 103, 105, and 100, respectively). The most recent data available at the time of publication echo these patterns. Not one show ranked in the Top 10 list for both groups in 1998 (Hass, 1988). The number 1 and 2 shows among European American viewers, *ER* and *Seinfeld* (NBC), ranked 18 and 52 for African American viewers. The top-rated show for African Americans, *Between Brothers* (Fox), was the 107th most watched show among European Americans.

As you read through our descriptions comparing the viewing habits of European Americans and African Americans, you have probably been considering your own personal choices when it comes to prime-time programming. How would your Top 10 programs compare to others within your own racial/ethnic group? If recent research is correct, your age may play as important a role as race/ethnicity in your viewing habits. Consider the following conclusion drawn from audience analysis research (Farhi, 1997; Hass, 1988): The racial/ethnic divisions among television viewing is most apparent among middle-aged adults. When focusing on younger viewers (ages 12–17), research indicates that they are much more likely to watch shows on either Top 10 lists. The same goes for viewers over the age of 50. Both African American and European households in this age group watched 13 of the same 20 shows (Dorsey, 1997). These findings are consistent with a central theme of our book (see Chapter 5 in particular): Focusing on race/ethnicity is helpful in understanding behaviors, but not as useful as analyzing intersections of race, ethnicity, and other cultural elements like age. Take some time to reflect on your television viewing habits. In addition to your race/ethnicity and age, what are some other elements of your cultural identity (socioeconomic status, spirituality, gender, etc.) that influence them?

TV Sitcoms

The situation comedy is currently the only genre to appear in the Top 10 programs every year since 1949. It has also emerged as most responsible for addressing controversial issues with humor (Whetmore, 1998). It was through the show *All in the Family* that producer Norman Lear was able to present realistic commentary addressing racial and ethnic issues. With the development of other shows such as *The Jeffersons, Maude*, and *Good Times*, Lear was able to bring some diversity to television programming. Lear's programs were also unique because he took a risk and centered his sitcoms around controversial racial and social issues that other networks and programs avoided. Although Lear is to be recognized and commended for his attempts to include racial/ethnic issues in television, it appears that representations of microcultural groups with any success with viewers have been relegated to sitcoms (e.g., *The Cosby Show, A Different World, Living Single*) and not television dramas (e.g., *Frank's Place* or *Under One Roof*). Such disparity reinforces the stereotype that people of color cannot be taken seriously. Instead, the use of humor and stereotypes may potentially reinforce bigotry (T. M. Harris & Hill, 1998) targeted toward different racial/ethnic groups.

❖ BOX 11.3

STUDENT REFLECTION

I wanted to sit down and watch the movie *Crash* with the family and see how they felt about the movie. Boy was I in for a treat. The only person grumbling during the film was my father. He kept complaining about how slow the movie was, and how it was more like a documentary rather than a movie. After the movie was over he gave a very audible sigh of relief, and remarked, "Thank God that's over." I asked him, "What did you not like about the movie?" and the only response that I could get out of him was that he just didn't like the movie. So I kept asking, and he kept rebutting, "I just don't like the [expletive] movie!" and shortly thereafter, he actually raised his voice and commented about how I'm just like my mother in that I keep asking him the same [expletive] questions. I think I really got to him at some point.

My entire family all sat there and watched the same movie about race in today's society from a more modern perspective, and my dad was the only one who had a problem with it. I don't know if he just didn't like seeing these types of issues thrown in his face, or if race is something that he prefers not to think about on a regular basis or what. It just bothered me that all I got out of him about the movie was that he didn't like it because it was boring and "more of a documentary than a movie, and I don't like documentaries." The funny part is that Dad is the open-minded one, and I had assumed going into the movie that he would like it and my mother wouldn't, but as it turns out, I had that completely backwards. After the movie my dad flipped to the History Channel . . . where he proceeded to watch a documentary on the lives of WWII pilots. I just smiled and left the room. My dad had been affected by the movie to some degree, but finding out how is a completely different battle.

Hass (1988) describes prime-time comedy shows as "one of the last bastions of public segregation" (p. D3). As described earlier, the increasing racial divide behind audience viewing patterns is relatively new, however. This is because, until the early to mid-1990s, there were not enough shows with microcultural casts (predominantly Latino/a, African American, etc.) to fragment the audience. An increased awareness of the large numbers of African American and Latino viewers in a highly competitive market prompted new networks (Fox, WB, and UPN) to establish an audience base by offering shows featuring predominantly African American (and a few Latino/a) casts (*In Living Color, Buggin' Out, South Central, The Parent Hood, Martin, Living Single, Between Brothers*). Although considerably successful with viewers of color, as well as young European Americans, these shows seemingly follow a similar network life: They are abandoned for more traditional shows (with more mainstream appeal) once they have helped secure an audience viewer base for the network. The logic of the network executives is that although these shows are popular with some segments of the population, they can never achieve "true success" because European American viewers will not watch programs with predominantly microcultural casts. Various sources of media research support their reasoning.

One of the only exceptions that was able to transcend the racial (and generational) divide of viewer habits was *The Cosby Show*, which aired on NBC from 1984 to 1992. Like many of the shows in the 1980s (*227*, *Amen*, *Benson*), this situation comedy featured representations of a successful African American middle class—one that had greater universal appeal (Merritt, 1991). In fact, *The Cosby Show* has been recognized as paving the way for other shows featuring African Americans because it was a "real life example of a previously unrecognized class of Black Americans who are making it in American society" (L. R. Tucker, 1997, p. 103). Both adult characters on the show (Claire and Cliff Huxtable) were accomplished professionals (lawyer, doctor) and supportive parents to five children (all of which were in—or on their way to—various stages of higher education). Ranking as the number-one watched show by both African American and European American viewers, the crossover appeal of *The Cosby Show* was unprecedented for modern-day television. In fact, it was the first situation comedy with a predominantly African American cast to accomplish the feat of being the number-one watched program. According to research, African American viewers appreciated the positive cultural images presented on the show, and European Americans enjoyed the universal appeal of the show (Jhally & Lewis, 1992). Although his ratings have not been as impressive, Bill Cosby's most recent sitcom, *Cosby*, has also enjoyed similar crossover appeal (Hass, 1988).

The Internet as a Mass Media Venue

The Internet was first introduced in the 1990s as a free and open system of information. In order to bring some semblance of order to this technology, the World Wide Web (WWW) was used by the Internet to standardize the information accessible to users across the world. One unique aspect of the Internet that distinguishes it from other media is that it allows users to engage in simulated interface exchanges. Instead of communicating with individuals face to face, people can become a part of a "virtual community" (Campbell, 1999). This cyberspace site allows users to transcend space and time and engage in on-screen conversations with people who share similar interests. Within this mass media venue, interracial communication can occur between individuals whose racial/ethnic identity is unknown. Some see one of the greatest benefits of cyberspace communication is its ability to nurture interactions that occur within a "color-blind" context.

The Southern Poverty Law Center (SPLC) has created a Web site devoted to fighting hate and promoting tolerance (http://www.tolerance.org/hate_internet/index.jsp). The Web site offers its browsers resources, information, and event announcements that can aid them in becoming an active member in the fight against hate of any kind. The benefit of this Web site is that people are provided with detailed and practical information that can aid them in actively engaging in this process on an individual and organizational level. More important, the Web site visitor is challenged to engage in a variety of activities that require them to self-reflect and think about their own biases and prejudices. Ultimately, the visitor is encouraged to become a part of the solution to ending racism and hate.

Case Study: Hate Groups on the Internet

Since the September 11 attacks, there has been an upsurge in the number of hate crimes committed in the United States. According the Southern Poverty Law Center Web site, there are a total of 805 hate groups in the United States, which is a 58% increase since its previous report in 1997 (pre–September 11) when there were 474. Within this number were different types of hate groups (as defined by the Center) including Ku Klux Klan (179), neo-Nazi (157), skinhead (56), Christian Identity (35), Neo-Confederate (99), and Black separatist (108) groups, and other/unnamed groups (171). In a 2004 newsletter, the U.S. Department of Justice Hate Crime Statistics stated that there were 7,649 criminal incidents reported to law enforcement agencies that were "motivated by a bias against a race, religion, disability, ethnicity, or sexual orientation—and [the publication] includes information on 9,035 offenses, 9,528 victims, and 7,145 known offenders" (U.S. Department of Justice, 2004). On this Web site, there are roughly 14 tables that present various information about hate crime incidents, the types of offenses committed, and some aspects of the victims and the offenders. The remaining tables contain hate crime data aggregated by state or agency type and show the parameters of participation for law enforcement agencies that contributed data to the program.

In 2005, the number of hate groups jumped to almost 550! California had the most hate groups (52), followed by Florida (50), South Carolina (46), Texas (43), Tennessee (36), and North Carolina (35) (Estes, 1999). According to those who track the growth of hate groups in the United States, the Internet is the primary factor in this large increase. Many hate groups use radio, magazine, newspaper, and telephone hot lines to support their movements. However, the Internet has provided these groups with a new way to communicate. As reported in a number of articles, the Internet has been used to promote an increased visibility and accessibility of hate groups. Between 1997 and 1998, for instance, there was a 60% increase in the number of White supremacist Web sites (Raspberry, 1999). According to Mark Potok, a researcher for the Southern Poverty Law Center, "The Internet is allowing the white supremacy movement to reach places it has never reached before" (quoted in Estes, 1999, p. 5). The heightened visibility on the Internet has also had another effect. Traditionally, individuals who believed in racial supremacy were typically isolated within their own communities, alone or with a few compatriots. However, the Internet has allowed these individuals to connect with one another and obtain a sense of a national movement. The result is a drastic increase in organized hate groups in the United States.

To date, there is very little research available on the nature of interracial communication on the Internet. There is only one known study by Heidi McKee (2002) who conducted a textual analysis of Internet postings by 75 students around the country who participated in an online discussion forum on affirmative action/diversity and five interviews conducted with students enrolled at four colleges or universities. McKee describes her analysis of "interracial electronic communication" as follows:

> I examine the misunderstandings that arose in this interracial discussion, situating the causes and consequences of the students' discourse within both the local context of the electronic forum and within wider cultural patterns. I show that flaming cannot be easily identified as destructive communication because posts that seem to be violent attacks intended to shut down dialogue may be attempts by writers to educate other, and posts that do not seem to be violent attacks may actually perpetuate an "othering" that is more destructive to interracial communication than online shouting. (p. 411)

McKee's (2002) analysis reveals that the Internet is a convenient, yet strategic form of communication used by "interactants" to discuss a very difficult topic. Individuals posting messages to the discussion forum were oftentimes misunderstood or failed to fully convey the intended meaning of their message. Comparing this increasingly popular form of communication, McKee concludes that "interracial dialogue is as 'rare and difficult to develop and sustain' in electronic exchanges as it is in the face-to-face forums" (p. 428).

Cyberspace anonymity provides a forum where individuals with racist beliefs can make quality interracial communication difficult. According to Estes (1999), the presence of hate groups on the Internet is growing (see accompanying box on p. 5 of Estes, 1999). Some persons associated with these groups may engage in hostile and threatening interactions with people of color communicating online (even those in forums dedicated specifically to one microcultural racial/ethnic group). However, Shannon (1997) reported that African Americans experience a larger problem during interracial communication in cyberspace. During many online conversations, African Americans are confronted with postings from European Americans that reflect cultural ignorance and racist ideologies. The presence (and subsequent defense) of these anonymous messages may work to foster a disconnection between different racial and ethnic groups. In this regard, they act as a constant reminder to people of color in the United States that racist beliefs are still prevalent despite not always being apparent in face-to-face interactions.

Another related concern regarding information accessed from the Internet is that the content on these Web sites is not always accurate (Campbell, 1999). Because few regulations prevent misinformation from being leaked to the masses, the Internet is not as accurate as other media (e.g., information via newspapers, magazines, television). An example of how difficult it is to regulate Internet access occurred on February 8, 1996, when Congress passed and President Clinton signed a law restricting children's access to obscene, indecent, or harassing material. However, the Communications Decency Act (CDA) was later ruled as violating First Amendment rights. The judge's position was that the law is too broad and goes against the very democratic nature of the Internet.

The Internet is a definite asset in society because it provides us with unlimited access to resources and information that may not be available in newspapers, magazines, or on television. This unlimited access, however, does not appear equally across the different racial and ethnic groups in the United States. Research consistently reports that Asian Americans and European Americans have much greater access to the information superhighway than others. Although some reports indicate this gap is closing ("Blacks Closing Gap," 1999), others point to the growing disparity between specific groups. For instance, data from the Computer and Internet Use supplement of the August 2000 Current Population Source (Fairlie, 2004) study found that 50.3% of European Americans use the Internet, while 29.3% of African Americans and 23.7% of Latino/a Americans use the Internet. The disparity between the groups indicates an economic and educational divide that is preventing racial ethnic groups from acquiring the resources necessary to purchase computers and become actively engaged with the information superhighway.

As this section illustrated, the Internet has proven to be a mixed blessing when it comes to issues of race and interracial communication. It's been a blessing because it provides us with a forum to access information and become a part of a worldwide community. The Internet offers people the freedom to share ideas and opinions with others across the globe; however, it runs the risk of communicating inaccurate and potentially damaging information to users. It also creates opportunities for productive discourse to turn into destructive communication that widens the gap in the racial divide. As a medium that continues to gain momentum and is ever-evolving, issues of democracy, equity, and globalized freedom of speech will remain at the center of the debate surrounding the use of the Internet for years to come.

❖ BOX 11.4

STUDENT REFLECTION

This issue was addressed in an episode of *Desperate Housewives*. During this episode, Gabrielle and her husband are attempting to adopt a baby because Gabrielle is unable to have children. They have searched for the right mother and finally came across a young woman who Gabrielle thought was a perfect mother for their future child. However, this young mother did not believe that Gabriel and her husband should be able to adopt her daughter purely because of the fact that Gabriel and her husband were Mexicans. During this episode, this young Caucasian woman immediately judged Gabrielle and her husband once she found out that they were Mexican rather than Hispanic.

I think that this was an excellent topic for *Desperate Housewives* to address because Mexicans are constantly fighting against stereotypes. Some of the stereotypes that I have heard about the Mexican culture are that they are poor, dirty, and will do hard labor for a very small amount of money. I am sure if I thought harder I could come up with many more stereotypes. I believe that oftentimes people forget to discuss how this culture is constantly discriminated against in the United States, and I am thankful that *Desperate Housewives* has brought this issue to the forefront. Besides appearing in *Desperate Housewives*, the issue has grown in popularity because of the new government bills that attempt to send home illegal immigrants, with a focus on the immigrants from Mexico. There are so many different views about this issue, but personally I believe that they should be welcomed into this culture. While I know that I am not aware of all the issues surrounding the issue of illegal immigrants, I do believe that we have a right to attempt to allow anyone willing to work and find a better life into this country. Personally, I believe that this is why our country was founded in the first place, an attempt to find a better life away from the government and hardships of our motherland.

Implications and Consequences of Media Images

If media images had no effect on how we communicate within our everyday lives, there would be little need for concern. However, research clearly demonstrates that the racial/ethnic images that appear in the media work to reinforce societal stereotypes of others (Omi, 1989). According to D. Kellner (1995), mass media images are a central beginning in how "many people construct their sense of 'us' and 'them'" (p. 1). Therefore, they play a central role in all of our everyday lives (Brooks & Jacobs, 1996)—especially whenever "we" come into contact with "them" (however those categories are created along racial/ethnic boundaries). As indicated throughout this chapter, mass media images of underrepresented group members are especially powerful given the quality and quantity of portrayals. The power of these mostly negative images has not gone unnoticed by people of color in the United States. For instance, think about the comments of Henry Louis Gates (1992):

> Historically blacks have always worried aloud about the image that white Americans harbor of us, first because we have never had control of those images and, second, because the greater number of those images have been negative. And given television's immediacy and its capacity to reach so many viewers so quickly, blacks . . . have been especially concerned with our images on screen. (p. 311)

Clearly, one effect that mass media images have had on interracial communication can be seen in how they have reinforced existing racial/ethnic stereotypes. However, an equally important effect is related to how the mass media has presented examples of interracial communication. According to some scholars (e.g., H. Gray, 1995), most media texts create separate worlds for different racial/ethnic groups. For instance, the vast majority of television programs and films feature casts of one racial or ethnic group. And although some may include one or two token representations of outgroup members, their presence is marginal to the overall plot. When interracial communication does occur, it is done with little, or no, attention to any sort of racial/ethnic barriers. These depictions are too simplistic to model any concrete strategies for effective interracial communication for viewers. Some scholars, as explained in the next section, even see how these more positive images of race/ethnicity contribute to a new form of racism.

Case Study: Asian Pacific Culture Week

Rarely do audiences become proactive in response to the images projected from their televisions. We have the liberty of changing the channel, turning off the television, or making a conscious decision not to watch a certain show or negative image we believe is being culturally insensitive. This is the reaction of the Asian American and Pacific Island students of Orange County, California, in response to television network FOX's program The O.C. (Zou, 2005). The show has an all-Caucasian cast, which does not accurately reflect the racial composition of the residents of Orange County. The 2000 U.S. Census Bureau states that nearly 15% of the Orange County population is Asian American or Pacific Islander (AAPI).

In 2005, AAPI students, who make up 40% of the University of California–Davis undergraduate population, held the 32nd annual Asian Pacific Culture Week in an effort to empower students and educate the community about this diverse racial/ethnic group. Although the weeklong celebration was not coordinated in direct response to their invisibility on *The O. C.* (Zou, 2005), Asian American Studies Student Affairs Coordinator Anita Poon is concerned that, "You rarely see accurate portrayals of AAPI in the media. . . . There are many unrealistic stereotypes."

Television audiences who are genuinely concerned with these issues can make a difference. Audiences of color and those committed to diversity in the media can do the following to start a letter writing campaign and make a difference: (1) initiate a letter and e-mail writing campaign expressing their specific concerns; (2) submit letters to network executives; (3) take the time to clearly express your appreciation of or concern with the show; (4) be polite and courteous in your message, even if the mere thought of NBC fills you with uncontrollable rage; (5) write letters by hand if possible (a hand-written letter is a rarity these days and would receive more attention); (6) contact your local network; (7) write to television critics and entertainment writers; (8) download the episodes on iTunes; and (9) buy the DVD sets. (This is adapted from the letter writing campaign currently under way to save the NBC sitcom *Scrubs* at www.supportscrubs.com.)

Fostering an "Enlightened Racism"

As described earlier, one of the most positive images of race/ethnicity on television was *The Cosby Show*. In terms of its representation of race relations in the United States, however, the success of the show was called into question by several media scholars (Jhally & Lewis, 1992; L. R. Tucker, 1997). Their primary criticism focused on how the show presented a candy-coated snapshot of the African American family that ignored the devastating social conditions of many African Americans in the United States. The show, according to Jhally and Lewis (1992), never offered viewers even the slightest glimpse of the economic disadvantages and deep-rooted discrimination that pervade the lives of most African Americans. Instead, the show was criticized for featuring African American characters with the values of European American middle-class culture (L. R. Tucker, 1997). The Huxtables, then, were proof that issues related to family had universal appeal among all viewers—as long as certain areas of African American life (e.g., racism) were made invisible.

According to Jhally and Lewis (1992), the Huxtables' accomplishments in their personal, family, and professional lives worked to perpetuate the myth of the "American Dream": We live in a just world where hard work and perseverance are rewarded and racial barriers no longer exist. In other words, the Huxtables proved that Black people can succeed. However, in doing so, they also promoted the perception that when African Americans do not succeed (like the Huxtables), they have only themselves to blame (L. R. Tucker, 1997). In this regard, the show cultivated the perception, particularly for European Americans, that racism is no longer a significant problem in the United States. The reason why most African Americans do not succeed, according to this line of thinking, is because they use racism as a crutch. Within these perceptions is the development of a new form of "**enlightened racism**" (Jhally & Lewis, 1992). This perspective of racial relations acknowledges the historical significance of racism in the United States. However, it sees the 21st century as a time when the effects of racism have been greatly reduced to the point that the American Dream is now available for all those who are willing to work to achieve it.

Television is not the only mass medium where a new form of enlightened racism has been promoted. Other researchers (e.g., Artz, 1998; Bogle, 1994) have demonstrated how the growing number of "interracial buddy films" have also perpetuated the idea of individual equality while ignoring realities of race relations in the United States. A number of well-publicized and highly popular movies depict (mostly, but not exclusively) European American–African American partnerships: *Silver Streak, 48 Hours, Beverly Hills Cops, The Last Boy Scout, Die Hard, Lethal Weapon, The Money Train, Men in Black, Rush Hour*, and *Wild, Wild West*. Beyond their attraction as action-adventure-comedy pictures, these films use the name recognition of stars (e.g., Bruce Willis, Eddie Murphy, Mel Gibson, Danny Glover, Tommy Lee Jones, and Will Smith) within their respective communities to draw diverse audiences to the box office. According to Artz (1998), however, different segments of the audience are attracted to interracial buddy films for different reasons. African Americans enjoy seeing African American actors in roles that exhibit strength, dignity, and intelligence. They are also drawn to these movies because African American culture is recognizable and portrayed in positive ways. European Americans are attracted to these films because they represent the fantasy of interracial cooperation. Artz (1998) argues that what is most appealing is that these partnerships exist without challenging the status quo. For instance, he notes that in most interracial buddy films two things exist: (1) European American authorities are ultimately in charge, and (2) the lone African American hero is separated from his community.

So how do these films, like *The Cosby Show*, perpetuate an enlightened racism among media consumers? In their study of audience perceptions of *Rush Hour 2*, Park, Gabbadon, and Chernin (2006) found that while racial stereotypes do exist, Asian American, African American, and European American audiences engaged differently with the cinematic images in the film. Rather than focus on the negative framing of racial difference, most study participants found the racial jokes inoffensive. In particular, Asian and African American participants "found a positive source of pleasure in the negative portrayals of their own race and did not produce oppositional discourse ... [suggesting that] the generic conventions and textual devices of comedy encourage the audience to naturalize racial differences rather than to challenge racial stereotypes" (Park et al., 2006, p. 157).

Conclusion

This chapter described the crucial role that the mass media play in our perceptions of race relations in the United States. Specifically, we discussed how different racial and ethnic groups are portrayed in the media. In addition, by examining specific areas of the media we focused our attention on media use and its influence on viewers' attitudes and beliefs. We hope that the material shared throughout the chapter enhanced your understanding of the key role that mass media images play in terms of everyday life interactions.

Although many may think that reading the newspaper, watching television, and using the Internet are activities that do not directly involve issues of racial/ethnic representation, we now know such is not the case. All media images—whether ignoring, stereotyping, or advancing racial and ethnic diversity—play some role in shaping how people come to understand race relations in the United States. In terms of mass media images of underrepresented group members, this means the presence or absence of each portrayal either "advances or retards the struggle" toward interracial understanding (Elise & Umoja, 1992, p. 83). Because the media play such a central role in how persons come to understand self and others, we must rethink how we use and interpret messages communicated via mass communication channels. Additionally, we must think critically about the media's role in contributing to perceptions that hinder effective interracial communication.

First, we can become active participants in decision-making processes that ultimately affect mass media images of underrepresented group members. Wilkinson (1996) suggests that viewers can increase their power in this struggle over representation by (1) participating in the Nielsen Media Research surveys when the opportunity arises, (2) orchestrating letter-writing campaigns, (3) advocating quality programming, (4) supporting the ownership and employment of underrepresented group members in the media industry, and (5) becoming familiar with the communication laws of the FCC. An example of viewer activism occurred in the spring of 1997 when fans of *Living Single* instigated a letter-writing, phone-calling, and e-mail campaign petitioning Fox TV to bring the sitcom back ("Popular Demand Brings 'Living Single' Back," 1997, p. 58). Second, on a more personal level, we can use a number of approaches to think critically about mass media representations of race/ethnicity. For instance, we can examine the *types* (e.g., friendship, family, professional) and *quality* of interactions (e.g., affirming, hostile, devaluing) occurring between the persons in the media. Just as important is to maintain an increased awareness of the obvious—and not so obvious—ways that visibility, marginalization, and stereotyping occur within various mass media texts.

As you read the newspaper, see an ad, watch television, or laugh at a cartoon, ask yourself several questions. What is being communicated here—explicitly or implicitly—about race/ethnicity? Am I being entertained, informed, or both? How are these images consistent with, or different from, what mainstream media typically portrays? Is there anything here that I or others might find offensive? What alternative images are present? By becoming more critical about our own use of the media, we can gain a better understanding of how influential the media are in shaping our attitudes, beliefs, and perceptions of self and others. If change does not start within ourselves, we will continue to be what we are: a society living in fear of difference and diversity.

OPPORTUNITIES FOR EXTENDED LEARNING ❖

1. Use the Internet to learn more about the "telenovela" and its significance in the Latin American community. Find reviews of the television show *Ugly Betty* and any observable trends in the viewing patterns of racial/ethnic groups and the degree to which they identify with the program. If available, find articles that speak to the motivations and intentions of the network ABC to create a show targeted toward Latin Americans.

2. Take a moment to reflect on your television viewing habits. Thinking about the television shows or news programs you have seen, how are the three European American ethnic groups previously discussed being depicted? What other ethnic groups from this race can you think of? How are they presented in the media? Does the label Whiteness or White appear to be preferred or used more so than ethnic group labels? List several explanations you believe may be offered to answer this question.

3. Have you ever seen Aaron McGruder's comic strip or television cartoon *Boondocks?* After being launched nationally in April 1999, the strip gained a significant amount of attention for its images of racism, race, and racial/ethnic identity. The comic strip was so popular that a television cartoon was created on the Cartoon Network and debuted in November 2005. After a very controversial strip attacking President Bush's past drug use and the Iraq war, several newspapers pulled the cartoon and the television network placed the show on hiatus until March 2007. You can also visit McGruder's Web site (www.theboondockstv.com).

4. Go to your library and complete a search for magazines targeted to a racial/ethnic group other than your own. After reading through at least three issues from different magazines, think about how these publications differ from those geared toward your own racial/ethnic group. Are the stories covered in each the same? What are some key similarities and differences?

5. In 1999, the National Association for the Advancement of Colored People (NAACP) contemplated actions against the top four television networks for the lack of diversity in the upcoming season (P. Shepard, 1999). The civil rights organization's criticism was based on the fact that none of the 27 new comedies and dramas premiering in the fall of 1999 had any lead, and few supporting, microcultural cast members. Consider how this reflects on the historical trend of racial/ethnic representation on TV. Use the Internet to locate and review the most recent programming lineups for each network. Then determine if these new programs continue marginalizing certain groups or create greater opportunities for a more balanced representation.

6. Locate a specific media text (e.g., film, music video, book, television program, etc.) that portrays realistic, positive images of effective interracial communication. Then share this source with others and discuss why you chose that particular mass media image. During this exchange, try and reach consensus in terms of how "realistic" and "positive" should be defined. What types of images were selected? How were they similar and/or different?

12

Moving From the Theoretical to the Practical

As the previous chapters have demonstrated, the issue of race has become incredibly complex. Although some may argue that race relations have improved, personal testimonies, research, and other resources tell us that such is not the case. Instead, racism, prejudice, and stereotyping remain a staple in the diet of many U.S. Americans.

Earlier we described theories that analyze the complexities associated with race and communication. In this chapter, we present some practical approaches to effective interracial communication. We hope that you will continue to apply concepts and new knowledge gathered from previous chapters to the issues here. We begin by identifying potential barriers to interracial communication, which includes discussion of unproductive assumptions and problematic communication approaches that perpetuate a cycle of ineffective interracial communication. From there, we explore communication strategies observed by some as most effective within an interracial context. The concept of dialogue is described as it relates to communication in the 21st century. The summary challenges you to extend your knowledge from the classroom into your real-world experiences.

Identifying Potential Barriers to Interracial Communication

As with any communication process, interracial communication may be hindered by potential barriers that prevent interactants from communicating effectively with each other. It is most often our prejudices, racist attitudes, stereotypes, and uncertainty that create barriers, and their mere presence or existence within the individual and society as a whole may complicate an otherwise natural communicative exchange. As we discussed earlier, interracial communication is so critical to the social and political success of our nation that several years ago President Clinton initiated a federally funded grant designed to assess the short- and long-term effects of racism on racial/ethnic groups living within the United States. People continue to assert that race relations have greatly improved over the past few decades; however, hate crimes, church burnings, murders, and contemporary forms of lynching (e.g., the 1998 dragging death of an African American man in Texas by three male self-described White supremacists) demonstrate the reality of racism in the United States. With the influx of racially diverse individuals entering many of our public and private institutions, we must examine the barriers to effective and positive interracial communication. T. F. Pettigrew (1981) collected survey data to better understand European Americans' attitudes toward and beliefs about the state of race relations in the United States. Twenty percent of the participants opposed racist propositions, 20% supported racist propositions, and 60% reportedly had no opinion. Although it may be encouraging to see a small percentage of people in support of a racist ideology, Bowser and Hunt (1996) assert that this 5-year trend of racism and apathy has remained constant over time. In other words, "the more things change, the more they stay the same."

Barriers and Unproductive Assumptions

According to Blubaugh and Pennington (1976), a **racial assumption** "is a consciously or unconsciously held premise that is considered to be true regarding a race or ethnic group and that is acted on as though it were true" (p. 45). Racial assumptions are held with no supporting evidence or they are based on hearsay, or generalizations. Stereotyping is one of the most natural cognitive behaviors we as humans engage in. This process involves efforts to categorize information in an effort to make sense of information to which we are exposed. Although this behavior brings order to chaos, the process of stereotyping becomes even more complex when it relates to racial/ethnic and sexual identities (among others). These stereotypes make interracial interactions problematic on three distinct levels. Stereotypes that affect our interracial interactions on an interpersonal level are often referred to as individual racism (Bowser & Hunt, 1996). It is on this level that stereotypes impede one of the most effective means for improving race relations.

Consider one of your interracial friendships as an example. More likely than not, both you and your friend had preexisting stereotypes of each other based on race or even personality. As your relationship developed and you got to know each other on a more intimate level, those stereotypes were probably challenged in some way. In your opinion, was this friendship more effective in diminishing racist thoughts and beliefs than hearing the news, reading the newspaper, or reading a journal article? The potency of any of the mass media varies from person to person; however, research indicates that interpersonal interaction is quite effective in improving race relations on a more humanistic level. Individuals are now able to place a face on the reality of racism. Institutionalized racism is different from individual racism in that group communication perpetuates racist ideologies in a much larger context. It is at this level that individual racist beliefs are reinforced by a larger body of like-minded people (Bowser & Hunt, 1996). Historically, people in positions of power have preserved racism by preventing various racial/ethnic group members from having equal access to institutions and organizations to which *all* people should have access (see Chapters 4 and 5 for more discussion of privilege and power).

Cultural racism is much like ethnocentrism in that people present their own racial/ethnic group's cultural preferences and values as superior to those of other groups (Bowser & Hunt, 1996). The consequences of this type of thinking is that all aspects of one culture and heritage are deemed culturally acceptable, thus negating the value of all other racial/ethnic groups. Although this ideology may appear antiquated, current events indicate otherwise. The rising number of hate groups on the Internet and society at large are a testament to the pervasiveness of racism in contemporary society. Although such groups use the First Amendment to support these extremist beliefs, their culture breathes life into a racist ideology that potentially leads to violence and, in some cases, death.

These forms of racism provide a context for understanding how people can individually and collectively adopt ideologies that have short- and long-term consequences. In any event, race relations and interracial contact are hindered in the process. These barriers ultimately make our communicative interactions problematic. In the next section, we explore the effects of racism on our communicative processes.

❖ **BOX 12.1**

"DECLARATION OF APPRECIATION"

It is our hope that now that you have completed this interracial communication course, you will put your newfound knowledge about and skills in interracial communication to use in effectively dealing with race relations beyond the college classroom. The following is a pledge adapted from the Southern Poverty Law Center to articulate a continued effort toward positive interracial communication. (We have renamed this from the "Declaration of Toleration" because the term *toleration* connotes an attitude of resistance and "putting up with" someone.)

Declaration of Appreciation

Appreciation is the purposeful decision I make to appreciate and value the differences and similarities that exist between myself and those who are different from me. Tolerance is a personal decision that comes from a belief that every person is a treasure. Diversity is the beauty of America and what it stands for. I embrace the opportunity to combat racism. I will do my part in recognizing and combating ignorance, insensitivity, prejudice, racism, discrimination, and bigotry. I will take this charge and apply it to my relationships and every aspect of my life. I pledge to operate with a spirit of respect, courtesy, sensitivity and respect concerning people whose abilities, beliefs, culture, race, sexual identity or other characteristics are different from my own.

To fulfill my pledge, I, [your name], will examine my own biases and work to overcome them, set a positive example for my family and friends, work for appreciation in my own community, and speak out against hate and injustice.

I embrace the challenge and accept the call with a glad heart!

Problematic Communication Approaches

As we have emphasized throughout this text, very little has happened to improve interracial communication nationally and/or globally. Although opportunities to communicate with others from different racial and ethnic groups are increasing, interracial communication in face-to-face and computer-mediated contexts (e.g., Internet) are difficult to manage (McKee, 2002). The research has shown that interracial communication is problematic for a variety of reasons, one of them being "a serious mismatch in racial perception[s] of change" (Patterson, 1995, p. 26). Patterson asserts that middle-class European Americans believe race relations and attitudes toward African Americans have improved, and African Americans believe and experience racism, which has led to feelings that the state of race relations has either not changed or gotten worse (see also J. H. Turner, Singleton, & Musick, 1984). Although perceptual difference is illustrative of European American–African American race relations, such beliefs are applicable to other interracial relations as well.

Researchers have asserted that interpersonal interactions contribute to improved race relations; however, this same relational context has the potential to increase ethnocentrism (Neuliep & McCroskey, 1997b). The racial difference between interactants becomes maximized and prevents them from evaluating their preconceived beliefs and attitudes toward their respective racial/ethnic groups. The following quotation is from a business manager discussing the need for organizations and society as a whole to acknowledge the existing barriers to interracial communication and their effect on the organizational climate:

> When you have a racial difference the assumption is driven by the stereotype and perceived prejudice. When you get into those cases, we usually find out that [the problem] is just good old-fashioned failure to communicate or a reluctance to interact in an open way for fear of being misinterpreted. So race does create a barrier but it's not a racism type barrier. It's an uncertainty, a lack of comfort or a lack of familiarity barrier and not wanting to be perceived as having difficulty working with a white person, a black person, or an Asian. (Laabs, 1993)

If effective interracial communication is to occur, members of society must have some level of consciousness and, ultimately, responsibility for engaging in dialogue about race and race issues. We must all examine our own roles in improving race relations. As the saying goes, "If you are not a part of the solution, you must be a part of the problem." In order for systematic change to occur, we must all make it our responsibility to deconstruct the existing racial hierarchy and create a democracy that provides opportunities and access to all citizens regardless of racial/ethnic identity.

Rebecca Raby's (2004) article entitled "'There's No Racism at My School, It's Just Joking Around': Ramifications for Anti-Racist Education" explores the **racialization process**, which can be described, in a sense, as the ways in which a person's racial identity is constructed, defined, and performed (see Chapters 4 and 5). We reemphasize this point to underscore how important it is that we recognize the privileges and powers that are associated with our racial identities. Although her interviews were with teenage girls, Raby's (2004) findings tell us that our attitudes, beliefs, and values about race impact those around us (e.g., family, friends, coworkers); therefore, in order to break the cycle of racism, we can do so through our interpersonal networks and relationships.

Another barrier that impedes interracial communication is metastereotypes (Sigelman & Tuch, 1997; Torres & Charles, 2004). Metastereotypes are perceptions that an individual has of the stereotypes that other individuals have for him or her. Although data exist suggesting that attitudes toward race are improving among European Americans, Sigelman and Tuch (1997) and Torres and Charles (2004) provide data stating otherwise. In each study, it was found that African Americans perceived European Americans to have negative perceptions of them as a racial group, including the belief that African Americans prefer to live off welfare, are violent, and are lazy. As predicted, the European Americans did report espousing such negative perceptions. These findings are troubling and demonstrate how African Americans, and quite possibly other racial/ethnic groups, are in the precarious position of exercising a double consciousness, or an awareness of the perceptions held of themselves through their own eyes and the eyes of European Americans (Torres & Charles, 2004). By expecting or anticipating that European Americans have negative perceptions of them, African Americans may purposely avoid all communication with them, which is problematic for those who don't espouse such beliefs. As such, barriers are erected that reduce the likelihood of intergroup relations from occurring and potentially perpetuate the stereotypes associated with outgroup members (Leonard & Locke, 1993).

Blatant forms of racism within the context of interpersonal relationships have changed since the 1950s and 1960s. Nevertheless, racist attitudes and beliefs are manifested in various ways and contexts. As we have already mentioned, people oftentimes experience uncertainty when they are interacting with a person from a different racial/ethnic or cultural group. This apprehension may stem from limited interracial contact, preconceived notions, stereotypes, prejudices, or general communicator apprehension (e.g., fear of losing face). Although there is not one clear answer to why people are uncertain about interracial/interethnic interactions, Neuliep and McCroskey (1997a) believe that this apprehension is essentially "the fear associated with either real or anticipated interaction with people from different groups, especially different cultural and ethnic groups" (p. 152). For some people, the idea and/or reality of contact and communication with a person from a racial/ethnic group different from their own is a very scary experience that induces anxiety. Have you ever been apprehensive about working with someone who is European American, Middle Eastern American, or Native American? If we are open and honest enough to examine the hows, whys, and whens of this uncertainty, we will then be able to deal with racist ideologies that prohibit effective interracial communication from occurring.

Privileged Checklist

Here are a few sample statements (from McIntosh's [1995b] original list of 26) designed to challenge European Americans to recognize and acknowledge how they potentially benefit from their social and racial positions in the United States.

1. I can if I wish arrange to be in the company of people of my own race most of the time.

2. If I should need to move, I can be pretty sure of renting or purchasing housing in an area which I can afford and in which I would want to live.

3. I can go shopping alone most of the time, pretty well assured that I will not be followed.

4. I can turn on the television or open to the front page of the paper and see people of my race widely represented.

5. When I am told about our national heritage or about "civilization" I am shown that people of my color made it what it is.

6. I can be sure that my children will be given curricular materials that testify to the existence of their race.

7. If I want to, I can be pretty sure of finding a publisher for this piece on white privilege.

8. I can go into a music shop and count on finding the music of my race represented, into a supermarket and find the staple foods which fit with my cultural traditions, into a hairdresser's shop and find someone who can cut my hair. (p. 94)

❖ **BOX 12.2**

"101 TOOLS FOR TOLERANCE"

On their Web site (www.tolerance.gov), the Southern Poverty Law Center offers 10 tips that people can use to combat racism on an individual level. Please consider these as possible strategies you can use in your own life to make a difference.

1. Attend a play, listen to music, or go to a dance performance by artists whose race or ethnicity is different from your own.

2. Volunteer at a local social services organization.

3. Attend services at a variety of churches, synagogues, mosques, and temples to learn about different faiths.

4. Visit a local senior citizens center and collect oral histories. Donate large-print reading materials and books on tape. Offer to help with a craft project.

5. Shop at ethnic grocery stores and specialty markets. Get to know the owners. Ask about their family histories.

6. Participate in a diversity program.

7. Ask a person of another cultural heritage to teach you how to perform a traditional dance or cook a traditional meal.

8. Learn sign language.

9. Take a conversation course in another language that is spoken in your community.

10. Teach an adult to read.

11. Speak up when you hear slurs. Let people know that bias speech is always unacceptable.

12. Imagine what your life might be like if you were a person of another race, gender, or sexual orientation. How might today have been different?

Currently, few scales in research are designed to assess the degree to which our (dis)comfort level with interracial communication is manifested in our interpersonal behaviors. In other words, there are no actual measures of the communication strategies or behaviors that create the barriers we believe exist and problematize communication between racially and ethnically different people. Can you recall a time when you felt or someone else appeared uncomfortable or awkward during an interracial interaction? What verbal or nonverbal cues did you observe that communicated discomfort? To what did you attribute this behavior? People who continually struggle with racial identity and racism may be more likely to have a higher level of consciousness to these cues within an interracial context. (This does not mean, however, that individuals sensitized to issues of race are not attuned to the significance of verbal and nonverbal cues.)

Neuliep and McCroskey's (1997a) Personal Report of Interethnic Communication Apprehension Scale (PRECA) explores one underlying dimension of this tension that sometimes arises in interracial/interethnic communication. This scale is a modified version of the Personal Report of Intercultural Communication Apprehension (PRICA), which explores the importance of culture in interpersonal interactions. PRECA is a very important tool used in research. The reality of racism in the United States is reflected in the reliability of this scale. The reliability of these scales has been tested, and if we examine the content items or statements to which participants respond, we are able to better understand how communication behaviors can potentially become problematic within an interracial exchange.

President Clinton's initiative on race relations must remain at the forefront of our national agenda. Coupled with self-examination of our communication behaviors and an understanding of the motivations guiding these behaviors (e.g., racism, uncertainty, personality), our interpersonal interactions provide an excellent context for identifying problematic communication approaches. According to the scale, factors used to assess apprehension and perceptions of communication competence are dislike, comfort level, tension, nervousness, calmness, relaxation, fear, and confidence. Neuliep and McCroskey (1997a) emphasize that racial, ethnic, and cultural diversity on college campuses and within organizations throughout the nation are in need of such measures that will educate students, faculty, employers, and employees alike about the important role of communication in our interracial interactions.

More importantly, studies designed with the organizational community in mind may have far-reaching implications. They describe this observation as follows: "Within multinational organizations, the scales could be administered to managers and employees to predict potential problems in culturally, ethnically, and/or racially diverse work settings" (Neuliep & McCroskey, 1997a, p. 154).

❖

TIP: THEORY INTO PRACTICE

A **hate crime** is legally defined as an offender attacking a victim "because of the victim's actual or perceived race, color, religion, disability, sexual orientation, or national origin" (K. Sun, 2006, p. 597) and is committed every hour in the United States (Carrier, 1999). Statistics indicate that these sorts of crimes are on the rise, especially since

September 11, 2001, and are primarily motivated by racial bias. According to the U.S. Department of Justice (n.d.), these heinous crimes, as well as many others, frequently go unreported. This may be attributed to feelings of powerlessness in confronting such crimes since the perpetrator(s) is usually a stranger. Here are several guidelines provided by the Southern Poverty Law Center (http://www.tolerance.org/10_ways/index .html) to respond effectively to hate crimes.

1. *Do something.* Lack of action will be interpreted as apathy or acceptance. Speak up and use your First Amendment rights too!

2. *Unite.* Call friends, colleagues, or neighbors. Organize diverse coalitions that can come together for a larger cause. Elicit the support of community leaders and public officials.

3. *Support the victims.* They may feel especially vulnerable, fearful, and alone; let them know that they are not facing this battle by themselves.

4. *Do your homework.* Obtain accurate information about the missions, agendas, and symbols of hate groups. Learn about how they use their legal rights, informal networks, and the media to promote their ideas.

5. *Commit yourself to teaching tolerance.* Racial/ethnic bias is learned early; however, these attitudes can also be unlearned through long-term programs and curricula. Never stop trying to make a difference.

6. *Dig deeper.* Press beyond the surface issues related to hate crimes. Develop more complex understandings of how other issues beyond race divide us. Continue to learn about self and others.

Setting the Stage for Effective Interracial Communication

Now that we have explored theories, concepts, and case studies to assist us in our understanding of interracial communication, we must challenge ourselves to set the stage for effective race relations. Let's use the theater as a metaphor to illustrate this point. Imagine you are an actor working with an improvisational ensemble with other actors who are equally committed to the production you are scheduled to perform. On the first day of the improvisation, you are given the theme comic-tragedy, which you are to perform that evening for an anxious audience. Because the performance is improvisational, no script guides the show and the team must work together to perform this comic-tragedy successfully. Of course, the cast must negotiate to determine what will work best for the night's performance. However, it is through trial and error that they learn what best achieves the designated goal of this particular play. Well, the same applies to those individuals committed to improving race relations on both the micro- and macrolevel.

No one methodology is most effective in fostering positive interracial communication. Therefore, individuals and organizations alike must employ multiple methods before they find the most appropriate and effective way to create the desired communication context. More importantly, people from historically oppressed racial and ethnic groups should not carry this burden alone. As McIntosh (1995b) has already suggested, European Americans must join in this fight against racist ideologies embedded within the psyche of Western culture. C. Crenshaw (1997) provides further support for this need in the following statement: "Whiteness functions ideologically when people employ it consciously or unconsciously, as a framework to categorize people and understand their social locations. Within this framework, whiteness as a social position has value and has been treated legally as property" (p. 255). Therefore, those who are not privileged have been oppressed in a society that places more value on skin color than character.

❖ **BOX 12.3**

AUTHOR REFLECTION

At the turn of the 21st century, scholars (e.g., Patterson, 1998) described productive discussions about race in the United States as null and void. Race, and related topics, remains a salient issue but one that is seldom explored in contexts where diverse perspectives are present, valued, and engaged. Given this reality, Hatch (2003) predicts that the current generation is tragically destined to pass on the problems of race to still another generation. I don't think that I am as pessimistic as Hatch; however, I am a realist and recognize that in all probability race will be an issue that my children's children will have to negotiate on some level.

The more I interact with my children—aged 14, 12½, and 11—and their friends, the more hopeful I am for the future. Clearly, each generation seems to be more and more open and less bogged down with negative racial baggage. As a parent of multiracial children, I believe that part of the job is to educate my children about race and empower them with strategies to deal with everyday racism. Despite these attempts—including those found in various "teachable moments"—my children appear much more comfortable and confident when it comes to discussing race. I oftentimes sit in awe as I observe them interact with others; I can't help but think how much more at ease they are with their racial identities (and overall self-concepts) than I was at their ages. Ideally, their self-confidence will spread to future generations.

Part of my teaching philosophy is based on the "each one, teach one" principle. In this regard, I expect students to share what they've learned with others—to create an ongoing ripple effect. So, as you conclude this semester, the question is: What will you do with the information that you learned? How will it affect how you go about your everyday lives? How, if at all, will your experiences contribute to a more equitable, harmonious society?

—MPO

Racial/ethnic diversity is inevitable as we begin the 21st century. We must learn about approaches that facilitate effective interracial communication and increase knowledge and understanding about the reality of racism. The next section provides a variety of approaches and communication strategies that have been used by communication scholars and consultants trained in the area of race relations and diversity. With each approach and strategy we suggest how we can employ these into our daily lives and interactions with others from diverse racial/ethnic groups.

Productive Approaches and Strategies

When it comes to the topic of racial reconciliation, some may wonder, "What for? Things are no longer 'separate but equal,' so there's no need to fight for change." As the rise in hate crimes indicates, a great wall of resistance to the goal of improving race relations remains. For those people who embrace a separatist and/or supremacist ideology, these efforts may appear futile. However, for those of us committed to this goal or interested in doing our part but do not know how, we must become aware of the approaches and communication strategies we can use to increase our interracial communication competence. You might be asking yourself, "How do these approaches come about? I'm sure they don't just appear." Through trial and error, people are able to determine ultimately what method is most effective in resolving the problem at hand.

For some researchers, applied research is the most appropriate means for achieving this goal. Applied communication research has three benefits: (1) to help people solve socially relevant problems, (2) to provide support for the "predictive validity of communication theory" based on the success of a real-world test (generalizability), and (3) to make clear the practicality of the communication discipline (Kreps, Frey, & O'Hair, 1991). These benefits are appropriate for all forms of communication, and they become imperative when we examine interracial communication. If we as a society cannot engage in public discourse regarding the pervasiveness of racism, are we able to communicate in private? Better yet, are we willing to leave our racial comfort zones and discuss race relations in racially mixed company? The following approaches and strategies address this tension directly by providing guidelines that will educate us about these very issues.

Race Relations Training

In Chapter 9, we discussed the importance of organizational communication and the far-reaching effect of race on the culture and the process of communication in this context. Now we must turn our attention to specific strategies that people have used to improve race relations on both the micro- and macrolevel. Again, we emphasize that one approach is not better than another. You must use discretion as you choose the tactic you deem most appropriate and effective in decreasing the tension levels associated with race.

When discussing the topic of race relations, many people think immediately of interpersonal conflict between racially/ethnically different people. However, this is not always the case. Oftentimes, ethnocentric thinking creates a site for conflict that prevents positive race relations from materializing. If a person believes her or his race is superior to all others, it is very likely that she or he will be very defensive when interacting with people from different racial/ethnic groups. This way of thinking is problematic for a variety of reasons.

First, ethnocentrism fosters an ingroup bias that allows those individuals to perceive (and believe) their racial/ethnic group possesses moral traits (e.g., trustworthiness, honesty, pacifism, virtue, obedience) that are lacking in all other groups (Deutsch, 1994). Thus, when the two (or more) groups interact, they compete for the same resources (e.g., jobs, housing, college education). This competition is natural because the resources may be limited. Nevertheless, the division along racial/ethnic lines only perpetuates racism and the unequal distribution of and/or access to those resources.

Second, this ethnocentric thinking prevents individuals from having interracial interactions. Therefore, interactions with ingroup members only magnify the perceived attitudes held of outgroup members. In other words, ingroup members' intragroup interactions discourage interracial contact. Even when they do occur, preconceived perceptions are reinforced (Deutsch, 1994).

The final factor that creates this adversarial climate is the pyramidal segmentary, where a societal organization is perceived as actively promoting ingroup ethnocentrism, which in turn creates intergroup strife on a macrolevel (Deutsch, 1994). In other words, micro- and macroculture group members are expected to accept the dominant culture (within that organization) as part of their sole identity. For those individuals who maintain a high level of ethnocentrism, it is very difficult for training to facilitate significant change in behavior unless greater emphasis is placed on the importance of skills. Additionally, individuals should be trained on how to transfer these learned skills from the training session to real-life situations.

You may be thinking that people who are ethnocentric would not choose to attend a race relations training session. This may be true, but what happens when they are part of an organizational culture that is becoming racially/ethnically diverse? More likely than not, they will be working directly with people who are different from them and, as a result of their beliefs they may be hostile, confrontational, or even ignore the very existence of those organizational members. In any event, it is very likely that the CEO or a human resources representative will require a race relations training session of all the employees. By acknowledging the crucial role of ethnocentrism within traditionally hegemonic cultures, proactive approaches to race relations training can work toward resolving "racial" conflict and changing intergroup prejudices, stereotyping, and discriminatory behaviors (Deutsch, 1994).

❖ **BOX 12.4**

AUTHOR REFLECTIONS

As I sit here working on the second edition of this textbook, I am thinking about this project and other tasks I have assumed as a communication scholar committed to addressing issues of race. For someone who couldn't fathom the idea of going to college after high school, I am truly humbled by the opportunity afforded me to engage in critical thought about race in very unique and socially significant ways. I enjoy the research that I do and get equal joy and satisfaction in the learning and growing opportunities that come with teaching courses specifically about race.

I have lamented on numerous occasions to colleagues, family, and friends how mentally, emotionally, and psychologically draining it sometimes is to engage in discourse about race on a constant basis. As an African American woman, I deal with these battles in my own life, and to compound those experiences with classroom instruction can become quite exhausting. I teach two race-related courses every spring semester, and by the end of the school year, I am wiped out. I am sometimes pushed to the edge, on the brink of giving up. After a quick episode of self-reflection (Tanno, 2004), however, I am quickly reminded that I am on this journey for the long haul. I know it is my purpose to be on this lifetime journey of self-discovery and eradicating racism.

I purpose to establish for my future children a legacy of peace, love, and appreciation in a racially diverse world. I can't wait for the day to come when I, first, get married, and second, create a family committed to healing the racial divide and fostering healthy relationships! It is my desire to remain in the good fight—one relationship, one moment, one step at a time.

—TMH

In her research on diversity training effectiveness, Marilyn Easter (2002) compared two groups of nontraditional students, those who were enrolled in a Managing Cultural Diversity (MCD) course and those enrolled in marketing classes. The goal of this study was to determine if seven weeks of "intensive training on cultural diversity, interracial differences, race relations, ethnicity and attitude, psychographics, prejudice and discrimination, and white privilege" (p. 1) would change negative attitudes toward workplace diversity. Using the Cross-Cultural Adaptability Inventory (CCAI), Easter found no statistically significant difference between the groups. She concluded that the students/employees were not affected or changed by the training because they had previous exposure to issues of diversity and, therefore, were not impacted by the information to which they were exposed.

Although this study was confined to the college classroom, it is questionable as to whether the findings would be replicated in the real world. The intense training that takes place in race-related classes that last between a quarter (10 weeks) and a semester (16 weeks) provides students with repeated exposure to discussions, information, and activities designed to challenge their thinking about race and proactive strategies to eradicate racism. In contrast, diversity training workshops in the workplace are sporadic. Some businesses may choose to offer a workshop infrequently (e.g., annually, quarterly) while others may offer repeated opportunities for workshop involvement in addition to departments, committees, and caucuses assembled for the sole purpose of strategically planning programs and training sessions and creating organizational or departmental goals and objectives that foster organizational diversity. These two examples demonstrate that organizational cultures are distinct, unique. As such, the likelihood of changing individual attitudes about race is in part influenced by organizational leadership and culture, whether diversity training is encouraged, and the degree to which their interpersonal networks support or discourage positive perceptions of racially different others. Therefore, it is imperative that individuals involved in creating diversity training workshops and organizational leaders who secure them consider these confounding factors and whether they involve strategic design and implementation of practical approaches to preparing organizations and their members for racial and ethnic diversity in the workplace and beyond.

Training Models

Foeman (1997) suggests five interpersonal behavioral objectives of race relations training: (1) discuss race-related issues (demystification); (2) articulate, (3) examine, and (4) find validity in the other groups' perspectives; and (5) utilize others' perspectives in order to work together effectively while striving toward common goals. During a race relations workshop or training session, information sharing and open discussion are frequently most effective (see Laabs, 1993). These processes are successful because they increase sensitivity among people who, for whatever reason, were not attuned to the significance of race prior to the workshop. By sharing their experiences and perceptions of racism, participants/coworkers have a better understanding of how racial/ethnic identity locates them in society as well as in the organizational context.

There are three training models (didactic, experiential training, and groupwork) that achieve the objectives just described and are designed to change the behaviors of macrocultural and microcultural group members. No matter which model is used to train people about race relations, all three have similar goals. The models vary in their approach to race relations. However, each provides information bases and social contexts designed to train participants, increase cross-racial dialogues, and encourage participants to apply this knowledge to their interpersonal interracial interactions and the larger social system (Foeman, 1997).

The **didactic model** is one of the most common forms of race relations training. The teaching mechanism used in this model is lecture, in which the trainer presents facts and information to participants. This linear, or one-way, approach confronts the macrocultural group members by making an information-based appeal. However, this style is very ineffective in bringing about change. First, the interpersonal goals of participants are not always met because they are not able to interact and exchange ideas and information. Second, macrocultural group members may perceive this approach as "defensive re-education," which may indicate an inability to personalize and internalize information gained from the social experiences of the "others" (Foeman, 1997).

The **experiential training model** centers on the assumption that interaction among race relations training participants is necessary. Unlike the didactic model, the experiential training model depends heavily on the personal experiences of individuals from various racial/ethnic groups. All persons are expected to share their racialized realities with fellow participants in an effort to reduce prejudice through personal contact, which may in turn facilitate change. One primary drawback of this model is that people of color take on the role of spokespersons for all members of their respective racial/ethnic groups. For example, in sharing her experiences with the group, a Filipina woman is then perceived as representative of all other Filipino/as. This can be harmful in that other participants may take this one perspective and generalize it to all other racial/ethnic minorities, which then can feed into the vicious cycle of stereotyping. As a result, the people of color participating in the training receive fewer benefits from the experience and have the additional stress of being a representative for all other racial/ethnic group members.

❖ **BOX 12.5**

STUDENT REFLECTION

The more I hang around my friends and actually listen to some of the things that come out of their mouths, the more I realize what a twisted world we live in. Before I began this class, I would venture to say that I felt as if I had a good understanding of what it means to be Black or White and everything else in between. I also have to admit that I was skeptical of the course and its content in general (being that some parts I felt I didn't agree with). So, now we are almost through with the semester and I feel as if I have changed a bit in that my eyes have been opened a little more to some of the small, less obvious injustices that take place on a daily basis. This is not to say that I never noticed them before, but I guess after hearing and seeing them for so long and having grown accustomed to them, I was desensitized in a sense that blinded me or made me indifferent to them in my path to achieving my own goals.

For some reason now, I feel the problem is more the absence of responsibility on the part of those who are being persecuted for whatever reason. In most situations I come in contact with the person that is being offensive [who] is no more knowledgeable about the problem than a dog drinking antifreeze. I am speaking of the interactions that are subtle and almost indiscrete. I feel as if most people are stuck in their ways and really use racism as an out or excuse for the things that bother them in life. A friend of mine and I were going through the bank drive-through, and I was completely cut off by a burgundy Mitsubishi. His first remark was "damn n*****." I turned to him and said, "Now why would you say some sh*t like that?" In this case I chose to engage the conversation and we ended up going on for about an hour about why he couldn't just attribute the person's actions to just being inconsiderate and rude rather than the fact they were Black. It almost makes me sick to even have to say that I had a conversation like that with someone I know. This is just one example of how it is more our responsibility to provoke this kind of awareness about these issues.

The **groupwork model** strikes a good medium between the didactic and experiential models in that trainers incorporate information and experience into the learning process. Doing so assists participants in discerning in what social contexts interracial contact will occur, which ultimately expands each person's frame of reference and their understanding of and responses to cross-race issues (Foeman, 1997). Because they are dealing with a variety of people who have different learning styles, trainers use film, discussion, and role play, among others, to encourage learner participation. The most appealing aspect of this model is that it promotes dialogue (see next section) among and between participants, particularly microcultural group members. It is hoped that participants will act on the information they are provided. Bowser and Hunt (1996) describe this newfound social consciousness as follows:

> European Americans are not one-dimensional in their racial identities and there is an important psychological connection, conditioned by historic culture, between racial identity and where one stands on the racism to antiracism continuum. By better understanding their own historic backgrounds, EAs' growth in racial identity is possible along with progression from individual racism to individual antiracism. (p. 250)

By becoming aware of their privileged location in the racial hierarchy, European Americans ideally are more educated about the reality of racism as experienced by their coworkers and colleagues. After participating in race relations training and developing some level of consciousness, they are then morally responsible (McIntosh, 1995b) for resolving racial tensions at a level they are most comfortable with. We must also acknowledge that racial/ethnic group members bear responsibility for this problem as well. If a Latino male is participating in a workshop with his European American colleagues, he must not directly blame them individually and/or collectively for his racist experiences with other European Americans. Although he has experienced cumulative racism (a series of racist experiences over a long period of time), the Latino male must recognize his role in this process of awareness. By educating his colleagues about racism and directing his anger at the racial hierarchy (society) and the perpetrators of racism, he is becoming a part of the solution to remedying unproductive interracial communication in the workplace.

Ideally, the use of any of these models will achieve the goal of sensitizing people to the reality of racism. Unfortunately, the possibility remains that not everyone will reach the same level of consciousness after completing one of the training sessions. Some European Americans may remain blinded or unconvinced by the evidence presented by the trainer and/or participants from other racial/ethnic groups. The accounts of racism may be perceived as atypical or unimportant, which only works to problematize race relations on a more complex level. Even though they are hearing the experiences about oppression from the oppressed, some individuals may choose to remain in denial about the saliency of racism in the United States.

As we have reiterated throughout the text, interpersonal contact and communication are critical to race relations if racism is to become a part of our past. Therefore, it is reasonable that approaches created to change intergroup prejudices, stereotyping, and discriminatory behaviors would promote intergroup contact (Deutsch, 1994). We must acknowledge that intergroup contact is influenced by context, power dynamics, time, status, individuality, and acquaintance potential. By receiving information, education, sensitivity training, and problem-solving workshops in addition to fostering relationships with people from other racial groups, all members of society can become more skilled in their approaches to interracial communication. Although personal relationships beyond the workplace may not "naturally" develop in most contexts, these skills and knowledge are necessary as we forge ahead into the 21st century. The changing racial demographics of our country will undoubtedly affect all areas of life in society—colleges, public schools, churches, restaurants, government, corporate America, among others. Therefore, we must be proactive in our efforts to educate ourselves and others about the importance we have placed on racial and ethnic identity. Not only should we acknowledge the saliency of our racial/ethnic identities in a society consumed by race, but we should make a conscious effort to combat racism in the public and private areas of our lives.

Fostering Interracial Dialogue

We believe, as does Johannesen (1971), that dialogue is best viewed as an attitude or orientation. Compare this approach to dialogue with popular myths that describe dialogue as simple, relatively effortless, and easy to maintain. Within this more common perspective, dialogue is seen as a strategy or technique—consciously achieved with little or no preparation. But our use of the concept of dialogue is different from "honest expression," "frank conversation, "or "good communication." To foster an environment where dialogue can emerge, community members must work hard to promote a supportive (caring) climate in which genuineness, empathic understanding, unconditional positive regard, and mutual equality are maintained (Johannesen, 1971). Setting the stage for dialogue also includes addressing existing power differentials from which speech is enacted and utilizing tactics to empower those persons who enter a specific situational context with less social, organizational, and/or personal power than others (Cooks & Hale, 1992).

According to Tanno (1998), six elements are crucial to the promotion of dialogue. The first involves recognition that our past, present, and future are inextricably tied together (*connection*). As a way to prepare for dialogue, community members must come to understand how their shared history (sometimes at odds, sometimes together) informs, to a certain extent, current interactions. Connection also involves simultaneously recognizing both similarities and differences.

The second element is a *commitment* over time. "Dialogue does not, or should not, have a discernible beginning and end" (Tanno, 2004, p. 2). One of the defining characteristics of dialogue is that it represents a process, one in which all parties are actively involved and committed. In other words, dialogue can *only* emerge through commitment and time.

❖ BOX 12.6

STUDENT REFLECTION

Something happened at dinner tonight with my family and my cousin that made me feel uncomfortable and also made me question how sensitive my parents were to issues concerning race. While we were eating dinner, my mom told my dad that if he kept eating so much unhealthy food, he would gain back all the weight that he had lost in the previous six months. My dad's response to this was, "It's okay. I'll just take my pants back to China Lady and she can fix them for me." My dad has been going to the same tailor for the past 13 years and it astounded me that he did not know her. Although I realize that my dad had had a few drinks, I still did not see this as an excuse for such an overtly racist remark.

Immediately I questioned my dad and asked him if he knew her name. After he told me that he did not know her name, it made me very upset and I launched into a tirade about how latent, subconscious prejudice and racism is more harmful than the blatant overt racism that most people think of when confronted with the topic of race. I told my family about the Crayola Activity that we had completed the day before in class and how it had made me aware of a lot of subconscious racial tension and prejudices that I had carried all my life. Seeing as how I have never been a minority, the Crayola Activity forced me to analyze my own behavior and to see things from a minority's point of view. Although it is entirely possible that my reaction to my dad's comment had a lot to do with the fact that the Crayola Activity was still very fresh in my mind, I would like to think that this would be my reaction in the face of any racist remarks for the remainder of my life.

As the world evolves and as the United States continues to become more diverse, my dad's remarks made me more aware of a necessary change that needs to occur in the way people interact with each other, especially when the people of a racial majority interact with people from racial minorities.

The second key element to dialogue is a developed *realness/closeness,* both in terms of physical and psychological distance. Genuineness, honesty, and candor—even that which initially may be potentially offensive—all are central to the emergence of dialogue (Johannesen, 1971). A central element of dialogue is the desire, ability, and commitment to "keep it real" even when such an endeavor may initiate tension or hostility.

As it relates to freedom of expression, a fourth element of dialogue is the *creation/maintenance* of space where everyone's *voice* is valued. This includes the recognition and an appreciation that each person may speak for a variety of voices (professional, personal, cultural).

The fifth element of dialogue includes an *engagement of mind, heart, and soul.* The mind may be where logic and reasoning are located; however, the heart and soul is where emotion, commitment, accountability, and responsibility reside (Tanno, 1998). Attempts to isolate some aspects (fact, logic, reason) with no or little consideration of others (emotions, experiences, intuitions) does not contribute to a healthy communication environment. Instead, it creates a traditional, hostile climate where certain voices are privileged over others.

The final element that is crucial in setting the stage for dialogue is *self-reflection.* According to Tanno (1998), all of the other elements previously described depend on each person's resolution to engage in self-reflection that is critical, constructive, and continuous. Such a process of self-examination can be initially difficult, and ultimately painful, especially when dealing with such issues as cultural oppression, societal power, and privilege. However, the process by which persons situate themselves—professionally, culturally, and personally—within the context of a healthy communication environment is crucial to establishing a readiness for dialogue. Through self-reflection, an understanding can emerge where individuals begin to recognize the relevance of their lived experience in perceptions of self and others. In this regard, "objective" positions stemming from a "neutral standpoint" are acknowledged as problematic. So, as we work to discuss the saliency of interracial communication, we must continue to engage in self-reflexivity. Through this process, we are encouraged to recognize that neutralization (apathy) only perpetuates the problem of racism. Strategic efforts must be made that challenge our socially conditioned behaviors. Instead of accepting racism, oppression, and discrimination as an inherent part of our social reality, we must become a collective body committed to changing the way we think, talk, and feel about race as we enter the 21st century.

Conclusion

It is our hope that this text has challenged you to think critically about interracial communication and your place on the "racism–antiracism continuum." Most people are either not challenged to think about race (European Americans) or are forced to think about it continually (microcultural racial/ethnic groups). Although this does not mean European Americans are not sensitized to issues of race and racism in the United States, racial/ethnic microcultural groups must deal with racism, stereotyping, prejudice, and discrimination more frequently than we care to admit.

On November 20, 2006, actor Michael Richards, who portrayed the character Cosmo Kramer on the television show *Seinfeld*, was caught on camera videotape flying into a 3-minute "racist tirade" while doing standup comedy at the Laugh Factory in Los Angeles, California. After being heckled by two African American men who vocalized that his routine was not funny, Richards is shown responding very angrily to the accusation posed by the men. Instead of throwing a zinger at the men or a comedic yet biting response that would quiet them, Richards insults the men by repeatedly calling them the N-word, referring to lynching practices, and threatening bodily harm. It eventually becomes apparent to the audience (and viewer) that Richards' behavior is inappropriate, disturbing, and quite possibly maniacal. The video clip is eventually released to the media and posted on the Internet for all to judge for themselves.

A media frenzy ensued shortly thereafter, and the details of this morally offensive encounter continue to unfold. Comedian Paul Rodriguez, co-owner of the Laugh Factory, stated that Richards declined to offer a public apology for his racist behavior as promised the following night when he was scheduled for a second performance at the club. His avoidant and insensitive behavior resulted in his being banned from the club altogether. Although Richards offered a fairly incoherent apology via satellite on *The Late Night Show with David Letterman,* per the request of his friend Jerry Seinfeld, many were left to question his motivations for engaging in such offensive behavior and whether the intentionality of his comments should be viewed as an emotional, temporal response to somewhat rude audience members or a public unveiling of his true racist self. Many lay people and people in the entertainment industry (e.g., Hollywood) concluded that Michael Richards' career was surely over.

Not so long ago there was another, more notable Hollywood actor who engaged in similarly offensive behavior. On the morning of July 28, 2006, Hollywood icon Mel Gibson was arrested for speeding and was eventually given a breathalyzer test, which proved he was also drunk (what a potentially deadly combination). Details of the police report were slowly leaked into the media despite the fact that the incident was "still under investigation." The public eventually learned that during his arrest, Gibson repeatedly hurled anti-Semitic slurs and sexist comments and repeatedly cursed at the arresting officers and, in his drunken stupor, fretted over the ramifications this incident would have for his career.

As the days passed and even more information was divulged concerning this incredibly offensive incident, we learned that, according to the police report, Gibson threatened the police officer with bodily harm and accused Jewish people of being responsible "for all of the world wars." The arresting officer was advised by an officer-in-charge to tone down the volatile nature of the report, fearing media coverage of the content would incite anti-Semitism in the public sphere, particularly in light of the war in the Middle East. The details of the tirade were eventually leaked into virtually every news outlet, and we were all consumed (or at least temporarily preoccupied) with what impact this incredibly racist outburst would have on Gibson's career and on the Jewish community at large.

Both of these incidents are social tragedies that were performed in public spheres and had potentially negative consequences for its "actors," per se. Only time will tell what the outcome will be. In the interim, however, Richards and Gibson extended public apologies to all offended parties, seeming to take responsibility for their reprehensible and unconscionable behavior. Each of them took their actions further and sought counsel from notable figures in the African American and Jewish communities in an attempt to identify and exorcize the demons of racism and hate that appeared to resided within them just below the surface in the subconscious (or was it?).

One positive outcome from the Richards incidents is the proclamation from eccentric African American veteran comedian Paul Mooney. In several newspaper interviews, Paul Mooney spoke about the shock he experienced after learning of his good friend Michael Richards' outburst and repeated use of the N-word. He was appalled by his friend's behavior and also became cognizant of his role in giving power to such a vile and racially oppressive word. Mooney states that as a comic writer for the late comedian Richard Pryor, the two purposely infused the word in Pryor's stand-up in an attempt to take away its power. Mooney even adapted this strategy in his own act, proclaiming that he used the word at *least* 100 times a day. After witnessing the tirade, Mooney, alongside the Reverend Jesse Jackson and other Black leaders, asked that all hip hop artists from any race, ethnicity, and culture join him and stop using the N-word. Mooney said he definitely used and abused the word, and through his "rant," Michael Richards is his Dr. Phil, curing him of ever uttering the N-word again.

While these tirades and rants may have affected us only from a distance, they brought to the foreground public discourse about what does and does not qualify as racist behavior in the 21st century. More specifically, we engaged in conversations, watched television shows, and saw news reports about these actors and were challenged to think about what we should do with this information. Each of us has quite possibly encountered someone who has made a covertly or overtly racist comment, which caused us to ponder their *intentionality* ("Did she or he mean to say that? Was their intention to harm?"), and whether they were racist or were just having a delusional moment, a comment that "just slipped out" and should be dismissed as an innocent faux pas. Regardless of the intent, we must direct our attention to the impact such behavior has not only on the offending party but on the offend*ed* party as well. When someone says something hurtful to us or someone we care about, or maybe a total stranger, we should see it as our moral responsibility to challenge the person on their comment. While some might hesitate to do so because of what might happen to the relationship, it is imperative that we become more proactive in eradicating racism on a micro-, interpersonal level, which will eventually lead to macrolevel change and a dismantling of institutionalism, one relationship at a time.

The fact that these racial tirades occurred is a sad commentary on the state of race relations as we know it. It is unfortunate that these men felt compelled to display such anger and hatred toward socially oppressed racial and ethnic groups in such a public manner. Their behaviors were at the very least a public display of inhumanity and insensitivity. But a positive outcome of these celebrity debacles are the public and private dialogues addressing the cross-section of race, racism, and public rhetoric that ensued as a result of media coverage surrounding the tirades. It is only through dialogue and communication that we can deconstruct the racist ideology that remains a pervasive part of Western culture.

OPPORTUNITIES FOR EXTENDED LEARNING ❖

1. Choose five friends outside of class and ask them to write on a piece of paper as many traits as possible that they feel describe Middle Eastern Americans, Japanese Americans, Mexican Americans, European Americans, and African Americans. Compile these different lists into one master list, and during one class session, in groups, compare the lists to those included in Andrea Rich's 1974 list of communication traits from her text, *Interracial Communication* (New York: Harper & Row). Discuss the differences and similarities between the lists. Also address how time has influenced (or not) the types of the stereotypes ascribed to each group.

2. Using Peggy McIntosh's list of privileges as a template, develop a "new" list of privileges that do not appear on the original. This assignment should be done outside of class with students from different racial

groups. From your informal discussions, identify privileges that currently exist and emerge in diverse social settings and contexts. In small groups during class, compile your lists, which will eventually be shared with the entire class. During the small group discussion, share with each other how different racial and gendered standpoints (among others) influenced how the new privileges were generated. As a class, list the new privileges on a dry erase board and discuss them collectively. Please make note of the general themes that emerge from the list and your discussion thereof. More importantly, the class should engage in honest discussion about feelings of guilt that privileged individuals may experience once they become cognizant of their social location in the racial hierarchy.

3. In groups of five, have the students create a template for identifying racist behaviors. Using the racial tirades as an example, the student groups should provide exemplars of behaviors that have racial (blatant) overtones and (subtle) undertones. Please refer to the concepts *intentionality versus emotionality* in Chapter 7. The list should include familiar and unfamiliar phrases or terms that serve as verbal markers of such behavior.

4. Neuliep and McCroskey's PRECA (1997a) is promoted as an effective measure of communicator apprehension and its effect on interracial/interethnic interactions. As a class, discuss the appropriateness of this scale. Would study participants be sensitized to the purpose of the study? Would their responses be accurate, or would they be hesitant to complete the questionnaire for fear of appearing racist or ethnocentric? What could the researchers do differently, if anything, to improve how we gather data on attitudes relative to race? If you were to complete this questionnaire, how would you respond to the manner in which the questions are presented? If you were asked to create your own scale, what would you do differently?

5. Search the Internet for articles and essays that examine racial conflict (keyword: *racial conflict* or *race relations + conflict*). What role does geography play in how the conflict originates and is resolved? Are certain racial/ethnic groups in conflict more than others? Is race a factor in the conflict, or is the conflict over a nonrace issue? Address whether race and/or racial/ethnic difference appears to contribute to the conflict. Compare and contrast those situations in which solutions are and are not utilized within those specific contexts. Consider the effectiveness of each strategy and, more importantly, apply strategies from this text that could resolve these racial conflicts effectively.

6. Using Andrea Rich's list of communication traits associated with four different racial/ethnic groups, you will be provided with four groups of 12 traits. (Instructor: Be sure there are no identifiers on each list.) Breaking into small groups, each group will discuss what racial/ethnic group they feel the grouped terms represent. After the discussion, the groups should share their findings with the class. Once each group has contributed to the discussion, the instructor will guide the class in a discussion designed to compare the class list to Rich's list. Students should also discuss the origins of these traits/stereotypes and how time has or has not influenced our perceptions of each other.

Glossary

abilities   The social effects of physical, emotional, and mental capabilities.

ability   A factor of co-cultural communication that refers to a person's access to enact certain communicative practices.

acceptance   A key theme to a Mexican American perspective to interracial communication that speaks to the importance of respecting and confirming one's culture and ideas.

accountability   When the leader in an organization ensures that human resource practices and decisions, such as those related to selection, promotion, and compensation, consider diversity goals and values.

acculturation   The process, as described by cross-cultural adaptation theory, that includes learning and acquiring the elements of a new culture.

administrative management theory   Discusses the organizational hierarchy and the flow of communication within that hierarchy; strict chains of communication among organizational members are an essential part of the organization, and the style of communication within this theory is vertical in nature.

African American   A label used to describe people living in the United States whose ancestors can be traced to Africa; sometimes used interchangeably with **Black**.

American Indian   A label used to describe people living in the United States whose ancestors can be traced to the indigenous people of the land; sometimes used interchangeably with **Native American** and **First Nations People**.

antimiscegenation laws   Laws that were enacted by 41 states that made intermixture between Whites and non-Whites through intermarriage illegal; born from fear that such unions would blur the lines of physiological differences (e.g., eye color, hair texture, facial features) between diverse ethnic and racial groups.

anxiety   An emotion triggered by anticipation of things yet to come; according to anxiety/uncertainty management theory, a basic cause of communication failure.

appreciation   The fourth stage of biracial identity development that involves a desire to embrace aspects of all of one's racial heritage.

arbitrary nature of words   The idea that words do not have inherent meaning; meaning is in people, not the words that they use.

ascription   An individual's perception of how others view her or him.

Asian American   A label used to describe people living in the United States whose ancestors can be traced to Asia.

assimilation (or **amalgamation**)   People adopting the dominant group's attitudes and beliefs while forsaking those of their primary racial/ethnic group.

autonomy   The final stage of macrocultural identity development whereby individuals work to maintain a positive nonracist perspective.

avowal   The perceived identity that an individual enacts in a particular context.

biracial Americans   A label used to describe people living in the United States who can trace their ancestors to two racial groups; sometimes used interchangeably with **multiracial Americans.**

Black   A label used to describe people across the world whose ancestors can be traced to Africa.

Brown v. Board of Education   The landmark U.S. Supreme Court case that desegregated all public educational institutions (e. g., elementary schools, high schools, and colleges and universities) throughout the nation.

bureaucracy theory   An organization described as bureaucratic is viewed as very formal, inflexible, and insensitive to the needs of its workers.

Caucasian   A label used to describe people of European descent that was created in reference to people from the Caucasus Mountain region who possessed superior beauty.

Charlie Chan   Emasculated stereotype portraying Asian men as eunuchs or asexual; Charlie Chan, a detective character, was "effeminate, wimpy," "dainty," and "a mysterious man, possessing awesome powers of deduction," yet was deferential to Whites, "nonthreatening, and revealed his 'Asian wisdom' in snippets of 'fortune-cookie'" (Shah, 2003, p. 658).

Chicana/o   A label used to describe people in the United States who can trace their ancestors to Latin America; most often used by those who maintain a political consciousness regarding race and culture.

chosen people   A belief that Europeans were the race chosen by God to reclaim the world in his name.

chronological context   The role of time in influencing the interaction (e.g., morning vs. afternoon meetings).

co-cultural group   Groups that share an aspect of culture—based on gender, race, ethnicity, sexual orientation, abilities, etc.—that traditionally has been marginalized in society; sometimes used interchangeably with **minority** or **subcultural group.**

code-switching   A communication strategy used by individuals who adapt their style of communication to the setting; also known as **style switching** and **language mobility.**

coherence   A concept, as articulated in complicity theory, that sees difference as complementary and constructs reality in a way that does not privilege one position at the expense of another.

collectivism   Cultural values that emphasize group identities, concerns, and needs over individual identities, concerns, and needs.

colonialism   A formal system of domination that removes the power of self-determination from one group and gives it to another.

commitment   One core element of community that refers to a strong willingness to coexist and work through any barriers that hinder a sense of community.

common intergroup identity model   Theory positing that bias toward outgroup members is reduced by changing a person's perceptions of an intergroup context from one that involves members of different groups to one that involves members of a single common or superordinate group; former outgroup members are recategorized as ingroup members within a superordinate category that they respectively share with one another.

communal frame   A layer of identity, according to communication theory of identity, that is situated through identification with a shared group identity.

communicare   Latin for "to make common"; serves as the root word for communication.

communication approach   A factor of cocultural communication that refers to nonassertiveness, assertiveness, and aggressiveness.

community   A group of individuals who practice inclusiveness, commitment, consensus, contemplation, vulnerability, and graceful fighting.

complicity   A concept, as articulated in complicity theory, that involves using language that highlights differences instead of commonalities, and emphasizes division at the expense of unity.

conformity   The second stage of microcultural identity development that includes an acceptance and internalization of macrocultural perspectives, values, and norms.

consensus   One core element of community that refers to efforts seeking general agreement on key values, assumptions, and decisions.

contact   The first stage in macrocultural identity development that typically involves an unawareness of one's own racial identity.

contact hypothesis   A theory by Allport (1958) that increased interactions with racially different others will reduce prejudiced thoughts and beliefs in optimal conditions.

contemplation   One core element of community that represents a reflective awareness of self, other, and the community itself.

convergence   A strategy, as described by communication accommodation theory, whereby individuals adapt their verbal and nonverbal communication to become more like the other person.

coping   Stage two of Foeman and Nance's (2002) interracial relational development model; in this stage, the couple pulling together toward each other and away from others solidifies their relationship, and they present themselves as a couple to outsiders.

cross-cultural adaptation   The process of change that occurs over time when individuals whose primary socialization is in one culture come into continuous, prolonged contact with a new and unfamiliar culture.

cultural racism   Much like ethnocentrism, this involves people presenting their own racial/ethnic group's cultural preferences and values as superior to those of other groups; all aspects of one culture and heritage are deemed culturally acceptable, thus negating the value of all other racial/ethnic groups.

cultural resources   How important an individual feels it is that both relational (romantic) partners share similar cultural or racial/ethnic backgrounds.

culture   A set of learned and shared values, beliefs, and behaviors common to a particular group of people.

decategorization   An awareness of individual distinctiveness.

decentering   A core concept of the Baha'i Faith that includes efforts to extend beyond one's own culture and seek understanding of other cultures.

deculturation   A process, as described in cross-cultural adaptation theory, that includes unlearning some cultural norms associated with one's native culture.

defining moments   Experiences with racism and sexism that help develop our inner strength to face adversities in spite of our circumstances.

didactic model   A teaching mechanism that uses lecture, wherein the trainer presents facts and information to participants; this is a linear, or one-way, approach that confronts the macrocultural group members by making an information-based appeal.

differentiated model   A model describing a person transitioning from thinking of racial groups as monolithic to seeing some distinctions between ingroup and outgroup members.

disintegration   The second stage of macrocultural identity development that typically involves a growing awareness of one's own privilege.

divergence   A strategy, as described by communication accommodation theory, whereby individuals stress verbal and nonverbal differences in order to emphasize ingroup/outgroup status.

emergence   Stage three of Foeman and Nance's (2002) interracial relational development model; in this stage, the couple has solidified their relationship and present themselves as a couple to outsiders.

emotionality   The negative emotions or feelings a party experiences as a result of experiencing firsthand, hearing, or observing the behavior she or he deems offensive.

enacted frame   A layer of identity, according to communication theory of identity, where one's sense of self is performed to others.

endogamy   Marriage that occurs when people marry within their group; this approach would include a person who prefers a marital partner from the same racial/ethnic background.

enlightened racism   A perspective of racial relations that acknowledges the historical significance of racism in the United States, but sees the 21st century as a time when the effects of racism have been greatly reduced to the point that the American Dream is now available for all those who are willing to work to achieve it.

enmeshment/denial   The third stage of biracial identity development characterized by emotional tension associated with an identity that does not fully express all aspects of one's racial identity.

Esperanto   The most widely spoken universal language created in 1887.

essentialism   The tendency to generalize cultural groups without recognition of ingroup differences.

ethnicity   A cultural marker that indicates shared traditions, heritage, and ancestral origins.

ethnocentrism   Belief in the normalcy or rightness of one's culture; consciously or unconsciously evaluating other cultures by using your own as a standard.

eugenics   The belief that intergroup breeding is a desirable mechanism to ensure the existence of a superior race.

European American   A label used by people living in the United States who can trace their ancestors to Europe; oftentimes used interchangeably with Caucasian, White, or Anglo.

experiential training model   Training model centered on the assumption that interaction among race relations training participants is necessary.

expressiveness   A central theme to a Mexican American perspective to interracial communication that values one's ability to express himself or herself in open and honest ways without a fear of rejection, judgment, or retaliation.

external bridges   The third category of the model of intergroup unity that features communication strategies used to unite individuals to the larger world.

eyeball test   A nonscientific, random measure of racial categorization used in everyday interactions by laypersons.

field of experience   A factor of co-cultural communication that refers to the sum of lived experiences that influence one's communication behaviors.

First Nations People   A label used primarily in Canada to describe people living in North America whose ancestors can be traced to the indigenous people of the land; sometimes used interchangeably with **American Indian** and **Native American**.

framing Communication from leaders to organizational members about diversity that positively frames it as a strategic learning opportunity for the organization and an opportunity to learn about new practices and markets that can improve and expand the business.

friend divorce Decision made by one or both friends to dissolve the relationship.

friendship A mutual involvement between two people that is characterized by affection, satisfaction, enjoyment, openness, respect, and a sense of feeling important to the other.

Fu Manchu An emasculated stereotype portraying Asian men as "a cruel, cunning, diabolical representative of the 'yellow peril'" (C. F. Sun, 2003, p. 658).

gender A socialized and psychological aspect of identity that refers to levels of femininity and masculinity.

generalized other A concept, central to symbolic interactionism, that refers to the collective body through which an individual sees oneself.

glass ceiling The invisible barriers that prevent women and people of color from advancing in the workplace, despite their qualifications or achievements.

glass escalator A new phenomenon in organizations referring to White men being promoted in the workplace at a much faster rate than women and minorities because of their status as a "new" minority group (e.g., being "marginalized" persons in a work environment where they are in the minority).

goal setting The establishment of diversity goals that can be measured by establishing relationships with minority communities in and outside of the organization, increasing the number of mentoring relationships available to female and minority employees, or raising retention rates of high-potential and minority managers.

graceful fighting One core element of community that involves a general acceptance that conflict should not be avoided but instead managed effectively to enhance the ultimate sense of community.

group categorization The second stage of biracial identity development characterized by an increased awareness of race to the point of being pushed to choose an identity.

group identification A desire to preserve the social history of one's racial/ethnic group, which directly influences their efforts to prevent interracial marriages from occurring.

group sanctions Institutions that traditionally oppose marriage between people from different racial/ethnic backgrounds.

groupwork model Training model that is a good medium between the didactic and experiential models in that trainers incorporate information and experience into the learning process; this assists participants in discerning in which social contexts interracial contact will occur.

hate crime   Legal definition of an offender attacking a victim because of the victim's actual or perceived race, color, religion, disability, sexual orientation, or national origin.

high context   A cultural value whereby people rely on inferred meanings and where differences may exist between what is said and what is meant.

Hispanic   A label used to describe people who can trace their ancestors to Spanish-speaking countries; sometimes used interchangeably with **Latino.**

homogamy   A person's preference for a mate who is close in social status.

homophily   A term that refers to the common experiences shared by two individuals.

human relations theory   The goal of the organization is to improve all interpersonal—including interracial—relationships among employees in the workplace; it takes into consideration the multiple identities of its organizational members.

hypergamy   When a person has an interest in or willingness to marry someone of a different status.

hypodescent   A social guideline that assigns a biracial or multiracial person solely to the racial group with the least social status.

identity emergence   The idea that people negotiate multiple, sometimes contradicting, messages about their identities.

immersion/emersion   The fourth stage of macrocultural identity development that is characterized by blaming microcultural groups for their own disadvantaged status.

implicature   A concept, according to complicity theory, that involves a basic acceptance of the belief that we are all implicated in each others' lives.

inclusiveness   One core element of community that refers to general acceptance and appreciation of differences.

individualism   A cultural value that emphasizes personal identity, rights, and needs over those of the larger group.

institutionalized contact   Contact occurring between independent nations; this type of contact is manifested through colonialism (subordination) or paternalism (sharply defined roles and status).

integration   The fourth stage of microcultural identity development that focuses on achieving a public racial identity that is consistent with one's inner sense of self; the final stage of biracial identity development characterized by individuals' ability to recognize and value each aspect of their racial identity.

intentionality   The degree to which a certain behavior is viewed by an offended party as purposeful in causing hurt or harm.

intercultural communication   A broad term used to describe interactions between two individuals who are culturally different.

interethnic communication   Interactions between two individuals from two different ethnic groups.

internal states   The second category in the model of intergroup unity that refers to the human influence that can impede intergroup unity.

international communication   Interactions between two individuals from two different countries; most often referring to interactions between representatives of different countries.

interpenetration   An idea, associated with communication theory of identity, that captures the ways in which different frames of identity influence, confirm, and contradict one another.

interpersonal communication   Interactions between two individuals regardless of race; often used synonymously with intraracial communication.

interpersonal intercultural communication   The second phase of third-culture building that includes both individuals exchanging information about one another.

interracial communication   Interactions between two individuals in a situational context where racial difference is salient issue.

intersectionality   An approach to understanding human communication through examinations of multiple aspects of cultural identity.

intracultural communication   The fifth, and final, phase of third-culture building when individuals identify with the newly created culture.

intrapersonal interpersonal communication   The first phase of third-culture building characterized by a new awareness (and curiosity) of other racial and ethnic groups.

intraracial communication   Interactions between two individuals who identify with the same racial group.

language mobility   See **code-switching**.

Latin/o American   A label used to describe people in the United States who can trace their ancestors to Latin America; most often used by those concerned with preserving language and culture.

linguistic profiling   Instances of racial discrimination when assumptions are made based on a person's vocalized patterns of speech (e.g., "sounding Black").

Lotus Blossom   Stereotype associated with Asian women; this caricature is a sexual-romantic object, utterly feminine, and delicate, which is a "welcome" respite from their often loud, independent American counterparts (e. g., China Doll, Geisha Girl, Shy Polynesian beauty).

low context   A cultural value whereby meanings are communicated via verbal messages, not embedded in the context or relational status of participants.

maintenance   Stage four of Foeman and Nance's (2002) interracial relational development model; in this stage, the couple see their vision of the relationship through for a lifetime; their communication can become a natural part of how they present themselves and how others speak about them.

Manifest Destiny   The idea that certain countries (e.g., European countries, the United States) had the right—granted by God—to spread across the entire North American continent.

metacultural communication   The fourth phase of third-culture building that includes the fine-tuning of an emerging third culture.

metastereotypes   Perceptions that an individual has of the stereotypes that other individuals have for him or her.

microculture   A group whose members are culturally different than those in the majority; used in place of less acceptable terms like minority or subgroup.

Middle Eastern Americans   A label used to describe people living in the United States who trace their ancestors to the Middle East.

minority   See **cocultural group.**

model minority   A stereotype ascribed to Asian Americans referring to the notion that a cultural work ethic leads to success, and by extension, the belief that other racial/ethnic minorities cannot achieve "the American Dream" due to a lack of work ethic.

mulatto/a   A term used historically in the United States to describe a person with one African American and one European American parent.

multicultural communication   The fourth category of the model of intergroup unity that features the creation and maintenance of a third culture that symbolizes group unity.

multicultural organization   A multiracial group of individuals that makes internal, structural changes to infuse diverse perspectives within its everyday functions.

multiracial Americans   A label used to describe people living in the United States who can trace their ancestors to two or more racial groups; oftentimes used interchangeably with **biracial Americans.**

mutual intergroup differentiation model   Positive contact with an individual from an outgroup should result in positive behavior and reactions toward individuals but not the entire group because the person is perceived as being "atypical."

nationality   Reference to the nation in which one is born; used interchangeably with nation of origin.

Native American   A label used to describe people living in the United States whose ancestors can be traced to the indigenous people of the land; sometimes used interchangeably with **American Indian** and **First Nations People.**

negative responses   Eleven negative relational strategies and communication behaviors (responses) that occur as a result of negative interracial/interethnic friendship experiences.

negative stereotyping   A central theme to a Mexican American perspective to interracial communication that recognizes cultural generalizations as a main source for dissatisfying communication.

normalization   The ultimate goal, according to Asante (A. Smith, 1973), of transracial communication; a process of identifying and moving toward common ground.

octoroon   A term used historically in the United States to describe a person with one African American and seven European American parents.

one-drop rule   A social and/or legal guideline used in the United States that defines a person with any African ancestry as African American.

organization   A social collectivity (a group of people) where coordinated activities achieve both individual and collective goals. These activities provide a structure that enables organizational members to deal effectively with each other within the larger organizational environment. In terms of communication, it is a process that has transactional (which involves two or more people interacting within that environment) and symbolic (communication transactions represent or stand for other things on some level of abstraction) perceived costs and rewards: a factor of co-cultural theory that refers to the conscious consideration of the potential advantages and disadvantages associated with different communication behaviors.

organizational culture   A pattern of basic assumptions—invented, discovered, or developed by a given group as it learns to cope with its problems of external adaptation and internal integration—that has worked well enough to be considered valid and, therefore, to be taught to new members as the correct way to perceive, think, and feel in relation to those problems.

perceived costs and rewards   A factor of co-cultural communication that refers to the ways in which individuals weigh the advantages and disadvantages of communicative choices.

peripheral contact   A minimal amount of contact between racial/ethnic groups that is transient (e.g., in classrooms, grocery shopping, riding the bus).

personal frame   A layer of identity, according to communication theory of identity, that encompasses one's sense of self.

personal identity   The first stage of biracial identity development that exists when individuals do not define themselves in terms of race.

personalization   When people respond to others in terms of their relationship to self (commonalities are found) and self-disclose positive information they otherwise would not know.

physical context   The physical environment where the communication takes place (e.g., boss's office, employee lounge).

pluralism   A societal phenomenon that occurs when racial/ethnic differences reflect variation in expected behavior and there is minimum social interaction.

political correctness A term popularized by the mass media to describe social movements to adopt a specific set of ideologies, concepts, and terms that reflect a sensitivity to issues of culture, power, and privilege, frequently abbreviated to "PC."

positive responses Eight positive relational strategies and communication behaviors (responses) that occur as a result of positive interracial/interethnic friendship relationships.

preferences for marriage candidates Refers to the resources romantic partners offer each other.

preferred outcome A factor of co-cultural communication that reflects one ultimate goal for a person's communication behavior (assimilation, accommodation, separation).

pseudo-independent The fourth stage of macrocultural identity development that is characterized by European Americans who unintentionally believe that their culture is more advanced and civilized than others.

quadroon A term used historically in the United States to describe a person with one African American and three European American parents.

race A sociopolitical construction that categorizes people into four primary groups.

racial assumption A consciously or unconsciously held premise that is considered to be true regarding a race or ethnic group and that is acted on as though it were true.

racial awareness Stage one of Foeman and Nance's (2002) interracial relationship development model; involves partners becoming aware of a mutual attraction and the possibility for an intimate involvement.

racial discrimination Acting upon your racial prejudice when communicating with others; all people can have racial prejudice and practice racial discrimination.

racial location An idea associated with standpoint theories that posits that racial and ethnic group members have similar vantage points from which they see the world.

racial motivation theory The theory that a person becomes involved in an interracial marriage (or relationship) *because* of racial difference.

racial perspective A largely unconscious social location, informed by race and other cultural group membership, that influences one's perception of self, other, and society.

racial prejudice Inaccurate and/or negative beliefs that espouse or support the superiority of one racial group.

racial reconciliation The process of healing the racial tensions and bridging the racial divide that exist between the races.

racial standpoint An idea associated with standpoint theories that refers to a racial location that is accompanied by a critical, oppositional understanding of how one's life is shaped by larger social and political forces.

racialization process The ways in which a person's racial identity is constructed, defined, and performed.

racism The systematic subordination of certain racial groups by those racial groups in power.

readiness An organizational leader's understanding of the complexities of diversity in the organization and society, engaging in self-exploration and understanding how privilege and ethnocentrism operate within their organizations and lives.

reintegration The third stage of macrocultural identity development that includes a sense of racial pride.

relational frame A layer of identity, according to communication theory of identity, that is negotiated through one's relationships with others.

resistance and separation The third stage of microcultural identity development that begins when individuals experience some tension trying to understand themselves in the context of ingroup/outgroup perceptions.

relational solidarity A central theme to a Mexican American perspective to interracial communication that relates to the positive value attributed to developing close relationships.

rhetorical intercultural communication The third phase in third-culture building that includes a conscious awareness of cultural similarities and differences and negotiation of the emergence of a third culture.

salience The attention or importance individuals place on their intergroup differences.

Sapir-Whorf Hypothesis The idea that language shapes one's perception of reality; also known as the **Whorfian Hypothesis.**

scientific management theory A subtheory of classical management theory, this theory posits that there is "one best way" to perform a task or job; employees should be scientifically selected and improved (based on skills and expertise to increase productivity); workers are monetarily motivated; management plans the work and laborers follow through with the plan (cooperation vs. individuality); clearly defined rules, regulations, and roles (creates harmony within the organization); and loafing should be eliminated.

self-construals One's self-perception as being either independent or interdependent of larger group influences; a concept that helps avoid essentializing entire groups as individualistic or collectivistic.

semantics of prejudice A concept that captures the ways that language choice can intentionally or unintentionally reveal an individual's internal thoughts steeped in cultural stereotypes.

sexual orientation An aspect of cultural identity that references the direction of an individual's sexuality, often in relation to their own sex: heterosexual (straight), bisexual (bi), and homosexual (lesbian and gay).

significant others A term, associated with symbolic interactionism, that refers to individuals who have substantial influence on how others see themselves; also known as orientational others.

situational context   A factor of co-cultural communication that recognizes the important role that the dynamics inherent in a particular setting play in communication behavior.

social context   The type of relationship that exists between the communicators.

societal privilege   An invisible package of unearned assets that majority members can rely on with much thought; a set of unearned entitlements only available to majority group members.

socioeconomic status   An aspect of cultural identity that refers to one's economic standing and the long-term values, norms, and behaviors that are associated with it.

speech code   A concept central to speech community theory that refers to a system of symbols, rules, and meanings related to communication behavior.

speech community   A concept central to speech community theory that describes when a group of people understand goals, norms, and styles of communication behavior in ways not shared by people outside the group.

spirituality   Reference to an individual's identification with, and belief in, a higher power or higher order of things.

stereotypes   Overgeneralizations of group characteristics or behaviors that are applied universally to all individuals of that particular group.

structural theory   Explains when relational partners develop a romantic relationship because of their similar backgrounds and interests (i.e., education, occupation, status).

style switching   See **code-switching.**

subcultural group   See **co-cultural group.**

theory   A way of seeing and thinking about the world; frameworks that provide insight into phenomena.

third-culture building   The idea that every culture emerges out of the prolonged, ongoing interactions between individuals from different cultures.

three social forces   Three difference variables that influence marriage patterns: (1) preferences for marriage candidates, (2) social group influence on mate selection process, and (3) constraints in the marriage market.

transnationalism   A concept that captures how modern-day immigrants participate in multiple social, political, economic, cultural, and national realities.

transracial communication   Interactions between individuals in a context where racial differences are transcended and commonalities are heightened.

typicality   Pleasant interaction among ingroup and outgroup members can be effective in reducing intergroup bias only if the outgroup members typify their group.

uncertainty   A cognition that represents doubt of one's ability to predict the outcome of interactions; according to anxiety/uncertainty management theory, a basic cause of communication failure.

unexamined identity   The first stage of microcultural identity development that is characterized by an absence of any awareness of racial identity.

unity of harmony   A concept central to the Baha'i Faith that emphasizes transcendence of cultural difference.

vulnerability   A core element of community that includes discarding masks of composure and exposing one's inner self to others.

Whiteness   A social construction associated with privilege based on how European American identity is unmarked, neutral, and invisible.

Whorfian Hypothesis   See **Sapir-Whorf Hypothesis.**

worldview   A central theme within a Mexican American perspective to interracial communication that points to the importance of shared common experiences and interests.

Yellow Peril   Unfounded fear of threatened Asian expansion by Whites, which led to the societal oppression and stereotyping of Asian Americans as a racial group deemed inferior.

References

Aamidor, A. (1994, February 27). The last word on PC. *Indianapolis (IN) Star*, pp. J1–2.

Acosta-Belen, E., & Santiago, C. E. (2006). *Puerto Ricans in the United States: A contemporary portrait*. Boulder, CO: Lynne Rienner.

Acuna, R. (1988). *Occupied America: A history of Chicanos*. New York: Harper & Row.

Adler, J. (1990, December 24). Taking offense. *Newsweek*, pp. 48–55.

Adler, J. (1991, September 23). African dreams. *Newsweek*, pp. 42–45.

African-Americans' viewing habits on the rise. (1994, March 26). *TV Guide*, p. 36.

Akiba, D., & Miller, F. (2004). The expression of cultural sensitivity in the presence of African Americans: An analysis of motives. *Small Group Research, 35*(6), 623–642.

Alba, R. D., & Chamlin, M. B. (1983). A preliminary examination of ethnic identification among whites. *American Sociological Review, 48*, 240–247.

Alba, R. D., & Golden, R. N. (1996). Patterns of ethnic marriage in the United States. *Social Forces, 65*, 202–223.

Alexander, L. (1998, November). Created equal: The principles of racial reconciliation. *Policy Review, 92*, 18–21.

Alexander, S. (1994). Vietnamese Amerasians: Dilemmas of individual identity and family cohesion. In E. P. Salett & D. R. Koslow (Eds.), *Race, ethnicity and self: Identity in multicultural perspective* (pp. 198–216). Washington, DC: MultiCultural Institute.

Allen, B. J. (1996). Feminist standpoint theory: A Black woman's (re)view of organizational socialization. *Communication Studies, 47*(4), 257–271.

Allen, B. J. (1998). Black womanhood and feminist standpoints. *Management Communication Quarterly, 11*, 575–586.

Allen, B. J. (2004). Sapphire and Sappho: Allies in authenticity. In A. Gonzalez, M. Houston, & V. Chen (Eds.), *Our voices: Essays in culture, ethnicity, and communication* (pp. 198–202). Los Angeles: Roxbury.

Allen, P. G. (1986). *The sacred hoop: Recovering the feminism in American Indian traditions*. Boston: Beacon Press.

Allport, G. W. (1958). *The nature of prejudice*. Garden City, NY: Doubleday.

Alperstein, N. (1994). Memories, anticipation, and self-talk: A cultural study of the inward experience of television advertising. *Journal of Popular Culture, 28*(1), 209–221.

American Psychological Association. (1996). *Publication manual of the American Psychological Association* (4th ed.). Washington, DC: Author.

Anderson, K., Harwood, J., & Hummert, M. L. (2005). The grandparent–grandchild relationship: Implications for models of intergenerational communication. *Human Communication Research, 31*(2), 268–294.

Andersen, P. A. (1998). Researching sex differences within sex similarities: The evolutionary consequences of reproductive differences. In D. J. Canary & K. Dindia (Eds.), *Sex differences and similarities in communication: Critical essays and empirical investigations of sex and gender in interaction* (pp. 83–100). Mahwah, NJ: Lawrence Erlbaum.

Antler, J. (2004). Jewish women on TV: Too Jewish or not Jewish enough? in G. Dines & J. M. Humez (Eds.), *Gender, race, and class in the media* (pp. 665–671). Thousand Oaks, CA: Sage.

Antonio, A. L. (2004). When does race matter in college friendships? Exploring men's diverse and homogeneous friendship groups. *The Review of Higher Education, 27*(4), 553–575.

Anzaldua, G. (1987). *Borderlands: La frontera*. San Francisco: Aunt Lute.

Artz, B. L. (1998). Hegemony in Black and White: Interracial buddy films and the new racism. In Y. R. Kamalipour & T. Carilli (Eds.), *Cultural diversity in the U.S. media* (pp. 67–78). Albany: State University of New York Press.

Asante, M. K. (1988). *Afrocentricity*. Trenton, NJ: Africa World Press.

Asante, M. K. (1991). The Afrocentric idea in education. *Journal of Negro Education, 60*(2), 170–180.

Asante, M. K. (1998a). *The Afrocentric idea*. Philadelphia: Temple University Press.

Asante, M. K. (1998b). Identifying racist language, linguistic acts, and signs. In M. L. Hecht (Ed.), *Communicating prejudice* (pp. 87–98). Thousand Oaks, CA: Sage.

Associated Press (2006). Immigration issue draws thousands into streets: LAPD estimates 500,000 at protest; Bush faces wedge issue for party. *MSNBC.* Retrieved November 21, 2006, from http://www.msnbc.msn.com/id/11442705

Astor, D. (1996, June 22). Laughs and gripes about stereotypes. *Editor & Publisher,* pp. 46–47.

Atkin, D. (1992). An analysis of television series with minority-lead characters. *Critical Studies in Mass Communication, 9,* 337–349.

Austin, A. (2006). *Achieving blackness: Race, black nationalism, and Afrocentrism in the twentieth century.* New York: New York University Press.

Ayres, J. (1996). Speech preparation and speech apprehension. *Communication Education, 45*(3), 228–235.

Ayres, J., Hopf, T. Brown, K., & Suck, J. M. (1994). The impact of communication apprehension, gender, and time on turn-taking behavior in initial interactions. *Southern Communication Journal, 59*(2), 142–152.

Ayres, J., Keereetaweep, T., Chen, P. E., & Edwards, P. (1998). Communication apprehension and employment interviews. *Communication Education, 47*(1), 1–17.

Ayers, K. (1994, April). *Life transitions: Exploring how retirement affects interpersonal communication.* Paper presented at the annual Women's Studies Conference, Indiana University at Kokomo.

Bahk, C. M., & Jandt, F. E. (2004). Being White in America: Development of a scale. *Howard Journal of Communications, 15,* 57–68.

Baia, L. R. (1999). Rethinking transnationalism: Reconstructing national identities among Peruvian Catholics in New Jersey. *Journal of Interamerican Studies and World Affairs, 41*(4), 93–109.

Bailey, B. (2000). Communicative behavior and conflict between African American customers and Korean immigrant retailers in Los Angeles. *Discourse and Society, 11,* 86–108.

Baker, J. R. (1974). *Race.* New York: Oxford University Press.

Baldwin, J. (1990). Quoted in Introduction: A way of images. In J. L. Dates and W. Barlow (Eds.), *Split image* (pp. 1–21). Washington, DC: Howard University Press.

Banaji, M. R., Hardin, C., & Rothman, A. J. (1993). Implicit stereotyping in person judgment. *Journal of Personality and Social Psychology, 65*(2), 272–281.

Banks, J. A. (1976). The emerging stages of ethnicity: Implications for staff development. *Educational Leadership, 34*(3), 190–193.

Banks, S. P. (1987). Achieving "unmarkedness" in organization discourse: A praxis perspective on ethnolinguistic identity. *Journal of Language and Social Psychology, 6,* 171–189.

Banton, M. (1967). *Race relations.* London: Tavistock.

Barge, J. K. (2006). Dialogue, conflict, and community. In J. G. Oetzel & S. Ting-Toomey (Eds.), *The Sage handbook of conflict communication: Integrating theory, research, and practice* (pp. 517–544). Thousand Oaks, CA: Sage.

Barker, V., & Giles, H. (2003). Integrating the communicative predicament and enhancement of aging models: The case of older Native Americans. *Health Communication, 15*(3), 255–275.

Basso, K. (1990). "To give up on words": Silence in Western Apache culture. In D. C. Carbaugh (Ed.), *Cultural communication and intercultural contact* (pp. 303–320). Mahwah, NJ: Lawrence Erlbaum.

Baugh, J. (1983). *Black street speech: Its history, structure and survival.* Austin: University of Texas Press.

Baugh, J. (2000a). *Beyond Ebonics: Linguistic pride and racial prejudice.* New York: Oxford University Press.

Baugh, J. (2000b). Racial identification by speech. *American Speech, 75*(4), 362–364.

Bawer, B. (1994, October 18). Confusion reigns. *The Advocate,* p. 80.

Baxter, L. A., & Goldsmith, D. (1990). Cultural terms for communication events among some American high school adolescents. *Western Journal of Speech Communication, 54,* 377–394.

Bednarski, P. J. (2003). PBS toon targets bilingual latinos. *Broadcasting & Cable, 10*(06), 133–172.

Beebe, S. A., & Beebe, S. J. (1991). *Public speaking: An audience-centered approach:* Englewood Cliffs, NJ: Prentice Hall.

Beech, H. (1996, April 8). "Don't you dare list them as other." *U.S. News & World Report,* p. 56.

Begley, S. (1995, February 13). Three is not enough. *Newsweek,* pp. 67–69.

Bell, D. (1992a). *Faces at the bottom of the well: The permanence of racism.* New York: Basic.

Bell, D. (1992b, July). Organizational communication techniques for managers. *Public Management, 79*(7), 24–25.

Bell, K., Orbe, M., Drummond, D. K., & Camara, S. K. (2000). Accepting the challenge of centralizing without essentializing: Black feminist thought and African American women's communicative experiences. *Women's Studies in Communication, 23*(1), 41–62.

Berger, C. R., & Douglas, W. (1981). Studies in interpersonal epistemology III: Anticipated interaction, self-monitoring, and observational context selection. *Communication Monographs, 48,* 183–196.

Bergman, M. (2004, March 18). *Census Bureau projects tripling of Hispanic and Asian populations in 50 Years; Non-Hispanic whites may drop to half of total population.* Retrieved March 9, 2007, from http://www

.census.gov/Press-Release/www/releases/archives/population/ 001720.html

Bernard, E. (2004). *Some of my best friends: Writers on interracial friendships*. New York: Harper Collins.

Berry, V. T. (1992). From *Good Times* to *The Cosby Show*: Perceptions of changing televised images among Black fathers and sons. In S. Craig (Ed.), *Men, masculinity, and the media* (pp. 111–123). Newbury Park, CA: Sage.

Billings, A. C. (2004). Depicting the quarterback in black and white: A content analysis of college and professional football broadcast commentary. *Howard Journal of Communications, 15*, 201–210.

Billings, A. C., & Eastman, S. T. (2002). Gender, ethnicity, and nationality: Formation of identity in NBC's 2000 Olympic coverage. *International Review for the Sociology of Sport, 37*, 349–368.

Birdwhistell, R. (1970). *Kinesics and context*. Philadelphia: University of Pennsylvania Press.

Blacks closing gap in use of technology. (1999, March 11). *Kalamazoo (MI) Gazette*, p. A11.

Blake-Beard, S., Murrell, A., & Thomas, D. (2006). *Unfinished business: The impact of race on understanding mentoring relationships* (Working Paper No. 06–060, 2006). Boston: Harvard Business School.

Blau, P., Blum, T. C., & Schwartz, J. E. (1982). Heterogeneity and intermarriage. *American Sociological Review, 47*, 45–62.

Blubaugh, J. A., & Pennington, D. L. (1976). *Crossing difference . . . Interracial communication*. Columbus, OH: Charles E. Merrill.

Blumenbach, J. F. (1969). *On the natural varieties of mankind* (T. Bendyshe, Trans.). New York: Bergman Publishers. (Original work published 1865)

Blumenbach, J. F. (1973). *The anthropological treatises of Johann Friedrich Blumenbach*. Boston: Milford House. (Original work published 1865)

Blumer, H. (1969). *Symbolic interactionism: Perspective and method*. Englewood Cliffs, NJ: Prentice-Hall.

Bogle, D. (1994). *Toms, coons, mulattoes, mammies, and bucks: An interpretive history of Blacks in American films*. New York: Viking Press.

Boswell, J. (1994). *Same-sex unions in premodern Europe*. New York: Villard.

Botan, C., & Smitherman, G. (1991). Black English in the integrated workplace. *Journal of Black Studies, 22*, 168–185.

Bourhis, R. Y. (1979). Language in ethnic interaction: A social psychological approach. In H. Giles & B. Saint-Jacques (Eds.), *Language and ethnic relations* (pp. 117–141). Oxford: Pergamon.

Bourhis, R. Y., & Giles, H. (1977). The language of intergroup distinctiveness. In H. Giles & R. St. Clair (Eds.), *Language, ethnicity, and intergroup relations* (pp. 119–135). London: Academic Press.

Bowe, F. (1978). *Handicapping America: Barriers to disabled people*. New York: Harper & Row.

Bower, L., & Schmid, J. (1997). Minority presence and portrayal in mainstream magazine advertising: An update. *Journalism and Mass Communication Quarterly, 74*, 134–146.

Bowers, L. B. (2006). *Becoming a multicultural church*. Cleveland, OH: Pilgrim Press.

Bowser, B. P. (1995). *Racism and anti-racism in world perspective* (Vol. 13). Thousand Oaks, CA: Sage.

Bowser, B. P., & Hunt, R. G. (1996). *Impacts of racism on White Americans*. Thousand Oaks, CA: Sage.

Braithwaite, C. (1990). Communicative silence: A cross cultural study of Basso's hypothesis. In D. Carbaugh (Ed.), *Cultural communication and intercultural contact* (pp. 321–327). Hillsdale, NJ: Lawrence Erlbaum.

Braithwaite, D. O. (1990). From majority to minority: An analysis of cultural change from able-bodied to disabled. *International Journal of Intercultural Relations, 14*, 465–483.

Braithwaite, D. O. (1991). Just how much did that wheelchair cost? Management of privacy boundaries by persons with disabilities. *Western Journal of Speech Communication, 55*, 254–274.

Braithwaite, D. O., & Braithwaite, C. A. (2000). Understanding communication of persons with disabilities as cultural communication. In L. A. Samovar & R. E. Porter (Eds.), *Intercultural communication: A reader* (pp. 136–145). Belmont, CA: Wadsworth.

Braithwaite, D. O., & Thompson, T. L. (Eds.). (2000). *Handbook of communication and people with disabilities: Research and application*. Mahwah, NJ: Lawrence Erlbaum.

Bramlett-Solomon, S., & Hernandez, P. (2003). Photo coverage of Hispanics and blacks in a southwestern daily newspaper. In D. I. Rios & A. N. Mohamed (Eds.), *Brown and Black Communication: Latino and African American conflict and convergence in mass media* (pp. 71–79). Westport, CT: Praeger.

Branch, S. (1998, July 6). What blacks think of corporate America. *Fortune*, pp. 140–143.

Brewer, M., & Campbell, D. T. (1976). *Ethnocentrism and intergroup attitudes*. New York: Wiley.

Brewer, M. B., & Miller, N. (1984). *Beyond the contact hypothesis: Theoretical perspectives on desegregation*. In N. Miller & M. B. Brewer (Eds.), *Groups in contact: The psychology of desegregation* (pp. 281–302). Orlando, FL: Academic Press.

Brewer, S. (2006). *Borders and bridges: A history of U.S.–Latin American relations*. Westport, CT: Praeger.

Brilhart, J. K., & Galanes, G. J. (1995). *Effective group discussion* (8th ed.). Dubuque, IA: WCB Brown & Benchmark.

Brooks, D. E., & Jacobs, W. R. (1996). Black men in the margins: Space Traders and the interpositional strategy against b(l)acklash. *Communication Studies, 47,* 289–302.

Brown, D. (2006). *Asian Americans go missing when it comes to TV.* Retrieved September 26, 2006, from http://www.imdiversity.com/villages/asian/arts_culture_media/pns_tv_emmys _0806.asp

Brown, J. C. (1993, June). In defense of the N word. *Essence,* p. 138.

Brown, P., & Levinson, S. (1978). Universals in language use: Politeness phenomena. In E. Goody (Ed.), *Questions and politeness* (pp. 56–289). London: Cambridge University Press.

Brummett, B. (1992, November). *Forget rhetoric, study "R" instead.* Paper presented at the annual meeting of the Speech Communication Association, Chicago.

Brummett, B. (1994). *Rhetoric in popular culture.* New York: St. Martin's Press.

Burke, P. J., & Franzoi, S. L. (1988). Studying situations and identities using experiential sampling methodology. *American Sociological Review, 53,* 559–568.

Burke, P. J., & Reitzes, D. C. (1981). The link between identity and role performance. *Social Psychology Quarterly, 44,* 83–92.

Burke, P. J., & Tully, J. (1977). The measurement of role/ identity. *Social Forces, 55,* 881–897.

Butcher, D. R. (2006). *Employee empowerment: Eliminate "us versus them."* Retrieved November 24, 2006, from http://news.thomasnet.com/IMT/archives/2006/10/employee_empowerment_eliminate_us_versus_them_environment.html?t=recent

Buttny, R., & Williams, P. L. (2000). Demanding respect: The uses of reported speech in discursive constructions of interracial contact. *Discourse & Society, 11,* 109–133.

Byers, L. A., & Hart, R. D. (1996, May). *I had my own identity for the first time in my life: The relational dialectics between self and society.* Paper presented at the annual meeting of the International Communication Association, Chicago.

Byers, P. Y. (1997). *Organizational communications: Theory and behavior.* Boston: Allyn & Bacon.

Byrd, J. (1997). Blacks, whites in news pictures. In S. Biagi & M. Kem-Foxworth (Eds.), *Facing difference: Race, gender, and mass media* (pp. 95–97). Thousand Oaks, CA: Pine Forge Press.

Byrne, D. (1971). *The attraction paradigm.* New York: Academic.

Cagney, K. A., Wallace, D., & Browning, C. R. (n.d.). *Interracial unease in an urban setting: The influence of neighborhood social context.* Retrieved November 23, 2006, from http:// www.spc.uchicago.edu/ prc/pdfs/ cagneyAbstract05.pdf

Calafell, B. M. (2004). Disrupting the dichotomy: "Yo soy Chicana/o?" in the new Latina/o South. *Communication Review, 7*(2), 175–204.

Calvert, C. (1997). Hate speech and its harms: A communication theory perspective. *Journal of Communication, 47*(l), 4–19.

Campbell, R. (1999). *Media and culture: An introduction to mass communication.* New York: St. Martin's Press.

Canary, D., & Dindia, K. (Eds.). (1998). *Sex differences and similarities in communication: Critical essays and empirical investigations of sex and gender in interaction.* Mahwah, NJ: Lawrence Erlbaum.

Carbaugh, D. (1987). Communication rules in Donahue discourse. *Research on Language and Social Interaction, 21,* 31–61.

Carbaugh, D. (1989). *Talking American: Cultural discourses on Donahue.* Norwood, NJ: Ablex.

Carbaugh, D. (1990). Intercultural communication. In D. Carbaugh (Ed.), *Cultural communication and intercultural contact* (pp. 151–176). Hillsdale, NJ: Lawrence Erlbaum.

Carbaugh, D. (1995). The ethnographic communication theory of Philipsen and associates. In D. Cushman & B. Kovacic (Eds.), *Watershed research traditions in communication theory* (pp. 241–265). Albany: State University of New York Press.

Carbaugh, D. (1999). "Just listen": "Listening" and landscape among the Blackfeet. *Western Journal of Communication, 63,* 250–270.

Carbaugh, D. (2002). "I can't do that! But I can actually see around the corners": American Indian students and the study of public communication. In J. N. Martin, T. K. Nakayama, & L. A. Flores (Eds.), *Reading in cultural contexts* (pp. 138–148). Mountain View, CA: Mayfield.

Carlson, C. I., Wilson, K. D., & Hargrave, J. L. (2003). The effect of school racial composition on Hispanic intergroup relations. *Journal of Social and Personal Relationships, 20*(2), 203–220.

Carrasco, R. (1996, January 8). Pivotal minority movements strive for racial unity. *Christianity Today,* p. 70.

Carrier, J. (1999). *Ten ways to fight hate: A community response guide.* Montgomery, AL: Southern Poverty Law Center.

Carroll, J. B. (1992). Anthropological linguistics: An overview. In W. Bright (Ed.), *International encyclopedia of linguistics* (pp. 33–49). New York: Oxford University Press.

Carson, C. (1981). *In struggle: SNCC and the Black awakening of the 1960s.* Cambridge, MA: Harvard University Press.

Carson, D. K., & Hand, C. (1999). Dilemmas surrounding elder abuse and neglect in Native American communities. In T. Toshio (Ed.), *Understanding the elder* abuse in minority populations (pp. 161–186). Philadelphia: Brunner/Mazel.

Carter, R. A. (1995, December). Improving minority relations. *FBI Law Enforcement Bulletin*, pp. 14–17.

Carter, R. T. (1990). The relationship between racism and racial identity among White Americans: An exploratory investigation. *Journal of Counseling and Development, 69*, 46–50.

Case, C. E., & Greeley, A. M. (1990). Attitudes toward racial equality. *Humboldt Journal of Social Relations, 16*(1), 67–94.

Casmir, F. L. (1993). Third-culture building: A paradigm shift for international and intercultural communication. *Communication Yearbook, 16*, 107–124.

Casmir, F. L., & Asuncion-Lande, N. C. (1989). Intercultural communication revisited: Conceptualization, paradigm building, and methodological approaches. *Communication Yearbook, 12*, 278–309.

Chan, S. (1989). You're short, besides! In Asian Women United of California (Eds.), *Making waves: An anthology of writing by and about Asian American women* (pp. 265–272). Boston: Beacon Press.

Chan, S. (Ed.). (2003). *Remapping Asian American history*. New York: AltaMira Press.

Chapa, J. (1998, June). Conquering the recruitment challenge. *Hispanic*, p. 62.

Chen, G. M., & Starosta, W. J. (1998). *Foundations of intercultural communication*. Boston: Allyn & Bacon.

Chen, V. (2002). (De)hyphenated identity: The double voice in *The Woman Warrior*. In A. Gonzalez, M. Houston, & V. Chen (Eds.), *Our voices: Essays in culture, ethnicity, and communication* (pp. 16–25). Los Angeles: Roxbury.

Cheng, H. L. (2005). Constructing a transnational multilocal sense of belonging: An analysis of *Ming Pao* (West Canadian edition). *Journal of Communication Inquiry, 29*(2), 141–159.

Chihara, M. (2000). Something about Lucy. *Boston Phoenix*. Retrieved October 3, 2006, from http://www.alternet.org/story/290/

Childs, E. C. (2005). Looking behind the stereotypes of the "angry black woman": An exploration of black women's responses to interracial relationships. *Gender & Society, 19*(4), 544–561.

Chism, N. V. N., & Border, L. L. B. (Eds.). (1992). *Teaching for diversity*. San Francisco: Jossey-Bass.

Cho, S. K. (1995). Korean Americans vs. African Americans: Conflict and construction. In M. L. Andersen & P. H. Collins (Eds.), *Race, class, and gender: An anthology* (pp. 461–469). Belmont, CA: Wadsworth.

Chong-Yeong, L. (2002). Language and human rights. *Journal of Intergroup Relations, 24*(3), 66–73.

Christian, S. E., & Lapinksi, M. K. (2003). Support for the contact hypothesis: High school students' attitudes toward Muslims post 9–11. *Journal of Intercultural Communication, 32*(4), 247–263.

Clark, K. D., & Diggs, R. C. (2002). Connected or separated? Toward a dialectical view of interethnic relationships. In T. McDonald, M. Orbe, & T. Ford-Ahmed (Eds.), *Building diverse communities: Applications of communication research* (pp. 3–26). Cresskill, NJ: Hampton Press.

Clayton, O., Jr. (1995, Winter). The churches and social change: Accommodation, moderation, or protest. *Daedalus*, pp. 101–117.

Clifton, J. A. (Ed.). (1989). *Being and becoming Indian: Biographical studies of North American frontiers*. Homewood, IL: Dorsey.

Close, E. (1997, January 13). Why ebonics is irrelevant. *Newsweek*, p. 80.

Cohen, G., & Faulkner, D. (1986). Does "elderspeak" work? The effect of intonation and stress on comprehension and recall of spoken discourse in old age. *Language and Communication, 6*, 91–98.

Cole, J. B. (1995). Commonalities and differences. In M. L. Andersen & P. H. Collins (Eds.), *Race, class, and gender: An anthology* (pp. 148–154). Belmont, CA: Wadsworth.

Coleman, L. M., & DePaulo, B. M. (1991). Uncovering the human spirit: Moving beyond disability and "missed" communications. In N. Coupland, H. Giles, & J. M. Wiemann (Eds.), *Miscommunication and problematic talk* (pp. 61–84). Newbury Park, CA: Sage.

Collier, M. J. (1988). A comparison of intracultural and intercultural communication among acquaintances: How intra- and intercultural competencies vary. *Communication Quarterly, 36*, 122–144.

Collier, M. J. (1991). Conflict competence within African, Mexican, and Anglo American friendships. In S. Ting-Toomey & F. Korzenny (Eds.), *Cross-cultural interpersonal communication* (pp. 132–154). Newbury Park, CA: Sage.

Collier, M. J. (1996). Communication competence problematics in ethnic friendships. *Communication Monographs, 63*, 314–336.

Collier, M. J. (2000). Cultural identity and intercultural communication. In L. A. Samovar & R. E. Porter (Eds.), *Intercultural communication: A reader* (pp. 16–33). Belmont, CA: Wadsworth.

Collier, M. J. (2002). Intercultural friendships as interpersonal alliances. In J. N. Martin, T. K. Nakayama, & L. A. Flores (Eds.), *Readings in cultural contexts* (pp. 301–309). Mountain View, CA: Mayfield.

Collier, M. J., & Bowker, J. (1994, November). *U.S. American women in intercultural friendships*. Paper presented at the Speech Communication Association conference, New Orleans, LA.

Collier, M. J., Ribeau, S. A., & Hecht, M. L. (1986). Intracultural communication rules and outcomes within three domestic cultures. *International Journal of Intercultural Relations, 10*, 439–457.

Collier, M. J., & Thomas, M. (1988). Cultural identity: An interpretive perspective. In Y. Y. Kim & W. B. Gudykunst (Eds.), *Theories in intercultural communication* (pp. 99–120). Newbury Park, CA: Sage.

Collier, M. J., Thompson, J., & Weber, D. (1996, November). *Identity problematics among U.S. ethnics.* Paper presented at the annual meeting of the Speech Communication Association, San Diego, CA.

Collins, P. H. (1986). Learning from the outsider within: The sociological significance of black feminist thought. *Social Problems, 33*(6), S14–S23.

Collins, P. H. (1990). *Black feminist thought: Knowledge, consciousness, and the politics of empowerment.* Boston: Unwin Hyman.

Collins, P. H. (1995). Pornography and Black women's bodies. In G. Dines & J. M. Humez (Eds.), *Gender, race, and class in media* (pp. 279–286). Thousand Oaks, CA: Sage.

Collins, P. H. (1998). *Fighting words: Black women and the search for justice.* Minneapolis: University of Minnesota Press.

Condit, C. M., & Lucaites, J. (1993). *Crafting equality: America's Anglo African word.* Chicago: University of Chicago Press.

Connaughton, S. L. (2004). Multiple identification targets in examining partisan identification: A case study of Texas Latinos. *Howard Journal of Communications, 15*, 131–145.

Connell, R. W. (2005). *Masculinities.* Cambridge, UK: Polity Press.

Cook, G. (2003, November 18). Study finds that racism can breed stupidity. *Kalamazoo (MI) Gazette*, p. A4.

Cooks, L. M., & Hale, C. L. (1992). A feminist approach to the empowerment of women mediators. *Discourse & Society, 3*(3), 277–300.

Coombes, W. T., & Holladay, S. T. (1995). The emerging political power of the elderly. In N. F. Nussbaum & J. Coupland (Eds.), *Handbook of communication and aging research* (pp. 317–343). Mahwah, NJ: Lawrence Erlbaum.

Cooper, M. (1990). Rejecting "femininity": Some research notes on gender identity development in lesbians. *Deviant Behavior, 11*, 371–380.

Coopman, S. J. (2003). Communicating disability: Metaphors of oppression, metaphors of empowerment. *Communication Yearbook, 27*, 337–394.

Corbett, C. (2003). Introduction: When God became red. In R. A. Grounds, G. E. Tinker, & D. E. Wilkins (Eds.), *Native voices: American Indian identity and resistance* (pp. 189–193). Lawrence: University Press of Kansas.

Cornett-DeVito, M. M., & Worley, D. W. (2005). A front row seat: A phenomenological investigation of learning disabilities. *Communication Education, 54*(4), 312–333.

Cornwell, N. C., Orbe, M., & Warren, K. (1999, May). *Hate speech/free speech: Using feminist perspectives to foster on-campus dialogue.* Paper presented at the annual meeting of the International Communication Association, San Francisco.

Cosby, B. (1995, November). 50 years of blacks on TV. *Ebony*, pp. 215–218.

Coser, L. A. (1956). *The functions of social conflict.* New York: Free Press.

Coward, J. M. (1993, August). *"The sculking Indian enemy": Colonial newspapers' portrayal of Native Americans.* Paper printed at the annual meeting of the Association for Education in Journalism and Mass Communication, Kansas City, MO.

Crawford, J. (2000). *At war with diversity: U.S. language policy in an age of anxiety.* Clevedon, England: Multilingual Matters Ltd.

Crawley, R. L. (1995, January). *Communicating about diverse people: An experiential workshop.* Presentation to the students at Indiana University Southeast, New Albany.

Crenshaw, C. (1997). Resisting whiteness' rhetorical silence. *Western Journal of Communication, 61*(3), 253–278.

Crenshaw, K., Gotanda, N., Peller, G., & Thomas, K. (Eds.). (1995). *Critical race theory: The key writings that formed that movement.* New York: New Press.

Crompton, R. (1993). *Class and stratification: An introduction to current debates.* Cambridge, UK: Polity.

Cross, W. E. (1971). The Negro-to-Black conversion experience: Toward a psychology of Black liberation. *Black World, 20*, 13–27.

Cross, W. E. (1978). The Thomas and Cross models of psychological nigrescence: A review. *Journal of Black Psychology, 5*(1), 13–31.

Cummings, M. C. (1988). The changing image of the Black family on television. *Journal of Popular Culture, 22*(2), 75–85.

Cupach, W. R., & Imahori, T. T. (1993). Identity management theory: Communication competence in intercultural episodes and relationships. *International and Intercultural Communication Annual, 17*, 112–131.

Dace, K. L. (1994). Dissonance in European-American and African-American communication. *Western Journal of Black Studies, 18*, 18–26.

Dace, K. L., & McPhail, M. L. (2002). Crossing the color line: From empathy to implicature in intercultural communication. In J. N. Martin, T. K. Nakayama, & L. A. Flores (Eds.), *Readings in cultural contexts* (pp. 344–350). Mountain View, CA: Mayfield.

Dalton, T. A. (1997). Reporting on race: A tale of two cities. *Columbia Journalism Review, 36*(3), 54–58.

Daly, J. A., Vangelisti, A. L., & Weber, D. J. (1995). Speech anxiety affects how people prepare speeches: A protocol analysis of the preparation processes of speakers. *Communication Monographs, 62*(4), 383–398.

Dart, B. (2006, May 10). One in three U.S. residents a minority. *Kalamazoo (MI) Gazette*, p. A12.

Davidson, J. R., & Schneider, L. J. (1992). Acceptance of Black-White interracial marriage. *Journal of Intergroup Relations, 24*(3), 47–52.

Davis, F. J. (1991). *Who is Black: One nation's definition.* University Park: Pennsylvania State University Press.

Davis, R. A. (1997). *The myth of Black ethnicity: Monophylety, diversity, and the dilemma of identity.* Greenwich, CT: Ablex.

Day, A. G. (1960). *Hawaii and its people.* New York: Duell, Sloan & Pearce.

Deetz, S. (1992). *Democracy in an age of corporate colonialization: Developments in communication and the politics of everyday life.* Albany: State University of New York Press.

Degler, C. N. (1971). *Neither Black or White: Slavery and race relations in Brazil and the United States.* New York: Macmillan.

De La Torre, W. (1997). Multiculturalism: A redefinition of citizenship and community. *Urban Education, 31*(3), 314–345.

Delgado, F. P. (1998a). Moving beyond the screen: Hollywood and Mexican American stereotypes. In Y. R. Kamalipour & T. Carilli (Eds.), *Cultural diversity in the U.S. media* (pp. 169–182). Albany: State University of New York Press.

Delgado, F. P. (1998b). When the silenced speak: The textualization and complications of Latino/a identity. *Western Journal of Communication, 62*, 420–438.

Delgado, R. (Ed.). (1995). *Critical race theory: The cutting edge.* Philadelphia: Temple University Press.

Deloria, V. (1985). *Behind the trail of broken treaties: An Indian declaration of independence.* Austin: University of Texas Press.

Deloria, V., Jr. (2003). The passage of generations. In R. A. Grounds, G. E. Tinker, & D. E. Wilkins (Eds.), *Native voices: American Indian identity and resistance* (pp. 318–324). Lawrence: University Press of Kansas.

Demo, A. (2005). Sovereignty discourse and contemporary immigration politics. *Quarterly Journal of Speech, 91*(3), 291–311.

Denham, B. E., Billings, A. C., & Halone, K. K. (2002). Differential accounts of race in broadcast commentary of the 2000 Men's and Women's Final Four Basketball Tournaments. *Sociology of Sport Journal, 19*, 315–332.

Deutsch, M. (1994). Constructive conflict resolution: Principles, training, and research. *Journal of Social Issues, 50*(1), 13–32.

DeVito, J. (1998). *The interpersonal communication book* (8th ed.). New York: Longman.

DeVos, G. A. (1982). Ethnic pluralism: Conflict and accommodation. In G. A. DeVos & L. Romanucci-Ross (Eds.), *Ethnic identity: Cultural continuities and change* (pp. 5–41). Chicago: University of Chicago Press.

Diamond, J. (1994, November). Race without color. *Discover*, pp. 83–89.

Diggs, R. D., & Clark, K. D. (2002). It's a struggle but worth it: Identifying and managing identities in an interracial friendship. *Communication Quarterly, 50*(3/4), 368–390.

Dixon, J., Durrheim, K., & Tredoux, C. (2005). Beyond the optimal contact strategy. *American Psychologist, 60*(7), 697–711.

Docan, T. (2003). *Building and sustaining intercultural relationships: Public perceptions and practical benefits of friendships and romantic relationships in intercultural contexts.* Conference paper presented at the International Communication Association Annual Meeting, San Diego, CA.

Dodd, C. H., & Baldwin, J. R. (1998). The role of family and macrocultures in intercultural relationships. In J. N. Martin, T. K. Nakayama, & L. A. Flores (Eds.), *Readings in cultural contexts* (pp. 335–344). Mountain View, CA: Mayfield.

Domke, D., McCoy, K., & Torres, M. (2003). News media, immigration, and priming of racial perceptions. In D. I. Rios & A. N. Mohamed (Eds.), *Brown and black communication: Latino and African American conflict and convergence in mass media* (pp. 123–142). Westport, CT: Praeger.

Donahue, W. A. (1985). Ethnicity and mediation. In W. B. Gudykunst, L. P. Stewart, & S. Ting-Toomey (Eds.), *Communication, culture, and organizational processes* (pp. 134–154). Beverly Hills, CA: Sage.

Donovan, S. (2004). *Stress and coping techniques in successful intercultural marriages.* Unpublished master's thesis, Virginia Tech, Blacksburg. Retrieved March 10, 2007, from http://scholar.lib.vt.edu/theses/available/etd-12222004-125301/

Dorsey, T. (1995, June 20). Many of the season's losers didn't deserve to be canceled. *Louisville (KY) Courier-Journal*, p. C3.

Dorsey, T. (1997, March). Blacks' viewing habits assessed. *Louisville (KY) Courier-Journal*, p. E2.

Dougherty, D. S. (1999). Dialogue through standpoint: Understanding women's and men's standpoints of sexual harassment. *Management Communication Quarterly, 12*, 435–468.

Dovidio, J., Gaertner, S. E., Kawakami, K., & Hodson, G. (2002). Why can't we just get along? Interpersonal biases and interracial distrust. *Cultural Diversity & Ethnic Minority Psychology, 8*, 88–102.

Dovidio, J. F., Kawakami, K., & Gaertner, S.L. (2002). Implicit and explicit prejudice and interracial interaction. *Journal of Personality and Social Psychology, 82*, 62–28.

Downing, J. D. H. (1999). "Hate speech" and "First Amendment absolutism" discourses in the U.S. *Discourse in Society, 10*(2), 175–189.

Drummond, D. K. (1997, November). *An exploration of multiple identity negotiation over the Internet.* Paper presented at the annual meeting of the National Communication Association, Chicago.

Drummond, D. (2002). Study circles and the creation of ideal social realities while addressing key social and political issues: A case study. In T. McDonald, M. Orbe, & T. Ford-Ahmed (Eds.), *Building diverse communities: Applications of communication research* (pp. 135–148). Cresskill, NJ: Hampton Press.

Du Bois, W. E. B. (1982). *The souls of Black folks.* New York: Signet. (Original work published 1903)

Duckitt, J., & du Toit, L. (1989). Personality profiles of homosexual men and women. *Journal of Psychology, 123*, 497–505.

Duncan, V. (2002). Interracial communication as a community builder within the university. In T. McDonald, M. Orbe, & T. Ford-Ahmed (Eds.), *Building diverse communities: Applications of communication research* (pp. 35–54). Cresskill, NJ: Hampton Press.

Durham, M. G. (2001). Displaced persons: Symbols of South Asian femininity and the returned gaze in U.S. media culture. *Communication Theory, 11*(2), 201–217.

Dwyer, E. (1993, December 10–12). The story behind "Geronimo." *USA Weekend*, p. 10.

Dyer, (1997). *The matter of Whiteness.* New York: Routledge.

Easter, N. (2002). *The rise and fall of diversity training.* Paper presented at the Annual Meeting of the American Educational Research Association, New Orleans, LA.

Eddings, J. (1996, October 23). The covert color war: A persistent stealth racism is poisoning black–white relations. *U.S. News & World Report*, pp. 40–42.

Eddings, J. (1997, July 14). Counting a "new" type of American. *U.S. News & World Report*, pp. 22–23.

Ehrenreich, B. (1989). *Fear of falling: The inner life of the middle class.* New York: HarperCollins.

Ehrenreich, B. (1990). Are you middle class? In M. L. Andersen & P. H. Collins (Eds.), *Race, class, and gender: An anthology* (pp. 100–109). Belmont, CA: Wadsworth.

Elise, S., & Umoja, A. (1992). Spike Lee constructs the new Black man: Mo' better. *Western Journal of Black Studies, 6*, 82–89.

Ellison, G. C., & Powers, D. A. (1994). The contact hypothesis and racial attitudes among Black Americans. *Social Science Quarterly, 75*(2), 385–400.

El Nasser, H. (2003, February 17). Black America's new diversity. *USA Today*, p. 3A.

El Nasser, H. (2006, October 27). Where will everybody live? *USA Today*, pp. A1–A2.

Ely, J. H. (1998). If at first you don't succeed, ignore the question next time? Group harm in *Brown v. Board of Education* and *Loving v. Virginia. Constitutional Commentary, 15*(2), 215–223.

Emry, R., & Wiseman, R. L. (1987). An intercultural understanding of ablebodied and disabled persons communication. *International Journal of Intercultural Relations, 11*, 7–27.

Entman, R. (1994). Representation and reality in the portrayal of blacks on network television shows. *Journalism Quarterly, 71*(1), 509–520.

Erikson, E. H. (1963). *Childhood and society* (2nd ed.). New York: Norton.

Erikson, E. H. (1968). *Identity: Youth and crisis.* New York: Norton.

"Esperanto: The international language that works!" (2006). Retrieved October 8, 2006, from http://www.esperanto-usa.org

Essed, P. (1991). *Understanding everyday racism: An interdisciplinary theory.* Newbury Park, CA: Sage.

Estes, A. (1999, February 25). Internet reported as major factor in hate speech group growth. *Western Michigan University Herald*, p. 5.

Ethridge, R. (1991, September 26). Politically correct speech. *Black Issues in Higher Education*, pp. B1–2.

Etzioni, A. (1996, September). From melting pot to mosaic: America's community of communities. *Current, 385*, pp. 8–13.

Evans, D. (1993, March 1). The wrong examples. *Newsweek*, p. 10.

Evoleocha, S. U., & Ugbah, S. D. (1989). Stereotypes, counter-stereotypes, and Black television images in the 1990s. *Western Journal of Black Studies, 12*, 197–205.

Ezekiel, R. S. (1997). *The racist mind: Portraits of American neo-Nazis and Klansmen.* New York: Penguin.

Fairchild, H. H. (1985). Black, Negro, or Afro-American? The difference are crucial! *Journal of Black Studies, 16*(1), 47–55.

Fairlie, R. (2004). *Race and the digital divide.* Retrieved November 30, 2006, from http://cjtc.ucsc.edu/docs/r_digitaldivide9.pdf

Falcon, A. (2004). *Atlas of stateside Puerto Ricans.* Washington, DC: Puerto Rican Federal Affairs Administration.

Falicov, C. J. (2005). Emotional transnationalism and family identities. *Family Process, 44*(4), 399–407.

"Families of many colors." (1998, February 9). *Scholastic Update*, pp. 12–21.

Farhi, P. (1997). A television trend: Audiences in black and white. In S. Biagi & M. Kem-Foxworth (Eds.), *Facing difference: Race, gender, and mass media* (pp. 202–204). Thousand Oaks, CA: Pine Forge Press.

Faulkner, S. L. (2006). Reconstruction: Being LGBTQ and Jewish. In M. Orbe, B. J. Allen, & L. A. Flores (Eds.), *The same and different: Acknowledging the diversity within and between cultural groups* (pp. 95–120). Washington, DC: National Communication Association.

Fayol, H. (1916). *General and industrial management*. London: Pitman.

Fears, D. (2003, August 25). Latinos or Hispanics? A debate about identity. *Washington Post*, pp. A1, A5.

Ferguson, R., Gever, M., Trinh, T. M., & West, C. (Eds.). (1990). *Out there: Marginalization and contemporary cultures*. Cambridge, MA: MIT Press.

Fernandez, C. A. (1992). La Raza and the melting pot: A comparative look at multiethnicity. In M. P. P. Root (Ed.), *Racially mixed in America* (pp. 126–143). Newbury Park, CA: Sage.

Ferre, I., Garlikov, L., Oppenheim, K., Spoerry, S., Keck, K., & Whitbeck, H. (2006). Thousands march for immigrant rights: Schools, businesses feel impact as students, workers walk out. *CNN*. Retrieved November 24, 2006, from http://www.cnn.com/2006/US/05/01/immigrant.day/ index.html

Field, D., & Travisano, R. (1984). Social history and American preoccupation with identity. *Free Inquiry in Creative Sociology, 12*, 51–56.

Fine, M. (1991). New voices in the workplace: Research directions in multicultural communication. *The Journal of Business Communication, 28*, 259–275.

Fink, B., & Wild, K.-P. (1995). Similarities in leisure interests: Effects of selection and isolation in friendships. *Journal of Social Psychology, 135*(4), 471–483.

Firth, J. (1991, November). A proactive approach to conflict resolution. *Supervisory Management*, pp. 3–4.

Fitch, N. E. (1992). Multiculturalism and diversity, or business as usual in the 20th century? *Diversity: A Journal of Multicultural Issues, 1*, 43–64.

Fitzgerald, M., & Hernandez, D. G. (1994, August 27). Diversity diversions: Entries from reporters' logs at the unity '94 conference. *Editor & Publisher*, pp. 26–28.

Fitzpatrick, K. M., & Hwang, S. S. (1992). The effects of community structure on opportunities for interracial contact: Extending Blau's macrostructural theory. *Sociological Forum, 7*(3), 517–536.

Flores, L. A. (1996). Creating discursive space through a rhetoric of difference: Chicana feminists craft a homeland. *Quarterly Journal of Speech, 82*, 142–156.

Flynn, G. (1998a). Experts explain the evolution of diversity programs. *Workforce, 77*(12), 32.

Flynn, G. (1998b). The harsh reality of diversity programs. *Workforce, 77*(12), 26–31.

Foeman, A. K. (1997, July). Managing multiracial institutions: Goals and approaches for race-relations training. *Communication Education, 40*(3), 255–265.

Foeman, A. K., & Nance, T. (1999). From miscegenation to multiculturalism: Perceptions and stages of interracial relationship development. *Journal of Black Studies, 29*(4), 540–557.

Foeman, A. K., & Nance, T. (2002). Building new cultures, reframing old images: Success strategies of interracial couples. *The Howard Journal of Communications, 13*, 237–249.

Folb, E. A. (1997). Who's got room at the top? Issues of dominance and nondominance in intracultural communication. In L. A. Samovar & R. E. Porter (Eds.), *Intercultural communication: A reader* (pp. 138–146). Belmont, CA: Wadsworth.

Fong, M. (2000). The crossroads of language and culture. In L. A. Samovar & R. E. Porter (Eds.), *Intercultural communication: A reader* (pp. 211–216). Belmont, CA: Wadsworth.

Fong, M. (2004). Identity and speech community. In M. Fong & R. Chuang (Eds.), *Communicating ethnic and cultural identity* (pp. 3–18). New York: Rowman & Littlefield Publishers.

Forbes, H. D. (1997). Ethnic conflict and the contact hypothesis. In H. D. Forbes (Ed.), *Ethnic conflict: Commerce, culture, and the contact hypothesis*. New Haven, CT: Yale University Press.

Ford-Ahmed, T., & Orbe, M. (1992, November). *African American graduate students, their majority host institution and ethnic prejudice: A bright side?* Paper presented at the annual meeting of the Speech Communication Association, Chicago.

Foster-Fishman, P. G., & Keys, C. B. (1997). The person/environment dynamics of employee empowerment: An organizational culture analysis. *American Journal of Community Psychology, 25*(3), 345–369.

Fox, S. A., & Giles, H. (1997). "Let the wheelchair through!" In W. P. Robinson (Ed.), *Social psychology and social identity: Festschrift in honor of Henry Tajfel*. Amsterdam: Elsevier.

Fox, S. A., Giles, H., Orbe, M., & Bourhis, R. Y. (2000). Interability communication: Theoretical perspectives. In D. O. Braithwaite & T. L. Thompson (Eds.), *Handbook of communication and people with disabilities* (pp. 193–222). Mahwah, NJ: Lawrence Erlbaum.

Fox, S. A., Giles, H., Bourhis, R. Y., & Orbe, M. (in press). Communication between people with and without disabilities: A review, critique, and expansion of interability communication theories. In D. O. Braithwaite & T. L. Thompson (Eds.), *Handbook of communication and people with disabilities: Research and application.* Mahwah, NJ: Lawrence Erlbaum.

Frankenberg, R. (1993). *White women, race matters: The social construction of whiteness.* Minneapolis: University of Minnesota Press.

Frey, W. H. (1998). Minority majorities. *American Demographics, 20,* 6.

Frey, W. H. (2000). Multiple melting pots: America is forming broad regions that differ distinctly in their race-ethnic combinations. *World and I, 15*(50), 36–38.

Frey, W. H. (2001). Trails South. *American Demographics, 19,* 8–19.

Frey, W. H. (2002). Multilingual America. *American Demographics, 22,* 12–14.

Frey, W. H. (2004a). Generational pull. *American Demographics, 26*(4), 14–15.

Frey, W. H. (2004b). Zooming in on diversity. *American Demographics, 26*(6), 26–28.

Friedman, R. A., & Davidson, M. N. (2001). Managing diversity and second-order conflict. *International Journal of Conflict Management, 12*(2), 132–153.

Fujino, D. C. (1997). The rates, patterns, and reasons for forming heterosexual interracial dating relationships among Asian Americans. *Journal of Social and Personal Relationships, 14*(6), 809–828.

Funderberg, L. (1993). *Black, White, other: Biracial Americans talk about race and identity.* New York: Morrow.

Funderburg, L. (1998, December 14). Loving thy neighborhood. *Nation,* pp. 23–26.

Gaertner, S. L., & Dovidio, J. F. (2000). *Reducing intergroup bias: The common ingroup identity model.* Philadelphia, PA: Psychology Press.

Gaines, S. O., Jr. (1997). Communalism and the reciprocity of affection and respect among interethnic married couples. *Journal of Black Studies, 27*(3), 352–364.

Galen, M. (1994, January 31). White, male, and worried. *Business Week,* pp. 50–55.

Gallagher, C. A. (1994). White construction in the university. *Socialist Review, 1/2,* 167–187.

Gallois, C. (2003). Reconciliation through communication in intercultural encounters: Potential or peril? *Journal of Communication, 53,* 5–15.

Gallois, C., Giles, H., Jones, E., Cargile, A. C., & Ota, H. (1995). Accommodating intercultural encounters: Elaborations and extensions. In R. Wiseman (Ed.), *Intercultural communication theory* (pp. 115–147). Thousand Oaks, CA: Sage.

Gallois, C., Ogay, T., & Giles, H. (2005). Communication accommodation theory. In W. B. Gudykunst (Ed.), *Theorizing about intercultural communication* (pp. 121–148). Thousand Oaks, CA: Sage.

Gandy, O. H., & Matabane, P. W. (1989). Television and social perceptions among African Americans and Hispanics. In M. K. Asante & W. B. Gudykunst (Eds.), *Handbook of international and intercultural communication* (pp. 318–350). Newbury Park, CA: Sage.

Gangotena, M. (1997). The rhetoric of La Familia among Mexican Americans. In A. Gonzalez, M. Houston, & V. Chen (Eds.), *Our voices: Essays in culture, ethnicity, and communication* (pp. 70–83). Los Angeles: Roxbury.

Garcia, W. R. (1996). Respeto: A Mexican base for interpersonal relationships. In W. Gudykunst, S. Ting-Toomey, & T. Nishida (Eds.), *Communication in personal relationships across cultures* (pp. 55–76). Thousand Oaks, CA: Sage.

Garlington, W. (2005). *The Bahai faith in America.* Westport, CT: Praeger.

Garofalo, R. (1997). *Rockin' out: Popular music in the USA.* Boston: Allyn & Bacon.

Garner, T. (1994). Oral rhetorical practice in African American culture. In A. Gonzalez, M. Houston, & V. Chen (Eds.), *Our voices: Essays in culture, ethnicity, and communication* (pp. 81–91). Los Angeles: Roxbury.

Garza, R. T., & Herringer, L. G. (1987). Social identity: A multidimensional approach. *Journal of Social Psychology, 127,* 299–308.

Gates, D. (1993, March 29) White male. *Newsweek,* 48–53.

Gates, H. L. (1992). TV's Black world turns—but stays unreal. In M. L. Andersen & P. H. Collins (Eds.), *Race, class, and gender: An anthology* (pp. 310–316). Belmont, CA: Wadsworth.

Gates, H. L., Jr., (1994). War of words: Critical race theory and the first amendment. In A. P. Griffin, D. E. Lively, R. C. Post, W. B. Rubenstein, & N. Strossen, (Eds.), *Speaking of race, speaking of sex: Hate speech, civil rights, and civil liberties* (pp. 17–58). New York: New York University Press.

Geertz, C. (1976). From the native's point of view: On the nature of anthropological understanding. In P. Rabinow & W. M. Sullivan (Eds.), *Interpretive social science* (pp. 225–241). Berkeley: University of California Press.

George, D., & Yancey, G. (2004). Taking stock of America's attitudes on cultural diversity: An analysis of public deliberation on multiculturalism, assimilation and intermarriage. *Journal of Comparative Family Studies, 35*(1), 1–19.

Gergen, K. J. (1991). *The saturated self: Dilemmas of identity in contemporary life.* New York: Basic.

Giaridina, J. C. (1998). A program to celebrate human diversity. *Education Digest, 63*(7), 9–14.

Gibbs, J. T. (1987). Identity and marginality: Issues in the treatment of biracial adolescents. *American Journal of Orthopsychiatry, 57,* 265–278.

Giles, H. (1973). Accent mobility: A model and some data. *Anthropological Linguistics, 15,* 87–109.

Giles, H. (1977). Social psychology and applied linguistics. *ITL: Review of Applied Linguistics, 33,* 27–42.

Giles, H., & Coupland, N. (1991). *Language: Contexts and consequences.* Pacific Grove, CA: Brooks/Cole.

Giles, H., Coupland, N., Coupland, J., Williams, A., & Nussbaum, J. (1992). Intergenerational talk and communication with older people. *International Journal of Aging and Human Development, 34,* 271–297.

Giles, H., Mulac, A., Bradac, J. J., & Johnson, P. (1987). Speech accommodation theory: The first decade and beyond. *Communication Yearbook, 10,* 13–48.

Giles, H., Taylor, D. M., & Bourhis, R. Y. (1973). Towards a theory of interpersonal accommodation through language: Some Canadian data. *Language in Society, 2,* 177–192.

Gitlin, T. (1991). On the virtues of a loose canon. *New Perspectives Quarterly, 8,* 53–55.

Gladwell, M. (1996, April/May). Black like them. *The New Yorker,* pp. 74–80.

Glascock, J. (2003). Gender, race, and aggression in newer TV networks' primetime programming. *Communication Quarterly, 51,* 90–100.

Goffman, E. (1967). Interaction ritual: Essays on face-to-face behavior. Garden City, NY: Anchor.

Golden, D. R., Niles, T. A., & Hecht, M. L. (2002). Jewish American identity. In J. N. Martin, T. K. Nakayama, & L. A. Flores (Eds.), *Readings in intercultural communication: Experiences and contexts* (pp. 44–52). New York: McGraw-Hill.

Goldsmith, P. A. (2004). Schools' role in shaping race relations: Evidence on friendliness and conflict. *Social Problems, 51*(4), 587–612.

Gong, G. (2004). When Mississippi Chinese talk. In A. Gonzalez, M. Houston, & V. Chen (Eds.), *Our voices: Essays in culture, ethnicity, and communication* (pp. 104–112). Los Angeles: Roxbury.

Gonzalez, A., Houston, M., & Chen, V. (Eds.). (2004). *Our voices: Essays in culture, ethnicity, and communication.* Los Angeles: Roxbury.

Gonzalez, M. C. (2002). Painting the white face red: Intercultural contact presented through poetic ethnography. In J. N. Martin, T. K. Nakayama, & L. A. Flores (Eds.), *Readings in intercultural communication: Experiences and contexts* (pp. 386–397). New York: McGraw-Hill.

Gordon, M. M. (1964). *Assimilation in American life,* New York: Oxford University Press.

Gordon, M. M. (1978). *Human nature, class, and ethnicity.* New York: Oxford University Press.

Gose, B. (1996, May 10). Public debate over a private choice. *Chronicle of Higher Education,* pp. A45–A47.

Gosset, T. F. (1963). *Race: The history of an idea in America.* New York: Schocke.

Gould, S. J. (1994, November). The geometer of race. *Discover,* pp. 65–69.

Graham, J. A., & Cohen, R. (1997). Race and sex factors in children's sociometric ratings and friendship choices. *Social Development, 6*(3), 355–372.

Grant, M. (1970). *The passing of the great race.* New York: Arno. (Original work published 1918)

Graves, J. L. (2004). *The race myth: Why we pretend race exists in America.* New York: Dutton.

Gray, H. (1989). Television, Black Americans, and the American dream. *Critical Studies in Mass Communication, 6,* 376–386.

Gray, H. (1995). *Watching race: Television and the struggle for "Blackness."* Minneapolis: University of Minnesota Press.

Gray, J. (1992). *Men are from Mars, women are from Venus.* New York: HarperCollins.

Greene, C. (1996). "In the best interest of the total community"? Women-in-action and the problems of building interracial, cross-class alliances in Durham, North Carolina, 1968–1975. *Frontiers, 16*(2–3), 190–218.

Grimes, D. S. (2002). Challenging the status quo? *Management Communication Quarterly, 15*(3), 381–409.

Groscurth, C. R. (2003). Dialectically speaking: A critique of intergroup differences in African American language research. *Journal of Intergroup Relations, 30*(2), 47–64.

Gudykunst, W. B. (1985). A model of uncertainty reduction in intercultural encounters. *Journal of Language and Social Psychology, 4,* 79–98.

Gudykunst, W. B. (1988). Uncertainty and anxiety. In Y. Y. Kim & W. B. Gudykunst (Eds.), *Theories in intercultural communication* (pp. 125–128). Newbury Park, CA: Sage.

Gudykunst, W. B. (1993). Toward a theory of effective interpersonal and intergroup communication: An anxiety/uncertainty management (AUM) perspective. In R. L. Wiseman & J. Koester (Eds.), *Intercultural communication competence* (pp. 33–71). Thousand Oaks, CA: Sage.

Gudykunst, W. B. (1995). Anxiety/uncertainty management (AUM) theory: Current status. In R. L. Wiseman (Ed.), *Intercultural communication theory* (pp. 8–58). Newbury Park, CA: Sage.

Gudykunst, W. B. (2001). *Asian American ethnicity and communication.* Thousand Oaks, CA: Sage.

Gudykunst, W. B. (2005). An anxiety/uncertainty management (AUM) theory of effective communication: Making the mesh of the net finer. In W. B. Gudykunst

(Ed.), *Theorizing about intercultural communication* (pp. 281–322). Thousand Oaks, CA: Sage.

Gudykunst, W. B., & Hammer, M. (1988). The influence of social identity and intimacy of interethnic relationships on uncertainty reduction processes. *Human Communication Research, 14,* 569–601.

Gudykunst, W. B., & Kim, Y. Y. (1992). *Communicating with strangers.* New York: McGraw-Hill.

Guerrero, L. K., & La Valley, A. G. (2006). Conflict, emotion, and communication. In J. Oetzel & S. Ting-Toomey (Eds.), *The Sage handbook of conflict and communication* (pp. 69–96). Thousand Oaks, CA: Sage.

Gumperz, J. J., & Cook-Gumperz, J. (1982). Introduction: Language and the communication of social identity. In J. J. Gumperz (Ed.), *Language and social identity* (pp. 1–21). New York: Cambridge University Press.

Gurin, P. (1999). The compelling need for diversity in education. *The University of Massachusetts Schools of Education Journal, 3,* 36–62.

Gurung, R. A. R., & Duong, T. (1999). Mixing and matching: Assessing the concomitants of mixed-ethnic relationships. *Journal of Social and Personal Relationships, 16*(5), 639–657.

Guthrie, P. (1995). The impact of perceptions on interpersonal interactions in an African American/Asian American housing project. *Journal of Black Studies, 25*(30), 377–395.

Gutierrez, F. (1980, May). *Latinos and the media in the United States: An overview.* Paper presented at the annual meeting of the International Communication Association, Acapulco, Mexico.

Gwartney-Gibbs, P. A., & Lach, D. H. (1991). Research report: Workplace dispute resolution and gender inequality. *Negotiation Journal, 7,* 1–9.

Habke, A., & Sept, R. (1993). Distinguishing group and cultural influences in inter-ethnic conflict: A diagnostic model. *Canadian Journal of Communication, 18,* 415–436.

Hacker, A. (1992). *Two nations: African American and White, separate, hostile, unequal.* New York: Ballantine.

Hadley-Garcia, G. (1990). *Hispanic Hollywood: The Latins in motion pictures.* New York: Citadel Press.

Hajek, C., & Giles, H. (2002). The old man out: An intergroup analysis of international communication among gay men. *Journal of Communication, 52*(4), 698–714.

Hale-Bensen, J. E. (1986). *Black children: Their roots, culture, and learning styles.* Baltimore, MD: Johns Hopkins University Press.

Hall, C. C. I. (1980). *The ethnic identity of racially mixed people: A study of Black-Japanese.* Unpublished manuscript.

Hall, E. T. (1959). *The silent language.* New York: Doubleday.

Hall, E. T. (1966). *The hidden dimension.* New York: Doubleday.

Hallinan, M. T., & Williams, R. A. (1987). The stability of students interracial friendships. *American Sociological Review, 52,* 653–664.

Hallinan, M. T., & Williams, R. A. (1989). Interracial friendship choices in secondary schools. *American Sociological Review, 54,* 67–78.

Halualani, R. T. (1998). Seeing through the screen: "A struggle of culture." In J. N. Martin, T. K. Nakayama, & L. A. Flores (Eds.), *Readings in cultural contexts* (pp. 264–274). Mountain View, CA: Mayfield.

Halualani, R. T., Chitgopekar, A. S., Morrison, J. H. T. A., & Dodge, P. S.-W. (2004). Diverse in name only? Intercultural interaction at a multicultural university. *Journal of Communication, 54*(2), 270–286.

Hamlet, J. D. (1997). Understanding traditional African American preaching. In A. Gonzalez, M. Houston, & V. Chen (Eds.), *Our voices: Essays in culture, ethnicity, and communication* (pp. 94–98). Los Angeles: Roxbury.

Hamm, J. V., Brown, B. B., & Heck, D. J. (2005). Bridging the ethnic divide: Student and school characteristics in African American, Asian-descent, Latino, and White adolescents' cross-ethnic friend nominations. *Journal of Research on Adolescence, 15*(1), 21–46.

Hamri, S. (Director), & Turner, K. (Writer). (2006). *Something new* [Motion picture]. United States: Gramercy Pictures & Homegrown Pictures.

Haraway, D. (1988). Situated knowledges: The science question in feminism and the privilege of partial perspective. *Signs, 14,* 575–599.

Hardiman, R. (1994). White racial identity development in the United States. In E. P. Salett & D. R. Koslow (Eds.), *Race, ethnicity, and self: Identity in multicultural perspective* (pp. 117–142). Washington, DC: National Multicultural Institute.

Harding, S. (Ed.). (1987). *Feminism & methodology.* Bloomington: Indiana University Press.

Harding, S. (1991). *Whose science? Whose knowledge? Thinking from women's lives.* Ithaca, NY: Cornell University Press.

Harris, D. R., & Sim, J. J. (2001). *An empirical look at the social construction of race: The case of multiracial adolescents* (Research Report No. 00–452). Ann Arbor: University of Michigan, Population Studies Center.

Harris, M. (1964). *Patterns of race in the Americas.* New York: Norton.

Harris, T. M. (1997). *Black sitcoms of the 1990's: Friend or foe?* Paper presented at the conference "Situating the comedy: Celebrating 50 years of American television situation comedy, 1947–1997," Bowling Green, OH.

Harris, T. M. (2001). Student reactions to the visual texts "the color of fear" and "rosewood" in the interracial classroom. *Howard Journal of Communications, 12*(2), 101–117.

Harris, T. M. (2004). "I know it was the blood": Defining the biracial self in a Euro-American society. In A. Gonzalez, M. Houston, & V. Chen (Eds.), *Our voices: Essays in culture, ethnicity, and communication* (pp. 203–209). Los Angeles, CA: Roxbury.

Harris, T. M., & Donmoyer, D. (2000). Is art imitating life? The construction of gender and racial identity in imitation of life. *Women's Studies in Communication, 23*(1), 91–110.

Harris, T. M., & Hill, P. S. (1998). "Waiting to exhale" or "breath(ing) again": A search for identity, empowerment, and love in the 1990s. *Women & Language, 11*(2), 9–20.

Harris, T. M., & Kalbfleisch, P. (2000). Interracial dating: The implications for race in initiating a romantic relationship. *Howard Journal of Communications, 11*(1), 49–64.

Harter, L. M., Scott, J. A., Novak, D. R., Leeman, M., & Morris, J. F. (2006). Freedom through flight: Performing a counter-narrative of disability. *Journal of Applied Communication, 34*(1), 3–29.

Hartigan, J., Jr. (2003). Who are these white people? "Rednecks," "hillbillies," and "white trash" as marked racial subjects. In A. W. Doane & E. Bonilla-Silva (Eds.), *White out: The continuing significance of racism* (pp. 95–111). New York: Routledge.

Hartsock, N. C. M. (1983). The feminist standpoint: Developing the ground for a specifically feminist historical materialism. In S. Harding & M. D. Hintikka (Eds.), *Discovering reality: Feminist perspectives on epistemology, metaphysics, methodology, and philosophy of science* (pp. 283–310). Boston: D. Reidel.

Hartz, P. (2002). *Baha'i faith: World religions.* New York: Facts on File.

Harwood, J., Soliz, J., & Lin, M.-C. (2006). Communication accommodation theory: An intergroup approach to family relationships. In D. O. Braithwaite & L. A. Baxter (Eds.), *Engaging theories in family communication: Multiple perspectives* (pp. 19–34). Thousand Oaks, CA: Sage.

Hasian, M., & Delgado, F. (1998). The trials and tribulations of racialized critical rhetorical theory: Understanding the rhetorical ambiguities of Proposition 187. *Communication Theory, 8*(3), 245–270.

Hass, N. (1988, March 12). Black and white. *Kalamazoo (MI) Gazette,* pp. D1, D3.

Hatch, J. B. (2003). Reconciliation: Building a bridge from complicity to coherence in the rhetoric of race relations. *Rhetoric & Public Affairs, 6*(4), 737–764.

Hawkins, P. (1997, April). Organizational culture: Sailing between evangelism and complexity. *Human Relations, 50*(4), 417–440.

Hayman, R. L., Jr., & Levit, N. (1997). The constitutional ghetto. In R. Delgado & J. Stefancie (Eds.), *Critical White studies: Looking behind the mirror* (pp. 239–247). Philadelphia: Temple University Press.

Hean, S. & Dickinson, C. (1995). The contact hypothesis: An exploration of its further potential in interprofessional education. *Journal of Interprofessional Care, 19*(5), 480–491.

Heaton, T. B., & Albrecht, S. L. (1996). The changing pattern of interracial marriage. *Social Biology, 43*(3–4), 203–217.

Hecht, M. L., Collier, M. J., & Ribeau, S. A. (1993). *African American communication: Ethnic identity and cultural interpretation.* Newbury Park, CA: Sage.

Hecht, M. L., Faulkner, S. L., Meyer, C. R., Niles, T. A., Golden, D., & Cutler, M. (2002). Looking through *Northern Exposure* at Jewish American identity and the communication theory of identity. *Journal of Communication, 52*, 852–870.

Hecht, M. L., Jackson, R. L., II, & Ribeau, S. (2003). *African American communication: Exploring identity and culture* (2nd ed.). Mahwah, NJ: Lawrence Erlbaum.

Hecht, M. L., Larkey, L. K., & Johnson, J. N. (1992). African American and European American perceptions of problematic issues in interethnic communication effectiveness. *Human Communication Research, 19*, 209–236.

Hecht, M. L., & Ribeau, S. A. (1984). Ethnic communication: A comparative analysis of satisfying communication. *International Journal of Intercultural Relations, 8*, 135–151.

Hecht, M. L., Ribeau, S. A., & Alberts, J. K. (1989). An Afro-American perspective on interethnic communication. *Communication Monographs, 56*, 385–410.

Hecht, M. L., Ribeau, S. A., & Sedano, M. V. (1990). A Mexican American perspective on interethnic communication. *International Journal of Intercultural Relations, 14*, 31–55.

Hecht, M. L., Trost, M., Bator, R., & McKinnon, D. (1997). Ethnicity and gender similarities and differences in drug resistance. *Journal of Applied Communication Research, 25*, 75–97.

Hecht, M. L., Warren, J. R., Jung, E., & Krieger, J. L. (2005). The communication theory of identity: Development, theoretical perspective, and future directions. In W. B. Gudykunst (Ed.), *Theorizing about intercultural communication* (pp. 257–278). Thousand Oaks, CA: Sage.

Hegde, R. S. (1998). Swinging the trapeze: The negotiation of identity among Asian Indian immigrant women in the United States. In D. V. Tanno & A. Gonzalez (Eds.), *Communication and identity across cultures* (pp. 34–55). Thousand Oaks, CA: Sage.

Heidegger, M. (1962). *Being and time* (J. Macquarrie & E. Robinson, Trans.). New York: Harper.

Heilbron, C. L., & Guttman, M. A. (2000). Traditional healing methods with First Nations women in group counseling. *Canadian Journal of Counseling, 34*, 3–13.

Heller, S. (1991, November 27). Frame-up of multicultural movement dissected by scholars and journalists. *Chronicle of Higher Education*, pp. A15–A16.

Helms, J. E. (1990). *Black and White racial identity: Theory, research, and practice*. Greenwich, CT: Greenwood Press.

Helms, J. E. (1994). *A race is a nice thing to have: A guide to being a White person or understanding the White persons in your life*. Topeka, KS: Content Communications.

Helms, J. E., Malone, L. S., Henze, K., Satiani, A., Perry, J. & Warren, A. (2003). First annual Diversity challenge: "How to survive teaching courses on race and culture." *Multicultural Counseling and Development, 31*, 3–11.

Henderson, C. (2001). *2001 college freshmen with disabilities: A biennial statistical profile* [Electronic version]. Washington, DC: Health Resource Center, American Council on Education.

Herek, G. M. (2000). Sexual prejudice and gender: Do heterosexuals' attitudes toward lesbians and gay men differ? *Journal of Social Issues, 56*, 251–266.

Herring, R. D. (1994). Native American Indian identity: A people of many peoples. In E. P. Salett & D. R. Koslow (Eds.), *Race, ethnicity, and self: Identity in multicultural perspective* (pp. 170–197). Washington, DC: MultiCultural Institute.

Herrnstein, R. J., & Murray C. (1994). *The bell curve: Intelligence and class structure in American life*. New York: Free Press.

Heuterman, T. (1987). "We have the same rights as other citizens": Coverage of Yakima Valley Japanese Americans in the "missing decades" of the 1920s and 1930s. *Journalism History, 14*, 94–102.

Hewstone, M., & Brown, R. (1986). Contact is not enough: An intergroup perspective on the "contact hypothesis." In M. Hewstone, & R. Brown (Eds.), *Contact and conflict in intergroup encounters* (pp. 1–44). Oxford: Blackwell.

Hewstone, M., & Giles, H. (1986). Social groups and social stereotypes in intergroup communication: Review and model of intergroup communication breakdown. In W. B. Gudykunst (Ed.), *Intergroup communication* (pp. 10–26). London: Edward Arnold.

Hildebrandt, N., & Giles, H. (1984). The Japanese as subordinate group: Ethnolinguistics identity theory in a foreign language context. *Anthropological Linguistics, 25*, 436–466.

Hocker, J. L., & Wilmont, W. W. (1995). *Interpersonal conflict*. Dubuque, IA: Wm C. Brown.

Hodge, J. L. (1989). Domination and the will in Western thought and culture. In C. E. Jackson & E. J. Tolbert (Eds.), *Race and culture in America: Readings in racial and ethnic relations* (pp. 27–48). Edina, MN: Burgess.

Hoetink, H. (1967). *Caribbean race relations: A study of two variants*. New York: Oxford University Press.

Hofman, J. E. (1985). Arabs and Jews, Black and Whites: Identity and group relations. *Journal of Multilingual and Multicultural Development, 6*, 217–237.

Hoijer, H. (1994). The Sapir-Whorf hypothesis. In L. A. Samovar & R. E. Porter (Eds.), *Intercultural communication: A reader* (7th ed., pp. 194–200). Belmont, CA: Wadsworth.

Holloway, J. E. (Ed.). (1990). *Africanisms in American culture*. Bloomington: Indiana University Press.

hooks, b. (1992). *Black looks: Race and representation*. Boston: South End Press.

Horno-Delgado, A., Ortega, E., Scott, N. M., & Stembach, M. C. (Eds.). (1989). *Breaking boundaries: Latina writing and critical readiness*. Amherst: University of Massachusetts Press.

Houston, M. (1997). When Black women talk with White women: Why dialogues are difficult. In A. Gonzalez, M. Houston, & V. Chen (Eds.), *Our voices: Essays in culture, ethnicity, and communication* (pp. 187–194). Los Angeles: Roxbury.

Houston, M. (2000). Writing for my life: Community-cognizant scholarship on African American women and communication. *International Journal of Intercultural Relations, 24*, 673–686.

Houston, M. (2002). Seeking difference: African Americans in interpersonal communication research, 1975–2000. *Howard Journal of Communications, 13*, 25–41.

Houston, M. (2004). When Black women talk with White women: Why dialogues are difficult. In A. Gonzalez, M. Houston, & V. Chen (Eds.), *Our voices: Essays in culture, ethnicity, and communication* (pp. 119–125). Los Angeles: Roxbury.

Houston, M., & Wood, J. T. (1996). Difficult dialogues, expanded horizons: Communicating across race and class. In J. T. Wood (Ed.), *Gendered relationships* (pp. 39–56). Mountain View, CA: Mayfield.

Hout, M., & Goldstein, J. (1994). How 4.5 million Irish immigrants became 40 million Irish Americans: Demographic and subjective aspects of the ethnic composition of White Americans. *American Sociological Review, 59*, 64–82.

Howard, A. (1980). Hawaiians. In S. Thernstorm (Ed.), *Harvard encyclopedia of American ethnic groups* (pp. 449–452). Cambridge, MA: Harvard University Press.

Howell, W. S. (1982). *The empathic communicator*. Belmont, CA: Wadsworth.

Hughes, M., & Tuch, S. A. (2003). Gender differences in whites' racial attitudes: Are women's attitudes really more favorable? *Social Psychology Quarterly, 67*, 384–401.

Hummert, M. L., Wiemann. J. M., & Nussbaum, J. F. (1994). *Interpersonal communication in older adulthood:*

Interdisciplinary theory and research. Newbury Park, CA: Sage.

Huntington, S. P. (2005). Hispanic immigration threatens to divide America. In J. D. Toor (Ed.), *Race relations: Opposing viewpoints* (pp. 62–79). New York: Greenhaven Press.

Hurtado. S. (1992). The campus racial climate. *Journal of Higher Education, 63*(5), 539–566.

Hymes, D. (1974). *Foundations in sociolinguistics: An ethnographic approach.* Philadelphia: University of Pennsylvania Press.

Infante, D. A., Rancer, A. S., & Womack, D. F. (1990). *Building communication theory.* Prospect Heights, IL: Waveland Press.

Inniss, L. B., & Feagin, J. (1995). *The Cosby Show:* The view from the Black middle class. *Journal of Black Studies, 25*(6), 692–711,

Jaasma, M. A. (2002). Friendship: The core value of sixth graders engaged in interethnic encounters. *Communication Education, 51*(2), 152–167.

Jackson, B. W., & Hardiman, R. (1983). Racial identity development. *The NTL Managers' Handbook, 13*(2), 107–119.

Jackson, C. E., & Tolbert, E. J. (Eds.). (1989). *Race and culture in America: Readings in racial and ethnic relations.* Edina, MN: Burgess.

Jackson, L. A., Sullivan, L. A., & Hodge, C. N. (1993). Stereotype effects on attributions, predictions, and evaluations: No two social judgments. *Journal of Personality and Social Psychology, 65*(1), 69–84.

Jackson, R. L. (2000). So real illusions of black intellectualism: Exploring race, roles, and gender in the academy. *Communication Theory, 10*, 48–63.

Jackson, R. L. (2006). *Scripting the black masculine body: Identity, discourse, and racial politics in popular media.* Albany: State University of New York Press.

Jacobs, J. H. (1992). Identity development in biracial children. In M. P. P. Root (Ed.), *Racially mixed people in America* (pp. 190–206). Newbury Park, CA: Sage.

Jacobs, J. J., & Furstenberg, F. F. (1986). Changing places, conjugal careers, and women's marital mobility. *Social Forces, 64,* 714–732.

Jacoby, T. (2006, April 16). *Illegal immigration: A border is crossed.* Retrieved March 9, 2007, from http://www .ocregister.com/ocregister/opinion/homepage/arti cle_1103566.php

James, A. D., & Tucker, M. B. (2003). Racial ambiguity and relationship formation in the United States: Theoretical and practical considerations. *Journal of Social and Personal Relationships, 20*(2), 153–169.

James, N. C. (1997). Classroom climate and teaching (about) racism: Notes from the trenches. In A. Arseneau Jones & S. P. Morreate (Eds.), *Proceedings of the National Communication Association Summer Conference on Racial and Ethnic Diversity in the 21st Century* (pp. 195–201). Annandale, VA: National Communication Association.

James, N. C. (2004). When Miss America was always white. In A. Gonzalez, M. Houston, & V. Chen (Eds.), *Our voices: Essays in culture, ethnicity, and communication* (pp. 61–65). Los Angeles, CA: Roxbury.

Jeanquart-Barone, S. (1993). Trust differences between supervisors and subordinates: Examining the role of race and gender. *Sex Roles, 29*(1–2), 1–11.

Jeter, K. (1982). Analytic essay: Intercultural and interracial marriage. *Marriage and Family Review, 5,* 105–111.

Jhally, S., & Lewis, J. (1992). *Enlightened racism:* The Cosby Show, *audiences, and the myth of the American dream.* San Francisco: Westview Press.

Jiobu, R. M. (1988). *Ethnicity and assimilation.* Albany: State University of New York Press.

Jo, M. H. (1992). Korean merchants in the black community: Prejudice among victims of prejudice. *Ethnic and Racial Studies, 15,* 395–411.

Johannesen, R. L. (1971). The emerging concept of communication as dialogue. *Quarterly Journal of Speech, 57,* 373–382.

Johnson, E. P., & Henderson, M. G. (Eds.). (2005). *Black queer studies: A critical anthology.* Durham, NC: Duke University Press.

Johnson, P. C. (1999). Reflections on critical White(ness) studies. In T. K. Nakayama & J. N. Martin (Eds.), *Whiteness: The communication of social identity* (pp. 1–12). Thousand Oaks, CA: Sage.

Johnson, R. A. (1980). *Religious assortative marriage in the United States.* New York: Academic Press.

Jones, J. M. (1972). *Prejudice and racism.* Reading, MA: Addison-Wesley.

Jordan, K. (1998). Diversity training in the workplace today: A status report. *Journal of Career Planning and Employment, 59*(1), 46–51.

Jung, E., & Hecht, M. L. (2004). Elaborating the communication theory of identity: Identity gaps and communication outcomes. *Communication Quarterly, 52,* 265–283.

Kagan, S., Knight, G., & Martinez-Romero, S. (1982). Culture and the development of conflict resolution style. *Journal of Cross-Cultural Psychology, 13,* 43–59.

Kalish, R. (1979). The new ageism and the failure models: A polemic. *The Gerontologist, 19,* 398–402.

Kalmijn M. (1993). Trends in Black/White in intermarriage. *Social Forces, 72,* 119–146.

Kalmijn, M. (1998). Intermarriage and homogany: Causes, patterns, trends. *Annual Review of Sociology, 24,* 395–421.

Kamalipour, R., & Carilli, T. (Eds.). (1998). *Cultural diversity in the U.S. media.* Albany: State University of New York Press.

Kampeas, R. (2001, March 30). Que significa ser Hispanamericano? *Kalamazoo (MI) Gazette*, p. C1.

Kang, J. (2003). Ruminations on cyber-race. *Dissent, 50*(2), 58–63.

Kathman, J. M., & Kathman, M. D. (1998). What difference does diversity make in managing student employees? *College & Research Libraries, 59*(4), 378–389.

Kautzer, K. (1986). Growing numbers, growing force: Older women organize. In R. Lefkowitz & A. Withorn (Eds.), *For crying out loud: Women and poverty in the United States* (pp. 89–98). Cleveland: Pilgrim Press.

Kay, P., & Kempton, W. (1984). What is the Sapir-Whorf hypothesis? *American Anthropologist, 86*, 65–73.

Keep America's gates open. (2001, November 19). *Business Week*, p. 72.

Kellner, D. (1995). *Media culture*. New York: Routledge.

Kellner, O. D. (1994). *Hispanics and United States film: An overview and handbook*. Tempe, AZ: Bilingual Review/Press.

Kennedy, R. J. R. (1944). Single or triple melting pot? Intermarriage trends in New Haven, 1870–1940. *American Journal of Sociology, 49*, 331–339.

Kenyatta, K. (1998). *Guide to implementing Afrikan-centered education*. Detroit, MI: Afrikan Way Investments.

Kich, G. K. (1992). The developmental process of asserting a biracial, bicultural identity. In M. P. P. Root (Ed.), *Racially mixed people in America* (pp. 304–317). Newbury Park, CA: Sage.

Kilman, N. (2005, April 14). Native American TV to fight stereotypes. Retrieved October 2, 2006, from http://www.tolerance.org/news/article_print.jsp?id=1198

Kim, M.-S., & Leung, T. (2000). A multicultural view of conflict management styles: Review and critical synthesis. *Communication Yearbook, 23*, 227–269.

Kim, W. (2006, July/August). Asian Americans are at the head of the class. *DiversityInc*, pp. 40–43.

Kim, Y. Y. (1988). *Communication and cross-cultural adaptation*. Philadelphia: Multilingual Matters LTD.

Kim, Y. Y. (1994). Interethnic communication: The context and the behavior. *Communication Yearbook, 17*, 511–538.

Kim, Y. Y. (1995). Cross-cultural adaptation: An integrative theory. In R. L. Wiseman (Ed.), *Intercultural communication theory* (pp. 170–193). Thousand Oaks, CA: Sage.

Kim, Y. Y. (2001). *Becoming intercultural: An integrative theory of communication and cross-cultural adaptation*. Thousand Oaks, CA: Sage.

Kim, Y. Y. (2005). Adapting to a new culture: An integrative communication theory. In W. B. Gudykunst (Ed.), *Theorizing about intercultural communication* (pp. 375–400). Thousand Oaks, CA: Sage.

Kitano, H. H. L. (1991). *Race relations*. Englewood Cliffs, NJ: Prentice Hall.

Kitayama, S., Markus, H. R., Matsumoto, H., & Norasakkunkit, V. (1997). Individual and collective processes in the construction of self: Self-enhancement in the United States and self-criticism in Japan. *Journal of Personality and Social Psychology, 72*, 1245–1267.

Kitman, M. (1998). *"Trinity" shines through Irish stereotypes*. Retrieved October 8, 2006, from http://www.moirakelly.net/Articles/irish.htm

Kivisto, P. (2001). Theorizing transnational immigration: A critical review of current efforts. *Ethnic and Racial Studies, 24*(4), 549–577.

Knapp, M. (1973). Dyadic relationship development. In J. Wiemann & R. Harrison (Eds.), *Nonverbal interaction* (pp. 102–118). Beverly Hills, CA: Sage.

Knox, D. L., Zusman, M. E., Buffington, C., & Hemphill, G. (2000). Interracial dating attitudes among college students. *College Student Journal, 34*(1), 69–71.

Kochman, T. (1981). *Black and white styles in conflict*. Chicago, IL: University of Chicago Press.

Kochman, T. (1990). Cultural pluralism: Black and white styles. In D. Carbaugh (Ed.), *Cultural communication and intercultural contact* (pp. 219–224). Hillsdale, NJ: Lawrence Erlbaum.

Kohatsu, E. L., Dulay, M., Lam, C., Concepcion, W., Perez, P., Lopez, C., et al. (2000, Summer). Using racial identity theory to explore racial mistrust and interracial contact among Asian Americans. *Journal of Counseling & Development, 78*(3), 334–342.

Korgen, K., Mahon, J., & Wang, G. (2003). Diversity on college campus today: The growing need to foster campus environments capable of countering a possible "tipping effect." *College Student Journal, 37*(1). 16–26.

Kouri, K. M., & Lasswell, M. (1993). Black-White marriages: Social change and intergenerational mobility. *Marriage and Family Review, 19*(3–4), 241–255.

Kramarae, C. (1981). *Women and men speaking*. Rowley, MA: Newbury.

Kreps, G. L., Frey, L., & O'Hair, D. (1991). Applied communication research: Scholarship that can make a difference. *Journal of Applied Communication Research, 19* (1, 2), 71–87.

Krupansky, J. (1995, July/August). Clips. *Out*, p. 20.

Kuhn, M. H., & McPartland, T. S. (1954). An empirical investigation of self-attitudes. *American Sociological Review, 19*, 68–76.

Laabs, J. J. (1993, December). Employees manage conflict and diversity. *Personnel Journal*, pp. 30–33.

Labov, W. (1972). *Sociolinguistics patterns*. Philadelphia: University of Pennsylvania Press.

La Feria, R. (2004, January 4). Advertisers and Hollywood highlight the ethnically ambiguous. *New York Times*, p. E4.

Lahiry, S. (1994). Building commitment through organizational culture. *Training and Development, 48*(4), 50–52.

Langston, D. (1995). Tired of playing monopoly? In M. L. Andersen & P. H. Collins (Eds.), *Race, class, and gender: An anthology* (pp. 100–109). Belmont, CA: Wadsworth.

Larkey, L. K., & Hecht, M. L. (1995). A comparative study of African American and European American ethnic identity. *International Journal of Intercultural Relations, 19*(4), 483–504.

Larkey, L. K., Hecht, M. L., & Martin, J. N. (1993). What's in a name? African American ethnic identity terms and self-determination. *Journal of Language and Social Psychology, 12*, 302–317.

Larsen, L. J. (2004). *The foreign-born population in the United States: 2003. Current population reports.* Washington, DC: U.S. Census Bureau.

Lasker, G. W., & Tyzzer, R. N. (1982). *Physical anthropology.* New York: Holt.

Lawhon, T. (1997, Summer). Encouraging friendships among children. *Childhood Education, 73* (4), 228–231.

Lazerwitz, B. (1995). Jewish-Christian marriages and conversions, 1971 and 1990. *Sociology of Religion, 56*, 433–443.

LeCroy, C. (1988). Parent–adolescent intimacy: Impact on adolescent functioning. *Adolescence, 23*(89), 137–147.

Lee, H., & Rogan, R. (1991). A cross-cultural comparison of organizational conflict management behaviors. *International Journal of Conflict Management, 2*, 181–199.

Lee, J., & Zhou, M. (Eds.). (2004). *Asian American youth: Culture, identity, and ethnicity.* New York: Routledge.

Lee, S. (Writer/Director). (1991). *Jungle fever* [Motion picture]. United States: Universal Pictures.

Lee, S. M., & Edmonston, B. (2005). New marriages, new families: U.S. racial and Hispanic intermarriage. *Population Bulletin, 60*(2), 1–36.

Lee, S. M., & Fernandez, M. (1998). Trends in Asian American racial/ethnic intermarriage: A comparison of 1980 and 1990 census data. *Sociological Perspectives, 41*(2), 323–343.

Lee, W. S. (1993). Social scientists as ideological critics. *Western Journal of Communication, 57*, 221–232.

Leff, A., & Penn, Z. (1994, April 29). Puncturing political correctness. *USA Weekend Magazine*, p. 16.

Lehmiller, J. J., & Agnew, C. R. (2006). Marginalized relationships: The impact of social disapproval on romantic relationship commitment. *Personality and Social Psychology Bulletin, 32*(1), 40–51.

Leigh, P. R. (1997). Segregation by gerrymander: The creation of the Lincoln Heights (Ohio) school district. *Journal of Negro Education, 66*(2), 121–136.

Leonard, R., & Locke, D. C. (1993). Communication stereotypes: Is interracial communication possible? *Journal of Black Studies, 22*(3), 332–343.

Leslie, K. B., & Orbe, M. (1997, November). *"Medical crisis" and "miracle? A phenomenological inquiry of transplant recipient communication.* Paper presented at the annual meeting of the National Communication Association, Chicago.

Leung, K., Au, Y-F., Fernandez-Dols, J. M., & Iwawaki, S. (1992). Preference for methods of conflict processing in two collectivistic cultures. *International Journal of Psychology, 27*, 195–209.

Leveen, L. (1996). Only when I laugh: textual dynamics of ethnic humor. *Melus, 21*(4), 29–55.

Levin, J., & Levin, W. C. (1980). *Ageism: Prejudice and discrimination against the elderly.* Belmont, CA: Wadsworth.

Lewis, B. (1998). Diversity training should focus on appreciating different perspectives. *InfoWorld, 20*(20), 110.

Lian, K. F. (1982). Identity in minority group relations. *Ethnic and Racial Studies, 5*, 42–52.

Lichter, S. R., Lichter, L. S. Rothman, S., & Amundson, D. (1987, July/August). Prime-time prejudice: TV's images of blacks and Hispanics. *Public Opinion*, pp. 13–16.

Lieberson, S. (1963). *Ethnic patterns in American cities.* New York: Free Press of Glencoe.

Lind, A. H. (1980). *Hawaii's people* (4th ed.). Honolulu: University Press of Hawaii.

Linnehan, F., Chrobot-Mason, D., & Konrad, A. (2006). Diversity attitudes and norms: The role of ethnic identity and relational demography. *Journal of Organizational Behavior, 27*, 419–442.

Lobe, J. (2005, July 21). Interracial marriages on the increase. *New York Amsterdam News, 96*(30), 32.

Lopez, I. F. H. (1997). *White by law: The legal construction of race.* New York: New York University Press.

Lovaas, K. E., & Jenkins, M. M. (Eds.). (2006). *Sexualities and communication in everyday life: A reader.* Thousand Oaks, CA: Sage.

Lorde, A. (1984). *Sister outsider.* Freedom, CA: Crossing Press.

Lozano, E. (1997). The cultural experience of space and body: A reading of Latin American and Anglo American comportment in public. In A. Gonzalez, M. Houston, & V. Chen (Eds.), *Our voices: Essays in culture, ethnicity, and communication* (pp. 195–202). Los Angeles: Roxbury.

Lui, M., Robles, B. J., Leondar-Wright, B., Brewer, R. M., & Adamson, R. (2006). *The color of wealth: The story behind the U.S. racial wealth divide.* New York: New Press.

Luna, A. (1989). Gay racism. In M. S. Kimmel and M. A. Messner (Eds.), *Men's lives* (pp. 440–447). New York: Macmillan.

Lundy, B., Field, T., McBride, C., Field, T., & Largie, S. (1998). Same-sex and opposite-sex best friend interactions among high school juniors and seniors. *Adolescence, 33*(130), 279–290.

MacDonald, J. F. (1992). *Black and white TV: Afro-Americans in television since 1948.* Chicago: Nelson-Hall.

MacIntyre, P. D., & MacDonald, J. R. (1998). Public speaking anxiety: Perceived competence and audience congeniality. *Communication Education, 47*(4), 359–365.

Mackenzie, G. (1991, September 4). Fallacies of PC. *Chronicle of Higher Education,* pp. B1–B2.

Mahalingam, R. (2006). Cultural psychology of immigrants: An introduction. In R. Mahalingam (Ed.), *Cultural psychology of immigrants* (pp. 1–12). Mahwah, NJ: Lawrence Erlbaum.

Mallinson, C., & Brewster, Z. W. (2005). "Blacks and bubbas": Stereotypes, ideology, and categorization processes in restaurant servers' discourse. *Discourse & Society, 16*(6), 787–807.

Maloney, B. (2006, August 1). *Mitt to be tied: With latest campaign controversy, some smell a rat.* Retrieved November 21, 2006, from http://radioequalizer.blogspot.com/2006/08/mittromney-talk-radio-tar-baby-remark.html

Maltz, D., & Borker, R. (1982). A cultural approach to male-female miscommunication. In J. J. Gumperz (Ed.), *Language and social identity* (pp. 196–216). Cambridge: Cambridge University Press.

Maly, M. T. (2005). *Beyond segregation: Multiracial and multiethnic neighborhoods in the United States.* Philadelphia, PA: Temple University Press.

Mandelbaum, D. G. (Ed.). (1949). *Selected writings of Edward Sapir.* Los Angeles: University of California Press.

Marable, M. (1997, March 6). What's in a name: African American or multiracial? *Black Issues in Higher Education,* p. 112.

Marable, M. (2005). White denial of racial issues contributes to poor race relations. In J. D. Toor (Ed.), *Race relations: Opposing viewpoints* (pp. 56–61). New York: Greenhaven Press.

Márquez, L. (2004, Dec. 14). UCLA Chicano studies research center study finds many TV series set in diverse cities, yet feature few minority regular characters. Retrieved November 23, 2006, from http://www.chicano.ucla.edu/press/reports/current.html

Marrow, L. (1995, October 9). O. J. and race: Will the verdict split America? *Time,* p. 28.

Marsiglia, F. F., & Hecht, M. L. (1999). The story of Sara: Raising a Jewish child around the Christmas tree. In D. O. Braithwaite & J. T. Woods (Eds.), *Case studies in interpersonal communication processes and problems* (pp. 44–51). Belmont, CA: Thomson Learning.

Marsiglia, F. F., Kulis, S., & Hecht, M. L. (2001). Ethnic labels and ethnic identity as predictors of drug use and drug exposure among middle school students in the Southwest. *Journal of Research on Adolescence, 11,* 21–48.

Martin, J. N., Hecht, M. L., & Larkey, L. K. (1994). Conversational improvement strategies for interethnic communication: African American and European American perspectives. *Communication Monographs, 61,* 236–255.

Martin, J. N., Krizek, R. L., Nakayama, T. K., & Brodford, L. (1996). Exploring Whiteness: A study of self labels for White Americans *Communication Quarterly, 44,* 125–144.

Martin, J. N., & Nakayama, T. K. (1997). *Intercultural communication in contexts.* Mountain View, CA: Mayfield.

Martin, J. N., & Nakayama, T. K. (1999). Thinking dialectically about culture and communication. *Communication Theory, 9*(1), 1–25.

Martindale, C. (1997). Only in glimpses: Portrayal of America's largest minority groups by The New York Times, 1934–1994. In S. Biagi & M. Kem-Foxworth (Eds.), *Facing difference: Race, gender, and mass media* (pp. 89–94). Thousand Oaks, CA: Pine Forge Press.

Mastro, D. E., & Behm-Morawitz, E. (2005). Latino representation on primetime television. *Journalism & Mass Communication Quarterly, 82*(1), 110–130.

Mastro, D. E., & Stern, S. R. (2003). Representations of race in television commercials: A content analysis of prime-time advertising, *Journal of Broadcasting & Electronic Media, 47*(4), 638–647.

Matsuda, M. J., Lawrence, C. R., Delgado, R., & Crenshaw, K. W. (Eds.). (1993). *Words that wound: Critical race theory, assaultive speech, and the First Amendment.* San Francisco: Westview Press.

Mayall, A., & Russell, D. E. H. (1995). Racism in pornography. In G. Dines & J. M. Humez (Eds.), *Gender, race, and class in media* (pp. 287–297). Thousand Oaks, CA: Sage.

McAllister, G., & Irvine, J. (2000). Cross-cultural competency and multicultural communication. *Review of Educational Research, 70,* 3–24.

McCall, G. J., & Simmons, J. L. (1978). *Identities and interaction* (Rev. ed.). New York: Free Press.

McCann, R. M., & Giles, H. (2002). Ageism and the workplace: A communication perspective. In T. D. Nelson (Ed.), *Ageism* (pp. 163–199). Cambridge, MA: MIT Press.

McCann, R. M., Kellerman, K., Giles, H., Gallois, C., & Viladot, M. A. (2004). Cultural and gender influences on age identification. *Communication Studies, 55*(1), 88–106.

McClenahan, C., Cairns, E., Dunn, S., & Morgan, V. (1996). Intergroup friendships: Integrated and desegregated schools in northern Ireland. *Journal of Social Psychology, 136*(5), 549–558.

McCutcheon, A. L. (1988). Denominations and religious intermarriage: Trends among White Americans in the twentieth century. *Review of Religion Research, 29,* 213–227.

McDonald, K. B. (2007). *Embracing sisterhood: Class, identity, and contemporary black women.* New York: Rowman & Littlefield Publishers.

McGreevy, J. T. (1996). *Parish boundaries: The Catholic encounter with race in the twentieth century urban North.* Chicago: University of Chicago Press.

McIntosh, P. (1992). White privilege and male privilege. In A. L. Andersen & P. H. Collins (Eds.), *Race, class, and gender: An anthology* (pp. 65–69). Belmont, CA: Wadsworth.

McIntosh, P. (1995a). White privilege and male privilege: A personal account of coming to see correspondences through work in women's studies. In M. L. Andersen & P. H. Collins (Eds.), *Race, class, and gender: An anthology* (pp. 78–86). Belmont, CA: Wadsworth.

McIntosh, P. (1995b). White privilege: Unpacking the invisible backpack. In A. Kesselman, L. D. McNair, & N. Schneidewind (Eds.), *Women, images, and realities: A multicultural anthology.* Mountain View, CA: Mayfield.

McIntosh, P. (2002). White privilege: Unpacking the invisible knapsack. In P. S. Rothenberg (Ed.), *White privilege: Writings on the other side of racism* (pp. 97–101). New York: Worth Publishers.

McKay, V. C. (2000). Understanding the co-culture of the elderly. In L. A. Samovar & R. E. Porter (Eds.), *Intercultural communication: A reader* (pp. 180–188). Belmont, CA: Wadsworth.

McKee, H. (2002). "Your views showed true ignorance!!!": (Mis)Communication in an online interracial discussion forum. *Computers & Composition, 19*(4), 411–434.

McKissack, F., Jr. (1997). The problem with black T.V. *Progressive, 61*(2), 38–40.

McLean, S. (1998). Minority representation and portrayal in modern newsprint cartoons. In Y. R. Kamalipour & T. Carilli (Eds.), *Cultural diversity in the U.S. media* (pp. 23–38). Albany: State University of New York Press.

McMahon, E. (1995). *What parish are you from? A Chicago Irish community and race relations.* Lexington: University Press of Kentucky.

McPhail, M. L. (1991). Complicity: The theory of negative difference. *Howard Journal of Communications, 3*(1&2), 1–13.

McPhail, M. L. (1994a). The politics of complicity: Second thoughts about social construction of racial equality. *Quarterly Journal of Speech, 80*(3), 343–357.

McPhail, M. L. (1994b). *The rhetoric of racism.* Lanham, MD: University Press of America.

McPhail, M. L. (1996a). Race and sex in black and white: Essence and ideology in the Spike Lee discourse. *Howard Journal of Communications, 7*(2), 127–138.

McPhail, M. L. (1996b). *Zen in the art of rhetoric: An inquiry into coherence.* Albany: State University of New York Press.

McPhail, M. L. (1998a). From complicity to coherence: Rereading the rhetoric of Afrocentricity. *Western Journal of Communication, 62,* 114–140.

McPhail, M. L. (1998b). Passionate intensity: Louis Farrakhan and the fallacies of racial reasoning. *Quarterly Journal of Speech, 84*(4), 416–429.

McPhail, M. L. (2002). *The rhetoric of racism revisited: Reparations of separation?* Lanham, MD: University Press of America.

Mead, G. H. (1934). *Mind, self, and society.* Chicago: University of Chicago Press.

Means Coleman, R. (2000). *African American viewers and the black situation comedy: Situating racial humor.* New York: Garland.

Means Coleman, R. (2003). Black sitcom portrayals. In G. Dines & J. M. Humez (Eds.), *Gender, race, and class in media: A text-reader* (2nd ed., pp. 79–88). Thousand Oaks, CA: Sage.

Meek, B. A. (2006). And the injun goes "how!": Representations of American Indian English in white public space. *Language in Society, 35,* 93–128.

Mehrabian, A. (1982). *Silent messages: Implicit communication of emotion and attitudes* (2nd ed.). Belmont, CA: Wadsworth.

Meltzer, B. N., & Petras, J. W. (1970). The Chicago and Iowa Schools of symbolic interactionism. In T. Shibutani (Ed.), *Human nature and collective behavior* (pp. 74–92). Englewood Cliffs, NJ: Prentice-Hall.

Melville, M. B. (1988). Hispanics: Race, class, or ethnicity? *Journal of Ethnic Studies, 16*(1), 67–84.

Méndez-Méndez, S., & Alverio, D. (2002). *Network brownout 2003: The portrayal of latinos in network television news.* Report prepared for the National Association of Hispanic Journalists.

Merrill, H. (2006). *An alliance of women: Immigration and the politics of race.* Minneapolis: University of Minnesota Press.

Merritt, B. (1991). Bill Cosby: TV auteur? *Journal of Popular Culture, 24*(4), 89–102.

Merskin, D. (1998). Sending up signals: A survey of Native American media use and representation in the mass media. *The Howard Journal of Communications, 9,* 333–345.

Merskin, D. (2001). Winnebagos, Cherokees, Apaches, and Dakotas: The persistence of stereotyping of American

Indians in American advertising brands. *The Howard Journal of Communications, 12,* 159–169.

Merskin, D. (2004). The construction of Arabs as enemies: Post–September 11 discourse of George W. Bush. *Mass Communication & Society, 7*(2), 157–175.

Merton, R. K. (1941). Intermarriage and the social structure. *Psychiatry, 4,* 361–374.

Messner, M. (1989). Sports and the politics of inequality. In M. S. Kimmel & M. A. Messner (Eds.), *Men's lives* (pp. 187–190). New York: Macmillan.

Metzger, J. G., Springston, J. K. (1992). The skillful, the loving, and the right: An analysis of ethical theories and an application to the treaty rights debate in Wisconsin. *Howard Journal of Communications, 4*(1&2), 75–91.

Milburn, T. (2002). Collaboration and the construction of Puerto Rican community. In T. McDonald, M. Orbe, & T. Ford-Ahmed (Eds.), *Building diverse communities: Applications of communication research* (pp. 289–306). Cresskill, NJ: Hampton Press.

Miller, A. N., & Harris, T. M. (2005). Communicating to develop white racial identity in an interracial communication class. *Communication Education, 54*(3), 223–242.

Miller, J. B. (2003). "Legal or illegal? Documented or undocumented?" The struggle over Brookhaven's Neighborhood Preservation Act. *Communication Quarterly, 51*(1), 73–85.

Miller, K. (1999). *Organizational communication: Approaches and processes* (2nd ed.). Belmont, CA: Wadsworth.

Miller, N. (2002). Personalization and the promise of contact theory. *Journal of Social Issues, 58*(2), 387–410.

Miller, R. L., & Rotheram-Borus, M. J. (1994). Growing up biracial in the United State. In E. P. Salett & D. R. Koslow (Eds.), *Race, ethnicity and self: Identity in multicultural perspective* (pp. 143–169). Washington, DC: Multicultural Institute.

Mills, J. K., Daly, J., Longmore, A., & Kilbride, G. (1995). A note on family acceptance involving interracial friendships and romantic relationships. *Journal of Psychology, 129*(3), 349–351.

Min, P. G. (Ed.). (2006). *Asian Americans: Contemporary trends and issues.* Thousand Oaks, CA: Pine Forge Press.

Miner, S., & Tolnay, S. (1998). Barriers to voluntary organizations membership: An examination of race and cohort differences. *Journals of Gerontology, 53B*(5), S241–S248.

Mirande, A., & Enriquez, E. (1979). *La Chicano: The Mexican American woman.* Chicago: University of Chicago Press.

Miyahara, A., Kim, M. S., Shin, H. C., & Yoon, K. (1998). Conflict resolution styles among "collectivist" cultures: A comparison between Japanese and Koreans.

International Journal of Intercultural Relations, 22, 505–525.

Mizuno, T. (2003). Government suppression of the Japanese language in World War II assembly camps. *Journalism and Mass Communication Quarterly, 80*(4), 849–865.

Monahan, T. P. (1976). An overview of statistics on interracial marriage in the United States, with data on its extent from 1963–1970. *Journal of Marriage and the Family, 38,* 223–231.

Montagu, A. (1964). *The concept of race.* New York: Free Press of Glencoe.

Montagu, A. (1972). *Statement on race: An annotated elaboration and exposition of the four statements on race issued by the United Nations Educational, Scientific, and Cultural Organization.* New York: Oxford University Press.

Montagu, A. (1997). *Man's most dangerous myth: The fallacy of race* (6th ed.). Walnut Creek, CA: AltaMira Press.

Moody, L. (1993, December 26). Politically correct dictionary updated. *Louisville (KY) Courier-Journal,* p. A8.

Moon, D. G. (1998). Performed identities: "Passing" as an inter/cultural discourse. In J. N. Martin, T. K. Nakayama, & L. A. Flores (Eds.), *Readings in cultural contexts* (pp. 322–330). Mountain View, CA: Mayfield.

Moon, D. G., & Rolison, G. L. (1998). Communication of classism. In M. L. Hecht (Ed.), *Communication prejudice* (pp. 122–135). Thousand Oaks, CA: Sage.

Moore, M. M. (1980). *Small voices & great trumpets: Minorities & the media.* New York: Praeger.

Moore, Q. (1993/1994). A "whole new world of diversity." *Journal of intergroup relations, 20*(4), 28–40.

Morganthau, T. (1995, February 13). What color is Black? *Newsweek,* pp. 63–65.

Morris, R., & Stuckey, M. E. (1998). Destroying the past to save the present: Pastoral voice and native identity. In Y. R. Kamalipour & T. Carilli (Eds.), *Cultural diversity in the U.S. media* (pp. 137–148). Albany: State University of New York Press.

Morrison, T. (1991). *Playing in the dark: Whiteness and the literary imagination.* Cambridge, MA: Harvard University Press.

Moss, K., & Faux, W. V. II (2006). The enactment of cultural identity in student conversations on intercultural topics. *Howard Journal of Communications, 17,* 21–37.

Munoz, C. (1989). *Youth, identity, power: The Chicano movement.* London: Verso.

Muraco, A. (2005). Heterosexual evaluations of hypothetical friendship behavior based on sex and sexual orientation. *Journal of Social and Personal Relationships, 22*(5), 587–605.

Murstein, B., Merigihi, J. R., & Malloy, T. E. (1989). Physical attractiveness and exchange theory in interracial dating. *Journal of Social Psychology, 129*(3), 325–334.

Muthuswamy, N., Levine, T., & Gazel, J. (2006). Interaction-based diversity initiative outcomes: An evaluation of an initiative aimed at bridging the racial divide on a college campus. *Communication Education, 55*(1), 105–121.

Muwakkil, S. (1998). Real minority, media majority. *In These Times, 22*(15), 18–19.

Myra, H. (1994, March 7). Love in black and white. *Christianity Today*, pp. 18–19.

Nakane, C. (1984). The social system reflected in the interpersonal communication. In J. Condon & M. Saito (Eds.), *Intercultural encounters with Japan*. Tokyo: Simul Press.

Nakashima, C. (1992). Blood quantum: Native American mixed bloods. In M. P. P. Root (Ed.), *Racially mixed people in America* (pp. 162–180). Newbury Park, CA: Sage.

Nakayama, T. (1998). Communication of heterosexism. In M. L. Hecht (Ed.), *Communicating prejudice* (pp. 112–121). Thousand Oaks, CA: Sage.

Nakayama, T. K. (2004). Dis/orienting identities. In A. Gonzalez, M. Houston, & V. Chen (Eds.), *Our voices: Essays in culture, ethnicity, and communication* (pp. 26–31). Los Angeles: Roxbury.

Nakayama, T. K., & Martin, J. N. (Eds.). (1999). *Whiteness: The communication of social identity*. Thousand Oaks, CA: Sage.

Names for minorities undergo constant change. (2003). *Ascribe News, Inc*. Retrieved April 30, 2003, from http://www.hispanicbusiness.com

Nance, T. A., & Foeman, A. K. (1993). Rethinking the basic public speaking course for African American students and other students of color. *Journal of Negro Education, 67*(4), 448–458.

Nance T. A., & Foeman, A. K. (2002). On being biracial in the United States. In J. N. Martin, T. K. Nakayama, & L. A. Flores (Eds.), *Readings in intercultural communication: Experiences and contexts* (pp. 35–43). New York: McGraw-Hill.

Narine, D. (1988, March). Black TV and movie scriptwriters: The write stuff. *Ebony*, pp. 92–98.

National Council of La Raza. (1997). Don't blink: Hispanics in television entertainment. In S. Biagi & M. Kem-Foxworth (Eds.), *Facing difference: Race, gender, and mass media* (pp. 29–31). Thousand Oaks, CA: Pine Forge Press.

National Research Council (2004). *Measuring racial discrimination*. Washington, DC: National Academies Press.

Neergaard, L. (2006, September 12). Where you live a significant factor in how long you live, new study finds. *Kalamazoo (MI) Gazette*, p. A8.

Negra, D. (2001). The new primitives: Irishness in recent US television. *Irish Studies Review, 9*(2), 229–239.

Nero, C. I. (1997). Black queer identity, imaginative rationality, and the language of home. In A. Gonzalez, M. Houston, & V. Chen (Eds.), *Our voices: Essay in culture, ethnicity, and communication* (pp. 61–69). Los Angeles: Roxbury.

Neuliep, J. W., & McCroskey, J. (1997a). The development of intercultural and interethnic communication apprehension scales. *Communication Research Reports, 14*(2), 145–156.

Neuliep, J. W., & McCroskey, J. (1997b). The development of the U.S. and generalized ethnocentrism scale. *Communication Research Reports, 14*(4), 385–398.

Neuliep, J. W., & Ryan, D. J. (1998). The influence of intercultural communication apprehension and socio-communicative orientation on uncertainty reduction during initial cross-cultural interaction. *Communication Quarterly, 46*(1), 88–99.

Ng, M. T. (2004). Searching for home: Voices of gay Asian American youth in West Hollywood. In J. Lee & M. Zhou (Eds.), *Asian American youth: Culture, identity, and ethnicity* (pp. 269–284). New York: Routledge.

Nguyen, L. T. (1998). To date or not to date a Vietnamese: Perceptions and expectations of Vietnamese American college students. *Amerasia Journal, 24*(1), 143–169.

No place for mankind. (1989, September 4). *Newsweek*, p. 17.

Nuessel, F. (1982). The language of ageism. *The Gerontologist, 22*, 273–276.

Nwanko, R. L. (1979). Intercultural communication: A critical review. *Quarterly Journal of Speech, 65*, 324–346.

O'Brien Hallstein, D. L. (2000). Where standpoint stands now: An introduction and commentary. *Women's Studies in Communication, 23*(1), 1–15.

Oetzel, J. G. (1998). The effects of self-construals and ethnicity on self-reported conflict styles. *Communication Reports, 11*, 133–144.

Ogunwole, S. U. (2006). *We the people: American Indians and Alaska Natives in the United States*. Washington, DC: U.S. Department of Commerce.

O'Hanlon, K. (2000, September 16). American Indian Catholics mix tribal beliefs with their Christian faith. *Kalamazoo (MI) Gazette*, p. D5.

Ohlemacher, S. (2006a, March 7). Hispanics chase jobs into Middle America. *Kalamazoo (MI) Gazette*, pp. A1–A2.

Ohlemacher, S. (2006b, October 15). As U.S. population hits milestone, consumption of resources in question. *Kalamazoo (MI) Gazette*, p. A5.

Oliver, J. E., & Wong, J. (2003). Intergroup prejudice in multiethnic settings. *American Journal of Political Science, 47*, 567–582.

Olsen, K. (2006, Fall). "We were still the enemy." *Teaching Tolerance*, pp. 36–41.

Omi, M. (1989). In living color: Race and American culture. In I. Angus & S. Jhally (Eds.), *Cultural politics in contemporary America* (pp. 111–122). New York: Oxford University Press.

Orbe, M. (1994). "Remember, it's always Whites' ball": Descriptions of African American male communication. *Communication Quarterly, 42*(3), 287–300.

Orbe, M. (1995). Intergroup relations in the classroom: Strategies for cultivating a sense of true community. *Journal of Intergroup Relations, 22,* 28–38.

Orbe, M. (1996). Laying the foundation for co-cultural communication theory: An inductive approach to studying "non-dominant" communication strategies and the factors that influence them. *Communication Studies, 47,* 157–176.

Orbe, M. (1997). A co-cultural communication approach to intergroup relations. *Journal of Intergroup Relations, 24,* 36–49.

Orbe, M. (1998a). *Constructing co-cultural theory: An explication of culture, power, and communication.* Thousand Oaks, CA: Sage.

Orbe, M. (1998b). Constructions of reality on MTV's "The Real World": An analysis of the restrictive coding of Black masculinity. *Southern Communication Journal, 64,* 32–47.

Orbe, M. (1998c). From the standpoint(s) of traditionally muted groups: Explicating a co-cultural communication theoretical model. *Communication Theory, 8,* 1–26.

Orbe, M. (1998d). An outsider within perspective to organizational communication: Explicating the communicative practices of co-cultural group members. *Management Communication Quarterly, 12,* 230–279.

Orbe, M. (1999). Communicating about "race" in interracial families. In T. Socha & R. Diggs (Eds.), *Communication, race, and family: Exploring communication in black, white, and biracial families* (pp. 167–180). Mahwah, NJ: Lawrence Erlbaum.

Orbe, M. (2003). African American first-generation college student communicative experiences. *Electronic Journal of Communication, 13*(2–3).

Orbe, M. (2005). "The more things change . . . ": Civil rights health assessment in a "majority–minority" U.S. community. *Howard Journal of Communications, 16*(3), 177–200.

Orbe, M., Allen, B. J., & Flores, L. A. (Eds.). (2006). *The same and different: Acknowledging the diversity within and between cultural groups.* Washington, DC: National Communication Association.

Orbe, M., Drummond, D. K., & Camara, S. K. (2002). Phenomenology and black feminist thought: Exploring African American women's everyday encounters as points of contention. In M. Houston & O. I. Davis (Eds.), *Centering ourselves: African American feminist and womanist studies of discourse* (pp. 123–144). Cresskill, NJ: Hampton Press.

Orbe, M., & Everett, M. A. (2006). Interracial and interethnic conflict and communication in the United States. In J. Oetzel & S. Ting-Toomey (Eds.), *The Sage handbook of conflict communication* (pp. 575–594). Thousand Oaks, CA: Sage.

Orbe, M., & Knox, R. J. (1994, September). *Building community among diverse peoples: Strategies in the classroom and larger global community.* Paper presented at the annual Enhancing Minority Attainment Conference, Kokomo, IN.

Orbe, M., Seymour, R., & Kang, M. E. (1998). Ethnic humor and ingroup/outgroup positioning: Explicating viewer perceptions of *All-American Girl.* In Y. R. Kamalipour & T. Carilli (Eds.), *Cultural diversity in the U.S. media* (pp. 125–136). Albany: State University of New York Press.

Orbe, M., & Spellers, R. E. (2005). From the margins to the center: Utilizing co-cultural theory in diverse contexts. In W. B. Gudykunst (Ed.), *Theorizing about intercultural communication* (pp. 173–192). Thousand Oaks, CA: Sage.

Orbe, M. P., & Warren, K. T. (2000). Different standpoints, different realities: Race, gender, and perceptions of intercultural conflict. *Communication Quarterly, 48,* 51–57.

Orbe, M. P., Warren, K. T., & Cornwell, N. C. (2001). Negotiating societal stereotypes: Analyzing *The Real World* discourse by and about African American men. In M. J. Collier (Ed.), *Constituting cultural difference through discourse* (pp. 107–134). Thousand Oak, CA: Sage.

Order Sons of Italy in America. (2003). *Sons of Italy report reveals pattern of Italian American stereotyping in advertising.* Retrieved March 12, 2007, from http:// www .osia.org/public/newsroom/pr07_7_03 .asp

Owen, M. (1998, August 14). A desegregation success story in the making in Louisiana. *Chronicle of Higher Education,* pp. A27–A28.

Pacheco, G. K. (1990). On native Hawaiians: Lost in the shuffle? *Focus, 4,* 6–7.

Padden, C., & Humphries, T. (1988). *Deaf in America: Voices from a culture.* Cambridge, MA: Harvard University Press.

Page, C. (1994, January 5). Uneasy journey to political correctness. *Louisville (KY) Courier-Journal,* p. A19.

Page, S. (2006, June 23). Survey: Suspicion separates Westerners, Muslims. *USA Today,* p. 7A.

Pagnini, D. L., & Morgan, S. P. (1990). Intermarriage and social distance among U.S. immigrants at the turn of the century. *American Journal of Sociology, 96,* 405–432.

Pal, K. S. (2005). Racial profiling as a preemptive security measure after September 11: A suggested framework for analysis. *Kennedy School Review, 6,* 119–129.

Palmer, P. J. (1993). *To know as we are known: Education as a spiritual journey.* San Francisco: Harper.

Palmore, E. B. (1990). *Ageism: Negative and positive.* New York: Springer.

Parham, T. A., & Helms, J. E. (1985). Relation of racial identity attitudes to self-actualization and affective states in Black students. *Journal of Counseling Psychology, 32,* 431–440.

Parham, T. A., & Williams, P. T. (1993). The relationship of demographic and background factors to racial identity attitudes. *Journal of Black Psychology, 19,* 17–24.

Park, J. H., Gabbadon, N. G., & Chernin, A. R. (2006). Naturalizing racial differences through comedy: Asian, black, and white views on racial stereotypes in *Rush Hour 2. Journal of Communication, 56,* 157–177.

Parrillo, V. N. (1996). *Diversity in America.* Thousand Oaks, CA: Pine Forge Press.

Paset, P. S., & Taylor, R. (1991). Black and white women's attitudes toward interracial marriage. *Psychological Reports, 69,* 753–754.

Patterson, O. (1995, November 6). The paradox of integration. *The New Republic,* pp. 24–27.

Patterson, O. (1998). The paradox of integration. In G. R. Weaver (Ed.), *Culture, communication, and conflict: Readings in intercultural relations* (pp. 90–123). Needham, MA: Simon & Schuster.

Patton, P. L. (1998). The gangstas in our midst. *Urban Review, 30*(1), 49–76.

Patton, T. O. (2004). In the guise of civility: The complicitous maintenance of inferential forms of sexism and racism in higher education. *Women's Studies in Communication, 27*(1), 60–87.

Paulin, D. R. (1997). De-essentializing interracial representations: Black and white border-crossings in Spike Lee's *Jungle Fever* and Octavia Butler's *Kindred. Cultural Critique, 36,* 165–193.

Pearson, J. C., & Davilla, R. A. (2001). The gender construct. In L. P. Arliess & D. J. Borisoff (Eds.), *Women and men communicating: Challenges and changes* (pp. 3–14). Prospect Heights, IL: Waveland Press.

Peart, K. N. (1994, May 6). Where do you stand: Race relations. *Scholastic Update,* pp. 6–9.

Peck, M. S. (1987). *The different drum: Community making and peace.* New York: Simon & Schuster.

Peck, M. S. (1992). The true meaning of community. In W. B. Gudykunst & Y. Y. Kim (Eds.), *Readings in communicating with strangers* (pp. 435–444). New York: McGraw-Hill.

Pedraza, S. (2006). Assimilation or transnationalism? Conceptual models of the immigrant experience in America. In R. Mahalingam (Ed.), *Cultural psychology of immigrants* (pp. 33–54). Mahwah, NJ: Lawrence Erlbaum.

Pennington, D. L. (1979). Black-white communication: An assessment of research. In M. K. Asante, E. Newark, & C. A. Blake (Eds.), *Handbook of intercultural communication* (pp. 383–402). Beverly Hills, CA: Sage.

Perkins K. R. (1996). The influence of television images on black females' self-perceptions of physical attractiveness. *Journal of Black Psychology, 22*(4), 435–469.

Peterson, M. S. (1998). Personnel interviewers' perceptions of the importance and adequacy of applicants' communication skills. *Communication Education, 46*(4), 287–291.

Petrie, P. (1991, August). Afrocentrism in a multicultural democracy. *American Visions,* pp. 20–26.

Petronio, S., Ellemers, N., Giles, H., & Gallois, C. (1998). (Mis)communicating across boundaries: Interpersonal and intergroup considerations. *Communication Research, 25*(6), 571–595.

Petrozzello, D. (1998, October 26). Civil rights and more: "Any Day Now." *Broadcasting & Cable,* p. 52.

Pettigrew, T. D., & Tropp, L. R. (2004). *A meta-analytic test and reformulation of intergroup contact theory.* Retrieved November 21, 2006, from http://www.cbrss.harvard.edu/events/ppbw/papers/ tropp.pdf

Pettigrew, T. F. (1981). Race and class in the 1980s: An interactive view. *Daedalus, 110,* 233–255.

Pettigrew, T. F. (1998). Intergroup contact theory. *Annual Review of Psychology, 49,* 65–76.

Pettigrew, T. F., Fredrickson, G. M., Knoble, D. T., Glazer, N., & Ueda, R. (1982). *Prejudice: Dimensions of ethnicity.* Massachusetts: Belknap Press of Harvard University Press.

Philipsen, G. (1975). Speaking "like a man" in Teamsterville: Culture patterns of role enactment in an urban neighborhood. *Quarterly Journal of Speech, 61,* 13–22.

Philipsen, G. (1976). Places for speaking in Teamsterville. *Quarterly Journal of Speech, 62,* 15–25.

Philipsen, G. (1992). *Speaking culturally: Explorations in social communication.* Albany: State University of New York Press.

Philipsen, G. (1996). A theory of speech codes. In G. Philipsen and T. Albrecht (Eds.), *Developing communication theory* (pp. 119–156). Albany: State University of New York Press.

Philipsen, G. (1997). A theory of speech codes. In G. Philipsen & T. L. Albrecht (Eds.), *Developing communication theories* (pp. 119–156). Albany: State University of New York Press.

Philipsen, G., Coutu, L. M., & Covarrubias, P. (2005). Speech codes theory: Restatement, revisions, and response to criticisms. In W. B. Gudykunst (Ed.), *Theorizing about intercultural communication* (pp. 55–68). Thousand Oaks, CA: Sage.

Phillips, N. (1993). Afrocentricity "purposeful." *Black Issues in Higher Education, 9,* 10.

Phinney, J. S. (1993). A three-stage model of ethnic identity development in adolescence. In M. E. Bernal & G. P. Knight (Eds.), *Ethnic identity: Formation and transmission among Hispanics and other immigrants* (pp. 61–79). Albany: State University of New York Press.

Phinney, J. S., & Rotherham, J. J. (Eds.). (1987). *Children's ethnic socialization: Pluralism and development.* Newbury Park, CA: Sage.

Pino, F. (1980). The "great" cultural tradition of Hispanics. *Agenda, 10*(3), 38–42.

Ponterotto, J. G. (1989). Expanding directions for racial identity research. *The Counseling Psychologist, 17,* 264–272.

Ponterotto, J. G., & Pedersen, P. B. (1993). *Preventing prejudice: A guide for counselors and educators.* Newbury Park, CA: Sage.

Popular demand brings "living single" back for fifth season. (1997, September). *JET Magazine, 92*(17), 52–61.

Porterfield, E. (1982). Black American intermarriage in the United States. *Marriage and the Family Review, 5,* 14–34.

Portes, A., Guarnizo, L. E., & Landolt, P. (1999). The study of transnationalism: Pitfalls and promise of an emergent research field. *Ethnic and Racial Studies, 22*(2), 217–237.

Poston, W. S. C. (1990). The biracial identity development model: A needed addition. *Journal of Counseling and Development, 69,* 152–155.

Poussaint, A. (1988, October). The Huxtables: Fact or fantasy? *Ebony,* pp. 72–74.

Powell, D. (1996). Group communication. *Communication of the ACM, 39*(4), 50–53.

Powell, R., & Collier, M. J. (1990). Public speaking instruction and cultural bias. *American Behavioral Scientist, 34*(2), 240–250.

Power, J. G., Murphy, S., & Coover, G. (1996). Priming prejudice: How stereotypes and counter-stereotypes influence attribution of responsibility and credibility among ingroups and outgroups. *Human Communication Research, 23*(1), 36–58.

Powers, D. A., & Ellison, C. (1995). Interracial contact and black racial attitudes: The contact hypothesis and selectivity bias. *Social Forces, 74*(1), 205–226.

Praeger, R. (1995). A world worth living in. In M. L. Andersen & P. H. Collins (Eds.), *Race, class, and gender: An anthology* (pp. 523–531). Belmont, CA: Wadsworth.

Pratt, S. B. (1998). Razzing: Ritualized uses of humor as a form of identification among American Indians. In D. V. Tanno & A. Gonzalez (Eds.), *Communication and identity across cultures* (pp. 80–99). Thousand Oaks, CA: Sage.

Price, D. (1998). *Civil rites: Arguments against same-sex marriage mirror those that kept the races apart.* Retrieved November 1, 2006, from http://www.ftm .org/loving/civil-rites.html

Provine, W. B. (1973). Geneticists and the biology of race crossing. *Science, 182,* 790–796.

Putman, A., & Thompson, S. (2006). Paving the way: First-generation Mexican American community college students in a border community. In M. Orbe, B. J. Allen, & L. A. Flores (Eds.), *The same and different: Acknowledging the diversity within and between cultural groups* (pp. 121–142). Washington, DC: National Communication Association.

Putnam, L. L. (2006). Definitions and approaches to conflict and communication. In J. G. Oetzel and S. Ting-Toomey (Eds.), *The SAGE handbook of conflict communication: Integrating theory, research, and practice* (pp. 1–32). Thousand Oaks, CA: Sage.

Qian, Z. (1998). Changes in assortative mating: The impact of age and education. 1970–1990. *Demography, 35*(3), 279–292.

Raby, R. (2004). "There's no racism at my school, it's just joking around": Ramifications for anti-racist education. *Race Ethnicity and Education, 7*(4), 367–383.

Radford, A. J. (1987). Ageism: Public prejudice and private preconceptions. *Australian Journal on Ageing, 6,* 4–9.

Ramsey, S. (1981). The kinesics of femininity in Japanese women. *Language Sciences, 3*(11), 104–123.

Randolph, L. B. (1994, May). Life after the Cosby show: Activist-actor celebrates 30 years of wedded bliss, continues fight against stereotypes on TV. *Ebony,* pp. 100–104.

Raspberry, W. (1989, January 4). When "Black" becomes "African American." *Washington Post,* p. A19.

Raspberry, W. (1999, March 2). Is racism getting better or worse? *Kalamazoo (MI) Gazette,* p. A8.

Reardon, K. K. (1996). The crossroads of organizational communication: Definition or dichotomy. *Management Communication Quarterly, 10*(1), 106–111.

Rebensdorf, A. (2001). *The network brown out.* Retrieved November 30, 2006, from http://www.alternet.org/ mediaculture/11197/

Reimers, D. M. (2005). *Other immigrants: The global origins of the American people.* New York: New York University Press.

Reiter, L. (1989). Sexual orientation, sexual identity, and the question of choice. *Clinical Social Work Journal, 17,* 138–150.

Remar, P. (1991, November). *Should college and universities prohibit "hate speech" on campus?* Paper presented at the annual meeting of the Speech Communication Association, Atlanta, GA.

Rhea, J. T. (1997). *Race pride and the American identity.* Cambridge, MA: Harvard University Press.

Ribeau, S. A. (1995, October). *African American communication and conflict resolution: A new dialogue.* B. Aubrey Fisher Memorial Lecture, Salt Lake City, UT. University of Utah.

Ribeau, S. A. (2004). How I came to know in self-realization there is truth. In A. Gonzalez, M. Houston, & V. Chen (Eds.), *Our voices: Essays in culture, ethnicity, and communication* (pp. 32–37). Los Angeles: Roxbury.

Ribeau, S. A., Baldwin, J. R., & Hecht, M. L. (1997). An African-American communication perspective. In L. A. Samovar & R. E. Porter (Eds.), *Intercultural communications: A reader* (pp. 147–154). Belmont, CA: Wadsworth.

Rich, A. L. (1974). *Interracial communication.* New York: Harper & Row.

Rich, A. L., & Ogawa, D. M. (1972). Intercultural and interracial communication: An analytical approach. In L. A. Samovar & R. E. Porter (Eds.), *Intercultural communication: A reader* (pp. 22–29). Belmont, CA: Wadsworth.

Richeson, J. A., Baird, A. A., Gordon, H. L., Heatherton, T. F., Wyland, C. L., Trawalter, S., et al. (2003). An fMRI investigation of the impact of interracial contact on executive function. *Nature Neuroscience, 6,* 1323–1328.

Rickford, J. R., & Rickford, R. J. (2000). *Spoken soul: The story of Black English.* New York: John Wiley & Sons.

Rinderle, S. (2006). Quienes son/quienes somos: A critical analysis of the changing names for people of Mexican descent across history. In M. Orbe, B. J. Allen, & L. A. Flores (Eds.), *The same and different: Acknowledging the diversity within and between cultural groups* (pp. 143–165). Washington, DC: National Communication Association.

Rios, D. I. (1997). Mexican American cultural experiences with mass-mediated communication. In A. Gonzalez, M. Houston, & V. Chen (Eds.), *Our voices: Essays in culture, ethnicity, and communication* (pp. 105–112). Los Angeles: Roxbury.

Rios, D. I. (2003). Introduction. In D. I. Rios & A. N. Mohamed (Eds.), *Brown and black communication: Latino and African American conflict and convergence in mass media* (pp. xiii–xiv). Westport, CT: Praeger.

Rivadeneyra, R. (2006). Do you see what I see? Latino adolescents' perceptions of the images on television. *Journal of Adolescent Research, 21*(4), 393–414.

Rivadeneyra, R., & Ward, L. M. (2005). From Ally McBeal to sábado gigante: Contributions of television viewing to the gender role attitudes of Latino adolescents. *Journal of Adolescent Research, 20*(4), 453–475.

Roberts, G., & Orbe, M. (1996, May). "Creating that safe place": Descriptions of intergenerational gay male communication. Paper presented at the annual meeting of the International Communication Association, Chicago.

Rockquemore, K. A., & Brunsma, D. L. (2002). *Beyond black: Biracial identity in America.* Thousand Oaks, CA: Sage.

Rockquemore, K. A., & Laszloffy, T. (2005). *Raising biracial children.* New York: AltaMira Press.

Rodriguez, A. (2002). Culture to culturing: Re-imaging our understanding of intercultural relations. *Journal of Intercultural Communication, 5.* Retrieved October 14, 2006, from http://www.immi.se/intercultural/

Rodriguez, D. (1998). Diversity training brings staff closer. *Education Digest, 64*(1), 28–31.

Roediger, D. R. (1994). *Towards the abolition of whiteness.* New York: Verso.

Roloff, M. E. (1987). Communication and conflict. In C. R. Berger & S. H. Chaffee (Eds.), *Handbook of communication science* (pp. 484–534). Newbury Park, CA: Sage.

Romano, L., & Trescott, J. (1992, February). Love in black and white. *Redbook,* pp. 88–94.

Romer, D., Jamieson, K. H., & de Coteau, N. J. (1998). The treatment of persons of color in local television news: Ethnic blame discourse or realistic group conflict? *Communication Research, 25,* 286–305.

Romer, D., Jamieson, K. H., Riegner, C., & Rouson, B. (1997). Blame discourse versus realistic conflict as explanations of ethnic tension in urban neighborhoods. *Political Communication, 14,* 273–291.

Root, M. P. P. (1992). Within, between, and beyond race. In M. P. P. Root (Ed.), *Racially mixed people in America* (pp. 3–11). Newbury Park, CA: Sage.

Root, M. P. P. (Ed.). (1996). *The multiracial experience: Racial borders as the new frontier.* Thousand Oaks, CA: Sage.

Root, M. P. P. (2001). *Love's revolution: Interracial marriage.* Philadelphia, PA: Temple University Press.

Root, M. P. P. (2002). The color of love. *American Prospect, 13*(7), 54–55.

Rosenblatt, P., Karis, T., & Powell, R. (1995). *Multiracial couples: Black and White voices.* Thousand Oaks, CA: Sage.

Rosenthal, D. A. (1987). Ethnic identity development in adolescents. In J. S. Phinney & M. J. Rotheram (Eds.), *Children's ethnic socialization: Pluralism and development* (pp. 156–179). Newbury Park, CA: Sage.

Ross, C. (1996, March). Blacks drawn to indy TV, cable. *Advertising Age,* pp. 4, 8.

Ross, M. H. (2000). Creating conditions for peacemaking: Theories of practice in ethnic conflict resolution. *Ethnic and Racial Studies, 23,* 1002–1034.

Rothenberg, P. S. (1992). *Race, class, and gender in the United States: An integrated study.* New York: St. Martin's Press.

Rowan, K. E. (1995). A new pedagogy for explanatory public speaking: Why arrangement should not substitute for invention. *Communication Education, 44*(3), 236–250.

Rowe, A. C., & Malhotra, S. (2006). (Un)hinging whiteness. In M. Orbe, B. J. Allen, & L. A. Flores (Eds.), *The same and different: Acknowledging the diversity within and between cultural groups* (pp. 166–192). Washington, DC: National Communication Association.

Rowe, D. M., & Ramos, R. G. (2003). Latino and African American relations in academia: A case study in solidarity between faculty of color. In D. I. Rios & A. N. Mohamed (Eds.), *Brown and black communication: Latino and African American conflict and convergence in mass media* (pp. 203–216). Westport, CT: Praeger.

Rubin, D., & Hampton, S. (1998). National performance standards for oral communication K–12: New standards and speaking/listening/viewing. *Communication Education, 47*(2), 183–193.

Rudman, L. A., Ashmore, R. D., & Melvin, L. (2001). "Unlearning" automatic biases the malleability of implicit prejudice and stereotypes. *Journal of Personality and Social Psychology, 81,* 856–868.

Ryoo, H.-K. (2005). Achieving friendly interactions: A study of service encounters between Korean shopkeepers and African-Americans customers. *Discourse & Society, 16*(1), 79–105.

Sachdev, I., & Bourhis, R. Y. (1990). Language and social identification. In D. Abrams & M. A. Hogg (Eds.), *Social identity theory: Constructive and critical advances* (pp. 211–229). New York: Harvester Wheatsheaf.

Saenz, R., Sean-Shong, H., Aguirre, B. E., & Anderson, R. N. (1995). Persistence and change in Asian identity among children of intermarried couples. *Sociological Perspectives, 38*(2), 175–195.

Sailer, S. (1997). Is love colorblind? *National Review, 49*(13), 30–33.

Salaita, S. (2006). *Anti-Arab racism in the USA: Where it comes from and what it means for politics today.* Ann Arbor, MI: Pluto Press.

Sanchez, V. E. (2001). Intertribal dance and cross cultural communication. Traditional powwows in Ohio. *Communication Studies, 51*(1), 51–69.

Sanchez-Burks, J., Nisbett, R. A., & Ybarra, O. (2000). Cultural styles, relational schemas, and prejudice against outgroups. *Journal of Personal and Social Psychology, 79*(2),174–189.

Sarup, M. (1996). *Identity, culture, and the postmodern world.* Athens: University of Georgia Press.

Schaefer, R. T. (1993). *Racial and ethnic groups.* New York: HarperCollins.

Schein, E. H. (1985). *Organizational culture and leadership.* San Francisco: Jossey-Bass.

Schemo, D. J. (2001, July 22). Study says segregation increasing. *New York Times,* p. F7.

Schmid, R. E. (1997, July 9). "Multiracial" category for census rejected. *Louisville (KY) Courier-Journal,* p. A5.

Schoen R., & Wooldredge, J. (1989). Marriage choices in North Carolina and Virginia, 1969–71 and 1979–81. *Journal of Marriage and the Family, 51,* 465–481.

Scott, K. D. (1996, June). *Style switching as ideological position in Black women's talk.* Paper presented at the annual meeting of the Speech Communication Association's Black Caucus/African American Communication and Culture Division Summer Conference, Frankfort, KY.

Sebring, D. L. (1985). Considerations in counseling interracial children. *The Personnel and Guidance Journal, 13,* 3–9.

Seeger, M. (1992). Responsibility in organizational communication: Individual, organizational, and environmental accounts. In J. Jaska (Ed.), *Proceedings of the 1992 National Communication Ethics Conference* (pp. 172–183). Annandale, VA: Speech Communication Association.

Seidman, S., Meeks, C., & Traschen, F. (1999). Beyond the closet: The changing social meaning of homosexuality in the United States. *Sexualities, 2*(1), 9–34.

Seiter, E. (1990). Different children, different dreams: Racial representation in advertising. *Journal of Communication Inquiry, 14,* 31–47.

Semmerling, T. J. (2006). *"Evil" Arabs in American popular film: Orientalist fear.* Austin: University of Texas Press.

Seymour, H. N., & Seymour, C. M. (1979). The symbolism of Ebonics: I'd rather switch than fight. *Journal of Black Studies, 9,* 397–410.

Shah, H. (2003). "Asian culture" and Asian American identities in the television and film industries of the United States. *Studies in Media & Information Literacy Education, 3*(3). Retrieved October 3, 2006, from http://www.utpress.utoronto.ca/journal/ejournals/ simile

Shah, H., & Thornton, M. C. (1994). Racial ideology in U.S. mainstream news magazine coverage of Black-Latino interaction, 1980–1992. *Critical Studies in Mass Communication, 11*(2), 141–161.

Shannon, V. (1997). Networking: When race meets life online, there's a disconnection. In S. Biagi & M. Kem-Foxworth (Eds.), *Facing difference: Race, gender, and mass media* (pp. 258–260). Thousand Oaks, CA: Pine Forge Press.

Shaver, L. D. (1998). The cultural deprivation of an Oklahoma Cherokee family. In D. V. Tanno & A. Gonzalez (Eds.), *Communication and identity across cultures* (pp. 100–121). Thousand Oaks, CA: Sage.

Shea, C. (1997, May 2). Intermarriage rates found to be on the rise. *Chronicle of Higher Education,* p. A14.

Shepard, C. A., Giles, H., & Le Poire, B. A. (2001). Communication accommodation theory. In W. P. Robinson & H. Giles (Eds.), *The new handbook of language and social psychology* (pp. 33–56). New York: John Wiley.

Shepard, P. (1999, July 13). NAACP to fight TV's "whitewash," too many guns. *Kalamazoo (MI) Gazette*, p. D4.

Shively, M. G., Jones, C., & DeCecco, J. P. (1984). Research on sexual orientation: Definitions and methods. *Journal of Homosexuality, 9*, 127–137.

Shotter, J., & Gergen, K. J. (Eds.). (1989). *Tests of identity*. London: Sage.

Shreeve, J. (1994, November). Terms of estrangement. *Discover*, pp. 57–63.

Shuter, R. (1993). On third-culture building. *Communication Yearbook, 16*, 407–428.

Shuter, R. M. (1998). Revisiting the centrality of culture. In J. N. Martin, T. K. Nakayama, & L. A. Flores (Eds.), *Readings in cultural contexts* (pp. 38–48). Mountain View, CA: Mayfield Publishing.

Shuter, R., & Turner, L. H. (1997). African American and European American women in the workplace: Perceptions of conflict communication. *Management Communication Quarterly, 11*(1), 74–96.

Siegel, G. (1995, May). Familia values. *Los Angeles Times*, p. 21.

Sigelman, L., Bledsoe, T., & Combs, M. (1996). Making contact? Black–white social interaction in an urban setting. *American Journal of Sociology, 101*(5), 1306–1332.

Sigelman, L., & Tuch, S. A. (1997). Metastereotypes: Blacks' perceptions of White's stereotypes of Blacks. *Public Opinion Quarterly, 61*, 87–101.

Sigelman, L., Tuch, S. A., & Martin, J. K. (2005). What's in a name? Preference for "black" versus "African-American" among Americans of African descent. *Public Opinion Quarterly, 69*(3), 429–439.

Sigelman, L., & Welch, S. (1993). The contract hypothesis revisited: Black–White interaction and positive racial attitudes. *Social Forces, 71*(3), 781–795.

Sikosek, Z. M. (2003). *Esperanto without myths*. Antwerp: Flandra Esperanto-Ligo.

Sing, B. (1989). *Asian Pacific Americans: A handbook on how to cover and portray our nation's fastest growing minority group*. Los Angeles: National Conference of Christians and Jews.

Smalls, J. (1998). Visualizing race: A lifelong process and training. *Art Journal, 57*(3), 2–3.

Smith, A. (1973). *Transracial communication*. Englewood Cliffs, NJ: Prentice-Hall.

Smith, A., & Ahuja, S. (1999). *Intergroup relations in the United States: Seven promising practices*. New York: The National Conference for Community and Justice.

Smith, B. (1983). Homophobia: Why bring it up? *Interracial Books for Children Bulletin, 14*, 112–113.

Smith, C. E. (1966). Negro–White intermarriage: Forbidden sexual union. *Journal of Sex Research, 2*, 169–177.

Smith, D. E. (1987). *The everyday world as problematic. A feminist sociology of knowledge*. Boston: Northeastern University Press.

Smith, D. E. (1992). Sociology from women's experiences: A reaffirmation. *Sociological Theory, 10*, 1–12.

Smitherman, G. (1995). Student's right to their own language: A retrospective. *English Journal, 84*(1), 21–27.

Snipp, C. M. (1986). Who are the American Indians: Some perils and pitfalls for data for race and ethnicity. *Population Research and Policy Review, 5*, 237–252.

Snowden, F. (1970). *Blacks in antiquity: Ethiopians in Greco–Roman experience*. Cambridge, MA: Belknap Press of Harvard University Press.

Sodowsky, R. G., Kwan, K. L. K., & Pannu, R. (1995). Ethnic identity of Asians in the United States. In J. Ponterotto, J. M. Casas, L. A. Suzuki, & C. M. Alexander (Eds.), *Handbook of multicultural counseling* (pp. 123–154). Thousand Oaks, CA: Sage.

Solomon, M. R., Ashmore, R. D., & Longo, L. C. (1992). The beauty match-up hypothesis: Congruence between types of beauty and product images in advertising. *Journal of Advertising. 21*(4), 23–34.

Spaights, E., & Dixon H. (1984). Socio-psychological dynamics in pathological Black–White romantic alliances. *Journal of Instructional Psychology, 11*(3), 133–138.

Speer, S., & Potter, J. (2000). The management of heterosexist talk: Conversational resources and prejudiced claims. *Discourse & Society, 11*, 543–572.

Speicher, B. L. (1995). Interethnic conflict: Attribution and cultural ignorance. *The Howard Journal of Communications, 5*, 195–213.

Spellers, R. E. (2002). Happy to be nappy! Embracing an Afrocentric aesthetic for beauty. In J. N. Martin, T. Nakayama, & L. A. Flores (Eds.), *Readings in intercultural communication: Experiences and contexts* (pp. 52–59). New York: McGraw-Hill.

Spencer, R. (2006). *Challenging multiracial identity*. Boulder, CO: Lynne Rienner Publishers.

Spickard, P. R. (1989). *Mixed blood: Intermarriage and ethnic identity in twentieth-century America*. Madison: University of Wisconsin Press.

Spickard, P. R. (1992). The illogic of American racial categories. In M. P. P. Root (Ed.), *Racially mixed people in America* (pp. 12–23). Newbury Park, CA: Sage.

Spielberg, B. J. (1980). The "little" cultural tradition of Hispanics. *Agenda, 10*(3), 30–36.

Spradlin, A. L. (1995, November). *The price of "passing": A lesbian perspective on authenticity in organizations*. Paper presented at the annual meeting of the Speech Communication Association, San Antonio, TX.

Squires, G., & Hartman, C. (Eds.). (2006). *There is no such thing as a natural disaster: Race, class, and Katrina.* New York: Routledge.

Stanton, M. (1971). A remnant Indian community: The Houma of southern Louisiana. In J. K. Moorland (Ed.), *The not so solid South: Anthropological studies in a regional subculture* (pp. 82–92). Athens: University of Georgia Press.

Starosta, W. J., & Olorunnisola, A. A. (1993, November). *A meta-model for third culture development.* Paper presented at the annual meeting of the International Communication Association, Sydney, Australia.

Stearns, E. (2004). Interracial Friendliness and the Social Organization of Schools. *Youth & Society, 35*(4), 395–419.

Stephan, W. G., & Stephan, C. W. (2001). *Improving intergroup relations.* Thousand Oaks, CA: Sage.

Stevens, G., Owens, D., & Schaefer, E. C. (1990). Education and attractiveness in marriage choices. *Social Psychology Quarterly, 53,* 62–70.

Stevens, S. (2004). *Reflecting reality: A Fordham professor testifies before congress about the dearth of Latinos on television and in film.* Retrieved October 28, 2006, from http://www.fordham .edu

St. Jean, Y. (1998). Let people speak for themselves: Interracial unions and the general social survey. *Journal of Black Studies, 28*(3), 398–414.

Stone, E. (1996). Family ground rules. In K. M. Galvin & P. Cooper (Eds.), *Making connections* (pp. 59–67). Los Angeles, CA: Roxbury.

Stonequist, E. V. (1937). *The marginal man: A study in personality and culture conflict.* New York: Russell & Russell.

Stowe, D. W. (1996, September/October). Uncolored people: The rise of Whiteness studies. *Lingua Franca,* pp. 68–72, 74–77.

Stroman, C. A. (1991). Television's role in the socialization of African American children and adolescents. *Journal of Negro Education, 60,* 314–327.

Stromberg, E. (Ed.). (2006). *American Indian rhetorics of survivance: Word medicine, word magic.* Pittsburgh, PA: University of Pittsburgh Press.

Stryker, S., & Statham, A. (1984). Symbolic interaction and role theory. In G. Lindzey & E. Aronson (Eds.), *Handbook of social psychology* (pp. 311–378). Reading, MA: Addison-Wesley.

Suarez-Orozco, M. (2000). Everything you ever wanted to know about assimilation but were afraid to ask. *Daedalus, 129,* 1–30.

Sun, C. F. (2003). Ling woo in historical context: The new face of Asian American stereotypes on television. In G. Dines & J. M. Humez (Eds.), *Gender, race, and class in media: A text-reader* (2nd ed., pp. 656–664). Thousand Oaks, CA: Sage.

Sun, K. (2006). The legal definition of hate crime and the hate offender's distorted cognitions. *Issues in Mental Health Nursing, 27*(6), 597–605.

Sung, B. L. (1990). Chinese American intermarriage. *Journal of Comparative Family Studies, 21*(3), 337–352.

Swahn, M. H., Mahendra, R. R., Paulozzi, L. J., Winston, R. L., Shelley, G. A., Taliano, J., et al. (2003). *Violent attacks on Middle Easterners in the United States during the month following the September 11, 2001 terrorist attacks.* Retrieved October 8, 2006, from http://ip.bmjjournals.com/cgi/content/full/9/2/187

Swarns, R. (2006). *A racial rift that isn't black and white.* Retrieved October 3, 2006, from http://www.nytimes .com/2006/10/03/us/03georgia.html

Swigonski, M. E. (1994). The logic of feminist standpoint theory for social work research. *Social Work, 39*(4), 387–393.

Tajfel, H. (1974). Social identity and intergroup behavior. *Social Science Information, 13,* 65–93.

Tajfel, H. (1978). Social categorization, social identity, and social comparison. In H. Tajfel (Ed.), *Differentiation between social groups* (pp. 61–76). London: Academic Press.

Tajfel, H. (1981). *Human categories and social groups.* Cambridge, UK: Cambridge University Press.

Tajfel, H., & Turner, J. C. (1979). An integrative theory of intergroup conflict. In W. Austin & S. Worchel (Eds.), *The social psychology of intergroup relations* (pp. 33–47). Pacific Grove, CA: Brooks/Cole.

Tan, A., Fujioka, Y., & Lucht, N. (1997). Native American stereotypes, TV portrayals, and personal contact. *Journalism and Mass Communication Quarterly, 74,* 265–284.

Tannen, D. (1990). *You just don't understand: Women and men in conversation.* New York: Morrow.

Tanno, D. V. (1997). Names, narratives, and the evolution of ethnic identity. In A. Gonzalez, M. Houston, & V. Chen (Eds.), *Our voices: Essays in culture, ethnicity, and communication* (pp. 28–34). Los Angeles: Roxbury.

Tanno, D. V. (1998, May). A characterization of dialogue. Paper presented at the biannual meeting of the National communication Association Ethics Conference, Gull Lake, MI.

Tanno, D. V. (2004). Names, narratives, and the evolution of ethnic identity. In A. Gonzalez, M. Houston, & V. Chen (Eds.), *Our voices: Essays in culture, ethnicity, and communication* (pp. 38–41). Los Angeles, CA: Roxbury.

Tanno, D. V., & Gonzalez, A. (1998). Sites of identity in communication and culture. In D. V. Tanno & A. Gonzalez (Eds.), *Communication and identity across cultures* (pp. 3–10). Thousand Oaks, CA: Sage.

Tatum, B. D. (1992). Talking about race, learning about racism: The application of racial identity development theory in the classroom. *Harvard Educational Review, 62*(1), 1–24.

Tatum, B. D. (1997). *"Why are all the black kids sitting together in the cafeteria?" and other conversations about race.* New York: Basic Books

Taylor, C. (1992). *Multiculturalism and the politics of recognition.* Princeton, NJ: Princeton University Press.

Taylor, C. R., & Stern, B. (1997). Asian-Americans: Television advertising and the "model minority" stereotype. *Journal of Advertising, 26*(2), 47–62.

Taylor, F. W. (1911). *The principles of scientific management.* New York: Harper Row.

Taylor, J. (1991, January 21). Thought police on campus. *Reader's Digest,* pp. 99–104.

Taylor, J., & Richardson, B. (2006). Powerlessness, resistance, and the understood "They": Sexual harassment at the intersection of race and gender. In M. Orbe, B. J. Allen, & L. A. Flores (Eds.), *The same and different: Acknowledging the diversity within and between cultural groups* (pp. 68–94). Washington, DC: National Communication Association.

Taylor, R. (2000). *Indian in the Cupboard:* A case study in perspective. *Qualitative Studies in Education, 13*(4), 371–384.

Thibaut, J. W., & Kelley, H. H. (1959). *The social psychology of groups.* New York: Wiley.

Thomas, K. M., & Davis, J. L. (2006). Best practices in diversity management. In M. Karsten (Ed.), *Gender, race, & ethnicity in the workplace: Issues and challenges for today's organizations* (Vol. 3, pp. 69–84). Westport, CT: Praeger/Greenwood.

Thomas, R. R., Jr. (2006). Diversity management: An essential craft for leaders. *Leader to Leader, 41,* 45–49.

Tierney, S., & Jackson, R. L. (2002). Deconstructing whiteness ideology as a set of rhetorical fantasy themes: Implications for interracial alliance building in the United States. *International and Intercultural Communication Annual, 25,* 81–107.

Ting-Toomey, S. (1986). Conflict communication styles in Black and White subjective cultures. In Y. Y. Kim (Ed.), *Interethnic communication: Current research* (pp. 75–88). Newbury Park, CA: Sage.

Ting-Toomey, S. (1988). Intercultural conflict styles: A face negotiation theory. In Y. Y. Kim & W. B. Gudykunst (Eds.), *Theories in intercultural communication* (pp. 213–235). Newbury Park, CA: Sage.

Ting-Toomey, S. (2000). Managing intercultural conflicts effectively. In L. A. Samovar & R. E. Porter (Eds.), *Intercultural communication: A reader* (pp. 388–400). Belmont, CA: Wadsworth.

Ting-Toomey, S., & Oetzel, J. G. (2001). *Managing intercultural conflict effectively.* Thousand Oaks, CA: Sage.

Ting-Toomey, S., Yee-Jung, K. K., Shapiro, R. B., Garcia, W., Wright, T. J., & Oetzel, J. G. (2000). Ethnic/cultural identity salience and conflict styles in four U.S. ethnic groups. *International Journal of Intercultural Relations, 24,* 47–81.

Tirodkar, M. A., & Jain, T. (2003). Food messages on African American television shows. *American Journal of Public Health, 93*(3), 439–441.

Toale, M. C., & McCroskey, J. C. (2001). Ethnocentrism and trait communication apprehension as predictors of interethnic communication apprehension and use of relational maintenance strategies in interethnic communication. *Communication Quarterly, 49,* 70–83.

Todd, J., McKinney, J. L., Harris, R., Chadderton, R., & Small, L. (1992). Attitudes toward interracial dating: Effects of age, sex, and race. *Journal of Multicultural Counseling and Development, 20,* 202–208.

Tolbert, E. J. (1989). General introduction. In C. E. Jackson & E. J. Tolbert (Eds.), *Race and culture in America: Readings in racial and ethnic relations* (pp. 1–21). Edina, MN: Burgess.

Torres, K. C., & Charles, C. Z. (2004). Metastereotypes and the black white divide: A qualitative view on an elite college campus. *DuBois Review, 1,* 115–149.

Troy, A. B., Lewis-Smith, J., & Laurenceau, J.-P. (2006). Interracial and intraracial romantic relationships: The search for differences in satisfaction, conflict, and attachment style. *Journal of Social and Personal Relationships, 23*(1), 65–80.

Trubisky, P., Ting-Toomey, S., & Lin, S-L. (1991). The influence of individualism-collectivism and self-monitoring on conflict styles. *International Journal of Intercultural Relations, 15,* 65–84.

Tucker, L. R. (1997). Was the revolution televised? Professional criticism about "The Cosby Show" and the essentialization of black cultural expression. *Journal of Broadcasting and Electronic Media, 41*(1), 90–108.

Tucker, M. B., & Mitchell-Kernan, C. (1995). Social structural and psychological correlates of interethnic dating. *Journal of Social and Personal Relationships, 12*(3), 341–361.

Turner, J. C. (1987). *Rediscovering the social group.* London: Basil Blackwell.

Turner, J. H., Singleton, R., & Musick, D. (1984). *Oppression: A sociohistory of Black–White relations in America.* Chicago: Nelson-Hall.

Turner, R. (1990, June). Interracial couples in the South. *Ebony,* pp. 41–49.

TV roles for minorities declining. (1999, May 11). *Kalamazoo (MI) Gazette,* p. D7.

Uchida, A. (1997). Doing gender and building culture: Toward a model of women's intercultural communication. *Howard Journal of Communications, 8*(1), 41–76.

University of Waterloo. (2000, May 25). *Professor studies stereotypes and impacts* [press release]. Retrieved

March 14, 2007, from http://newsrelease.uwaterloo.ca/news.php?id=1438

Uotinen, V. (1998). Age identification: A comparison between Finnish and North American cultures. *International Journal of Aging and Human Development, 46*, 109–124.

U.S. Bureau of the Census (1993). Washington, DC: Government Printing Office.

U.S. Department of Justice. (n.d.). *Introduction and overview: Defining and recognizing bias crime.* Retrieved March 12, 2007, from http://www.ojp.gov/ovc/publications/infores/responding/files/sessionA.pdf

U.S. Department of Justice. (2004). *Hate crime statistics 2004.* Retrieved March 11, 2007, from http://www.fbi.gov/ucr/hc2004/openpage.htm

U.S. Office of Management and Budget. (1997, October 30). Revisions to the standards for the classification of federal data on race and ethnicity. *Federal Register,* pp. 58782–58790.

Vacquera, E., & Kao, G. (2005). Private and public displays of affection among interracial and intra-racial adolescent couples. *Social Science Quarterly, 86*(2), 484–507.

Valdivia, A. N. (1998). Big hair and bigger hoops: Rosie Perez goes to Hollywood. In J. N. Martin, T. K. Nakayama, & L. A. Flores (Eds.), *Readings in cultural contexts* (pp. 243–249). Mountain View, CA: Mayfield.

Valdivia, A. N. (2004). Latino/a communication and media studies today: An introduction. *The Communication Review, 7*, 107–112.

Valentine, G. (1995, Spring). Shades of gray: The conundrum of color categories. *Teaching Tolerance,* p. 47.

Van Buren, H. J., III (1997). Ending the culture of corporate discrimination. *Business & Society Review, 98*, 20–23.

Vance, D. C. (2002/2003). The same yet different: Creating unity among the diverse members of the Baha'i faith. *Journal of Intergroup Relations, 24*(4), 64–88.

Van den Berghe, P. L. (1960). Hypergamy, hypergenation, and miscegenation. *Human Relations, 13,* 83–91.

Vargas, L. (1996). *When the "other" is the teacher: Teaching as a transcultural practice within systems of inequality.* Paper presented at the Eastern Communication Association Conference, New York.

Vertovec, S. (2001). Transnationalism and identity. *Journal of Ethnic and Migration Studies, 27*(4), 573–582.

Viswanath, K., & Arora, P. (2000). Ethnic media in the United States: An essay on their role in integration, assimilation, and social control. *Mass Communication and Society, 3,* 39–56.

Vox pop. (1994, April 4). *Time,* p. 12.

Waldinger, R., & Lichter, M. I. (2003). *How the other half works: Immigration and the social organization of labor.* Los Angeles: University of California Press.

Waldron, V. R., & Di Mare, L. (1998). Gender as a culturally determined construct: Communication styles in Japan and the United States. In D. J. Canary & K. Dindia (Eds.), *Sex differences and similarities in communication: Critical essays and empirical investigations of sex and gender in interaction* (pp. 179–202). Mahwah; NJ: Lawrence Erlbaum.

Waldrop, J., & Stern, S. (2003). *Disability status 2000: Census 2000 brief.* Washington, DC: U.S. Department of Commerce/Economics and Statistics Administration.

Wander, P. C., Martin, J. N., & Nakayama, T. (1999). Whiteness and beyond: Sociohistorical foundations of Whiteness and contemporary challenges. In T. K. Nakaywna & J. N. Martin (Eds.), *Whiteness: The communication of social identity* (pp. 13–26). Thousand Oaks, CA: Sage.

Wardle, F. (1987, January). Are you sensitive to interracial children's special identity needs? *Young Children,* pp. 53–59.

Warfield, W. (2006). Managing racial/ethnic conflict for community building. In J. G. Oetzel & S. Ting-Toomey (Eds.), *The Sage handbook of conflict communication: Integrating theory, research, and practice* (pp. 479–500). Thousand Oaks, CA: Sage.

Warren, J. T., & Hytten, K. (2004). The faces of whiteness: Pitfalls and the critical democrat. *Communication Education, 53*(4), 321–339.

Warren, K. T., Orbe, M., & Greer-Williams, N. (2003). Perceiving conflict: Similarities and differences between and among Latino/as, African Americans, and European Americans. In D. I. Rios & A. N. Mohamed (Eds.), *Brown and black communication: Latino and African American conflict and convergence in mass media* (pp. 13–26). Westport, CT: Praeger.

Waters, H., Jr. (1992). Race, culture, and interpersonal conflict. *International Journal of Intercultural Relations, 16,* 437–454.

Waters, M. (1999). *Black identities: West Indian dreams and American realities.* Cambridge, MA: Harvard University Press.

Watson, D. (April 5, 2005). Fox's *24:* Propaganda thinly disguised as television programming. Retrieved September 26, 2006, from http://www.wsws.org

Weber, M. (1947). *The theory of social and economic organization* (A. M. Henderson & T. Parsons, Trans.). New York: Oxford University Press.

Weedon, C. (1987). *Feminist practice and poststructuralist theory.* New York: Basil Blackwell.

Wei, W. (1993). *The Asian American movement.* Philadelphia: Temple University Press.

Weick, K. (1979). *The social psychology of organizing.* New York: Random House.

Weinberger, A. D. (1966). Interracial intimacy. *Journal of Sex Research, 2,* 157–168.

Wellner, A. S. (June, 2005). *U.S. attitudes toward interracial dating are liberalizing.* Retrieved November 23, 2005, from http://www.prb.org/Template.cfm?Section =PRB_Country_Profiles&template=/Content Management/ContentDisplay.cfm&ContentID =12690

Wells, L., Jr. (1998). Consulting to Black–White relations in predominantly White organizations. *Journal of Applied Behavioral Science, 34*(4), 392–396.

Welner, K. G. (2006). K–12 race-conscious student assignment policies: Law, social science, and diversity. *Review of Educational Research, 76*(3), 349–382.

West, C. (1982). *Prophecy deliverance: An Afro-American revolutionary Christianity.* Philadelphia: Westminster Press.

West, C. (1993). *Race matters.* Boston: Beacon Press.

Weston, M. A. (1992, August). *Native Americans in the news: Symbol, stereotype, or substance?* Paper presented at the annual meeting of the Association for Education in Journalism and Mass Communication, Montreal, Canada.

Weston, M. A. (2003). Post 9/11 Arab American coverage avoids stereotypes. *Newspaper Research Journal, 24*(1), 92–106.

What constitutes a mulatto? (1995, Spring). *Teaching Tolerance,* p. 47.

Whelan, S. A., Murphy, D., Tsumura, E., & Kline, S. F. (1998). Member perceptions of internal group dynamics and productivity. *Small Group Research, 29*(31), 371–393.

Whetmore, E. (1998). *Mediamerica, mediaworld: Form, content, and consequence of mass communication* (5th ed.). Belmont, CA: Wadsworth.

Whetstone, M. L. (1996, October). The '96 TV season: Cosby is back, but Black oriented shows decline. *Ebony,* pp. 54–58.

Why do more Blacks have disabilities? (2006, October). *DiversityInc,* p. 16.

Why interracial marriages are increasing. (1996, September 15). *Jet Magazine,* pp. 12–15.

Why more Black women are dating White men. (1997, October 20). *Jet Magazine,* pp. 12–16.

Wilkinson, D. M. (1996). Power beyond the remote control. *Black Enterprise, 27*(5), 75–82.

Williams, A., & Giles, H. (1998). Communication of ageism. In M. L. Hecht (Ed.), *Communicating prejudice* (pp. 136–162). Thousand Oaks, CA: Sage.

Wilson, C. C., & Gutierrez, F. (1985). *Minorities and media: Diversity and the end of mass communication.* Beverly Hills, CA: Sage.

Wilson, K. H. (1999). Towards a discursive theory of racial identity: The Souls of Black Folks as a response to nineteenth-century biological determinism. *Western Journal of Communication, 63*(2), 193–215.

Wilson, M., & Russell, K. (1996). *Divided sisters: Bridging the gap between Black women and White women.* New York: Anchor.

Winker, K. J. (1994, May 11). The significance of race. *Chronicle of Higher Education,* pp. A10–A11.

Winn, P. (1995). *Americas: The changing face of Latin America and the Caribbean.* New York: Pantheon.

Witteborn, S. (2004). Of being an Arab woman before and after September 11: The enactment of communal identities in talk. *Howard Journal of Communications, 15,* 83–98.

Woman who changed laws that prevented mixed marriages tells what it was like then. (1992, November 9). *Jet Magazine,* pp. 12–15.

Wong (Lau), K. (2002). Migration across generations: Whose identity is authentic? In J. N. Martin, T. K. Nakayama, & L. A. Flores (Eds.), *Reading in cultural contexts* (pp. 95–100). Mountain View, CA: Mayfield.

Wong, P., Manvi, M., & Wong, T. H. (1995). Asiacentrism and Asian American Studies? *Amerasia Journal, 12,* 137–147.

Wong, W. (1997). Covering the invisible "model minority." In S. Biagi & M. Kern-Foxworth (Eds.), *Facing difference: Race, gender, and mass media* (pp. 97–101). Thousand Oaks, CA: Pine Forge Press.

Wood, J. T. (1992). Gender and moral voice: Moving from women's nature to standpoint epistemology: *Women's Studies in Communication, 15*(1), 1–24.

Wood, J. T. (1993). Diversity and commonality: Sustaining tension in communication courses. *Western Journal of Communication, 57,* 367–380.

Wood, J. T. (Ed.). (1996). *Gendered relationships.* Mountain View, CA: Mayfield.

Wood, J. T. (1997a). *Communication theories in action: An introduction.* Belmont, CA: Wadsworth.

Wood, J. T. (1997b). Gender, communication, and culture. In L. A. Samovar & R. E. Porter (Eds.), *Intercultural communication: A reader* (pp. 164–173). Belmont, CA: Wadsworth.

Wood, J. T. (2005). Feminist standpoint theory and muted group theory: Commonalities and divergences. *Women and Language, 28*(2), 61–64.

Wood, J. T., & Dindia, K. (1998). What's the difference? A dialogue about differences and similarities between women and men. In D. J. Canary & K. Dindia (Eds.), *Sex differences and similarities in communication: Critical essays and empirical investigations of sex and gender in interaction* (pp. 19–40). Mahwah, NJ: Lawrence Erlbaum.

Woods, J. D. (1993). *The corporate closet: The professional lives of gay men in America*. New York: Free Press.

Woodward, K. L. (1993, June 12). The rites of Americans. *Newsweek*, pp. 80–82.

Woodyard, J. L. (1995). Locating Asante: Making use of the Afrocentric idea. In D. Ziegler (Ed.), *Molefi Kete Asante and Afrocentricity: In praise and criticism* (pp. 27–43). Nashville: James C. Winston.

Wright, L. (1994, July 25). One drop of blood. *The New Yorker*, pp. 46–55.

Wright, S., Aron, A., McLaughlin-Volpe, T., & Ropp, S. (1997). The extended contact effect: Knowledge of cross-group friendships and prejudice. *Journal of Personality and Social Psychology, 73*(1), 73–90.

Wu, F. H. (2002). *Yellow: Race in America beyond black and white*. New York: Basic Books.

Xie, Y., & Goyette, K. (1997). The racial identification of biracial children with one Asian parent: Evidence from the 1990 census. *Social Forces, 76*(2), 547–571.

Yale-Loehr, S., & Kowalski, D. M. (2006, October 1). Cut through the notes: Trends in immigration law. *Texas Lawyer*, p. 15.

Yancey, G. (2002). Who interracially dates: An examination of the characteristics of those who have interracially dated. *Journal of Comparative Families, 33*, 179–190.

Yancey, G. (2003). A preliminary examination of differential sexual attitudes among individuals involved in interracial relationships: Testing "jungle fever." *The Social Science Journal, 40*, 153–157.

Yang, J. (1994, October 4). Anything but the girl. *Village Voice*, p. 47.

Yates, E. L. (2000). Helping students build bridges across racial division. *Black Issues in Higher Education, 17*, 36–38.

Yep, G. A. (2002). Navigating the multicultural identity landscape. In J. N. Martin, T. K. Nakayama, & L. A. Flores (Eds.), *Readings in cultural contexts* (pp. 60–66). Mountain View, CA: Mayfield.

Youngblood, J. D., & Winn, J. E. (2004). Shout glory: Competing communication codes experienced by the members of the African American Pentecostal Genuine Deliverance Holiness Church. *Journal of Communication, 54*(2), 355–370.

Zaharna, R. (1989). Self-shock: The double-binding challenges of identity. *International Journal of Intercultural Relations, 13*(4), 501–525.

Zarefsky, D. (1998). *Public speaking: Strategies for success* (2nd ed.). Boston: Allyn & Bacon.

Zinsmeister, K. (1998). When black and white turn gray. *American Enterprise, 9*(6), 4–7.

Zook, K. B. (1995, January 17). Warner brothas. *Village Voice*, pp. 36–37.

Zou, J. (2005, April 18). *Asian Pacific culture week aims to dispel stereotypes, empower students: Entertainment events offer glimpse of diverse culture*. Retrieved November 30, 2006, from http://www.californiaaggie.com/home/

Zuberi, T. (2000). Deracializing social statistics: Problems in the quantification of race. *Annals of the American Academy of Political and Social Science, 568*, 172–175.

Author Index

Subject Index

About the Authors

Mark P. Orbe received his undergraduate degree in organizational communication from Ohio University, followed by a master's degree in higher educational administration from the University of Connecticut. After holding several student affairs positions, he returned to Ohio University to complete his doctoral degree in interpersonal/intercultural communication. His first faculty position was at Indiana University Southeast, and he is now Professor of Communication and Diversity at Western Michigan University, where he also has a joint appointment in the Gender and Women's Studies Program. Born and raised in New London, Connecticut, he currently resides in Kalamazoo, Michigan, with his wife, Natalie, and three children, Isaiah, Gabrielle, and Victoria.

Tina Maria Harris, Ph.D., is an Associate Professor at the University of Georgia in the Department of Speech Communication. She is a communication scholar who has special research interests in the areas of interracial communication, pedagogy, diversity in the media, and race and ethnic disparities and religious frameworks in health communication. She first coauthored the textbook *Interracial Communication: Theory Into Practice* with African American communication scholar Mark P. Orbe in 2001. It was the first textbook to be written on this topic since 1974. Professor Harris has been honored by the University System of Georgia Board of Regents (BOR) with its 2005 Award for the Scholarship of Teaching and Learning for her research. Her research explores individual understandings of race and its influence on the ways in which people communicate about race and non–race-related topics and issues both within and outside of the college classroom.